Multiple Intelligences Around the World

Multiple Intelligences Around the World

Jie-Qi Chen
Seana Moran
Howard Gardner

Editors

JOSSEY-BASS
A Wiley Imprint
www.josseybass.com

Published by Jossey-Bass
A Wiley Imprint
989 Market Street, San Francisco, CA 94103-1741—www.josseybass.com

Library of Congress Cataloging-in-Publication Data
Chen, Jie-Qi.
Multiple intelligences around the world / Jie-Qi Chen, Seana Moran, and Howard Gardner.—1st ed.
p. cm.
Includes bibliographical references and index.
ISBN 978-0-7879-9760-1 (cloth)
1. Multiple intelligences—Cross-cultural studies. I. Moran, Seana, date- II. Gardner, Howard. III. Title.
BF432.3.C43 2009
153.9—dc22
2009004211
Printed in the United States of America
FIRST EDITION
HB Printing   10 9 8 7 6 5 4 3 2 1

CONTENTS

THE CONTRIBUTORS

Thomas Armstrong is a former elementary and middle school special education teacher who has been working with MI theory since 1986. He completed his doctoral dissertation on MI in 1987, and over the past twenty years he has been writing and lecturing full time to parents and educators on multiple intelligences and related topics. Armstrong has written five books on multiple intelligences, including *Multiple Intelligences in the Classroom,* which has been translated into fifteen languages. He has had the opportunity to visit many countries in the course of his lecturing on MI, including Brazil, Mexico, Canada, Norway, Iceland, Denmark, the United Kingdom, Austria, the Netherlands, the principality of Andorra, the People's Republic of China, Japan, Singapore, Australia, and New Zealand.

María Ximena Barrera is an educator and technology specialist. She has been working with Project Zero ideas for ten years and provides professional development to educators in Latin America and Spain. She offers workshops and talks focusing on teaching for understanding and multiple intelligences. During the past seven years, she has worked with WIDE World as coach and instructor for courses taught in Spanish. She is an active member of FUNDACIES and Vision Action, nonprofit organizations dedicated to educational research and professional development for educators.

Antonio M. Battro is the chief education officer of One Laptop Per Child and a member of the Pontifical Academy of Sciences and the Academy of Education, Argentina. He earned his M.D. from the University of Buenos Aires and his Ph.D. in psychology from the University of Paris. He is a former member of the Centre International D'épistemologie Génétique, University of Geneva; associate director of Ecole Pratique des Hautes Études, Laboratoire de Psychologie Expérimentale et Comparée, Paris; and Robert F. Kennedy Visiting Professor at the Graduate School of Education at Harvard University. His recent books are *Half a Brain Is Enough* (2000), *The Educated Brain* (with K. Fischer and P. Lena, editors, 2008), and *Hacia una Inteligencia Digital* (with P. J. Denham, 2008).

Brian Boyd is emeritus professor of education at the University of Strathclyde in Glasgow, Scotland, and codirector of Tapestry, an organization that aims to bring creativity to Scottish education. He is editor of the Continuing Professional Development in Education series and has written three books for it. He was previously a head teacher (the principal) of two secondary schools, for students between the ages of eleven and eighteen. Much of his work has focused on the practice of streaming and setting, and he has worked tirelessly to challenge the traditional practice of labeling learners based on the measurement of intelligence.

Mary Joy Canon-Abaquin founded the first multiple intelligence institution in the Philippines, creating an alternative school culture that respects children's individual differences. Spearheading the vision for the Multiple Intelligence International School, she has taken a leadership role in educational reform through the exemplary practices of the school. She has brought together educators, political leaders, and business leaders to advocate for the Filipino children through the MI lens. She runs her school with a passion, tirelessly advocating that her students use their intelligences to make a difference in the lives of other people and their country.

Kyung-Hee Cha is a senior researcher of the Center for Teaching and Learning at Hanyang University in Seoul, Korea. Currently she is concentrating on curriculum development for medical education. Since the mid-1990s, she has spearheaded MI-based program development in Korea. In 2008 she published

Multiple Intelligences Class Examples: Children Who Enjoy Class, which introduces examples of MI-based education in Korea. She has particular interest in the field of communication in an education context such as question-and-discussion in the classroom and qualitative interview for research.

⌒

Jie-Qi Chen, professor of child development and early education at Erikson Institute in Chicago, has been involved in MI-related research and practice since 1989 when she began working at Harvard Project Zero. Chen is a frequent speaker to educators interested in MI. As a Fulbright senior specialist in multiple intelligences, Chen has traveled to many countries and regions, including China, Peru, Italy, Turkey, Saudi Arabia, Russia, Hong Kong, and Taiwan. She has written and edited several books, including *Building on Children's Strengths,* which describes a ten-year research project at Project Zero that applied MI theory to early childhood education and assessment.

⌒

Happy Hoi-Ping Cheung is originally from Hong Kong. A recipient of the M.Ed. from the Harvard Graduate School of Education, she is now the chair of the Multiple Intelligences Education Society of China and the publisher of *Multiple Intelligences* magazine. She is the founder of Sino Capital Education Foundation in Hong Kong. She is also the cohost of a radio show on family education issues and the guest speaker of Chinese Central TV Channel 10 on education, science, and technology issues. She is devoted to philanthropy and education in China.

⌒

Kwok-cheung Cheung is professor of curriculum and instruction at the University of Macau, Macao, China. He is also director of the Educational Testing and Assessment Research Centre and national project manager of the Macao-China Programme for International Student Assessment 2009 Reading Literacy Study. His two main areas of research are school-based MI-inspired pedagogy and assessment, including print and electronic assessment, and international assessment of mathematical, scientific, and reading literacy and modeling of school system data. He has written and edited ten books and monographs on these research topics, as well as many academic articles, and he has made numerous conference presentations.

⌒

Anna Craft is professor of education at the University of Exeter and the Open University, both in England. She leads the CREATE research group at Exeter.

With a small team, she also acts as government advisor in England on creative and cultural education. She is currently lead editor of the peer-refereed international journal, *Thinking Skills and Creativity*, and founding co-convenor of the British Educational Research Association Special Interest Group, Creativity in Education. Her areas of research and development are creativity in education and the futures of educational provision. She has written and edited sixteen books and many articles on these topics.

René Díaz-Lefebvre is professor of psychology at Glendale Community College, Glendale, Arizona. His research interests include cognitive psychology, intelligence, and assessment in higher education. In the 1990s, he pioneered methods of applying MI research in the college setting through Multiple Intelligences/Learning for Understanding (MI/LfU). Díaz-Lefebvre has presented more than 150 keynote addresses, academic papers, seminars, and workshops at national conferences and faculty institutes around the world. He has published twenty-five articles and written two books on MI/LfU in English and Spanish. He received a fellowship from the Maricopa Community College International and Intercultural Education Program to present his research and teach seminars on *inteligencias múltiples* at la Universidad Veracruzana, Xalapa, Veracruz, México. He is currently working on a project, Somos Inteligentes/We Are Intelligent, to use ideas presented in his chapter in this book.

Michael Fleetham is a learning consultant and author. He works with schools and businesses across the United Kingdom to help make their learning more effective, enjoyable, and relevant to twenty-first-century contexts. He has worked as an engineer, designing communications equipment for an international defense company, and as a classroom teacher and assistant head teacher in inner-city schools.

Tomoe Fujimoto is president of Tomoe Soroban (Japanese Abacus) Ltd. and head of Tomoe MI Academy. Her professional interest is in implementing MI in teaching abacus to young children. She is a cofounder of the Japan MI Society and invited honorary president Howard Gardner to speak in 2003 and 2006.

Howard Gardner is the Hobbs Professor of Cognition and Education at the Harvard Graduate School of Education. He is the author of more than twenty books translated into twenty-seven languages. Gardner also holds positions as adjunct professor of psychology at Harvard University and senior director of Harvard Project Zero.

Carissa Gatmaitan-Bernardo has been working in the Multiple Intelligences International School in the Philippines for the past ten years, first as a classroom teacher and currently as coordinator of special projects for the school. As well, she heads the MI-Comprehensive School Reform Project in Tagbilaran City, where she works closely with local government officials and the city's day care workers. She also helps the school in providing professional development to educators who are interested in integrating MI theory with their practice.

Thomas R. Hoerr is the headmaster of the New City School in St. Louis, Missouri. Under his leadership, the faculty began using MI in 1988. The school has hosted four MI conferences and produced two MI books for teachers. Hundreds of educators still visit New City School each year, and in 2005 the school opened the world's first MI library. Hoerr is the author of *Becoming a Multiple Intelligences School* and the facilitator of the ASCD MI Network, and he has written many articles on the implementation of MI. He is also the author of two books for principals, *The Art of School Leadership* and *School Leadership for the Future.*

David Howland is an arts-based learning specialist. He is active as a consultant, writer, and teacher in Tokyo and Yokohama. Originally from the United States, he has called Japan home for fourteen years.

Áine Hyland has recently retired as professor of education and vice president of University College, Cork Ireland. During the 1990s, she led a university-based research project on multiple intelligences, curriculum, and assessment in collaboration with colleagues and with thirty teachers in primary and secondary schools in the city of Cork. She chaired a government-appointed national committee on criteria for admission to university education in Ireland (the Points Commission) and advised the national Ministry for Education and Science on issues relating to curriculum and assessment. Her research interests encompass different aspects of inclusive education: social, cultural, religious, ethnic, and linguistic.

Keiko Ishiwata is an assistant professor and foreign student advisor at Yokohama National University. Previously she worked as a senior high school English teacher for twenty years. She has directed several research projects applying MI and teaching for understanding to English pedagogy. She is a cofounder of the Japan MI Society.

⌒

Masao Kamijo is the president of the Japan MI Society (JMIS), emeritus adjunct lecturer at the graduate school of Nagoya University, and a representative of Office Kannonzaki Consulting. He began his study and application of MI outside the academic world while in his prior position at the Sony Corporation as chief manager in market research.

⌒

Osman Nafiz Kaya is one of the first researchers to investigate the effects of the implementation of MI theory on Turkish middle school students' achievement and affective dispositions in science. He developed MI-oriented methods courses for preservice elementary and middle school teachers on the Faculty of Education, Gazi University, Ankara. He served as a staff developer and consultant for MI theory and practices in the Private Gazi Elementary School, one of the key MI schools in Turkey.

⌒

Mia Keinänen is a professional dancer and a scholar researching art and cognition and creativity. She holds a doctorate in education from Harvard University with Howard Gardner as her advisor. After having lived and worked in London, New York, Boston, Ljubljana, Paris, Oslo, and Helsinki, she is currently based in Moscow, where she conducts research on intuition as a postdoctoral fellow of the Academy of Finland and teaches dance. She is also a lecturer on modern dance at the Theater Academy in Finland.

⌒

Myung-Hee Kim is a professor of education at Hanyang University in Seoul, Korea. In 1996, she was the first scholar in Korea to apply MI theory in the Korean classroom with a grant from the Ministry of Education. Since then, she has been instrumental in spreading MI theory to Korean schools, especially at the primary level. Her efforts eventually led to the application of MI theory in national curriculum development. In 2002, she founded the Multiple Intelligences Society, which has organized numerous teacher training sessions. She also led a series of qualitative studies on schools that adopted MI theory. With particular interest in linguistic intelligence, Kim is currently developing diagnostic tools for communication ability. She has numerous MI theory research papers and two translated works to her credit.

⌒

Hans Henrik Knoop is associate professor of psychology at the University of Aarhus and director of the Universe Research Lab, committed to studying learning, creativity, teaching, and innovation in ways that bridge theory and practice. Knoop has been responsible for the Nordic branch of the GoodWork Project led by Howard Gardner, Mihaly Csikszentmihalyi, and William Damon. He has served on a number of important governmental and international committees, has worked with companies such as LEGO and Danfoss, and has presented his work through more than eight hundred invited talks in many countries. He is on the board of directors of the International Positive Psychology Association.

⌒

Mindy L. Kornhaber is an associate professor in the Department of Education Policy Studies at the Pennsylvania State University. Her scholarship explores how human potential can be advanced to both a high level and on an equitable basis. At the Harvard Graduate School of Education, she pursued studies in cognitive development and social policy. She continued to explore these areas at Harvard Project Zero and the Civil Rights Project at Harvard University. She has extensively examined the relationship between high-stakes testing systems and the equitable development of students' disciplinary understanding.

⌒

Chris Kunkel joined the Key School group in 1990 to develop the Key Middle School. When Key Renaissance Middle School opened in 1993, she was the science teacher. She continued to work on the design and implementation team as plans for the Key High School got under way. When the high school opened in 1999, she accepted the assistant principalship while continuing to teach. In 2003 she completed her Ph.D. and became principal of the Key Program after the untimely death of Patricia Bolaños, founding principal.

⌒

Patricia Kyed is executive assistant to Charlotte Sahl-Madsen, CEO of Danfoss Universe. Before moving to Danfoss Universe in 2005, she worked for LEGO Company for twenty-five years, several of them as executive assistant.

⌒

Patricia León-Agustí founded Colegio San Francisco de Asís and for eleven years was director of Colegio Rochester in Bogotá, Colombia. She has completed her course work in community psychology at Javeriana University and has a master's in educational research and human development from CINDE, in Bogotá. She led a reform movement in Colombia centered on teaching for understanding and MI. She is an instructor for WIDE World Spanish online courses and offers professional development to teachers in Latin America and Spain. She is an active member of FUNDACIES and Vision Action, nonprofit organizations dedicated to educational research and professional development for educators.

C. June Maker is professor of special education, rehabilitation, and school psychology at the University of Arizona in Tucson. She is senior researcher and director of the DISCOVER Project, a pioneering program to infuse MI theory into culturally responsive curricula and develop performance-based assessments. Her research teams have designed assessments that can be used effectively with small groups of students of all ages, languages, and cultures in classroom settings; curriculum and teaching models for enhancing problem-solving abilities; and instructional strategies for challenging gifted students in regular classrooms. With colleagues and students, she has conducted many studies of the effectiveness of assessments and curricula. She has written numerous books and articles about these projects and about the education of gifted and talented students.

Marian McCarthy is a lecturer in education and is program coordinator of certified courses in teaching and learning in higher education at University College Cork. She has supported teaching and learning initiatives in the university since 1995 and has been influenced in particular by the work of Project Zero at the Harvard Graduate School of Education and that of the Carnegie Foundation for the Advancement of Teaching.

Seana Moran is a research associate at the Stanford Center on Adolescence, examining how young people age twelve to twenty-six develop purpose in their lives. Her research interests address how people contribute to their environments, especially extraordinary contributions such as creativity and wisdom, and the internal motivational mechanisms that drive contribution, such as purpose and commitment. She has written several papers addressing extraordinary achievements, creativity, commitment, executive function, collaboration, and multiple intelligences. Her work has been supported by the Arete Initiative/Templeton Foundation, Spencer Foundation, American Association of University Women, and Harvard University. She earned her doctorate in human development and psychology from Harvard University and holds a master of education and a master of business administration.

 ⌒

Paula Pogré is a professor of education at General Sarmiento University. Trained in social psychology, her research focuses on teacher change through professional development. She is cofounder of L@titud and has directed many research projects in Argentina applying MI theory and Harvard Project Zero's teaching for understanding framework. She serves on the faculty for Project Zero's Summer Institute. Collaborating in the national process of innovation and reform in Argentina, she worked as a consultant for the undersecretary of education in the 1990s.

 ⌒

Vincent Rizzo is the director of the Howard Gardner School for Discovery (HGSD) in Scranton, Pennsylvania, which he helped establish in 2005. Previous to this position, he served as head of the University of Scranton Campus School, the predecessor of HGSD. He was a public school teacher for sixteen years, followed by a curriculum supervisor, principal, and superintendent of schools. He currently serves on the board of directors of NALS: The International Association of University Affiliated and Laboratory Schools.

 ⌒

Marcela Rogé has been an English language teacher for over twenty years and has served as head of the English Department at primary and secondary school levels. A specialist in information and communication technology (ICT), she has worked on projects that aimed at including ICT in daily teaching practices. She codeveloped "The Symbolism of the Candle," a global classroom curriculum project, and an educational CD-ROM of study techniques.

 ⌒

Charlotte Sahl-Madsen is CEO of Danfoss Universe. She is also president of the Universe Foundation and works closely with Universe Research Lab. She was formerly employed as head of LEGO VisionLab (including LEGO Learning Institute and LEGO Serious Play), head of LEGO Research and Development and executive director of the Ebeltoft Glass Museum. She has been a board member of Aarhus Business School and MINDLAB (Ministry of Economic and Business Affairs Innovation Unit) and a member of the Minister of Business Affairs' Expert Group.

Ligia Sarivan is a curriculum expert, teacher trainer, and a senior researcher at the Institute for Educational Sciences (IES), Bucharest, Romania. In the mid-1990s, she was a pioneer in introducing MI to the Romanian public. She carried out small-scale MI experiments in the IES pilot schools and, as a result, published the first two articles about MI in Romanian literature. In the late 1990s, Sarivan introduced MI in her courses for undergraduate prospective teachers. More recently, she has started a partnership with Florence Mihaela Singer for an MI-based approach in teacher training programs.

Ketty Sarouphim is associate professor of psychology and education at the Lebanese American University in Beirut and was instrumental in introducing MI to her fellow Lebanese citizens. Her research on identifying gifted students through the performance-based assessment DISCOVER was unique in Lebanon. She has presented her work at international conferences and has published several articles on assessing giftedness using MI theory. Also, she has had many TV appearances on various topics related to children's development, including the application of MI in the classroom. She has given several workshops to teachers and parents on a variety of topics, such as preventing aggression in children, the effect of parenting styles on children's behavior, and using MI to enhance learning.

Ziya Selçuk is the founder of Private Gazi Elementary School, which was organized and structured around MI theoretical frameworks in 1998. He has organized hundreds of conferences, lectures, and panels about MI theory all over Turkey. In 2002, he and his colleagues published *Multiple Intelligences Practices,* which adapts MI theory to the Turkish education system. MI theory gained prime importance in the Turkish education system after Selçuk became chairman of the Turkish Board of Education in 2003.

C. Branton Shearer is a neuropsychologist who has taught about the creative and practical applications of multiple intelligences since 1990 at Kent State University in Kent, Ohio. He is the creator of the Multiple Intelligences Developmental Scales, which have been translated into twelve languages and implemented by educators and researchers in more than twenty countries. He is the founder of the American Educational Research Association Special Interest Group, Multiple Intelligences: Theory and Practice. Along with Mike

Fleetham, Shearer is the author of *Creating ExtraOrdinary Teachers* (2008). In 2009 Teachers College Press published a collection of critical essays that he commissioned by notable educators and theorists, *Multiple Intelligences After 25 Years: Reflections.* Also from Teachers College Press is his book *MIndful Education for ADHD Students: Differentiating Curriculum and Instruction Using Multiple Intelligences,* coauthored with Victoria Proulx-Schirduan and Karen I. Case.

⌣

Zhilong Shen is a professor of physical chemistry and a music educator in Beijing, China. He was attracted by MI theory in 1994 and accepted the idea because it accords with the experiences of his personal development and teaching in different fields. In order to study and popularize the theory, he visited Harvard twice, working with Howard Gardner in 1997 and 2006. He has given more than one hundred presentations in China and the United States, translated three of Gardner's books into Chinese, supervised translations of four more books by Gardner, and published his own book related to MI theory applications.

⌣

Florence Mihaela Singer is a professor at the University of Ploiesti, Romania. In the mid-1990s, she was deeply involved in the process of developing a national curriculum at the preuniversity education level. Later she found that a small-scale approach could be more effective. As a researcher and professor, she uses a student-centered approach. Currently she teaches modern theories of learning in a master's program and math teaching methods for primary teachers. In an attempt to bring to the Romanian public firsthand MI litera-ture, Singer obtained the rights to translate four of Howard Gardner's books, which are now on the Romanian market.

⌣

Wilma Vialle completed her Ph.D. in the United States after twelve years of teaching drama and English in Tasmania. That is where she first encountered MI theory, and it has been part of her professional life ever since, which has included writing one of the first Australian books on MI. She now lives in Wollongong, south of Sydney, where she lectures in educational psychology and research in gifted education. She teaches prospective teachers about MI and works extensively with practicing teachers to incorporate MI in their programs. She is currently researching children's spiritual development.

PART ONE

OVERVIEW

G ardner and Armstrong set the stage for exploring the many ways MI theory is applied in educational settings around the world. They outline the basics of MI theory and engage in processes that will be encountered throughout the book: description, analysis, evaluation, and synthesis. Their call for deeper thinking about MI theory precedes the book's journey from Asia to Europe through South America and back to the United States. The diverse cultures and educational contexts described in the book offer a unique opportunity to gain insights about the ways in which cultural contexts can shape educational practice. A great many people around the world are working diligently to apply MI theory and improve education for all students. Their vitality, excitement, and perseverance are notable.

CHAPTER 1

Birth and the Spreading of a "Meme"

Howard Gardner

In 1983, I published *Frames of Mind: The Theory of Multiple Intelligences*. At the time, I was a full-time research psychologist living in the Cambridge-Boston area. I divided my time between two research sites: the Boston Veterans Administration Medical Center, where I worked with and studied individuals who had suffered one or another form of cortical damage, and Project Zero, a research group at the Harvard Graduate School of Education that focused on issues of human development and cognition, particularly in the arts. My own work at Project Zero examined the development in children of various skills in several art forms. I had been trained as a developmental psychologist, in the traditions of Jean Piaget, Lev Vygotsky, and Jerome Bruner, and I thought of myself as belonging to, and addressing, that segment of the scholarly community.

Had I not worked in tandem with these populations—normal and gifted children, on the one hand, and once-normal individuals who had suffered brain damage—I would never have conceived of MI theory (as it later came to be called). Like most laypersons and most other psychologists, I would have continued to believe in the IQ orthodoxy: there is a single thing called intelligence; it allows us to do a variety of things more or less well, depending on how "smart" we are; we are born with a certain intellectual potential; this potential is highly heritable (that is, our biological parents are the principal determinants of our intelligence); and psychometricians can tell us how smart we are by administering some form of intelligence test.

But every working day, I was exposed to striking exceptions to this orthodoxy. I encountered brain-damaged individuals whose language was grossly impaired but who were able to find their way around unfamiliar settings; I observed brain-damaged patients who were lost spatially but could carry out all manner of linguistic tasks. Analogous double dissociations could be observed across the cognitive spectrum. I was so intrigued by such phenomena that in 1975, I published *The Shattered Mind: The Person After Brain Damage*.

Much the same anomaly cropped up in my studies with children. A young person might be excellent in poetry, fiction, and oral expression but have difficulty in drawing even a passable person, plant, or airplane. A classmate might be an excellent draftsman and yet have difficulty speaking, writing, or reading. Such ideas began to be expressed in my 1973 book, *The Arts and Human Development,* and my 1980 book, *Artful Scribbles*. Again, this pattern of dissociations did not comport with the orthodoxy that I had absorbed as a child growing up in the United States in the 1950s and as a student of developmental and cognitive psychology in the 1960s.

This vague intuition that "something is rotten in the state of intelligence theorizing" would probably have remained unredeemed had it not been for a Dutch philanthropic organization, the Bernard Van Leer Foundation. In 1979 the foundation presented a generous grant to the Harvard Graduate School of Education to elucidate the question, "What is known about the nature and realization of human potential?" A big question—I used to quip that it was "more of a West Coast than an East Coast question." In the event, I was asked to prepare a synthesis of what had been determined about human cognition from the biological, psychological, and social sciences.

BIRTH OF THE THEORY

Some years before, I had sketched the barest of outlines of a book called "Kinds of Minds," but that project had never been launched. Receipt of five years of generous support from the Van Leer Foundation gave me an invaluable opportunity. With the help of several gifted research assistants, I surveyed a wide literature about cognition, including studies in genetics, neuroscience, psychology, education, anthropology, and other disciplines and subdisciplines. This survey not only strengthened my growing intuition that cognition was not monolithic; it also provided the hard empirical evidence with which to substantiate this claim.

Two steps remained. The first was what to call these dissociable human faculties. I considered a variety of labels and finally determined to call them "human intelligences." This lexical turn has offended some ears, and it still generates an underscore when I type the word on my computer. But it had the advantage of drawing attention to the theory, in part because it poached on a territory that had hitherto belonged to a certain kind of psychologist.

(Never underestimate the backlash when you step on the toes of a group that sees itself as all-knowing.) I am pretty sure that I would not be writing this Introduction twenty-five years later had I written precisely the same book but called it "Seven Human Faculties" or "Seven Cognitive Talents."

The second step entailed a definition of an intelligence and a set of criteria for what should count as an intelligence. I came to think of intelligence as a biopsychological potential to process information in certain ways in order to solve problems or create products that are valued in at least one culture or community. More colloquially, I thought of an intelligence as a specially tuned mental computer. Whereas standard intelligence theory posited one all-purpose computer that determined one's strength across the landscape of tasks, MI theory posits a set of several computational devices. Strength or weakness in one does not predict strength or weakness in another. What I had observed in dramatic fashion in brain-damaged individuals, what Oliver Sacks and Alexander Luria have written about with poignancy, is in fact the human condition. What we typically term "intelligence" is really a combination of certain linguistic and logical-mathematical skills, particularly those that are valued in a modern secular school.

As for criteria, these followed from the several disciplines that I had been surveying. As I laid it out in Chapter Four of *Frames of Mind*, an intelligence fits eight criteria reasonably well:

1. Potential isolation by brain damage
2. The existence of idiots savants, prodigies, and other exceptional individuals with jagged cognitive profiles
3. An identifiable core operation or set of operations
4. A distinctive developmental trajectory, culminating in expert performances
5. An evolutionary history and evolutionary plausibility
6. Support from experimental psychological tasks
7. Evidence from psychometric findings
8. Susceptibility to encoding in a symbol system

I consider the set of criteria to be the most original and the most important feature of MI theory. Anyone can generate additional intelligences, but unless they fit some criteria, the positing of an intelligence becomes an exercise of the imagination, not a work of scholarship. Interestingly, neither supporters nor critics of the theory have paid much attention to the criteria. From the beginning, I made it clear that application of the criteria was to some extent a matter of judgment. There is no iron-clad rule for determining whether a candidate intelligence does or does not fit the criteria. That said, I have been very conservative in adding to the list of intelligences. As itemized in the next paragraph, in twenty-five years, I have added only one intelligence and am still on the fence about it.

As for the intelligences themselves, I have already mentioned the two that are typically valued in modern secular schools and are invariably probed in intelligence tests: skill in language (linguistic intelligence) and skill in logical-mathematical operations. The other intelligences are musical intelligence; spatial intelligence; bodily-kinesthetic intelligence (using your whole body or parts of your body to solve problems or to make things); interpersonal intelligence (understanding of others); intrapersonal intelligence (understanding oneself); naturalist intelligence; and a possible ninth intelligence, existential intelligence (the intelligence that generates and attempts to clarify the biggest questions about human nature and human concerns).

On a scientific level, the theory makes two claims. First, all human beings possess these intelligences; put informally, they are what make us human, cognitively speaking. Second, no two human beings—not even identical twins—possess exactly the same profile of intellectual strengths and weaknesses. That is because most of us are genetically different from our conspecifics, and even identical twins undergo different experiences and are motivated to distinguish themselves from one another.

INITIAL REACTIONS

When I introduced MI theory, I fully expected that it would be read, analyzed, and critiqued primarily by psychologists. In fact, the theory proved of interest primarily to educators (and to parents and the general public as well). This locus of interest fascinated me because there was relatively little about education in the book. And just because I had written nothing about the educational implications of MI theory, readers were free to make what uses they wanted.

Indeed, MI theory became a kind of Rorschach (inkblot) test of the reader-educator. Some saw the theory as about curriculum, others about pedagogy or assessment. Some thought that the theory was particularly relevant for gifted children, others for those with learning disabilities. Some used the theory to argue for homogeneous grouping and the utility of tracking, others for heterogeneous grouping and the elimination of tracking. You can see some of these contrasting predilections expressed in the chapters that follow. What was interesting is that none of these ideas was endorsed in *Frames of Mind*. Rather, readers used the book to support ideas that they had already favored for other reasons. Again, you can discern this trend in subsequent chapters of this book.

Not immune to what the market was telling me, I began to think about educational issues and to consider ways in which MI theory might be useful to educators. I also paid attention to the particular applications that educators were making and began to communicate directly with educators who had an interest in the theory. By the mid-1980s, I was in contact with the eight teachers who were shortly to launch the Key School (now the Key Learning Community) in Indianapolis, by all accounts the first MI school in the world (see Chapter Twenty-Four). And by the late 1980s, I had had considerable contact with Tom Hoerr, then and now the head of the St. Louis New City School, who used MI ideas in a way quite different from the teachers at the Key Learning Community (see Chapter Twenty-Five).

Because I had not put forth educational goals of my own and because I was intrigued by the multifarious ways in which the theory was being drawn on, I did not address this issue of an "MI education" for a decade. Finally, when I encountered a use that I particularly deplored, I spoke out. I went on television in Australia to denounce an educational program that, among other things, listed the various ethnic groups in a state and mentioned the intelligences that they had and the ones that they lacked. Of course, this was pseudoscience (as well as veiled racism) and deserved to be labeled as such. Fortunately, the program was cancelled shortly after.

MISUNDERSTANDINGS

I also began to delimit some of the common misunderstandings of the theory, including ones that were prominent among educators. In a 1995 article, "Reflections on Multiple Intelligences: Myths and Realities" (1995) and in subsequent publications, I cautioned educators on several points:

- An intelligence is not the same as a sensory system. There are no "visual" or "auditory" intelligences.

- An intelligence is not a learning style. Styles are ways in which individuals putatively approach a wide range of tasks. An intelligence is a computational capacity whose strength varies across individuals.

- An intelligence is not the same as a domain or discipline. A domain or discipline is a social construct. It refers to any profession, academic discipline, hobby, game, or activity that is valued in a society and features levels of expertise. Skill in a domain can be realized using different combinations of intelligences. And strength in a particular intelligence does not dictate in which domains it will be brought to bear.

- People are not born with a given amount of intelligence, which serves as some kind of limit. We each have potentials across the intellectual spectrum; the extent to which these potentials are realized depends on motivation, skill of teaching, resources available, and so forth.

- An individual should not be described, except in informal shorthand, as a "spatial" person, a "musical" person, or "lacking interpersonal intelligence," for example. All of us possess the full spectrum of intelligences, and intellectual strengths change over time through experience, practice, or in other ways.
- There are no official MI or Gardner schools. Many principles, goals, and methods are consistent with the principal assertions of MI theory.

MAJOR EDUCATIONAL IMPLICATIONS

After two decades of considering the educational implications of MI theory, I have concluded that two are paramount. First, educators who embrace MI theory should take differences among individuals seriously and should, inasmuch as possible, craft education so that each child can be reached in the optimal manner. The advent of personal computers makes such individuation easier than ever before; what was once possible only for the wealthy (personal tutoring) will soon be available to millions of learners around the world.

Second, any discipline, idea, skill, or concept of significance should be taught in several ways. These ways should, by argument, activate different intelligences or combinations of intelligences. Such an approach yields two enormous dividends. First, a plurality of approaches ensures that the teacher (or teaching material) will reach more children. Second, a plurality of approaches signals to learners what it means to have a deep, rounded understanding of a topic. Only individuals who can think of a topic in several ways have a thorough understanding of that topic; those whose understanding is limited to a single instantiation have a fragile grasp.

THE MI MEME

But of course I do not own MI theory. To use Richard Dawkins's term, MI is a meme—a unit of meaning, created at a certain place and time, that has spread widely in the past quarter-century. Initially it spread around educational circles in the United States. But soon it ventured abroad, and it became an item of discussion and application not only in schools, but in homes, in museums and theme parks, places of worship, the workplace, and the playground.

The goal of this book is to examine the way in which the "MI meme" has been apprehended and applied in a number of countries around the world. In 2006 Branton Shearer organized a symposium on multiple intelligences in global perspective at the American Educational Research Association meeting in San Francisco. In the wake of that symposium, the editors decided to invite individuals, most of whom were educators, to write about how MI ideas had been understood and applied in their school, community, region, or nation. To our pleasure, nearly everyone who was invited accepted our invitation. Lesley Iura, an editor at Jossey-Bass, lent her enthusiastic support to the project. Then in March 2008, a majority of the authors journeyed to New York City to discuss the ideas that they were developing in their papers. The papers were completed by the summer of 2008, and this resulting book followed shortly after.

THE GENERATION AND SPREADING OF A MEME

Once the "meme" of MI was created and began to spread in the United States, the question was whether it would be short-lived, like so many educational fads, or whether it would have a longer half-life, and if so, how broadly and in what forms.

I was both surprised and gratified to see the extent to which the meme spread. The MI meme was probably spread chiefly by books—translations of my books and more practically oriented books like those authored in English by Thomas Armstrong, David Lazear, Linda and Bruce Campbell, and many others, ultimately appearing in several languages. In my 1999 book *Intelligence Reframed,* the list of primary and secondary sources took over thirty-five pages, and today, even with powerful search engines, it would not be possible to list all of the works spawned in the "MI industry."

In 1995 the publication of Daniel Goleman's book *Emotional Intelligence* (1995) catalyzed an unexpected turn of events. Goleman's book, which generously cited my work, had a worldwide influence unequaled by any similar work in recent memory and qualitatively greater than any of my writings. His ideas were more accessible than mine, and often our works were confused with one another. In fact, sometimes we ourselves were confused with one another. In Latin America, I was frequently asked to sign copies of Dan's book. A whole industry developed around the assessment and training of what came to be called "emotional intelligence," or EQ. In the subsequent decade, the writings about multiple intelligences were complemented by books on a dizzying array of candidate intelligences: sexual intelligence, business intelligence, spiritual intelligence, and financial intelligence, to name just a few. Indeed, once the MI and EQ genies had been let out of the bottle, there was no way in which to limit the written works, training sessions, and media presentations done under the umbrella of a pluralistic view of intelligence. (If you doubt this claim, test it out on a search engine.)

Going beyond the United States, an indigenous coterie of authors arose. In China, for example, there are dozens of books about multiple intelligences by persons unknown to me. Other writings, such as popular articles in journals and, eventually, doctoral theses (by 1999, according to Clifford Morris, a Canadian scholar and archivist, there were over two hundred theses), also spread the wisdom. Note that there was discussion in psychology and other scholarly disciplines, but by far the bulk of the dissemination occurred in educationally oriented writings, even as criticism was heavily skewed to academics, such as John White in the United Kingdom, who seems to have devoted a sizable proportion of his career over the past decade to inveighing against MI. We might credit White and a few other authors with putting forth a meme to counter the MI meme, whether that meme be a reversion to a single intelligence or a proposal for another way of thinking about a plurality of intelligences.

Individuals can be very important in spreading ideas. Zhilong Shen was a big force in popularizing the ideas in China. My own trips to China over the years, and presentations by other colleagues like Jie-Qi Chen and Happy Cheung, also played a role. In 2003, a major conference on MI in Beijing attracted thousands of participants and hundreds of papers. In addition to the influential MI school that she founded, Mary Joy Canon-Abaquin presided over a huge conference in the Philippines in 2005 that honored individuals who had deployed their intelligences in ways that benefited the broader society.

Sometimes MI ideas were introduced along with other complementary ideas and practices. In Ireland, Áine Hyland and her colleagues combined the perspectives of MI and a Project Zero initiative called "teaching for understanding," and these efforts exerted influence at both the secondary and tertiary educational levels. In Scotland, Brian Boyd, Katrina Bowes, and the Tapestry group have been catalytic in linking the arts and creativity using the MI framework. Through contact with present and future teachers, the development of curricula and assessments, and the conduct of empirical research, Myung-Hee Kim and her associates in South Korea have familiarized much of the educational world (and many outside it) with the ideas of multiple intelligences.

Those who embraced MI were not always as successful in their home territory. Tim Brighouse featured MI ideas in the educational authority of Birmingham, England, but the ideas rarely traveled to other jurisdictions. The MI Society of Japan has been active for a decade and has warmly greeted my family and me in Japan on a number of occasions. But in comparison to Korea and China, Japan has proved quite uncongenial to the MI meme. I cannot know why, but I suspect that as a whole, the Japanese population is reluctant to think psychologically (as opposed to sociologically) and to recognize and honor individual differences. Also, the Japanese educational system has been seen as excellent for many years, and that consensus may have reduced the temptation to tinker with it. My books are translated into French, but to my knowledge, there has never been a strong advocate of these ideas in France, let alone an MI society or MI school. It is relevant to mention that the IQ test was developed in France and that this nation, more so than any other developed country, has long been organized around an elite set of schools that select attendees on the basis of measures of linguistic and logical intelligences. The possibility that MI ideas may be of help in dealing with individuals who are not smart in the traditional sense has not been widely embraced—at least not yet!

Although I used to think that the idea did not take hold in the Soviet Union because of economic reasons, there is so far little evidence of interest in the post-Communist Russia. I think that, like some of "old Europe," Russians think that they have education pretty well worked out and may see little reason to consult an American psychologist-turned-educationalist (and perhaps they are right). If it were not for the heroic advocacy of Michaela Singer, it is unlikely that my books would be available in Romania, and so far as I know, they are only rarely available in other former members of the Soviet bloc. My writings are widely available in Scandinavia and the Netherlands, in the Swedish and Danish languages, as well as in English. Individuals in these northern European societies seem to accept the idea of multiple intelligences, but a sense of stretch and discovery is less evident, perhaps because promoting MI ideas in a progressive educational terrain is akin to pushing a door that was already ajar.

In the past few years, I have noted two phenomena. One is that many educators in India are discovering MI ideas and are seeking to implement them. I suspect that as with China, the increasing affluence of the country and the opening of many for-profit schools has catalyzed interest in ideas that have already become trendy in the more developed countries. I also note a steady stream of people writing from the Middle East, including from Iraq and Iran, but not much interest at the ministry or publication level except in Israel. (Note, however, Thomas Armstrong's report of Islamic madrases that embrace MI ideas [see Chapter Two].)

In addition to the influence of authors or individual promoters, memes can be spread by charismatic institutions or powerful practices. Self-declared MI schools in the United States and abroad can prove to be a powerful Petri dish for spreading the ideas. In their twenty years of existence, the Key Learning Community in Indianapolis and the New City School in St. Louis have had thousands of visitors, many from abroad. These visits can have a powerful effect. When visitors from Norway attended the opening of the MI Library at the New City School, they pledged to open an MI library in their country and have just carried through on their pledge. Media that carry MI stories can exert great influence. When *ABC-TV News* and *Newsweek* featured the Key Learning Community, millions of persons learned about MI educational experiments. Happy Cheung's publications and broadcast have had similar reverberations in China. The existence of institutions based on MI ideas, such as the Explorama in Danfoss Universe, has exposed families and businesspeople to MI ways of thinking, even if these individuals never encounter the "MI meme" per se. Assessment instruments—qualitative ones, like Spectrum in Scandinavia, and quantitative ones, like the MIDAS in East Asia—spread the MI meme as effectively as books or soapbox speakers. Similarly, instruments designed for special populations, like the DISCOVER approach of June Maker and colleagues, introduce MI ideas beyond mainstream circles.

It is relatively straightforward to do a travelogue, to mention the places where MI ideas have taken hold and where they have not, and to speculate about the carriers of the ideas. But this *tour de horizon* raises two related and more searching questions: Why are certain regions more receptive than others? and What messages is MI bringing to these disparate soils?

The Nature of the Soil

It is useful to think of MI as a new plant (all the while being careful not to stretch the analogy too far). Having blossomed on its home soil, its seeds are now borne to distant terrains. The new soil, however, can be so resistant, so alien, that the seed cannot take hold, and it simply dies.

It may be that the soil is already so stocked with other seeds and plants that there is no room for any additional flora. Often schools and institutions are so busy, or so self-confident, or so beleaguered, that they show no interest in any new ideas or practices.

Or the soil may be so impoverished, so lacking in nutrients, that it cannot absorb any new living matter. I suspect that there are some institutions, regions, and even entire societies that lack resources to attempt anything new, to attend to any new ideas or practices.

At the opposite end of the continuum, some seeds grow naturally and easily in a rich but hitherto sparsely stocked terrain. An MI seed has little trouble in sprouting in a well-resourced environment that has long been receptive to ideas like individual differences, teaching in multiple ways, a focus on arts and creative activities, and so on. These institutions can embrace MI ideas, but they may not be much affected by them. They can rightly say, "We are already doing this, we are happy to wear the MI banner, but [to coin a phrase!] you have simply brought tulips to Holland."

Of course, there are also false positives. As Mindy Kornhaber and colleagues have observed, many places claim to be carrying out MI practices and may even feature banners, slogans, and the like. And yet shorn of the appurtenances, such institutions look indistinguishable from ones that have never heard of MI and ones that are in effect uniform schools (featuring a single way of teaching and assessing). These places may believe that the soil is receptive, but in fact the soil cannot, for whatever reason, actually absorb the seed. So to speak, the seed dies on the vine but continues to cling there, deceiving those who cannot see the difference between pseudo- and genuine MI practices.

Of most interest are those places, institutions, and leaders who initially offer resistance to MI or initially understand MI in the most superficial way. Using our analogy, these places at first prove quite resistant to the MI seed. And yet, over time either the ground becomes friendlier to the seed, or a mutant version of the MI seed is able to take hold and eventually flourish in the initially hostile environment. I am reminded of a poignant anecdote featuring Pat Bolaños, the charismatic founder of the Key Learning Community. At the fifteenth anniversary of the school, she addressed a large supportive audience gathered in a concert hall in downtown Indianapolis. After thanking the many who had supported Key over the years, she declared, "And finally, I'd like to thank the six superintendents who have been in Indianapolis since we first thought of the school. Without your steadfast opposition, we would never have achieved anything!"

Why MI Takes Hold in Certain Soils

As the progenitor of the idea of multiple intelligence, I'd like to think that its intrinsic power, beauty, and truth have accounted for its success in various venues. And in fact, I think that many advocates of MI are attracted to the idea on the basis of its merits. Yet for an idea like MI to spread in various regions, to go beyond the advocacy of a precious few, there have to be reasons that appeal to a wider group. In reviewing my own experiences and observations over the past twenty-five years, I have identified four factors that stand out.

Rediscovery of Traditions In some cultures, there is a belief that certain norms or practices, valued in the past, have been ignored or minimized in recent years. In Japan, for example, the formal schools and apprenticeships of an earlier era featured many practical arts and crafts (see Chapter Seven). By the same token, the Confucian tradition in China recognized a whole gamut of competences that distinguished the educated person (see Chapters Four through Six). The Diné group in the American Southwest used to honor various craft traditions, and approaches like the DISCOVER method devised by Maker allow a recognition of these practices and their associated cognitive and sensory faculties.

Sometimes this renewed embrace of traditional values can lead to unexpected and even humorous effects. In China in 2004, I attempted to discover the reasons that MI theory had taken such hold. The mystery was cleared up by a journalist in Shanghai who said to me, "Dr. Gardner, in the West, when people hear about the idea of multiple intelligences, they go directly to what is special about *their* child, to discover his or her 'unique genius.' In China, by contrast, the multiple intelligences are simply eight talents that we must nurture in every child."

A Desire to Broaden Curricula, Pedagogy, and Assessments In many regions of the world, there has been a steady narrowing of the curriculum, so that it highlights the STEM subjects (science, technology, engineering, and mathematics), while giving short shrift to the arts, physical education, and certain of the humanities and social sciences. MI can be a useful vehicle for broadening the remit of education: to include subjects that address the several intelligences and ways of thinking, as well as teaching methods that speak to individual differences, and assessments that go beyond standard, short-answer language-and-logic instruments (see Chapters Eight, Twelve, Fourteen, Fifteen, Twenty-Four, Twenty-Five, and Twenty-Nine). Even when the focus remains on science and mathematics, an MI approach can open new possibilities for mastery (see Chapters Fourteen and Nineteen).

A Desire to Reach Underserved Students Even as the curriculum has tended to narrow in recent years, so too in many regions, curricula are addressed to average or typical students; there has been relatively little effort to help students who fall outside the mainstream. Accordingly, MI ideas have been used widely in special education (Chapter Eleven), gifted education (Chapter Twenty-Seven), and the education of traditionally underserved students (Chapters Thirteen, Sixteen, Eighteen, Twenty-Three, and Twenty-Six). Alas, this laudable aim can be abused. Too often have I heard a specific ethnic or racial group described as "having" certain intelligences and "lacking others." There is no scientific warrant for such a statement, and considerable damage can be done in its wake.

An Affirmation of Democratic Practices and Values Nowadays, few if any countries in the world would declare that they are opposed to democratic values. Even the most authoritarian of countries call themselves democracies, indeed even incorporate the word *democracy* into the country's current name. And yet truly democratic practices are often elusive. Schools are often authoritarian institutions that stifle debate, controversy, and individual points of view—light-years away from democratic communities whose members participate in decision making and governance. In several of the chapters in this book, we see clear indication that those involved in MI education are dedicated to providing a model of a democratic institution in a soil that has been hostile to these ideas—for example, in Argentina (Chapter Twenty-One), Colombia (Chapter Twenty-Two), the Philippines (Chapter Nine), and Romania (Chapter Nineteen).

THE POLICY LEVEL

Many times these goals are put forth by individuals or single institutions that simply want to make changes at the local level. But as some of the chapters document, more ambitious efforts have been launched to alter practices on a wider scale. In England, Scotland, China, and Norway, for example, MI approaches are explicitly promoted as an alternative to practices that are currently regnant but are seen by some as shortsighted, counterproductive, or even destructive. At times, even in these countries, policies are announced that seem more congenial to MI approaches. Not surprisingly, supporters of MI are quick to embrace these reformist inclinations (China, Korea, Scotland, Turkey). So long as ministers of education around the world are focused largely on the comparative performance of countries on the Programme for International Student Assessment (PISA)[1] examinations, we can expect that supporters of MI will mount counterefforts. And in the event that these supporters find themselves in policymaking positions, they will attempt to institute policies that are more "MI friendly."

I am still mystified by one development. A few years ago, a colleague visited Pyongyang, the capital of North Korea. In a major library there, he saw only two books in English. One was Michael Moore's *Stupid White Men.* The other was *Frames of Mind: The Theory of Multiple Intelligences.* I cannot help wondering how these two memes managed to plant themselves in such seemingly resistant soil.

CONCLUDING NOTE: THE PERSONAL AND THE POLITICAL

The theory of multiple intelligences was developed by a psychologist; it was initially a proposal of how we should think of individual minds. This way of thinking initially proved most congenial to individuals who themselves have a psychological perspective on the world and who are excited rather than threatened by the idea of a plurality of individual differences.

I was surprised to see how this "inside psychology" meme spread quickly to education, first in the United States and then abroad. I was surprised by the staying power of the meme. And I am surprised that this meme has begun to be of interest to those in the policy realm, thus melding the personal and the political. It is striking that an idea that arose as an account of how the human brain/mind evolved and how it is organized today could end up joining forces with movements that give more voice to individuals and promote more democratic classes, schools, and perhaps even societies. I would like to think that this combination would please John Dewey, an American philosopher and psychologist who was perennially rooted in both the personal and the political.

Still, it is salutary to remember that the idea of multiple intelligences remains a minority view in psychology and that most schools around the world remain uniform schools, where a narrow group of topics is taught in the same way to all children and where modes of assessment are unadventurous, to say the least. My own view—or perhaps, to be more accurate, my own hope—is that the new digital media will allow so much individualized education in the future that the meme of multiple intelligences will be taken for granted. Should that be the case, the authors in this book will deserve considerable credit for sustaining and enriching MI ideas and practices in the interim.

Note

1. A triennial worldwide test of fifteen-year-old schoolchildren's scholastic performance for the purpose of crosscultural school learning comparison.

References

Gardner, H. (1973). *The arts and human development.* New York: Wiley.

Gardner, H. (1975). *The shattered mind: The person after brain damage.* New York: Knopf.

Gardner, H. (1980). *Artful scribbles.* New York: Basic Books.

Gardner, H. (1983). *Frames of mind: The theory of multiple intelligences.* New York: Basic Books.

Gardner, H. (1995). Reflections on multiple intelligences: Myths and realities. *Phi Delta Kappan, 77,* 200–209.

Gardner, H. (1999). *Intelligence reframed.* New York: Basic Books.

Goleman, D. (1995). *Emotional intelligence.* New York: Bantam Books.

Moore, M. (2004). *Stupid white men.* New York: HarperCollins.

CHAPTER 2

When Cultures Connect

Multiple Intelligences Theory as a Successful American Export to Other Countries

Thomas Armstrong

This chapter describes contacts between the theory of multiple intelligences (MI theory) and three different cultural contexts: the teaching of a high school lesson plan based on MI theory in a suburb of Beijing, China; the Norwegian practice of nature education in an *utskole* (outdoor school) and its relationship to the naturalist intelligence; and the paradox of a pluralistic theory (MI) being adopted by monistic Western religious traditions. In each case, the cultural contact is a favorable one, and reasons are explored as to why MI theory has been so successful in integrating its Western cultural bias with the values and beliefs of other cultures. The fact that MI theory has as part of its core structure a deep-seated appreciation for the manifestations of intelligences in cultures around the world is seen as a primary reason for its success as an American export to other shores.

Cultures are like chemical elements. You can mix two of them, and you might get something useful like water or table salt. But you might also blow up the kitchen. When Portuguese Jesuits came to the Mughal Emperor Akbar's court in sixteenth-century India, they were astonished when the Muslim emperor prostrated himself before images of Christ (Dalrymple, 2007). But when Admiral Perry sailed into Uraga Harbor near modern-day Tokyo in 1853 and was told by representatives of the Tokugawa shogunate to proceed to Nagasaki for limited trading, Perry threatened a naval bombardment before Japanese officials relented and reluctantly let him come ashore (Walworth, 1946).

In a similar though not nearly so dramatic way, Howard Gardner's theory of multiple intelligences (MI theory) represents an expression of American culture that has increasingly been exported to other cultures over the past two decades. In this chapter, I examine how MI theory has fared in these cultural contacts and determine where along the spectrum of cross-cultural acceptance, from enthusiastic prostration to threatened bombardment, MI theory can be placed in this potential collision of cultures. In particular, I explore three different cultural encounters that I have personally experienced: classroom observation in the People's Republic of China, the experience of *uteskole* in Norway, and reflections on the acceptance of MI theory in fundamentalist and orthodox cultural and religious traditions in the West.

There is a strong multicultural component in MI theory. At the core of Howard Gardner's theory of multiple intelligences is the assertion that each intelligence represents the manifestation of culturally valued products and the formulation and solving of culturally relevant problems. In establishing his set of criteria or prerequisites for what an intelligence must contain, Gardner writes, "I recognize that the ideal of what is valued will differ markedly, sometimes even radically, across human cultures, with the creation of new products or posing of new questions being of little importance in some settings. The prerequisites are a way of ensuring that a human intelligence must be genuinely useful and important, at least in certain cultural settings" (Gardner, 1983, p. 61). I believe that MI theory has been well received by cultures around the world precisely because the eight intelligences embody capabilities that are found in virtually all cultures. All cultures have systems of music, literature (or oral traditions), logic (even if hidden under symbolic structures; see, for example, Lévi-Strauss, 1966), social organization, physical formation, pictorial expression, intrapersonal integration, and nature classification. In essence, cultures can easily recognize themselves in these eight manifestations of intelligent activity. MI theory, in this way, has a bit of the chameleon in it, ever shifting its colors to meet the specific cultural expressions it encounters in each society around the world.

At the same time, MI theory itself is a culturally valued product (as well as the outcome of a set of problems posed and perhaps resolved) that is specific to a particular social and historical context: the United States in the late twentieth and early twenty-first centuries. As such, it brings with it certain types of cultural values that are implicit in American culture. Perhaps foremost among them is the idea of pluralism—the belief that there are many truths, not just one overarching truth, and many ways of knowing and thinking (see, for example, James, 1966; Berlin, 2000). In addition, MI theory reflects the American value of pragmatism, as seen, for example, in the works of John Dewey (a clear precursor to Howard Gardner in the history of American education), William James, and, more recently, Richard Rorty (Rorty, 1989;

James, 1991; Dewey, 1998; see also Menand, 2001). In this respect, MI theory is to be judged not by its ability to solve central truths in philosophy (such as an absolute definition of the nature of intelligence) but rather by its "cash value," that is, its operational ability to generate new questions, ideas, programs, discourses, and strategies in psychology and education. (This point deserves to be well taken by recent critics of the theory of multiple intelligences who have consistently attacked the theory for its "fuzziness" and lack of empirical support; see, for example, Waterhouse, 2006.) There is also a sense of the good old American values of optimism and individualism contained within MI theory, as can be seen in the work of many practitioners around the United States (see, for example, my own self-help books: Armstrong, 1999, 2000a, 2002). This includes the idea of American "can-do-ism"—the belief that every person can reach his or her full potential—as well as the value of using creativity or innovation to come up with novel solutions to difficult problems. Finally, MI theory embraces the value of egalitarianism, wherein each of the eight intelligences has relative equality with the other seven, and individuals possessed of superiority in the Western elitist academic domains of linguistic and logical-mathematical intelligence are no longer necessarily deemed worthy of retaining their unquestioned hegemony in the educational arena or in the intellectual marketplace of ideas.

Given this background, I examine my own experiences in observing multiple intelligences adopted or applied in three different cultural contexts. First, I look at a trip that I took to the People's Republic of China in August 2002 for a conference organized by the Beijing Institute of Education. At this conference, I presented a lecture and also had the opportunity of seeing a lesson taught using multiple intelligences at a high school in a suburb outside Beijing. My wife and I sat at the back of the classroom while a teacher in her twenties or thirties taught fourteen-year-old students a lesson about the Irish singer, songwriter, actor, and political activist Bob Geldof, who was one of the chief organizers of the Live Aid rock concert simulcast from London and Philadelphia in 1985 that raised $150 million for worldwide famine relief. While the students practiced their English, they proceeded to provide statistics about the event; share music, lyrics, and images; interact socially; plumb their own personal emotions; and even put on a role play about Geldof's life.

As I watched the lesson proceed, I found my jaw dropping as I realized that I was observing something that I had never seen before: an exact demonstration of an ideal multiple intelligences lesson plan as I had envisioned it in my book *Multiple Intelligences in the Classroom* (Armstrong, 2000b). My first reaction was one of elation. During previous visits to MI classrooms, I had never seen such a lean and tight presentation of a lesson that tied specific strategies to a clearly identified instructional objective. Too often what I had seen in previous classroom visits were simply typical examples of children working at projects in a manner consistent with the ideals of progressive education, open education, and constructivist learning (not that there is anything wrong with that). What was new for me here was an approach to learning that was distinctively multiple intelligences and not to be confused with any other approach. Of course, there was more than a little pride welling up in my throat as I watched my own book being demonstrated in living color in front of me six thousand miles from my own home shores.

But then another reaction set in. The question, "Am I looking at the real thing?" passed through my mind. Was what I was seeing in this classroom in a Beijing suburb simply an artificial orchestration of my lesson plan instructions designed to impress the author? Or was there something going on at a higher level that was more along the lines of "imitation is the sincerest form of flattery" or even reflections of a noble Chinese ideal? I had read Howard Gardner's book *To Open Minds* (1991) about his experiences visiting China in the 1980s and was aware of the Chinese proclivity in art toward copying as opposed to creativity. In the course of the book, Gardner struggles to reconcile himself with the Chinese value system of exact replication of artistic masterpieces and the way it contrasts with the American value placed on creating something brand new. He seemed by the end of the book to have reached a rapprochement, at least to some degree, with imitation as an artistic ideal alongside creative originality. Perhaps, here too I could appreciate the fact that the classroom teacher had created something that accurately reflected what I had spent years cultivating and refining in my own writings and practice.

When we were in the bus going back to the conference headquarters, the teacher of the lesson asked me what she could do to improve on what she had done. Frankly I was so impressed with the lesson that I couldn't think of a single thing, except, sad to say, a suggestion that she had spelled the name Bob Geldof wrong—that it was spelled Geldorf. This, I later found out, was not correct. The teacher was right; I was wrong. I had had a close friend with auditory discrimination problems tell me about Geldo[r]f's work a few years before (or perhaps it was I who had the auditory discrimination problems). This little gaff underlined for me again the fact that maybe exact imitation is not such a bad thing after all.

The second cultural encounter relates to my experience visiting Norway in 2005 when I attended a conference in Skien, Norway, Henrik Ibsen's boyhood home. During that trip, I had an opportunity to visit the Kollmyr Skole (School) in Skien to see elementary school children engaged in a variety of practical and academic tasks reflecting the wide range of multiple intelligences. What impressed me the most was what Norwegians call the *uteskole,* or outside school. *Uteskole* is part of a larger naturalist framework in education in Norway called *friluftsliv,* which can be roughly translated as "outdoor nature life"; it encompasses a range of physical activities in nature, most of which have environmental and cultural dimensions. The Web site of the Parliament of the United Kingdom notes that *friluftsliv* is a defining aspect of national identity in Norway (Higgins, 2004). One can certainly appreciate this, looking at the vast expanses of nature in Norway, the strong emphasis on winter sports like skiing and tobogganing, and the rich elements of nature in their folklore and literature (note, for example, Edvard Grieg's orchestral work, "In the Hall of the Mountain King," based on a section of Ibsen's marvelous play *Peer Gynt*). As a result of this all-embracing vision of nature education, most of Norway's elementary-school children spend a full day each week of the academic year engaged in outdoor learning, much of it occurring in a lean-to structure or hut, called a *gapahuk,* which is set apart from the regular school.

I happened to visit Kollmyr Skole during a day when nine- and ten-year-old students were at one of the two *gapahuker* at the school making replicas of prehistoric Norse cooking utensils from fallen branches of trees and other natural materials. I remember that it started to rain, and I reflected at the time that the typical reaction of an American educator to these circumstances would have been to round up all the students and head back to the warm school building, which in this case was located several hundred yards away along a winding dirt pathway. Nobody headed toward the school. There is a motto at another *uteskole* in Norway: "There isn't such a thing as bad weather, only bad clothing" (Ellevol Oppvekstsenter, n.d.). The backpack-bearing children had come to the *gapahuk* prepared for the rain, and they pulled out and put on their windbreakers, caps, jackets, and other "good weather" clothing and continued to engage in their activities.

Kari Birkeland, the principal of Kollmyr Skole, communicated to me that students who have been struggling with the indoors classroom (the regular classroom instruction) often do particularly well when they are outside. Another *uteskole* teacher commented, "I have noticed lots of children with 'ants in their back' [a Norwegian expression] who don't like our education in front of the class, and many teachers give them up and give them a diagnosis [attention deficit hyperactivity disorder, ADHD, is common]. But I have seen children bloom when they can be outdoors, and use their bodies. Children who can't spell their names, can dig a tunnel and be smart 'constructional [sic] engineers'" (I. M. Misje, personal communication, December 19, 2007). This appears to agree with research in the United States that green environments help individuals labeled ADHD concentrate and learn more effectively (Taylor, Kuo, & Sullivan, 2001).

This particular instance of cultural contact between MI theory and Norwegian outdoor education differs from the Chinese example cited above in that it is not MI theory that is bringing something new—a lesson planning strategy—to the table, as was the case in the People's Republic of China. Rather the Norwegian ideal of *friluftsliv* is offering something new to MI theory: a framework within which the naturalist intelligence (as well as each of the other intelligences) can develop and flourish. Up until my contact with the *uteskole,* most of my observations of the naturalist intelligence at work in schools in the United States consisted in the occasional garden, terrarium, ecology curriculum, or classroom pet that I would see during my classroom visits. What particularly impressed me about the *uteskole* was its all-encompassing vision of outdoor learning.

The educator who was my contact while visiting Skien, Mette Bunting, pointed out to me in a recent communication that all of the learning that can take place inside a school building can also take place outside in the *gapahuk.* This reminded me of various strategies that I had written about in my book *The Multiple Intelligences of Reading and Writing* that related to the outdoors—for example, "read outside," "spell outside," "write outside" (Armstrong, 2003). It is far more difficult to bring the outdoors inside than to do indoor activities outside. It also reminded me of certain exotic aphasias reported by psycholinguist Steven Pinker, wherein an afflicted individual has the ability to name things that are found outside but not inside or can name living things but not nonliving objects (Pinker, 1994). There seems to be a proclivity toward naturalist activities in the brain, which makes sense from an evolutionary perspective, since our species has spent far more time learning to survive in the wilds than living in framed and insulated buildings. This very fact seems to underscore the importance of using *friluftsliv* in other countries and cultures around the world. Mette Bunting told me that in some kindergartens in Norway, children spend the entire day outdoors. This flabbergasted me, coming from an American culture where kindergartens are increasingly having their nap, recess, and play time cut back to provide more time for developmentally inappropriate formal academic learning (Swidey, 2007). Clearly the *uteskole* is a cultural gift to the theory of multiple intelligences and in particular to the naturalist intelligence, especially in the way MI theory is practiced in the United States.

Finally, I make some reflections on what to me has been a somewhat puzzling phenomenon: the broad acceptance of the theory of multiple intelligences in at least certain segments of the orthodox and fundamentalist wings of all three major Western religious traditions: Judaism, Christianity, and Islam. The reason I say this is puzzling is that MI theory seems to be rooted in an American ideal of pluralism, where the concept of many truths is acknowledged. The fundamentalist or orthodox cultural and religious traditions that I have had experience with as an MI writer and practitioner seem to embrace more of an ideal of monism, the sense that there is only one truth embodied in the specific religious traditions, beliefs, and practices of a particular faith. I have done multiple intelligences training for Torah Umesorah, an orthodox Jewish educational organization; seen Gardner's work discussed favorably in fundamentalist Christian publications for parents (see, for example, Tobias, 1994); and had my book *Multiple Intelligences in the Classroom* (2006) translated into Arabic by a Saudi Arabian publisher. From my perspective as a non-Muslim, this last form of acceptance has been perhaps the most mind-boggling. I recognize that my reaction stems, perhaps in large part, from the onslaught of narrowly focused media coverage in the United States after the events of September 11, 2001, and in part from the distorted views that non-Muslim Western cultural sources have promulgated about Islam over the course of many centuries (Said, 2003). Yet it still startles me when I see an article on the Internet entitled "Reforming Pakistan's 'Dens of Terror,'" claiming that Howard Gardner's theory of multiple intelligences is being favorably taught and received in the madrasas of Pakistan (Schmidle, 2007).

I can venture several explanations as to why MI theory has been so well received in these seemingly narrowly focused cultural and religious contexts. First, there is a strong component of learning in each of these faiths, and MI theory is seen as a means of supporting that tradition. In Judaism, there is a folk tradition of providing a young child with his or her first alphabet board smothered in honey so that the child will always associate learning with sweetness. In *Frames of Mind,* Gardner cites the tradition in Islamic schools of memorizing the Qur'an (Gardner, 1983). One might add to this the long tradition in Islamic culture of explorations in philosophy, mathematics, astronomy, history, geography, poetry, and many other fields of study (Esposito, 2000). Second, there are in these religious traditions, elements that emphasize alternative ways of learning that are superior to a traditional academic intellectual approach. The story that I use most often to begin my multiple intelligences keynote speeches and workshops is "The Grammarian and the Boatman," which is from Sufi poet Jalal al din Rumi's monumental work the *Masnavi,* one of the masterpieces of Islamic and world literature (Jalal al din Rumi, 2002). In this story, a grammarian criticizes a boatman for making grammatical mistakes, only to encounter a storm in a boat and hear the boatman chide him for not being able to swim. The idea that there are many different kinds of abilities is a theme that runs through all religious traditions. In Christianity, there is the well-known story of the "investment of one's talents" in Matthew 25:14–30. An Algerian educator I have been in contact with recently is investigating the relationship between multiple intelligences and the multiple—there are ninety-nine—names of Allah (Abdelhak, 2008).

There is also the matter of looking at this acceptance from the other side of the equation as well. What has MI theory done to accommodate itself to these cultural and religious traditions? I suggest that perhaps the major contribution in this regard is Gardner's finding a place in the theory for the religious impulse (in the candidate existential intelligence), while rejecting the idea of a "spiritual" intelligence that could have brought with it a great deal of controversy among different religious groups. After all, whose idea of spiritual would be incorporated as authoritative? Gardner (2000) notes, "The believers or spokespersons for spirituality [claim] that spiritual concerns lead to an encounter with a deeper or higher truth. . . . There is a specific content—a spiritual truth—to which only some or only those who have followed a certain path can have access. And this slippery slope leads all too often to a belief that the world can be divided between those who qualify on some spiritual, religious, or metaphysical ground and those who do not. . . . Here, we have left the realm of intelligence and moved to the sphere of dogma" (p. 56).

Gardner has provisionally adopted the idea of an existential intelligence, which has no fixed dogma or belief connected with it yet acknowledges the existence of individuals who have a higher capacity than is common to see visions, influence others ethically, reflect on religious and philosophical questions, and engage in other pursuits related to ultimate life questions. Hence, there is something in MI theory for each religious faith to identify with in terms of a well-regarded scientific model with Harvard backing that validates their own practices. I might suggest also that even Gardner's giving only provisional status to existential intelligence—holding it apart, as it were, from the rest of the theory—may serve as a kind of pragmatic strategy to lessen the potential for conflict, were the intelligence given full-fledged membership in the MI pantheon.

Although each cultural encounter described in this chapter has its own unique features, in all three cases, there has been a favorable outcome in the interaction between MI theory and the values of the respective cultures. The Admiral Perry scenario was avoided! The reason for this goodness of fit between MI theory and diverse cultures appears to reside most strongly in the theory's capacity to validate each culture's traditions, not simply at the high culture level (published literature, music, science, and others), but also at the level of a nation's folk traditions, its core national identifications, its aesthetic ideals, and other subtle dimensions of a society's deep cultural practices.

In addition, a parting word should be appended here acknowledging Gardner's personal openness to the application of his theory to a wide range of contexts as a major reason for the theory's success worldwide. With regard to others taking his ideas and making them relevant to their own unique circumstances, Gardner (2000) has written, "In general, my advice has echoed the traditional Chinese adage: 'Let a hundred flowers bloom'" (p. 89). By taking this open approach, Gardner has ensured that MI theory will continue to flourish across cultures for many years to come.

References

Abdelhak, H. (2008). *Multiple intelligences theory and English language learning: A case study.* Unpublished doctoral dissertation, Ferhat Abbes University, Setif, Algeria.

Armstrong, T. (1999). *Seven kinds of smart: Identifying and developing your multiple intelligences.* New York: Plume.

Armstrong, T. (2000a). *In their own way: Discovering and encouraging your child's multiple intelligences.* New York: Tarcher/Penguin.

Armstrong, T. (2000b). *Multiple intelligences in the classroom* (2nd ed.). Alexandria, VA: Association for Supervision and Curriculum Development.

Armstrong, T. (2002). *You're smarter than you think: A kid's guide to multiple intelligences.* Minneapolis, MN: Free Spirit Publishing.

Armstrong, T. (2003). *The multiple intelligences of reading and writing: Making the words come alive.* Alexandria, VA: Association for Supervision and Curriculum Development.

Armstrong, T. (2006). *Multiple intelligences in the classroom* (2nd ed.) [Arabic translation] (H. Abdulghani, Trans.). Al Khobar, Saudi Arabia: Educational Book House and Dhahran Ahliyya Schools.

Berlin, I. (2000). *The proper study of mankind: An anthology of essays.* New York: Farrar, Straus, & Giroux.

Dalrymple, W. (2007, November 22). The most magnificent Muslims. *New York Review of Books, 27.*

Dewey, J. (1998). *The essential Dewey, Vol. 1: Pragmatism, education, democracy.* Bloomington: Indiana University Press.

Ellevol Oppvekstsenter (n.d.). *Outdoor schooling.* Retrieved March 10, 2008, from http://home.no.net/elvevoll/.

Esposito, J. L. (Ed.). (2000). *The Oxford book of Islam.* New York: Oxford University Press.

Gardner, H. (1983). *Frames of mind: The theory of multiple intelligences.* New York: Basic Books.

Gardner, H. (1991). *To open minds.* New York: Basic Books.

Gardner, H. (2000). *Intelligence reframed: Multiple intelligences for the 21st century.* New York: Basic Books.

Higgins, P. (2004, October). Memorandum submitted by Peter Higgins, Outdoor and Environmental Education Section, School of Education, University of Edinburgh, executive summary. Retrieved March 10, 2008, from http://www.publications. parliament.uk/pa/cm200405/cmselect/cmeduski/120/120we06.htm.

Jalal al din Rumi. (2002). *Tales from the Masnavi* (A. J. Aberry, Trans.). London: RoutledgeCurzon.

James, W. (1966). *A pluralistic universe: Hibbert Lectures at Manchester College on the present situation in philosophy.* Lincoln: University of Nebraska Press.

James, W. (1991). *Pragmatism.* Buffalo, NY: Prometheus Books.

Lévi-Strauss, C. (1966). *The savage mind.* Chicago: University of Chicago Press.

Menand, L. (2001). *The metaphysical club: A story of ideas in America.* New York: Farrar, Straus, & Giroux.

Pinker, S. (1994). *The language instinct.* New York: Morrow.

Rorty, R. (1989). *Contingency, irony, and solidarity.* Cambridge: Cambridge University Press.

Said, E. (2003). *Orientalism.* New York: Penguin.

Schmidle, N. (2007, January 22). *Reforming Pakistan's "dens of terror."* Retrieved March 10, 2007, from http://www.truthdig.com/report/item/20070122_nicholas_schmidle_reforming_pakistans_dens_of_terror/.

Swidey, N. (2007, October 28). Rush, little baby: How the push for infant academics may actually be a waste of time or worse. *Boston Globe.* Retrieved March 10, 2007, from http://www.boston.com/news/globe/magazine/articles/2007/10/28/rush_little_baby/.

Taylor, A. F., Kuo, F. E., & Sullivan, W. C. (2001). Coping with ADD: The surprising connection to green play settings. *Environment and Behavior, 33*(1), 54–77.

Tobias, C. U. (1994). *The way they learn: How to discover and teach to your child's strengths.* Colorado Springs: Focus on the Family Publications.

Walworth, A. (1946). *Black ships off Japan: The story of Commodore Perry's expedition.* New York: Knopf.

Waterhouse, L. (2006, Fall). Multiple intelligences, the Mozart effect, and emotional intelligence: A critical review. *Educational Psychologist, 41*(4), 207–225.

PART TWO

ASIA AND PACIFIC AREAS

E ncounters between the MI meme and long-standing educational traditions are readily visible in Asia. Despite differences between ancient
and modern traditions, Asian educators discover that some key values
and practices from the past are in confluence with MI educational principles.
The Japanese tradition of arts education and Confucian thinking are two examples of this confluence. Significant features of chapters in this section include
strong efforts in collaboration, emphasis on character education, and the positive effects of government support. The widespread use in Asia of standardized tests, such as college entrance examinations, poses a great challenge to
MI-inspired educational practices. A noticeable change documented in the chapters is the shift from teacher-centered curriculum to child-centered education.

CHAPTER 3

China's Assimilation of MI Theory in Education

Accent on the Family and Harmony

Jie-Qi Chen

The successful integration of MI theory in China's schools is seen at all grade levels and in all geographical areas. Political, cultural, and educational forces contributed to the theory's wide diffusion. Operating within China's cultural zone of proximal development, MI built on the momentum of Chinese educational reform and contributed to its advancement. MI implementation in China is not a direct transfer, but the result of a strong acculturation process. Specifically, the Chinese people conceptualize intelligence as an attribute of the family. Thus, MI practices in China involve the whole family. Committed to the value of harmony, Chinese MI educators seek to achieve balance among diverse teaching and learning components such as individual interests and group goals. The cultural assimilation process in China suggests new MI applications and deepens our understanding of the pivotal role that culture plays as MI extends around the world.

MI theory is widespread and has been well received in Chinese education (Using MI Theory to Guide Discovery of Students' Potential Project, 2007). As indicated elsewhere in the volume (see Chapters Five and Six), hundreds of thousands of teachers, school administrators, and educational researchers across China have completed MI training through international conferences, university-based professional development sessions, and provincial educational bureau programs. As a particularly compelling example of MI popularity, half the teacher population in Shanxi Province participated in an intensive summer training program on MI theory and practices. So far as I know, the scale of this initiative is unequaled in other countries, though of course the percentage of MI-trained Chinese educators is still small.

Although there is no official record of how many Chinese schools use MI theory as a guiding principle for curriculum reform, many different kinds of schools are involved in MI implementation: public and private; mainstream and special education; preschools, elementary, and high schools; vocational schools; city, urban, and rural schools; key schools that serve a highly select student population; and district schools that enroll primarily children from working-class families. Many schools have formed MI study teams, composed of the school principal, teachers, curriculum coordinators, and parents, that support and evaluate MI implementation effectiveness.

Print materials and information related to MI theory are readily accessible in big cities through bookstores, libraries, and Web sites. More than one hundred books on MI theory and its applications have been written or translated by scholars in Mainland China, Taiwan, Hong Kong, Macao, and Singapore. A national MI project sponsored by the Chinese Educational Society, Using MI Theory to Guide Discovery of Students' Potential Project, has published a dozen books describing MI implementation experiences in project schools. The project also produced, in DVD form, over three hundred exemplary case studies of MI implementation across a range of grade levels and in different types of schools. Centralizing educators' access to print materials, the project staff assembled a collection of more than three thousand MI-related essays and reports written by school leaders and teachers.

The degree of MI impact is all the more impressive considering that MI theory is a Western intelligence theory offering no solution to any specific Chinese educational problems. The popularity of the theory in China poses two questions related to the role of culture in MI dissemination. First, what factors account for the current status of MI theory among Chinese educators? Second, how has MI theory been transformed through implementation by Chinese educators? To address these two questions, I examine the acceptance and practices of MI theory in China in relation to political, societal, cultural, and educational contexts from historical and contemporary perspectives. In the analysis, I pay special attention to the Chinese recognition of family, rather than the individual, as the unit for conceptualizing intelligences, and I focus as well on the Chinese cultural commitment to harmony, which stresses a balance among components in the teaching and learning process. This contextual analysis helps to explain why China has welcomed MI theory and how Eastern and Western values have intermingled in the MI acculturation process.

FACTORS CONTRIBUTING TO THE STATUS OF MI THEORY IN CHINA

The success of a theory depends on both its internal features and external factors in the environment in which the theory is introduced (Feldman, 2003; Gruber, 1981). Major internal features that drew Chinese attention to MI theory are its distinctive accessibility to practitioners, the reliable data sources used to support the theory, and the theory's positive view of developing human potential. Four major external influences contributed to MI's success in China: the politics of the open door policy, societal needs for educational change, consonance with Chinese traditional thinking, and centralization of the Chinese educational system. While the internal features of MI theory may appeal to educators from around the world, the external factors are culture specific and therefore require a contextual analysis.

Change in Political Atmosphere with the Open Door Policy

Reflecting a strong, shared ideology, the political atmosphere in the People's Republic of China (PRC) is the ultimate force that directs society's educational thinking. For more than three decades following the establishment of the PRC in 1949, China was closed to the outside world. Everything—political ideology, economic development, education, and even social life—was controlled by the government. Western ideologies, particularly those of the United States, were condemned as imperialist or capitalistic poisoning of the proletarian revolutionists. John Dewey (1948), whose philosophy of education was once venerated as a breath of fresh air from the West, was condemned as an apologist for Western values. In this political environment, it would have been extremely difficult, if not entirely impossible, for a Western intelligence theory emphasizing individual differences to penetrate the heavily controlled ideological hegemony in China.

Deng Xiaoping's open door policy adopted in the early 1980s reestablished China's contact with the rest of the world. After more than thirty years of isolation, the Chinese people were eager to explore the world beyond China's borders. In its governing strategy, the Chinese political leadership became more utilitarian than ideological. Deng made the following statement, which was repeated so often it became famous: "It does not matter whether it is a black or yellow cat. As long as it catches mice, it will be a good cat." With this shift in political atmosphere, Chinese took a giant step toward embracing Western ideas and practices—among them capitalism-based competition, private ownership, Montessori teaching methods, and infant attachment theory, to name a few scattered examples. The change in the political atmosphere opened the way for changes in other aspects of the society, including education. This opening of the political context made the introduction of MI theory to China possible. Without the recent history of an open door policy and practice, there would be no MI theory in China.

Societal Needs for Educational Change

The most obvious consequence of China's open door policy has been rapid economic development, which creates strong demand for a workforce that is not only knowledgeable and skillful, but also creative and capable of problem solving. Chinese educators were not equipped to meet this demand. As alluded to in Chapter Six, with teachers trained in the use of traditional teaching practices and pressured to prepare students for the college entrance exam, the Chinese educational system has long been known for producing students with high test scores based on narrow skills, which cannot be mobilized to meet new challenges. Educators spoke out about the need for new teaching and learning practices to ensure continuing economic development in China.

In response to societal needs and educators' outcry, China's Ministry of Education issued a series of educational reform guidelines, including the Outlines of Chinese Educational System Reform (1985), the Outlines of Chinese Educational Reform and Development (1993), and the Outline of Curriculum Reform for Compulsory Education (2001). These guidelines established that for Chinese education to meet the challenges of modernization, the world, and the future, it was imperative to adopt curriculum and teaching methods with several attributes, among them respecting the developmental characteristics of children, attending to individual differences, and emphasizing active learning. As policy statements, these outlines did not specify particular theoretical foundations for educational reform. Because MI theory clearly supported the basic tenets of the outlines, educational leaders quickly identified it as a primary theoretical framework for China's curriculum reform.

Consonance with Chinese Traditional Thinking

As emphasized in Chapters Four through Six, the ideas of MI fit well with traditional Chinese thinking in philosophy and education. Philosophically the pluralistic view held by MI theory is familiar. Chinese society is characterized by diverse schools of thought. Pluralism rather than reductionism has dominated philosophical thinking for thousands of years. In the period of the Chinese Warring State (475–221 B.C.), for example, there were a hundred schools of thought or ideologies. Even after a long period of synthesis, there remained four major schools of thought: Confucianism, Daoism, Buddhism, and Legalism. Pluralism continues within each of these schools of thought.

Many Chinese sayings from ancient sages and sacred classics have stressed ideas similar to those proclaimed in MI theory. Confucius, for example, defined the term *humanity* (ren) in more than a dozen ways. His position was clear: a concept as complex as humanity incorporates many elements and should be studied from different angles and approached from a variety of perspectives. Individual differences in teaching and learning are a frequent topic discussed in such sacred classics as *Great Learning* (Da Xue). Using stories from sages such as Confucius and Mencius, as well as from ordinary parents and teachers, the classics articulated many individualized teaching principles, including *Yin Cai Shi Jiao* ("Suit instruction to the student's aptitude"), *Yin Ren Er Yi* (Vary teaching with each individual), and *Zhang Shan Jiu Shi* ("Enhance strengths to lift up weaknesses").

Given the brainwashing by the Chinese Communist party from 1949 to 1979, Westerners may question the extent to which Chinese educators understand these traditional philosophical and educational ideas. To address this question, I summarize evidence that the Communist party did not and could not destroy these traditional ideas. First, in contrast to the short-lived communist ideology in China, the characterization of Chinese culture as pluralistic with Confucian teaching principles is rooted in the five thousand years of history prior to 1949. Pluralism and Confucian principles are so deeply embedded in the culture that they penetrate almost every aspect of Chinese life. Deeply rooted, this cultural history cannot be easily destroyed or replaced. Second, Mao, the chairman of the Chinese Communist party from 1949 to 1979, was himself a diligent disciple of Confucian classics. Many of his sayings about education, such as "Analysis applies to specific situations" (*Ju Ti Wen Ti Ju Ti Fen Xi*) and "Do what is suited to each person" (*Yin Ren Zhi Yi*), were similar to the sayings of Confucius. For Chinese educators at the time, implementing Mao's educational thinking was the continuation of good pedagogy found in the sacred classics. Third, and perhaps the most important factor related to the long-lived Confucian tradition in Chinese society, is its language. There is a common saying, "The process of learning Chinese language is the process of converting to Confucianism." One does not have to go to a formal Confucian school to learn about its doctrines because numerous Chinese daily phrases are heavily influenced by Confucianism and sacred classics. Talk to any Chinese teachers, novice or veteran, in the city or the countryside: all will be familiar with many phrases derived from the Confucian classics despite the fact that they may not know the origins of these sayings.

As this brief historical review indicates, MI theory highlighted, reinforced, and renewed concepts and practices rooted in traditional Chinese pedagogy and embedded in Chinese language. It has been much more difficult for Western ideas, such as infant attachment, that have no corresponding term in the Chinese language to be contemplated and discussed. Because MI builds on what is familiar, many Chinese believe they understand MI theory. They support its use in education and feel psychologically connected to it.

Centralization of the Chinese Educational System

The Ministry of Education in China holds the ultimate power for making decisions about the direction of educational policy and practices. Because education is centralized in China, government policy statements, such as the outlines mentioned earlier, have a much larger impact on curriculum and classroom teaching than actions within a decentralized educational system such as the United States. Following the educational principles presented in the outlines, the People's Education Press in Beijing developed several sets of curricula for elementary and high schools that encouraged teachers and students to use multiple entry points to support learning. MI theory was explicitly mentioned in the teacher guides that accompanied the curricula. Because the People's Education Press operates under the auspices of the Ministry of Education, and schools across the country therefore trust its authority in developing curriculum, use of these MI-related curricula spread quickly throughout China.

Consider another example of how the power of China's centralized educational system accelerated the assimilation of MI theory. In 2002, the Chinese Educational Society selected Using MI Theory to Guide Discovery of Students' Potential as one of its key research and development projects. This endorsement provided financial support, garnered national attention, and attracted participants from all regions of the country. Most important, a systematic and large-scale implementation of MI in Chinese schools became a national priority. To ensure that the project work met high standards, two leading institutions of higher education, the Institute of Education in Beijing and East China Normal University in Shanghai, assumed leadership roles in the north and south of China. Many top educational leaders, such as Xiping Tao, former director of the Bureau of Education in Beijing, and Fang Li, the president of Beijing Institute of Education, served as leaders in the project and therefore played key roles in the MI implementation process across China. The voices of these top educational leaders attracted attention, gained support, and had considerable impact on educators' thinking and action.

The Optimal Environment

In concluding the discussion of factors that have contributed to the success of MI theory in China, the effects of Gardner's association with Harvard University and his personal relationship with China must be recognized. The birthplace of MI theory is Cambridge, Massachusetts, in the United States, a rarely mentioned but undeniable factor contributing to the popularity of MI theory in China. For Chinese, American higher education is the best in the world, and Cambridge-based Harvard University is the flagship of American higher education. If one wants the best of the best in education, Harvard is the destination. People and ideas associated with Harvard are admired and have a competitive edge in China. Gardner has traveled to China several times. His book *To Open Minds: Chinese Clues to the Dilemma of Contemporary Education* (1989) is the result of these trips as well as a residency in China. Many Chinese know that Gardner is genuinely interested in Chinese culture and friendly toward the Chinese people. Following Confucius's teaching, "To have friends coming in from afar, how delightful," Chinese embraced Gardner and MI theory with the warmest of welcomes.

The four factors mentioned above—open door policy, emerging workforce demands, a centralized educational system, and pedagogy in traditional Chinese thought—interacted to create an optimal environment for the successful diffusion of MI theory in China. Through their joint influence, these factors led to a state of readiness for the assimilation of new ideas. Extending Vygotsky's (1978) concept of an individual's zone of proximal development, I suggest the term *cultural zone of proximal development* to refer to the readiness level of a culture to accept new ideas and engage in alternative practices. When China was ready to embrace external ideas and practices useful for its advancement, MI theory was introduced. Because MI theory aligned with critical factors, its reception was strong, and implementation has been effective. MI has continued to function in this cultural zone of proximal development in China for the past decade.

IMPLEMENTATION OF MI THEORY THROUGH AN ACCULTURATION PROCESS

Throughout its five-thousand-year history, China has accepted foreign ideas by assimilating them into its own cultural traditions (Spence, 2002). The introduction of Buddhism, Marxism, and Christianity into China is an example of this assimilation process. MI theory is no exception. MI implementation in China is not a direct transfer, but the result of a strong acculturation process. Among many intriguing issues embedded in the assimilation process, I highlight two here for their contrast with the implementation of MI theory in American culture: differing conceptions of intelligence and different values guiding the educational process.

The Conceptualization of Intelligence

The individual mind is central in the Western intelligence theories that have been developed over the past century. Whether the theory of intelligence is singular or pluralistic, innate or ecological, the focus of Western conceptions centers on the individual. From birth through adulthood, the individual is seen as the primary agent and expression of intelligence. Representing a shift over the past twenty years, context is now recognized as influential in the development of intelligence. Gardner's (1993) multiple intelligence theory, Sternberg's (1988) triarchic theory of intelligence, and Ceci's (1996) bioecological theory of intelligences are among those that draw attention to context. However, compared to the mind of the individual, context frequently remains in the background rather than the foreground in studies of intellectual development.

The Chinese conception of intelligence is different. The origin of this conception can be traced to the Confucian tradition so fundamental in Chinese culture. Intelligence is attributed to the family rather than to the individual. Particularly when children are young, the family is regarded as a collective agent of intelligence. There is no clear boundary between parents and their offspring, either existentially, emotionally, or intellectually. The relationship between family and family members can be likened to the relationship between a body and its parts. Although parts such as an arm or a leg can be distinguished, they do not function independent of the body. From the perspective of the Confucian tradition, the family is a fundamental and irreducible unit of intelligence when children are young. Any attempt to reduce a family to a set of isolated individuals violates the integrity and meaning of the family unit.

The Chinese have implemented MI theory in ways that are consistent with their conception of intelligence. For example, the distinctive intellectual profile of a child is examined in the context of the family, not treated as representing an isolated individual. Parents are often asked to portray a family intellectual profile, indicating existing strengths, interests, or skills of the parents and the child, as well as those they are developing. A family profile is not viewed as separate bar graphs, but rather a dynamic intellectual system in which each member complements, supports, or contributes to the development of another member. Looking at family profiles, MI educators explore to what extent a child's particular strengths reflect parental interests and how a home environment may support the education of the child's intelligences.

For Chinese MI educators, intelligences as attributes of the family are shared resources rather than the property of an individual. The intelligences of all family members are applied to reach goals, solve problems, and engage in the activities of daily living. One of the key family goals is the child's education, which is understood as an extension of the family's intelligences. Instead of focusing solely on how to use an individual child's intellectual strengths, Chinese MI educators constantly search for ways to mobilize the unit of the family as an educational resource and an active agent in helping to develop a child's intellectual strengths. Family occupies a distinctive position in the Chinese MI implementation process.

Based on the belief that developing a child's intellect is a responsibility shared by parents, children, and teachers, many MI-focused schools hold classes in the evenings and on weekends to help parents learn about MI theory and its applications in the classroom. As described in Chapter Four, for Chinese MI educators, educating parents is an integral element of educating children because parents and children grow together in a family. From the parents' perspective, their active involvement helps to ensure that they clearly understand what teachers expect of the child and that they are providing related educational opportunities at home.

This same focus on the family unit can be seen in MI curriculum. Many Chinese MI educators emphasize that a priority curricular goal for the development of children's interpersonal intelligence is learning to understand their parents' feelings, values, needs, interests, and efforts expended in bringing them up. Because intelligences are shared by the individuals who make up a family, children's understanding of their parents is as important as parents' knowing a great deal about their children. The more that children understand their parents, the more likely it is they will appreciate their parents' efforts and recognize when their behavior mirrors or deviates from their parents' values and expectations. Understanding how they resemble or differ from their parents contributes also to the emergence of a child's self-awareness and identity formation. Thus, parents contribute uniquely to the development of a child's interpersonal and intrapersonal intelligences.

Another instance of recognizing the centrality of family in intellectual development is building on children's understanding of family roles and members' responsibilities. This factor leads to teachers' frequent use of a team approach in Chinese schools. Drawing on their experience in the family, team members take on the role of siblings. They act as brothers and sisters, working together inside as well as outside school. In teams, students build on each other's strengths and knowledge for project-based learning. Assuming the roles of brother and sister, both older and younger students are more willing to share ideas and materials and help each other complete tasks. Teachers report that the brother and sister teams produce a higher quality of work than other teams do. It is important to point out that using children's understanding of family to structure teams is not related to the practice of forming mixed-age groups, an educational approach used in many American schools. Rather, it grows out of the practice of mutual support as a key value in Chinese families and emphasizes as well the pivotal role the family plays in the consciousness of the child.

Harmony as a Fundamental Cultural Value

MI theory promotes pluralism and egalitarianism in conceptualizing intelligence. According to Gardner (1993), human beings have evolved over millennia to use several distinct, relatively autonomous intelligences, and these multiple intelligences have equal claims to priority, validation, and importance. MI theory focuses on independence rather than dependence and equality among individuals rather than unity of the group.

For Chinese, relationship and mutual benefit are appreciated as much as, if not more than, independence and equality because they are the keys to harmony, one of the values most dear to Chinese society. Because its influence spans thousands of years and touches so many aspects of Chinese life, *harmony* is not a term that can be translated easily. For the purpose of this chapter, the term is interpreted with a focus on balance. Balance refers to the relationships among different components in a system, such as different generations in a family and different members of the workforce. Harmony acknowledges differences; these differences call for adjustment and synchronization among components. The varied components in a system are not autonomous, existing for their own sake. Rather, they fit into a greater whole in which different components are complementary and beneficial to one another.

With the culture valuing and practicing harmony, Chinese educators have implemented MI through assimilations that preserve harmony. Consider the case of viewing a child's intellectual profiles and identifying strengths, a hallmark of MI practice elsewhere. However, Chinese MI educators are reluctant to use the term *strength*. In their view, people too often see strengths as achievements related to a single intelligence, such as the use of linguistic intelligence to compose a novel or musical intelligence to perform onstage. For Chinese, these characterizations run the risk of suggesting that an intelligence can work in isolation and be uniquely correlated with a certain type of achievement.

Rather than focusing primarily on strengths, Chinese see strengths and weaknesses as parts of a larger whole. Strengths are relative to weaknesses and vice versa. The two coexist for a purpose. Identification of a student's particular intellectual strengths must be accompanied by an understanding of his or her vulnerabilities. Otherwise understanding of the child is unbalanced and incomplete. In practice, building on students' strengths is one way MI education helps students to succeed. Helping students realize their vulnerabilities or weaknesses and working to overcome them is another way MI can be effective. To develop a balanced person, teachers need to know the complete intellectual profile of each student based on a range of curricular and extracurricular areas. They also need to help the student become aware of his or her strengths and weaknesses.

A second example of preserving harmony when assimilating MI practice concerns balancing the relationship between more and less in curriculum and teaching. As advocated by the national project Using MI Theory to Guide Discovery of Students' Potential, "less is more" became a pedagogical principle among some Chinese schools. Initially, to expose students to diverse learning areas, these schools added elective courses—as many as fifty in some schools. Gradually they realized that quantity must be balanced with quality to achieve harmony in teaching and learning. Attention to key concepts and skills that support development in disciplinary areas is as important as introductory exposure to a wide range of curricular areas.

Teachers in these schools have begun to grasp the significance and value of teaching "less" using the MI framework. Teaching "less" means that teachers and their students pursue deep knowledge of related concepts that can be applied in everyday activities. Mastery of this deep knowledge, in the form of key concepts and skills, leads students to explore concept applications across a range of curricular areas. As they explore applications, the students encounter new core concepts and skills in different areas that may become goals for the next cycle of learning. Through these cycles, teachers balance depth of knowledge and understanding with breadth of exposure and diversity of learning opportunities.

Development of the individual through collective education offers a final example of the unique approach to MI practice based on the Chinese value of harmony. Collective education refers to the practice that regards the betterment of the collective, rather than development of the individual, as the purpose of education. Members of a collective share goals and values, which lead to support and cooperation among individuals. In collective education, the success of all students is dependent on the success of each group member. Each student is responsible for helping others to learn and achieve.

For many Westerners, the concepts of individual and collective are incompatible and opposite. From the Chinese view, the two concepts are complementary. Harmony is achieved when individuals complement each other while maintaining their identity. A simple example is the yin and yang symbol. While yin and yang are opposite in shape and color, their union forms a complete whole. Collective education is an important condition for the development of individual intelligence. At the same time, the diversity of individuals contributes to the richness of the collective. A healthy collective respects and appreciates, rather than diminishes, individuality. In turn, individuals benefit from a healthy collective. Individualized collective education—that is, education that takes into consideration individual differences in the context of group activities—is the goal that Chinese educators now strive to achieve.

When implementing MI education, Chinese educators have devoted considerable effort to move toward individualized collective education. Consider the

Chinese college entrance examination, a necessary, though often unwelcome, requirement in contemporary China. In the past, to prepare students for the college entrance exam, senior high school teachers reviewed all possible testing materials while all students spent tremendous amounts of time studying the same test items and memorizing the same facts. Inspired by MI-related curriculum reform, teachers now ask students to generate questions based on the review materials instead of simply answering questions presented by teachers. Rather than giving equal attention to all testing review materials, each senior student has a notebook for recording his or her frequent mistakes, particularly those related to the misunderstanding of key concepts. These mistakes are shared with members of the student's study team and become that student's review focus.

No longer emphasizing one or a few "best" study approaches, many high schools now ask seniors to write essays about their choice of study methods or their preferred forms of teacher assistance. The reflection involved in writing these essays helps seniors to become more conscious of the approaches that best meet their learning needs. In the process, students strengthen their intrapersonal intelligence. Working with students in large groups, teachers meet individual differences through students' active involvement in identifying content and selecting study methods for the test review process. The goal of bettering the performance of all students is reached by recognizing the needs and strengths of each student.

Rather than competing with other group members, each student adds his or her strengths to the team, and the team works as a whole. Individuals contribute to the collective effort. They also gain from the support and help the team provides. Individual differences are understood in relation to common goals. One student's weakness is offset by another student's strength. The deep appreciation of harmony and balance, so fundamental in Chinese culture, leads naturally to the relationship between the individual and the collective in terms of balance. As practices related to MI theory are implemented, this relationship is becoming more balanced.

CONCLUSION

Over the past decade MI theory has had a sweeping influence on Chinese educational reform. In fact, it is more popular and has had a larger impact in China than in the Untied States, the homeland of the theory. The infusion and dissemination of MI theory in China have been a process of acculturation set in motion by the increasing frequency of exchanges between East and West. Successful implementations of MI in China are not replications of the theory's use in the United States. Welcoming MI's valid and authentic perspective on the nature of human intellectual abilities, the Chinese people have assimilated MI ideas into their cultural traditions while maintaining the core values of the theory. This acculturation process in itself exemplifies the Chinese value of harmony and was a prerequisite for successful implementation of MI in China.

Chinese MI educators have reached the stage of reflective MI practice. After the initial stage of MI exploration, followed by widespread implementation activities, they now feel the urge to engage in what is called "calm thinking process." At the center of this reflection process is how to integrate the theory further into the contemporary Chinese context. The goal of the reflective practice is to use MI theory to serve the needs of Chinese educational reform and implement MI practices that are marked with distinctive Chinese characteristics. China faces many educational challenges. The typical class size of fifty to sixty students, for example, makes it nearly impossible to individualize the teaching process. Scarce resources and the college entrance examination are major obstacles to the nurturance of individual students' diverse strengths. China is becoming a more and more individualistic and market-driven society. As a result of the One Child Policy, China soon will be a country dominated by generations of single children. Although harmony and balance continues to be a value and a goal, it remains to be seen how it will fare in a fast-growing, fast-changing, competitive, market-driven, one-child environment. For MI practice to reach the next level of success in China, these and many other challenges must be addressed directly and creatively. With the insights gained from reflection, Chinese educators will be ready to enter new territory. Building on their successes with MI, they will continue to help students reach their individual as well as collective potentials and to help China achieve its global aims.

References

Ceci, S. J. (1996). *On intelligence: A bio-ecological treatise on intellectual development* (2nd ed.). Cambridge, MA: Harvard University Press.

Dewey, J. (1948). *Reconstruction in philosophy.* New York: Holt.

Feldman, D. H. (2003). The creation of multiple intelligences theory: A study in high-level thinking. In R. K. Sawyer, V. John-Steiner, S. Moran, R. Sternberg, D. H. Feldman, J. Nakamura, et al. (Eds.), *Creativity and development* (pp. 139–185). New York: Oxford University Press.

Gardner, H. (1993). *Multiple intelligences: The theory in practice.* New York: Basic Books.

Gardner, H. (1989). *To open minds: Chinese clues to the dilemma of contemporary education.* New York: Basic Books.

Gruber, H. (1981). *Darwin on man: A psychological study of scientific creativity* (2nd ed.). Chicago: University of Chicago Press.

Spence, J. (2002). *To change China: Western advisers in China*. Penguin: New York.

Sternberg, R. J. (1988). *The triarchic mind: A new theory of human intelligences*. New York: Viking.

Using MI Theory to Guide Discovery of Students' Potential Project. (2007). *Multiplicity and harmony: Reports from the field of multiple intelligences theory practice*. Shanxi, China: Shanxi Teachers University Press (in Chinese).

Vygotsky, L. (1978). *Mind in society*. Cambridge, MA: Harvard University.

CHAPTER 4

Multiple Intelligences in China

Challenges and Hopes

Happy Hoi-Ping Cheung

The Chinese believe that people's intelligences are diversified, and should be used to cultivate well-rounded development of students who are good in three areas: ethics, sports, and academics. Chinese traditional pedagogy can be understood as individualized teaching and apprenticeship, but we have a long history of using examinations to select the qualified elite. The pressure of college entrance exams today, coupled with sparse educational resources, has caused many problems in education, a situation that has caught the attention of Chinese educators and the government. MI theory became the theoretical support to government's educational policies. The Chinese have embraced the idea of MI yet question the realities of implementing MI practices. In this chapter, I address the efforts that the Multiple Intelligences Education Society of China (MIESC) has made outside educational settings. Through seminars, magazine articles, radio programs, and TV interviews, it tries to influence teachers, parents, and policymakers in order to bring the idea of multiple intelligences to the fields of family education, vocational education, and even examination reform.

At the time that Chinese educators were making every effort to relieve pressure on students while preparing them to excel in a rapidly changing world, multiple intelligences theory was introduced to China. MI theory is consistent with the Chinese new educational policy referred to as "Quality Education" (*Su Zhi Jiao Yu*), which puts an accent on diverse ways of learning and development. Academic excellence should not be the only measurement of students' achievement. Teachers and parents should pay equal attention to students' other abilities, such as in the arts, sports, music, and moral education. People have embraced the concept enthusiastically.

China has a large population but limited resources invested in education. It has a long history of examination, and that practice is regarded as the fairest assessment of talents. Moreover, when people believe a college diploma is the only ticket to a better career and a better life, the national college entrance examination will surely persist. When people swing between "Quality Education" and "examination education," MI practices in the classroom are likely to remain an experiment rather than a universally accepted approach.

Some Chinese question how this Western psychological theory can apply to the Chinese condition. As one of the significant cognitive findings in the twentieth century, we hope that more Chinese will learn about and understand it. We seek to introduce this theory throughout society rather than only within traditional educational settings. Other colleagues have described how MI theory has been applied in Chinese schools in this book (see Chapters Three and Five). In this chapter, I briefly look at what the Multiple Intelligences Education Society of China has done outside traditional educational settings.

CONDITIONS SURROUNDING THE INTRODUCTION OF MI: OBSTACLES AND FACILITATORS

"Quality Education" and Examination Education

For more than one thousand years, Chinese people attained social mobility by taking the imperial examination, an approach that reflected hierarchical talent selection. In the past three decades, the Chinese college entrance examination (known as *GaoKao*) has become a bridge for millions of students to pass through and enter college.

The academic result has become an overwhelming concern in teaching and learning. Students who excel on exams are regarded as "good students," while those with low scores are labeled "poor students." Examination-oriented education has produced quite a lot of students who received high scores but are viewed as having "low capability." As the pressure of study and school life has created emotional pressure and frustration to both parents and children, student suicides started to crop up more frequently.

This destructive cycle has captured the attention of Chinese educators and the government. Both are seeking more effective ways to prepare students to excel in a rapidly changing world. In 1999 the Government introduced the concept of Quality Education.

In an effort to find a theoretical support for this idea, MI theory has served almost as a magic elixir to China's Quality Education.

Introducing MI to China

Multiple intelligences became well known and popular nationwide in China in the late 1990s when Howard Gardner's *Frames of Mind* (1983) was translated into Chinese.

In teacher's colleges, MI theory became one of most important educational theories in the curriculum for education students. From kindergarten to high school, MI practice has been applied to classrooms all over the country, and numerous books on MI have been translated and published in Chinese. MI theory enriches teachers' criteria for assessing their students. One teacher had this to say: "Unlike before, when I look at my students now, they are all good students. Everyone has shining points to appreciate." Another teacher said, "I noticed some of my students who did not have high scores in school turned out to be more successful. MI theory shows me the reason. Those students' interpersonal intelligences might be higher. Each of them is unique." In the past, test and IQ scores were the only way teachers evaluated their students. MI theory now offers teachers a new perspective to appreciate students' other talents.

Limited Educational Resources

Most primary schools, middle schools, and high schools in China are public schools, financially supported by the government. The "key" (or most prestigious) schools have better teachers and better facilities, and they receive more financial support from government than ordinary schools do. Compared to regular schools, key schools usually have a long history of strong academic performance records. To keep the high promotion rate, these schools prefer to recruit students with high scores in math, Chinese, and English, and perhaps on an IQ test as well. The parents enroll their children in English or "Math Olympics" classes to help the students obtain the high scores they need to enter and remain in the key schools.

To promote more student-centered classroom teaching is also difficult in China because of the huge class sizes. In most cities, the standard class size in a key school is forty to fifty students and in an ordinary school, sixty to ninety students. Moreover, every teacher usually teaches two classes or more. Some teachers complain that using individual initiative in their classrooms is too difficult because of large class sizes. Traditional ways of teaching, by following a schedule and encouraging students to be passive, allow teachers to control the class more easily. Moreover, teachers' salaries are pegged to the scores of their students. To make sure their students achieve high academic scores, many schools practice what is referred to as "quality education in words, exam-oriented education in deeds."

New Criteria for Success

Nevertheless, some students who failed academically in high school have become successful; they have become, for example, popular authors, sports stars, dancers, or singers. Han-Han, who did not graduate from high school, became a famous novelist whose novels are so popular among the young that he has become the highest-paid writer in China. When Ding Jun-hui regularly failed in mathematics tests in high school, his father took him out of school and trained him to become a snooker champion. In addition, many successful entrepreneurs who have impressed the public with their special talents and amassed fortunes do not have college degrees.

Such examples have been noted and have inspired Chinese educators to think of the truths embedded in the notion of multiple intelligences. Should people struggle to develop themselves more fully, or spend significant time developing their special talents? As Chinese society starts to accept the existence of various types of success, such as in singing, acting, and sports, the Chinese saying that "every trade has its masters" becomes a vivid reality.

Misunderstanding of MI

In China, the idea of MI theory has a stronger influence in people's minds than in their practice, however. Moreover, they practice and appreciate MI more in kindergartens and lower grades than in middle schools and high schools and better in special education institutes such as schools for children with learning disabilities and teenagers with behavior problems than in grammar schools. In general, the further students are from the time when they must take the college entrance examination, the better that MI is practiced. Among schools and educators who practice MI, however, many of them do not really understand what it is.

A journalist in Shanghai once made this interesting observation: "In the United States, people are interested in MI because they are looking for what is special in each child, and they want to nurture the special gifts and bring out the child's individuality. In China," she speculated, "the multiple intelligences indicate eight areas where children can now be expected to excel."

In fact, MI theory and Quality Education reflect somewhat different perspectives. The tradition of the Chinese is to cultivate what are referred to as "all-round" students (*San Hao Sheng*), that is, those who excel in ethics, sports, and academics. Whereas MI urges the individualized development of a distinctive blend of innate talents, Quality Education emphasizes mastering all multiple intelligences through cultivating students' abilities to think critically and creatively and to problem-solve.

MULTIPLE INTELLIGENCES EDUCATION SOCIETY OF CHINA

China has rich soil to grow the seed of multiple intelligences, though some obstacles remain. After several years of studying and practicing MI, some teachers, administrators, and policymakers sought to reflect together on their experiences. In May 2004, when MI influence had reached its peak, more than a thousand educators took part in the International Conference on Theory of Multiple Intelligences held in Beijing. When the conference preparatory committee asked me to invite Howard Gardner to give a keynote speech to the conference, I had an opportunity to pay attention to MI practice in China and began to talk with many Chinese teachers and administrators who are interested in MI theory and practices.

As Gardner's former student, I was lucky to learn MI theory when I was at Harvard. Though many years have passed, I still believe it is one of the most important theories of the mind; moreover, it embodies important Chinese traditional educational thought and can inspire educational reforms in China today.

By 2004, MI theory had become well known and influential in China. Indeed, it was all the fashion. Schools, especially private schools, were looking for new selling points to attract parents. No matter how little they understood MI, some schools claimed they were MI schools. A kindergarten in the South distributed violins to each child and promised to train them to be good players before graduation. The headmaster said that their curriculum was designed according to MI ideas that emphasize the importance of arts study. To train every child's musical potential certainly meshed with the idea of MI.

Our research, however, showed that relatively few educators understand MI well. Fortunately, many teachers are eager to learn more about the theory and methods if they can find the right training. Based on a request from teachers and administrators and supported by the Sino Capital Education Foundation, the Multiple Intelligences Education Society of China (MIESC) was founded as a nonprofit in April 2003. It is composed of schools, teachers, and parents dedicated to MI ideas and practices. It endeavors to introduce MI to more educators and train them so that they have a better understanding of MI theory and practice.

The MIESC tries to build a platform for teachers, parents, school administrators, and educational policymakers who are interested in MI. These educators can share their experiences and questions related to MI theory and practice.

Working Within Schools

During the past five years, the MIESC has organized workshops, seminars, and conferences for teachers, school administrators, and policymakers. Most of these activities are carried out in cooperation with the local education commission, which provides access to the majority of teachers and school administrators. The MIESC also helps MI practice schools share their experiences with other schools, national and international; helps to assess their curriculum, facilities, teacher training programs, and parenting programs; introduces MI research results and information to Chinese schools; and conducts research and academic exchange and cooperation.

Working with staff, we at MIESC help schools set their own goals for children in general and for each child in particular. MI is not an educational goal but a tool. Only after the goals have been articulated can personnel decide how MI might help them achieve those goals.

Because of the competitive college entrance examination, the struggle between "examination education" and "Quality Education" continues. MI practice in formal grammar schools faces difficulties and limitations. However, special education does not have the pressure of public examination because they are intellectually or developmentally disabled, and do not expected to get into the college. The MIESC found that MI works well with two types of special education: intellectual and developmental disabilities training centers and what are called "opportunity schools."

Beijing Xicheng Peichi School has over two hundred students with different levels of intellectual or developmental disabilities. Before applying MI theory to their teaching, Peichi School personnel followed the traditional assessment and curriculum based on linguistics and mathematics. They classified students based on IQ scores and grouped similar scorers by class despite differences of age. Teachers were exhausted by teaching students counting and writing day in and day out, and students were tired of try to do things they could hardly understand.

The most significant contribution of MI to Peichi School has been to reformulate its special educational goal: to prepare these students so that they can take care of themselves and adapt socially. The concept of MI gave the school and its teachers a new way to look at each student's unique abilities and weaknesses and design activities for them. The students loved the new programs and became more confident because their talents were found and encouraged and their weaknesses avoided. Several students joined the Special Olympics and won prizes.

As an example, a teacher found that one of her students, a girl named SiruiJia, was good at body-kinesthetic activities, and she trained her to be a gymnast specializing on the balance beam. Jia won a gold medal in the Special Olympics and became an international ambassador for the organization. She was invited to the White House twice, first to meet President Bill Clinton and then President George W. Bush. She gave fine speeches in public. Now she is working as a trainer in the department of corporate relations in China's Bayer Group, a global leading healthcare enterprise.

Jia's story encourages Peichi School and teachers to embrace MI ideas and practices. The music and crafts classes at the school became very popular as well. It is amazing to watch students control hammers and chisels to pit porcelain plates carefully (the pits on the plate display different pictures).

In sharp contrast to traditional Chinese practices, the school does not require all students in a class to learn the same things. Some learn cooking, while some others work on painting. When the students, with big smiles, present me their embroidery and brush paintings or serve me the food they cook, I am touched and amazed by what has been achieved by curriculum reform in this special school.

The other example I touch on here is Beijing Haidian Opportunity School, which has about two hundred students from eighth through twelfth grade. These students are former dropouts or were deemed likely to drop out of their former middle schools. They had behavior or emotional problems, used illegal substances, were frequently absent, or were involved with juvenile court. Most lacked the passion and motivation to sit still and listen to the lectures and did not like the formal school curriculum. Moreover, they were not expected to go to college. This school decided to it had to reform its curriculum to reach these students.

The MIESC consulted and recommended that Haidian Opportunity School cut down lecturing time. For example, there are twelve units in the subject of Chinese during a semester, and teachers choose four of them to teach, so they now have enough time to help students individually understand what they are being taught. After the school decreased lecturing time, it increased hands-on experiments and other selected courses. Students now show more interest in learning. For instance, in physics, students use plastic basins and barrels to make electronic guitars and drums. Students who are good at music, physics, or handcraft work together, using their knowledge of music and electronics to create instruments. They also learn the importance of teamwork. A rocket project by a group of students won second prize in a national science competition. The school now invites some traditional Chinese handcraft artists to campus to give interested students apprenticeship training.

Without the pressure of public examination, teachers in these schools are able to create flexible teaching plans. Students' special talents in this school are found, appreciated, encouraged, and cultivated, and in the process, students gain confidence and self-esteem. The MIESC intends to extend this experience to vocational schools.

In 2005, the Department of Personnel of China invited the MIESC to conduct a research project on applying multiple intelligences in training professionals and technicians. It became one of the most influential research projects in the Department of Personnel that year and was the first effort for the MIESC to introduce MI theory to vocational education.

The National Association of Vocational Education of China, the nongovernmental organization with the longest history of vocational education in China, would like to organize regular forums on vocational education and entrepreneurship and has invited the MIESC to join the organization committee. These forums will offer guidance to policymakers, and the hope is that MI theory will provide the theoretical foundation for China's vocational education policy.

Working with Teachers

The mastery of disciplines and disciplinary concepts is important to education. MI can be used to determine different ways of introducing these challenging concepts and the different ways to reflect different intelligences.

When we work with teachers, we focus on showing them how to assess students' intellectual strengths and weaknesses and how to use different kind of entry points to introduce disciplinary concepts to different students. We invite experienced teachers to demonstrate MI ideas in classroom teaching and let them discuss and raise more issues. We also collect teachers' research papers and cases to share with others. Many teachers learn from others and become creative in teaching.

Some teachers want to know how others practice and how they can "copy" specific procedures in their own classrooms. This can cause a problem. We stress to teachers that there is no a formula here: each class and each student is unique and different, and all teachers should find their own ways of delivering teaching. Nevertheless, a few teachers persist in trying to follow these demonstrations exactly, step by step, while failing to grasp the spirit of MI. When those who do not understand the spirit face new problems, they do not know how to create solutions and do not achieve their expected goals and results. Copying leads to stereotypical practices and undermines the idea that we are seeking to convey. Moreover, when teachers pay rigid attention to the curriculum and follow teaching schedules to the letter rather than focusing on students, they come to see MI practice as a burden.

Working with Parents

Many books, textbooks, and teaching materials have been published based on MI theory, and many daycare centers, kindergartens, and playgroups have been set up or have names identifying them as MI schools; even some toys are touted as being produced "according to MI theory." Although many of these benefit children, some used the name of MI to raise tuition. It is difficult for parents to judge which schools truly base themselves on MI theory, and many parents have sought our help in this area.

In order to make sure their children will get into good schools and eventually prestigious colleges, parents want their children to be excellent in many areas. MI theory indicates eight areas where parents think their children can be expected to excel.

Most parents hope their children will achieve high scores on academic tests, without regard to their children's special intelligences and strengths and weaknesses in these areas. When parents and teachers are cognizant of children's capability to survive in this rapidly changing world, they choose "Quality Education"; however, when they think of the pressure of college entrance examination, they choose "examination education." Their slogan is, "Do not let your child lose at the starting point," in reference to getting into every level of school. Parents want their children to do what others are doing, and more. Otherwise they think they might be left behind.

In March 2004, Shanxi Province Radio Channel invited me to cohost a parenting program, "MI Parents Time," which reaches 25 million listeners, including, of course, many parents. For more than four years, I have been the guest speaker of this program, which has been recognized as the most popular program for this radio station four years in row. On this one-hour live program every Saturday morning, we answer parents' questions. We try not just to give standard answers but to present cases that inspire them and other listeners to find solutions. In this program, MI idea is the soul and core. We convince parents that each child has a unique combination of strong and weak intelligences. If we encourage each child to develop his or her strengths, and not to perseverate on his or her weaknesses (especially if they happen to lie in the area that the exam system prioritizes), children will achieve more and grow up happier.

Parents provide us successful stories about how they have raised their children according to MI theory. For example, a high school boy failed in most of the subjects disliked school, and had low self-esteem. He often skipped school and spent his time at garages. Cars fascinated him, and he learned a great deal about them. He eventually failed the college entrance examination two years running, but his mother asked him to repeat one more year of high school in order to prepare for the examination again. He did not want to return to school and wanted to work at the garage, and he asked his mother to listen to our program. One day his mother called and told us that she decided to respect her son's choice. Parents gradually accept that college is not the only way forward for their children.

As another example, a girl was labeled by her teacher in fourth grade as having attention deficit disorder. She was afraid to go to the school. She could not sit still and listen to the teacher's lecture in the classroom, and she was in fact afraid to go to school. Her father took her to a golf course once and found she had special talent at this game. He then started to train her to be a professional golfer. Over the years, she won many prizes at national and international tournaments. As she became interested in developing skills to manage a golf course, she came to realize that mathematics and logical thinking were important so she hired private tutors to help her in these subjects.

These and other inspirational stories offer hope to those who are not successful on school tests. More and more parents are coming to accept that children who have intelligences different from the usual academic ones can be successful.

Using the Media

Media represent a powerful way to spread ideas about MI. As a guest speaker and commentator on CCTV Channel 10, the China Central channel of science and education, I use MI ideas to analyze social and educational topics. We interview professionals and celebrities in our program. From their vivid stories of their school experiences and careers, viewers see which intelligences are their strengths and how they developed these strengths and avoid their weaknesses. The strong intelligences are not necessarily linguistic or mathematics-logical. A popular social worker whose major was music could not make a living until he found out that music was not his talent; his interest lay in helping others. A famous writer said mathematics had bored him a lot until he found that he could impress others by telling stories. These examples encourage people to recognize and develop their own intelligences.

We hope that MI theory will become well known to the public and have an influence over all Chinese society. Through the power of the media, we seek to broaden the use of MI theory. We hope that people will understand the essential ideas of MI, develop appropriate attitudes to human intelligences, and appreciate their own special talents. There is a Chinese saying, "Whatever occupation you have, you could excel to the top notch." When people are happy with what they are and what they do, society will be more harmonious.

Many books on multiple intelligences have been translated and introduced to Chinese readers, and Chinese educators are also writing books to share their experiences of practicing or studying MI. Different authors may give different perspectives and suggestions, and readers who are not familiar with MI theory may well be puzzled. Not many Chinese readers are able to access or understand Howard Gardner's original works in English. In order to give Chinese readers a more systematic idea of MI theory, the MIESC planned to translate a series of Gardner's books into Chinese. I facilitated the translation and publication of Chinese versions of Gardner's *The Disciplined Mind* and *The Unschooled Mind.*

At the request of teachers and administrators who were interested in MI theory and practice, the first issue of a magazine, *Multiple Intelligences,* was published in China and Hong Kong in January 2004. It provides a platform for MI teachers and parents to share their experiences, connect classroom teaching and policymaking, and inspire Chinese educational reform. The magazine is under the supervision of the MIESC and financially sponsored by the Sino Capital Education Foundation.

The magazine introduces MI theory, implementation, and projects; reports MI events; reviews MI books; and interviews people whose work is related to MI. Among the articles, the family education cases and book reviews are the most popular columns. The authors include teachers who practice MI in their classrooms, principals who apply MI in school management, parents who benefit from MI in communicating with their children, and policymakers and researchers who are interested in MI theory and practices. Our articles provide actual cases and are practical and interesting. Our readers include school administrators, policymakers, researchers, teachers, and parents.

In 2007, the magazine title was changed to *Multiple Intelligences Science Magazine,* by the most respected and renowned Confucian in modern China, Nan HuaiJin. Master Nan believes MI is cutting-edge science. This new version of the magazine is digital and will be readily accessible to many readers.

FUTURE CHALLENGES

The National Education Examinations Authority of China (NEEAC) is under the direct supervision of the Ministry of Education. Its task is to undertake educational examinations, including the college entrance examination, and to provide administrative authority. MI theory is one of the theories that the staff in the NEEAC should study. We hope that immersion in the principal ideas of MI theory will have an impact on China examination policy.

In fact, the college entrance examination system has been changing gradually. Universities and high schools have started to accept special talented students (*Te Chang Sheng*) who have extraordinary skills in music, visual or performing arts, or sports (usually they have received awards in competitions). This gives a message to the public that academic results are no longer the only measurement for college entrance. The cut-off score for these special talented students can be 10 percent lower than other students in college admission.

Some parents are now sending their children to schools where they will be exposed to expanded curriculum and become *Te Chang Sheng.* They believe that "effort rather than talents and mastery brings creativity." Nevertheless, many parents care more about which program will help their children enter college easily than about their children's talents and interests. As long as parents still believe that a college diploma is the only guarantee to a better future, the idea of MI theory will always remain a stronger influence in people's mind rather than in their practice.

Nevertheless, after implementing "Quality Education," the government has embraced college independent enrollment: universities may reserve a small percentage of seats for the top students or students with special talents. Students who are interested in a particular university (usually a prestigious one) can apply directly to that university before taking the college entrance examination. The admission procedure includes a personal statement, an interview, and a written test given by that university. Although the system needs to be improved, it reveals that society has begun to recognize an individual's special talents, clearly a big leap forward in the college entrance examination reform.

In addition, the government has greatly increased investment in education, including teachers' salaries, teaching facilities, and equipment. Class sizes are getting smaller, and the curriculum has been reconstructed as well. Creative study and creative research are the criteria used to evaluate teaching. Taken together, these ideas and trends provide better soil for MI in China.

References

Gardner, H. (1983). *Frames of mind: The theory of multiple intelligences.* New York: Basic Books.

Gardner, H. (1995). *The unschooled mind: How children think and how schools should teach.* New York: Basic Books.

Gardner, H. (1999). *The disciplined mind: Beyond facts and standardized tests, the K–12 education that every child deserves.* New York: Simon & Schuster.

CHAPTER 5

Multiple Intelligences Theory on the Mainland of China

Zhilong Shen

Multiple intelligences theory has been accepted and welcomed widely by countless educators, teachers, administrators and supervisors of education, artists, and even chemists on the mainland of China because it coincides with Chinese culture and ancient educational ideology, the new steps of the reform, and the popular principle of education: character education. Under the guidance of MI theory, Chinese have changed their perspectives of students, educational goals and policies, teaching methods, and learning and assessment in schools. Some art educators confirm the existence of existential intelligence and its connection with the arts. They try to inspire students' crystallizing experience of existential intelligence through the appreciation of music.

China is a vast country with the largest population in the world. As befits a country of such size, countless stories related to MI theory have circulated since 1985 when Howard Gardner visited the country and introduced the theory to Chinese musicians. As a Chinese educator, I have twice visited Project Zero and worked with Gardner; I was also one of his hosts when he visited China in 2004. I bear significant responsibility for introducing the stories referring to MI theory in China.

A WELCOME THEORY FOR EDUCATION

When MI theory was imported into China in 1985, some musicians showed interest in it immediately. Unfortunately, most Chinese psychologists and educators did not pay much attention to it at that time.

However, the situation has been changing quickly since the end of the twentieth century. At that time China adopted a new educational principle: character education. By coincidence, Gardner's book, *Multiple Intelligences: Theory in Practice* (1993), which I translated into Chinese, was published at the same time. Since then, more and more people, including professional educators, teachers from a variety of schools, administrators and supervisors of education, policymakers and legislators, students, and parents on the mainland of China have learned about the theory and realize its significance. Numerous people have been attracted by and accepted MI theory, with converts and supporters ranging from teachers and parents to top leaders of the Central Government of PRC.

As these ideas became better known, the China Education Association set up a key project, Applied Research of Multiple Intelligences Theory on Developing Students Potential, in February 2002. Over 150 schools, from kindergartens to universities in thirteen provinces, have been involved in research and practice on MI. The project sponsored an international conference every year from 2002 to 2005 where participants could discuss MI theory.

By my calculation, 3,145 papers from members of the project have been published in newspaper, magazines, and journals or exchanged at the annual meetings. Since 2000 about a hundred books referring to MI theory have been translated into or written in Chinese. At the beginning of 2004, an article in *China Educational Daily* declared that the translation of *Multiple Intelligences: Theory in Practice* now occupied first place on the list of the one hundred best-selling books on education in 2003.

These events had a profound effect on my own life. I left my position as the chair of a university department of chemistry to devote my efforts to studying and popularizing the theory. I now have invitations to give more than one hundred presentations about MI theory in fifteen provinces in China and at Harvard University and the University of Illinois at Urbana-Champaign. I have translated three of Gardner's books and supervised the translation of four of his other books, and I have published my own book: *Howard Gardner, Arts, and Multiple Intelligences* (Shen, 2004).

Some people thought that MI theory might be welcome only in cities of China, but my own experience belies that. In the winter of 2004, I gave a presentation about MI theory in a city in Shanxi Province. More than eleven hundred principals gathered to listen to the presentations in a huge, cold hall that lacked heating since the organizers could not afford to pay for it (I gave my three-hour presentation wrapped in two blankets). Because most of the principals came from poor and remote villages and could not pay expenses for even the cheapest hotel in the city, they had gotten up at 3:00 A.M. and walked two or three hours in the mountain area in order to catch the bus going to the city and listen to the lectures on MI theory. I was deeply moved by their enthusiasm and passion.

IMPLEMENTING MI IN CHINA

In three ways, MI theory has changed Chinese perspectives on students, educational goals and policy, methods of teaching, and learning and assessment in schools. First, as an educational philosophy, MI theory widens Chinese perspectives. Chinese educators have been stimulated to rethink their assumptions with respect to intelligence, student abilities, the organization of schools, and methods of assessment. For example, the principal of an Islamic primary school located in Chongwen District of Beijing bought 120 copies of Gardner's book for his employees to study. The director of the Educational Bureau of Changzhou City from Jiangsu Province bought 300 copies of Gardner's book and presented them as gifts to all principals in the city's schools. The teachers in schools who received the books were asked to write papers after intensive reading and study.

In the past, Chinese educators directed their attention largely to students who possess higher linguistic and logical-mathematical intelligence as measured by paper-and-pencil examinations. The educators identified the top scorers and gave them special opportunities, often in selective schools. Now a growing number of educators and teachers are paying attention to students who are good at other intelligences as well. After studying and practicing MI theory, a teacher in Beijing wrote, "There are no students who cannot be educable, and there are teachers who should be educated." These new ideas have led people to accept the new principle of character education and try to find the intellectual strengths of students whose performance on traditional tests was not good.

At the Third High School at Changping District of Beijing, a student had apparently been poor in linguistic intelligence. He was unable to recite even a short poem from the Tang dynasty with only twenty Chinese characters. But his teacher was struck by this strength in the area of bodily performance, so she had the student play the role of hero in a drama performed in the classroom, which gave him confidence to master linguistic tasks and progress academically. Finally he was able to recite a famous essay with one thousand characters.

The theory has also pushed forward the reform of teaching and learning methods in the schools. Teachers in the Second Experimental Primary School of Beijing no longer use the method of "explaining words though words" in teaching the Chinese language. Rather, pupils now use multiple ways, such as using pictures or music, to recount their life experiences in order to show their understanding of words, phrases, and proverbs. Their vocabulary has become part of their life activities, with the result that the classroom atmosphere has become very lively.

At the Fourth Primary School of Hepingli in Beijing, teachers develop teaching and learning methods for student projects according to the experience of Key School in Indianapolis in the United States (see Chapter Twenty-Four). The school featured many themes. A focus on the theme of spring stimulated students to observe everything around them in spring, write diaries about the natural changes, and raise questions about the seasons. This project involves not only students' naturalist intelligence but also other intellectual capacities. In this case six- and seven-year-old children raised thirty-four questions, such as "Why is there sandstorm in spring?" Subsequently the teacher guided the students to select six themes for further discussion. The students collected numerous words to describe the spring, plotted the statistical temperature data in the spring of Beijing, and displayed the data with variety of diagrams. Such exercises have enriched pupils' knowledge and understanding and developed their interpersonal intelligence.

At a secondary school in Zhucheng City in Shandong Province, the principals and teachers have nurtured students' intelligences through assessment in a range of contexts inside and outside schools. One assessment system has seven categories with forty-two items, including the different methods designed for assessing seven intelligences. Consequently, nearly 90 percent of students have received awards and are inspired to make further progress—and their ranks include many who would have been considered unintelligent on standard examinations.

As a third area of change, Chinese educators promote effective international exchanges of education. In May 2004, as part of the annual meeting of the project cited above, Howard Gardner was invited to deliver a keynote address on his reflections on the theory of multiple intelligences. More than seven hundred scholars, teachers, and officers from thirteen provinces in China and the United States, United Kingdom, Canada, Australia, Japan, and Singapore journeyed to Beijing to listen to Gardner's talk and attend the group discussions. As a result of this and similar meetings, many cross-cultural ties have been forged, with mutual benefit to Chinese and other educational systems.

REASONS MI THEORY IS ACCEPTED WIDELY IN CHINA

Combination of Both Western and Eastern Cultures

Multiple intelligences theory is a cross-cultural undertaking, combining the essences of Western and Eastern cultures. In a number of ways, it coincides with Chinese culture and ancient education ideology. These confluences help Chinese citizens grasp the principal concepts.

There are two principles of Confucian thoughts on education. One is *You Jiao Wu Lei*, which means "no distinction between different social strata and intelligent profile of students for education." The others is *Yin Cai Shi Jiao*, which means, "to teach students using different materials and approaches according to their different facets of intelligences."

These two ideas express the same thought as MI theory: varied human intelligences, and all combinations of these intelligences must be recognized and nurtured. Gardner argued that students strike us as different largely because they have different profiles of intelligences.

Chinese self-cultivation and the ability to be an accepted member in a group or community are the cores of ancient moralities in China. What are the indicators of the morality in students' behavior? Possessing the higher interpersonal and intrapersonal intelligences and using them correctly are the answers according to MI theory.

Character Education and Educational Reform

Multiple intelligences theory happened on the scene in 1999 when the Central Government of China issued a document: *The Decision on Deepening Education Reform and Promoting Character Education.* Character education applies to all students; it means that no student should be left behind and that the purpose of education is to promote students' development morally, intellectually, physically, and aesthetically.

A major purpose for conducting character education is to provide, through diverse instructional methods, the opportunity for children to bring out the best from their individual aptitudes and passion while receiving a unified education in basic courses.

The introduction of character education has been the most significant education reform in recent years. It is a reform of the content and methodology of teaching, of assessments of teaching and learning, and of methods of developing and selecting able professionals. The reform movement received a boost when Li Lanqing, former vice premier of China, published a book of reflections (Li, 2004). In the sixth chapter, "The Philosophy of Character Education," he introduced Howard Gardner and MI theory to China and wrote: "Dr. Gardner's theory of multiple intelligences eschews traditional theories on intelligence and asserts that every person has his or her own strengths due to differences in these eight categories. His theory offers a broader picture of people's individual abilities and vindicates such adages as 'heaven has bestowed genius upon us and will also find its use definitely some day' and 'every trade produces its own masters.' . . . It has furnished some important inspiration and valuable references for our efforts to carry out character education (Li, 2004, p. 316).

According to MI theory, the purpose of school should be to develop a variety of intelligences in students and to help them reach vocational goals that are appropriate to their spectrum of intelligence. MI theory strongly supports the principal tenets of character education; it emboldens those involved in educational reform. In addition, clues for achieving educational reform can be gleaned from MI Theory.

Aesthetic Education and Art Education

Both Chinese ancient culture and MI theory stress the importance of art education. While Confucius (551–479 B.C.) is known as a politician, philosopher, and educator, many people are not aware that he was an excellent musician, composer, aesthetician, and musical educator as well (Shen & Zhao, 1999). He preached the importance of teaching poetry and music, believing them to be a necessity in life. He also argued that the development of morality begins with training in literature and art, then moves on to the topic of moral responsibility, and ends with exhibiting skill in musical performance. He said: "Draw inspiration from the poems, steady your morality with rites, and find your fulfillment in music" (Confucian Disciples, 1977, p. 33). More generally, Confucius valued the emotional features and social function of art and emphasized, in particular, the association of aesthetic education as the means to moral education.

The educational reform put into effect a decade ago included a new emphasis on arts and aesthetic education. This emphasis reflects a reaction to the Cultural Revolution, which was in many ways devastating for the arts, particularly for the classical arts associated with the Confucian tradition. The emphasis also reflected the growing feeling on the part of many Chinese—leaders as well as ordinary persons—that the arts ought to receive more emphasis.

MI theory has stressed not only the importance of the interaction among disciplines but also the connection between sciences and arts. As a developmental psychologist, neuroscientist, pianist, and consumer of the literature on genetics, Gardner has both called attention to the centrality of the arts in education and embodied this belief in his own theories and practice.

Gardner argues that any intelligence can function artistically. Indeed four of the intelligences—musical, spatial, bodily-kinesthetic, and linguistic—are used directly in artistic production, performance, and appreciation. In addition, interpersonal intelligence and intrapersonal intelligence are featured in the arts. They relate to the emotions and are crucial to artistic processes. Arts also feature communication, a process that draws on personal intelligence. I also believe that students possessing higher interpersonal and intrapersonal intelligences understand artistic works more deeply; quite possibly, aesthetic education and moral education are more effective than is the case with persons who are weak in the above two intelligences.

As for the connection between naturalist intelligence and art, it is indicated in many musical works and artistic works. Examples are Beethoven's Symphony No. 6 in F major, *Pastorale*; the symphonic poem *La Mer* by Claude Debussy; and *The Carnival of Animals* by Saint-Saëns. For all these reasons, MI theory is inextricably connected to a variety of art forms and artistic processes. It is no wonder that many Chinese artists and arts educators have expressed an interest in MI theory.

In October 2004 the president of Beijing Dance Academy invited me to give a talk. He wanted his students to understand bodily-kinesthetic intelligence, bringing it into play better in their studies and performances. A dramatic and unexpected event occurred: one of my audience at the presentation was international dance theorist and critic Ou Jianping. He told me that the only book except on dance he read was my book on MI Theory, and he read it in one sitting! Shortly after he sent me a short essay regarding his acquaintance with the theory of multiple intelligences.

Family Planning Policy

Since 1979, China has enforced the one-child family policy. Perhaps unexpectedly this policy has stimulated an interest in MI theory. If one believes that there is only one kind of intelligence that matters and an only child is not strong in that intelligence, it can be quite depressing for the parents. Now that additional intelligences are recognized and fostered, families have renewed hope that their child can excel in some area.

Scientific Support

Multiple intelligences theory is presented as scientific. It can and will be evaluated in the light of evidence drawn from various disciplines. Chinese people have learned to judge the varieties of psychological and educational theories from the Western world since the country opened in 1979.

MI theory is a result of interdisciplinary research and innovation. It draws on and synthesizes findings from developmental psychology, neuroscience, evolutionary biology, and genetics, as well as anthropology, linguistics, literature, artistic cognition, fine arts, performing arts, athletics, and others. Determination of the nature and extent of an intelligence is based on eight criteria, laid out in *Frames of Mind: The Theory of Multiple Intelligences*. Possibly another reason for the appeal of MI theory in China is the growing interest in studies of the brain. MI theory was the first approach to intelligence built on newly emerging knowledge of the specialized brain functions.

EXISTENTIAL INTELLIGENCE IN CHINA

So far, Gardner is sticking to his 8½ intelligences. The eight intelligences are well known but the "½ intelligence," existential intelligence, has been almost forgotten or neglected by many people all over the world, including Chinese. Nevertheless, I find this ninth intelligence to be a plausible candidate for an intelligence.

Lao Zi, the founder of Taoism and a major figure of Chinese philosophy lived in the fourth century B.C. In Chapter Thirty-Three of his book *Lao Zi,* he wrote: "The person who understands others is intelligent; the person who has self-knowledge is wise; the person who can locate himself has a much longer life"(Lao, 2003, p. 73). The first part of the sentence implies interpersonal intelligence, the second, intrapersonal intelligence, and the third, existential intelligence.

I ask: Who can escape from birth, old age, illness, and death? Who never ponders the meaning and value of life? It is not possible for human beings to be involved in the "peak experience" defined by humanistic psychologist Abraham Maslow and immersed in the exultation and great happiness throughout one's life (LeBon, 2006). Suffering, loneliness, oppression, anxiety, and desperation cannot be denied. The philosophical consideration of existence entails the gamut of feelings and experiences—those of pain no less than those of pleasure. Like language, existential capacity is also a distinctive trait of humans, a domain that separates us from other species. I see existential intelligence as closely connected with the existential philosophy associated with Jean-Paul Sartre and Martin Heidegger.

As Gardner suggests, one of the important characteristics of existential intelligence is the close connection with art and artistic works. Some artists, including Vincent van Gogh and Fyodor Dostoyevsky, suffered from temporal lobe epilepsy yet channeled their symptoms and pain into powerful, dramatic works of art with existential considerations (Gardner, 1999). Moreover, I suggest that a great number of composers did so in their monumental symphonic works—among them Beethoven, Gustav Mahler, and Peter Tchaikovsky. The famous French painter Paul Gauguin described the philosophical theme of existentialism more than half-century earlier than Jean-Paul Sartre did in his powerful painting, *Where do we come from? What are we? Where are we going?*

To sum up, Howard Gardner has not confirmed the existence of existential intelligence yet, but I believe that our knowledge, intuition, and insights in daily life about nature, society, philosophy, and artistic works confirm its plausibility.

PROBLEMS AND IMPACTS IN THE CONTEXT OF CHINESE CULTURE

There are several problems associated with the ways in which the idea of multiple intelligences has been grasped and implemented in China.

Disharmonic Sound

In my presentation at Harvard on April 14, 2006, one member of the audience did not trust the statistical data I presented about the ratio of the number of people who oppose MI theory to the number who accept the theory in China. My data suggest that 99.9 percent of people in China who know about MI theory accept it. When I told him the source of the data, the skeptic finally was silent. I had skimmed through more than three thousand articles and papers on the research and practice of MI theory; only one of them doubted the theory, and all others endorsed it.

That single article was written by a well-known psychologist in Beijing ("Doubtable MI Theory," September 7, 2004). I did not find any talking points and grounds of argument in the article to support the author's point of view. I doubt that he knew about the eight criteria. The article expresses his distrust of MI theory but offers no proof.

Doubtful Understanding and Application

Multiple intelligences theory is a psychological one and a kind of educational philosophy as well, but many Chinese teachers think of it as a goal of education. They faithfully follow a strange and doubtful slogan—"to teach for MI theory." In their mind, the main purpose of education is to develop the eight intelligences in their students.

In some schools, MI theory has been applied to all educational programs, new and old, no matter whether the programs are actually built on an understanding of the assertions and implications of the theory. In some schools, educators and teachers treat MI theory as a new tool to serve the Chinese test-oriented education. They try to develop all intelligences according to the list in MI theory, but their only purpose is to have their students score high on examinations.

Moreover, some teachers and scholars make no effort to understand the precise claims of MI. Instead, they invoke some suspicious conceptions, such as rhythmic-musical intelligence and visual-spatial intelligence. As Gardner has pointed out, rhythm is not restricted to music since it is also an integral component of linguistic and bodily-kinesthetic intelligence. Also, he could have noted that some modern music and electronic music has no rhythm. I doubt that scholars and teachers who insist on the concept of rhythmic-musical intelligence understand the basic elements of music or the features of modern music.

In Gardner's point of view, there is no certain connection between spatial intelligence and visual sensitivity. He pointed out that research with blind subjects has indicated that spatial knowledge is not totally dependent on the visual system and that blind individuals can appreciate certain aspects of pictures (Gardner, 2006). So I doubt that Chinese scholars who insist on the concept of visual-spatial intelligence have read Gardner's books.

Commercial and Misused Implements

Many businesspeople wanted to work with me to establish schools, kindergartens, and training classes labeled with MI theory, but I have refused these overtures.

I saw an advertisement in which a company will hold a national MI competition in order to select eight children, with each representing the best in each of eight intelligences. My name appeared on the list of experts who were going to judge the best child in each of eight intelligences, but I had known nothing about the competition and nobody had invited me before. Of course, the parents must pay for the registration of their children to participate in the competition.

Wrong Channel of Learning and Doubtable Translation

Some confusions about MI theory come about because some teachers and scholars have not read Gardner's original work or authorized translations. Instead they rely on the doubtful second-hand, third-hand, fourth-hand, even sixth-hand materials in Chinese that relate to MI theory.

In the summer of 2003, the manager of a publisher I was unfamiliar with asked me to translate one of Gardner's books on MI theory in one month. I replied that I needed at least six months to provide a good translation even though I had read the book many times. The manager never got back to me. Soon after, the publisher issued the translation, which had been done by several students, with the name of their teacher listed as the first author. I found in the translation many evident mistakes, which have since confused many readers who have not had the opportunity to read Gardner's books in English or authorized translations.

CONCLUSION

Innumerable educators, teachers, administrators and supervisors of education, artists, and parents have accepted and welcomed MI theory in China. As I have shown, this theory happens to tally with Chinese culture and ancient educational ideology, the new steps of the reform, and the popular principle of education—character education. It also offers solace to parents who are permitted to have only one child.

Under guidance of this theory, the Chinese have changed their perspectives of students, educational goals and policies, teaching methods, learning, and assessment in many schools at many educational levels. Some Chinese musicians and I have confirmed the existence of existential intelligence and discerned it at work in the arts. We try to inspire students' crystallizing experience of existential intelligence through the appreciation of music in the education of aesthetics.

References

Confucian Disciples. (1977). *The analects of Confucius* (S. Leys, Trans.). New York: Norton.

Gardner, H. (1993). *Multiple intelligences. The theory in practice: A reader*. New York: Basic Books.

Gardner, H. (1999). *Intelligence reframed: The multiple intelligences for the 21st century.* New York: Basic Books.

Gardner, H. (2006). *Multiple intelligences: New horizons.* New York: Basic Books.

Lao, Z. (2003). *Lao Zi.* Beijing: China Social Science Publishing House.

LeBon, T. (2006). *Peal Experiences & Maslow.* http://www.timlebon.com/PeakExperiences .html.

Li, L. (2004). *Education for 1.3 billion: On 10 years of education reform and development.* Beijing: Foreign Language Teaching and Research Press.

Shen, Z. (2004). *Howard Gardner, arts, and multiple intelligences.* Beijing: Beijing Normal University Press.

Shen, Z., & Zhao, C. (1999). Aesthetic education in China. *Journal of Multicultural and Cross-cultural Research in Art Education, 17,* 91–102.

CHAPTER 6

A Decade of School-Based MI Teaching Experiments in Macao

Kwok-cheung Cheung

This chapter describes a decade-long effort to initiate school-based MI teaching experiments in Macao, China. Three aspects of this effort are detailed: comparing MI theory with traditional Chinese educational thought, developing MI-inspired assessments, and fostering individualized educational practices. Individualized educational practices include four ways to think about the relationship between teaching and MI theory: teaching of MI, teaching with MI, teaching about MI, and teaching for MI. Each of these terms is explained with the results of action research. The chapter concludes with implications of the Macao experience for international MI educators.

As a professor of curriculum and instruction at the University of Macau in Macao, China, my areas of research interest and expertise are theories of educational psychology, assessment and evaluation, and classroom practices. Before I knew of Gardner's MI theory, I had pondered the question of how our understanding of human beings and our school practices could better take into account individual differences, which are so evident in children's development. For the past decade, my colleagues and I have used MI theory to guide our research and fieldwork. Specifically, we have pursued three strands of scholarly inquiries: theory adaptation, assessment development, and teacher capacity building. In the sections that follow, I share each of these pursuits in the context of educational systems and recent school reform efforts in Macao.

CULTURAL AND EDUCATIONAL CONTEXT

Since 1991, Macao schools, of which most are private Chinese schools, have been protected by law and given complete autonomy in matters related to instruction and curricular provisions. The Macao school system does not have public examination of children from kindergarten to twelfth grade. Assessments are essentially school based and wholly in the hands of the teachers and principals. Macao's flexible educational system places it in an ideal position to adapt new ideas such as MI. Indeed, Macao has been fertile ground for my colleagues and me to conduct MI teaching experiments over the last decade.

After the 1999 sovereignty transition from Portugal back to China, more and more schools, including the English schools whose students are ethnic Chinese, have been influenced by the newly promulgated Chinese national curriculum. Happily, by the turn of the century, Mainland China showed genuine interest in using MI to guide its curriculum reform toward individualized education. Macao schools have been influenced by this MI wave because students use textbooks and instructional materials imported from China.

At the dawn of this century, the aims of education for all school subjects in Macao were subjected to adaptation and revision in the light of the new Chinese curriculum standards. The new standards argue that education should be responsive to the individual character and intellectual potentials of children. The following excerpt from the new Chinese *Mathematics Curriculum Standards* is a case in point (Ministry of Education, People's Republic of China, 2001, p. 1):

> The basic, general, and developmental characteristics of the mathematics curriculum for compulsory basic education should be exhibited visibly so that mathematics education is responsive to all children it serves. The following should be realized:
>
> 1. Everybody learns valuable mathematics;
> 2. Everybody is able to acquire mathematics indispensable for them;
> 3. In mathematics each student will have his/her own distinctive kind of development.

In response to the third aim of mathematics education, practitioners were looking for a sound theory to guide their practice. The promise of MI-inspired pedagogy to fulfill this aim had great appeal to them. Central to MI theory is the notion of individual differences. Using a wide range of data sources, including brain research, Gardner laid out a clear framework for why focusing on diverse intellectual strengths of individual children is central to quality education for all. MI theory confirmed many Macao teachers' long-held beliefs and practices. Its sound theoretical framework with strong supporting evidence convinced many educators that this was the way to go.

Another impetus for MI infusion in Macao came from the government. The policy address for fiscal year 2002 was delivered by the chief executive, Edmund Ho. The address presented multiple intelligences as an important means to foster all-around development for the new generation. Citizens should understand that academic achievements are not the only benchmark of success in learning. Equally important, if not more so, is the development of students' self-confidence and self-concepts. Only when students have a better sense of who they are and what they want and can do can they take full advantage of their natural as well as environmental resources to succeed in school and in life.

In this context, my colleagues and I have made a concerted effort to bring MI theory into the Macao school system over the past decade. For example, I have written Chinese textbooks introducing Gardner's original work on frames of mind and ideas of individually configured education. I have also given talks, provided workshops, and written articles to help clarify misunderstandings and curb inappropriate uses of MI. Translating the theory into classroom practice in the Chinese context is not without difficulty. Does MI theory fit with traditional Chinese educational thought? If so, is it more easily adapted by Chinese teachers and educators? How can we use MI theory as a means to reach educational goals set by the government and society? How can we practice MI theory so that practitioners have classroom tools to understand the intellectual strengths of individual students? With these and many other related questions in mind, I initiated three scholarly inquiries into the application of MI theory: comparing MI theory with traditional Chinese educational thought, developing MI-inspired assessments, and fostering individualized educational practices.

COMPARING MI THEORY WITH TRADITIONAL CHINESE EDUCATIONAL THOUGHT

To compare MI theory with traditional Chinese educational thought, I studied many Chinese classics. With more than five thousand years of uninterrupted history, China has rich educational practices rooted in Confucian thought. After extensive reading and literature review, I decided to make three attempts to revitalize MI theory from the Chinese educational perspective, using three types of Chinese classics known to most Chinese even today.

I started with an analysis of the *Analects* (Lun Yu), a record of the words and acts of the Confucius and his disciples. Written between 479 B.C. and 221 B.C., the *Analects* is the representative work of Confucianism and continues to have a tremendous influence on Chinese and East Asian thought and values today. Confucius, an educator himself, stated in the *Analects* many educational principles and told many stories about education based on the individual characteristics of his students. For example, he said, "A gentleman is no vessel (*Jun Zi Bu Qi*)." This short statement embraces a rich message that there are multiple talents of the generalized kinds in our people (and state governors) and one should not consider them to have just one kind of specialty that fits just one kind of task. Putting Confucius's statement into contemporary MI context, educational practitioners need to nourish students' multiple intelligences to develop the multiple competences needed to keep pace with the ever-changing skill demands of the job market in the postmodern era (Cheung, 2003).

Having determined that there are numerous principles from Confucian canonical scriptures that have a bearing on MI, I next analyzed the contribution of *Book of Odes* (*Shi Jing*) to the genesis and evolution of MI in Chinese culture and society (Cheung, 2004). The *Book of Odes* is one of the earliest Confucian classics and highly regarded by the ancient Chinese state governors. It played a pivotal role because the evolution of the eight intelligences relied on the germination, nurturing, and development of the culture we live in. I hypothesized that the genesis and evolution of multiple intelligences stemmed from the three kinds of odes (Lessons from the States, Odes of the Kingdom, and Odes from the Temple and the Altar [*Feng, Ya, Song*]), as well as the three practical ways of expressing these three kinds of odes (*Fu, Bi, Xing*). For instance, "In hewing an axe-handle, in hewing an axe-handle, the pattern is not far off (*Fa Ge Fa Ge, Qi Ze Bu Yuan*)" is an excerpt of *Fa Ke* in *The Book of Odes*. It may be explained as the Chinese notion of Gardner's principle of individually configured education. This excerpt captures the essence of the first chapter of *Zhong Yong* (also known as *Doctrine of the Mean*), which is one of the Four Books and Confucian canonical scriptures. The first chapter of *Zhong Yong* says, "What heaven confers is called *nature*. Accordance with this nature is called the *way*. Cultivating the way is called *education* (*Tian Ming Zhi Wei Xing, Shuai Xing Zhi Wei Dao, Xiu Dao Zhi Wei Jiao*)."

My third effort was more challenging and ambitious. I sought to analyze the potential contributions of the ancient *Thousand Characters Classics* (*Qian Zi Wen*) of the sixth century to the design of basic textbooks for MI-inspired liberal education in this century (Cheung, 2003). For more than thirteen hundred years, this classic has proved itself the most popular reading material in China for children's general education. Content analyses of the text revealed that despite its varied topical areas, there are four overarching themes: learning to know, learning to do, learning to live together, and learning to be. These correspond to MI theory in that the purpose of developing multiple intelligences is to put them to good use by contributing to personal well-being and the betterment of society. The conclusion of the content analysis is that by referencing *Thousand Characters Classics* in today's curriculum design, teachers can relate it to MI theory by helping students realize their fullest potential (learning to know and learning to do) and understand the responsibility of being a member of society (learning to live together and learning to be).

DEVELOPING MI-INSPIRED ASSESSMENTS

One thorny issue central to the successful application of MI theory for individually configured education is the assessment of the intellectual configurations of children and their developmental progression. I am a specialist in testing, measurement, and evaluation, so my second strand of MI-related scholastic inquiry in Macao is to develop MI-inspired assessments and conduct school-based research on their use and validity. To date, my colleagues and I have developed two computerized MI assessment software programs: SMILES (School-Based Multiple Intelligences Learning Evaluation System) and BRIDGES (Brain-Based Recommendations for Intellectual Development and Good Education—a Self-Rating System). Both computerized assessment systems have been disseminated for teachers' use in Macao (see Cheung, Wai, & Chiu, 2000/2002; Cheung, 2005).

Based on teacher ratings of observed behavior, SMILES was designed for kindergartners and students in the primary grades. BRIDGES, which relies on students' self-ratings, was developed for use in secondary school. Either teachers or students complete a series of Likert-type items composing the eight intelligence scales. The result of the assessment is a profile chart of multiple intelligences. These profiles are commonly known as MI spectra in Macao and the region. Developmental progressions included in SMILES and BRIDGES are both norm referenced and criterion referenced. Teachers can use the MI spectrum charted for each student to learn about that student's intellectual profile, that is, strengths and weaknesses.

Admittedly MI assessment cannot be done with precision. Nevertheless, Macao's experiences confirm that the MI spectrum, together with other data routinely collected, such as teacher observations and students' sample work, can be validly deployed for strength-based scaffolding. As in the case of Chinese medicine, the MI spectrum provides a holistic diagnosis with attention paid to building on students' strengths to overcome weaknesses (Cheung & Lou, 2003; Cheung, Tang, & Lam, 2003; Cheung & Lee, 2006). We are now in the process of developing a system that will integrate the MI spectrum with an individual student's school database to monitor the development of MI as students advance in grade level during their fifteen years of compulsory basic education in Macao.

FOSTERING INDIVIDUALIZED EDUCATIONAL PRACTICES

My third strand of scholastic inquiry is to build teachers' capacity to integrate MI theory into their daily classroom practice. The primary purpose of the capacity building is to empower teachers to practice individually configured education. Inspired by the work of both Western and Chinese MI scholars, I developed an MI-inspired curriculum and pedagogy inquiry framework (see Figure 6.1). The framework consists of four interrelated components: teaching of MI, teaching

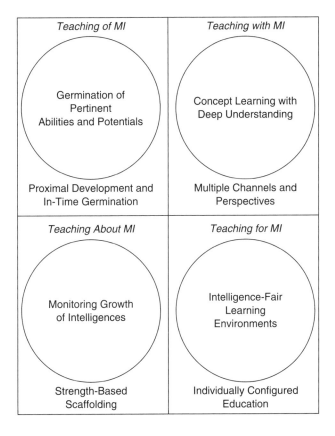

Figure 6.1 MI-Inspired Curriculum and Pedagogy Inquiry Framework
Source: Adapted from Cheung (2003, p. 47).

with MI, teaching about MI, and finally, teaching for MI. The four components create a synergy in classrooms that is conducive to individually configured education. Using this framework, I conducted a series of action research studies in a range of schools in Macao.

Teaching of MI

Teaching of MI refers to the process of helping children acquire knowledge and skills at the optimal time and using developmentally appropriate approaches. For example, to develop emergent literacy skills, early childhood teachers in a Macao kindergarten engaged children in a range of reading activities. Teachers provided a literacy-rich classroom environment, used reciprocal teaching methods for reading instruction, and conducted storybook and storyboard assessment, to name a few of their literacy enrichment activities (see Sit, 2007, for the lesson study approach). As the result of this intentional teaching approach, the children became familiar with the four reading strategies: questioning, clarifying, predicting, and summarizing. These emergent literacy skills pave the way for these children to learn to read at higher grade levels.

Sit (2007) is exemplary of teaching of MI because reading ability and the proximal development of associated reading strategies during the preschooler growth period are of paramount importance to young children's cognitive and language development.

Teaching with MI

Teaching with MI refers to the teaching practice of multiple entry points and multiple representations. Among the four components of the MI-inspired curriculum and pedagogy inquiry framework, this is the most successful one in my action research, particularly at the preprimary level. For example, kindergarten curriculum usually introduces a large number of concepts, such as big/small, family, and friends. Each of these concepts can be introduced through multiple channels, such as music, story, movement, and science experiment. When a concept is introduced through multiple channels, it offers more entry points for children to grasp the concept, and they are more likely to understand the concept at a deeper level. In the case of the size concepts of big and small, a teacher can blow air into several balloons of different sizes and vary the size after each comparison. Children can join their hands together, mimicking the changing sizes of balloons. Furthermore, the teacher and children can use their big voice as well as small voice to sing and talk. In this process, children use not only their hands, but also their eyes and voices to observe and experience the concepts of big and small.

Teaching with MI is enthusiastically welcomed by kindergarten teachers in Macao, who have found it helpful for guiding the thematic teaching approach that is often used in the preprimary curriculum. This instructional approach urges teachers to plan activities to reach diverse learners by tailoring instruction to varied ways of learning. The results are more motivated learners and deeper understanding of concepts (Cheung, 2003). Teaching with MI does not imply that every concept needs to be taught in eight different ways. The channels or entry points that teachers choose to introduce a concept have to be meaningful and conducive to understanding.

Teaching About MI

Teaching about MI involves the use of MI-inspired assessment results to inform curriculum planning and teaching. For example, my colleague and I conducted a research study of senior secondary students in a school in Macao (Cheung & Lee, 2006). Using BRIDGES, we generated an MI spectrum for each of the students assessed based on their responses to the MI self-rating scales. Complementing the MI spectrum chart for each student is a description of his or her distinctive characteristics in each of the eight intelligences. Teachers found both the chart and the description useful. Based on these diagnostic reports, they can carry out strength-based scaffolding for academic advancement or career counseling.

It is important to point out that teaching about MI does not entail labeling students. Rather, MI-inspired assessment such as SMILES and BRIDGES allows us to identify each student's unique intellectual configuration. The strengths can be capitalized on as a vantage point for overcoming or elevating weaknesses. Intervention strategies congruent with the MI philosophy can also help students who have trouble with particular learning areas.

Teaching for MI

Teaching for MI relates to the design and use of intelligence-fair environments. In the intelligence-fair environment, children have equal opportunity to access a range of intellectually stimulating and challenging areas rather than being limited to narrowly defined school learning areas. In the past few years, for example, I have worked with a group of kindergarten teachers to implement teaching for MI practices (Cheung, 2007). Using SMILES, kindergarten teachers observed their children's MI spectrum as either individuals or in groups. To ensure that the classroom learning environments are fair in terms of exposing children to all kinds of learning experiences, we created a template or grid to guide teachers' design of MI-inspired activities and to record each child's activities in relation to different intelligences. The intelligence-fair learning environment provides ample opportunities for children to demonstrate their areas of strength as well as strengthen their areas of weakness.

Designing intelligence-fair learning environments helps teachers support diverse learners through meaningfully connected activities. Meaningful connection is a key to true MI learning experiences. If activities are not meaningfully connected to the concepts studied or to each other, children's learning will be haphazard and effective learning will not take place.

CONCLUSION

This chapter briefly describes my scholarly pursuits to apply MI theory in Macao through school-based teaching experiments. Because most of these research results were published in Chinese, the influence of the work is limited to the Chinese-speaking community: Mainland China, Taiwan, Hong Kong, and Macao.

No formal evaluation of my school-based teaching experiments has been conducted so far. Through word of mouth, when teaching experiments are successfully implemented in one school, the idea and practice are adapted and replicated in another school. Based on my decade-long MI implementation experiences, the following aspects of the work done in Macao are worthy of attention for an international audience. First, many MI ideas can be found in the ancient Chinese classics, and Gardner's MI theory can be adapted for Chinese culture more easily when they are attached to the ideas in these classics. In addition, teaching with MI, together with the use of a template or planning grid, is useful in designing MI-inspired activities. Furthermore, SMILES and BRIDGES, computer-based MI assessment systems, are versatile tools that can assist teachers in identifying each student's unique intellectual profile as well as in designing intelligence-fair learning environments based on the assessment results. Finally, Macao's experiences in using MI-Spectrum for academic guidance and career counseling can be applied universally.

References

Cheung, K. C. (2003). *Raindrops soothing amidst the spring wind: Exemplary case studies of multiple intelligences inspired education.* Hong Kong: Crystal Educational Publications.

Cheung, K. C. (2004). The contribution of Shi Jing to the genesis of multiple intelligences in Chinese culture and society. *New Horizons in Education, 50,* 49–54.

Cheung, K. C. (2005). Development of a self-rating multiple intelligences computerized assessment system for intellectual development and student counseling. *Educational Research Journal, 20*(1), 57–72.

Cheung, K. C. (2007). Intimate integration of assessment and instruction in the design of thematic study units: The Macao experiences. In J. X. Zhu (Ed.), *Preprimary education from the Chinese perspective.* Shanghai: East China Normal University Press.

Cheung, K. C., & Lee, C. L. (2006). *Liberating talents and potentials in accordance with developmental regularities: An experimental research study on brain-based recommendations for intellectual development and good education—a self-rating system.* Macao: University of Macau Publication Centre.

Cheung, K. C., & Lou, L. H. (2003). *Children thank teachers for being educated: An experimental research study on the exploitation and evaluation of multiple intelligences.* Macao: University of Macau Publication Centre.

Cheung, K. C., Tang, H. S., & Lam, I. S. (2003). *Every child is talented: An experimental study of self-ratings of students' multiple intelligences.* Macao: University of Macau Publication Centre.

Cheung, K. C., Wai, F. L., & Chiu, K. H. (2000/2002). *School-Based Multiple Intelligences Learning Evaluation System (SMILES).* Hong Kong: Crystal Educational Publications.

Ministry of Education. People's Republic of China. (2001). *Full-time obligatory education: Mathematics curriculum standards (experimental version).* Beijing: Beijing Normal University Press.

Sit, P. S. (2007). Lesson study as a means to help kindergarten teachers develop children's reading comprehension ability. *Journal of Research on Elementary and Secondary Education, 18*, 145–164.

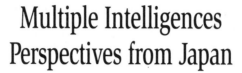

CHAPTER 7

Multiple Intelligences
Perspectives from Japan

David Howland
Tomoe Fujimoto
Keiko Ishiwata
Masao Kamijo

Although MI is still relatively new in Japan, it shows striking compatibility with traditional Japanese education models, particularly within the arts and the *terakoya*, community schools within local temples that provided the nation with universal public education until the opening of Japan in the Meji era (1868–1912), when they were replaced by Westernized systems. As Japan now begins to experience a rediscovery of those elements in its cognitive history that links it with MI, the need for MI implementation in education and industry is apparent, and in fact it is already beginning to have an impact on Japanese culture. This chapter traces Japan's journey from *terakoya* to technology and looks at ways in which MI has begun to play an important role as the country moves forward in reshaping ideas about thinking and learning.

Though perhaps encountering a slow start, MI theory is gradually becoming known in Japan. In this chapter we present a brief history of Japanese education and traditional arts, suggesting their compatibility with MI theory, and we look at a representative sampling of the practical applications of MI today with implications for its future in both Japan and the rest of the world.

Our special thanks go to Naohiko Furuichi, head teacher of school affairs at Midorimachi Junior High School, for permission to use information based on an interview with him by the editorial office of the Japanese MI Society.

In 2004, the Japan Multiple Intelligence Society (JMIS) was formed by alumni of the Project Zero Summer Institute, and Howard Gardner was named honorary president. Since its inception, JMIS has been striving to make MI theory known throughout Japan. Since 2000, Gardner has returned to Japan three times. During this period, enthusiastic teachers, researchers, and practitioners in a wide range of fields continue to spread the word. As part of this interest in MI, there has also been an emphasis on other ideas developed at Project Zero, such as an education for understanding, the importance of arts education, and the use of multiple, more qualitative means of assessment as opposed to standardized, fact-based tests.

Nurturing creativity has been a great challenge in Japan, as it is hindered by a system that places tremendous emphasis on school entrance examinations, particularly at the university level. However, some universities are beginning to require applicants to exhibit deep understanding of their discipline, not just the regurgitation of facts on an entrance exam. We hope this will be a pivotal point in Japan's system of education at all levels.

Whether Japan will prove to be fertile soil for MI theory remains debatable, but without MI theory, how can Japan manage to improve education? Since the 1980s, education in Japan has been experiencing a downward spiral and is in dire need of help to reverse this. But we suggest perhaps Japan was once the perfect environment for MI, since traditional Japanese education and traditional arts institutions seem so compatible with MI theory. A key to understanding this begins with a look at the *terakoya.*

MULTIPLE INTELLIGENCES SPIRIT IN *TERAKOYA*

The official national educational system in Japan was established in 1873, at the end of a two-hundred-year-closure of the country (Ueno, 2002). Until then, the *terakoya,* literally "temple school," was the major institution of learning in Japan. It naturally came into existence in response to people's need for education and spread to small towns and villages with the development of the monetary system. Its teachers were volunteers, not licensed, and received only honorariums from parents. However, it provided people from every walk of life with literacy and numeracy skills (Wada, 2006; Fujimoto, 2006). Indeed, the ratio of the people with numeracy skill was higher than that of people in any other country at that time (Ministry of Education, Culture, Sports, Science and Technology, 1999). In the middle of the fifteenth century, there were seventeen *terakoya,* and at their peak, from 1854 to 1867, the number of *terakoya* had increased to 4,293. In 1868 boys' attendance was 43 percent and girls' attendance was 10 percent (Kito, 2002), indicating the wide spread of education at that time.

In a *terakoya* classroom, the teacher worked individually with each student, carefully considering his or her practical needs; for example, the *terakoya* located in the agricultural area nurtured naturalist intelligence in students. In this way, *terakoya* provided each student with deep understanding and the skills he or she would need as an adult (Ministry of Education, Culture, Sports, Science, and Technology, 1999b). The curriculum was flexible and spontaneous, unlike today's rigid system, and it provided festivals and calligraphy exhibitions in order to motivate student learning. The *terakoya* provided students with multiple entry points to a variety of intelligences in addition to linguistic and logical-mathematical. Therefore, the Terakoya's educational philosophy was compatible with MI theory.

MULTIPLE INTELLIGENCES SPIRIT IN JAPANESE TRADITIONAL PERFORMING ARTS

Japanese traditional performing arts are also compatible with MI because of the multiple entry points for learners and potentiality for fostering intelligences. One of the Japanese forms of poetry, haiku (a traditional seventeen-syllable poetic form), is relevant to MI-based learning in that through one art form, various intelligences are tapped. Koshiro Matsumoto (2007), one of the foremost *kabuki* actors today, stated that studying haiku helps him to refine his performance. Since the Edo era (1603–1867), some *kabuki* actors have studied haiku to understand how they can express themselves in each gesture and movement, just as haiku poets express a theme succinctly and beautifully in just seventeen syllables.

The teaching for understanding (TfU) framework developed at Project Zero can be applied to learning traditional Japanese arts. One of the through lines across Japanese traditional arts is an aphorism, *"Shu-Ha-Ri,"* first used by tea master Sen Rikyu (1522–1591). He redefined and reformed the traditional tea ceremony in the sixteenth century, perhaps the best example of MI compatibility in traditional Japanese arts. The aphorism best illustrates this and it conveys the literal meaning "keep-break-leave," meaning learners should observe the conventions of the form, improve their own form, and then create their own art with the original form in mind. In doing so, they are expected to preserve the original form and pass it down to the next generation of learners. Traditional Japanese performing arts require individual instruction, generative topics, and ongoing assessments—all facets of a TfU approach. Elementary learners need to show deep understanding initially by performing under the guidance of the master. Over time, learners refine their performance with creativity.

The tea ceremony, a highly cultivated art in Japan that is still revered today, provides practitioners with a variety of multiple entry points, and requires several intelligences to appreciate and understand. It integrates pottery, china, textiles, and painting (spatial intelligence); poetry and literature (linguistic intelligence); and flower arrangement (naturalist and spatial intelligences). Moreover, it requires learners to master an understanding of tea etiquette (intrapersonal and interpersonal intelligences); correct gestures and movements (bodily-kinesthetic intelligence); communication skills (linguistic intelligences); spiritual awareness, ethics, and morality (intrapersonal and interpersonal intelligences); and the Japanese way of thinking: simplicity and economical living (logical-mathematical intelligence).

This panoply of intelligences seems to be just what Tenshin Okakura, art curator and principal founder of Japan's first academy of fine arts, has described in *A Book of Tea.* Okakura (1906) argues that teaism is not merely aestheticism, but rather a Japanese perspective on man and nature, religion and ethics. Okakura also asserts that teaism is hygiene, emphasizing cleanliness. It is economic, advocating comfort in simplicity rather than in the complex and costly. And it is moral geometry, defining human proportion with the universe.

Indeed this perspective holds true for the tea ceremony today. Before beginning the ceremony, practitioners clean the tearoom and the tea set. They pick fresh flowers and arrange them in a prescribed way, simple and humble. They choose the porcelain and a decorative scroll for hanging, and their costume. They then prepare simple cuisine for the ceremony. Everything should suit the season, the occasion, and the guests' tastes. During the ceremony, every movement must be graceful, and the tea service should be arranged impeccably on the *tatami* (woven rush floor mat). Everyone involved in the tea ceremony is a performer in the small tearoom, which symbolizes a microcosm of the world (Sen, 1981). The ceremony involves serving and enjoying tea, writing poems, and enjoying the beauty of the tea set, flowers, and calligraphy.

Traditional Japanese culture, arts, and education thrived in what clearly was a haven for multiple intelligences. Together with *terakoya,* Japan was well suited for MI.

AFTER TERAKOYA, A FADING OF THE MI SPIRIT

In 1853, Commodore Perry's visit from the United States forced Japan to open up to the world. In 1871, an official educational system was established by the Japanese government, which set out to make Japan a rich and powerful country, and ultimately the ruler of all Asia (Meech-Pekarik, 1986). For this purpose, it organized educational policy based on nationalism. Simultaneously, the educational system was instituted on the basis of utilitarianism. Thus, all academic institutions became the arena where people were provided with facts and information in order to pass the exams to be certified as doctors, lawyers, high officials, teachers, and so on. The insufficient number of schools limited people from obtaining a higher education because of scarcity of financial resources. After the Industrial Revolution in Japan in 1894–1895, the number of privileged social class applicants to junior high school began to soar, which caused strong competition. The Imperial University was considered to be the main avenue for obtaining a successful position in society (Ito, 2006; Amagi, 1979; Katagiri & Kimura, 2008; Tachibana, 2001).

It was not until after World War II that Japan dramatically shifted to a truly modernized and civilized country (Kito, 2002). In 1947, the Fundamental Law of Education was enacted, and Japan's rigid system of education was established. Since that time, the Ministry of Education, Culture, Sports, Science, and Technology (MEXT) has determined the basic standards of Japanese national education: educational objectives, curricula, length of the school year, and subjects to be studied at each level of the system. The objectives and content of every course are stipulated under the national courses of study. All schools are required by law to observe it, so that men and women, poor and rich alike, obtain a standardized education that is of the same quality everywhere in Japan (Kubo, 2001). The courses of study also forces teachers to observe regulations and cover the required materials.

During the 1960s, with the development of the Japanese economy, increasing numbers of people pursued higher education and were involved in academic competition, and an academic-oriented society formed (Kubo, 2001). The pencil-and-paper entrance examination required applicants to learn detailed facts by rote memorization, not deep understanding (Hirahara, 1993; Kubo, 2001; Morishima, 1985; Tachibana, 2001). The utilitarian idea toward education remained, and students were trained to pass exams. For their part, teachers endeavored to improve their pedagogy so as to cover the materials on which the students would be examined. In the affluent 1970s, when high school education was available to almost all Japanese people (education in Japan is compulsory from seven to fifteen years old), this system turned out to be ineffective. Moreover, it has not changed to address modern problems such as school violence, crime, bullying, truancy, dropouts, and corporal punishment in school. Some educators say these problems were caused by the ordeal of the entrance examination and the government policy on education that every student should be provided with the same education (Sakata, 2007). Still other problems plague Japanese education today, such as stress, parents' complaints, and student Internet addiction problems, which have backed teachers into a corner. They have to deal with those problems without adequate support. Whenever a problem occurs, the public requires teachers' accountability, which often adds more burden on teachers. They are stressed out. (Osaka Bunka Center, 1996; Refusal to Go to School, 2007; Wada, 2006).

MULTIPLE INTELLIGENCES: A TOOL FOR THE FUTURE

Some solutions to these problems were posed in 2002 by MEXT. The first one is individualized instruction. Ironically, this is exactly what the *terakoya* did. By applying the strategies of *terakoya,* and therefore MI principles, this solution is feasible. It is clear that the application of MI can help to reach every student, motivating each one to learn and pursue individual interests.

The second solution is an amendment in the course of study. MEXT relaxed the standardized education by decreasing the number and range of required subjects. Thus, a school is allowed to offer more elective courses to students. Now students can pursue their interests and study in depth the subject they are interested in (Okabe et al., 2008). This shift in requirements means that students have an opportunity to achieve deep understanding.

The third solution is integrated studies, which serves Japanese students' individual interests. The courses of study delineated by MEXT requires all schools in Japan to offer integrated studies, where students can pursue their interests across the curriculum. Through integrated studies, students are encouraged to undertake research on a topic that interests them, to learn from hands-on experiences—not from teachers' lectures—and to integrate what they have learned into a content area (Ministry of Education, Culture, Sports, Science, and Technology, 1999a). Through this study, students not only gain real-world experience, but they apply this learning to classroom study and develop their intellectual curiosity through this synthesis.

Kanagawa Prefectural High School of Foreign Studies, a prestigious school for 450 students with highlinguistic skills, has been particularly successful in fostering intellectual stimulation through integrated studies. The school is proud of its achievements, particularly because it sends a significant number of students to prestigious universities. One of the integrated studies, "English Camp" for first-year students, is discussed below.

Integrated studies encompasses all of the intelligences and meets the demands of modern society. Nobel laureate Ezaki (2007) reiterates the need for this kind of learning in Japan. He emphasizes that educators should nurture each student's individual abilities because Japan needs people with creativity, originality, and individuality rather than a nation of people who are good only at absorbing facts. This message signals a need for deep understanding.

MI is beneficial to Japan in an additional important way. Recently the important university entrance examination has been undergoing a drastic change. The stimulus is the demographic change in the school-age population, which has dropped significantly. Universities are now looking for qualified applicants who can demonstrate high degrees of uniqueness or individuality, and the notion that everyone should be exactly alike is changing.

University applicants within the past fifteen years have decreased because of this drop in the school-age population. In the next few years, the number of places available at Japanese universities will equal the number of applicants, so most universities will face the problem of filling places with qualified applicants.

Interestingly, where universities used to require only a passing grade on extremely difficult pencil-and-paper entrance examinations, admissions officers now look to a variety of tools in assessing applicants. In addition to the test, an interview, a recommendation from the school, and a writing sample from the applicant make up the admission's portfolio. In essence, a student can demonstrate strengths in any or all of the intelligences, and he or she has the opportunity to provide proof of deep understanding. For example, a student who wants to become a historian can demonstrate the ability to think like a historian. Conscious awareness of MI theory, TfU, and deep understanding on the part of students, teachers, administrators, and admissions officers can facilitate the process.

Nonetheless, there is still considerable distance to traverse at the university level. Teachers' other jobs are demanding and time-consuming: accounting, career consulting, counseling, coaching, administrating, and so on. Japanese society regards education as a tool for obtaining a higher position in society. Only a small number of universities offer liberal arts education (Tachibana, 2001). Nevertheless, considering the history of Japan and its impact on the current educational environment, there is no time like the present for thinking about the future. MI could play a crucial role in Japan for generations to come.

In what follows, we describe a number of programs in which ideas of multiple intelligences have played a guiding role. It should be noted that with the exception of the final one, which is connected with university study, these programs do not explicitly use MI terminology or concepts. Rather, the individuals who have conceptualized the programs, as well as those who teach in them, have embedded the spirit of MI into their activities.

LINGUISTIC, INTRAPERSONAL, AND INTERPERSONAL INTELLIGENCES

The Kanagawa Prefectural High School of Foreign Studies has been designated as a "Super English High School (SELHi)" by MEXT from 2003 to 2008. SELHi schools develop unique approaches to teaching and serve as models to other schools.

The school's four-day English Camp has been a highlight of the English program for nearly forty years. In 2003, Keiko Ishiwata wanted to emphasize the efficacy of the camp in her SELHi report. Some colleagues, ignorant of MI, doubted that a four-day camp could enhance students' communicative skills in English. However, through MI frameworks, it was shown that students' language skills benefited from the camp; every activity at English Camp provides students with multiple entry points that develop and reinforce their intelligences as they progress in English language learning (Ishiwata, 2003). An analysis of the activities used at the camp revealed that those that were most compatible with MI theory were also the ones that teachers felt motivated the students to learn English and develop leadership and cooperation skills.

An activity that proved successful at the start of English Camp was "Find the Teacher." Since the students' goals were to be more confident and comfortable using spoken English, this activity got them to use English immediately with teachers who were native speakers of English. Each of the teachers submitted one interesting fact about their life, and these were recorded on a list with no names attached—for example (Lacey, 2003):

1. I hit a golf ball to the North Pole.
2. I once drove a ferry in Sydney Harbor.
3. Former Vice President of the United States Al Gore came to my home for a soccer party.
4. I climbed the highest mountain in Africa. First, what mountain is it?
5. I was an All American three meter springboard diving champion.
6. I shot a crocodile that attacked and tried to eat me.
7. I lived in a cave for two months in Greece.
8. I went to Times Square in New York City for New Year's.
9. I sat on top of a pyramid in Egypt drinking a beer while the sun was setting over the desert.
10. I attended a one-room school for first grade.

Students were encouraged to meet with and speak to the teachers throughout the course of the four days and try to discover which teacher submitted each fact, but they were not allowed to ask the question directly; they had to start a conversation first and then ask questions related to the information.

At the dinner table on the first night, teacher-mentor Keiko Ishiwata sat with a shy boy named Makoto. She noticed that he was not talking to anyone and realized that this was probably because he was reluctant to speak English only, a rule at the camp. She struck up a conversation with him and asked him if he had met Bob, a teacher who was sitting in front of him. "Not yet," Makoto answered as he smiled awkwardly. She asked him if he had his "Find the Teacher" list. He said yes. She asked him if his group had found names to go with all the information on the list. He said no, and she urged him to speak to Bob.

Makoto introduced himself and immediately asked Bob, "Did you hit a golf ball to the North Pole?" Bob reminded Makoto that he could not ask the question directly. Slowly Makoto began formulating questions, and the conversation began. Through context clues, Makoto learned that it was not Bob who had hit the golf ball to the North Pole, but he did discover who had. Makoto found his information, and he also conversed in English.

Many Japanese students are reluctant to hold conversations in English not only because they are shy, but because Japanese and English conversation styles are completely different. Nancy Sakamoto, author of *Polite Fictions in Collision* (2006), concludes that every participant in a Japanese conversation waits for his or her turn to speak. The turn depends on age, relationship to the perceived main speaker, and social position. Thus, the students at camp were not confident about speaking with adults, but with their lists and exercising their multiple intelligences, they were able to make great strides in English communication.

After English Camp, their reflection sheets revealed that they developed not only linguistic intelligence but also intrapersonal, interpersonal, musical, and spatial intelligences.

MULTIPLE INTELLIGENCES TAPPED FROM THE SISTER SCHOOL EXCHANGE PROGRAM

Aside from English Camp, another peak experience for students at this school is the Sister School Exchange Program. This program, which has been sending and receiving delegations of students to and from France, the United States, China, Germany, and Australia for more than ten years, is the one where MI theory is implemented the most. Teachers of both schools exchange information about each participating student so that the students can be matched with appropriate host families. The participating faculty take great care to match students and families according to such details as hobbies, favorite sports, favorite subjects in school, and preferences in music. Once matches are determined, e-mail communication begins so that host families and students get to know one another before they meet.

Students prepare for the trip three months beforehand in a variety of ways, with careful attention to MI frameworks. They learn about the culture of the host country; they research the education system, politics, history, and geography of the host culture; and they share their research through presentations to each other. They also prepare presentations about Japan to take with them and share with students at the sister school.

Throughout this process, excitement is high, and students come to understand their own profile of intelligences. Some use musical intelligence by teaching songs to be used at the host school, some use interpersonal intelligence by becoming group leaders, and some use linguistic intelligence by editing group publications or learning the language of the host country.

When the students arrive in the host country, they attend the same classes as their host "sisters" and "brothers." They give their presentations at school or to their host families. But above all, they use their intelligences to communicate and live comfortably within another culture, speaking another language.

At the end of the program, the students participate in a farewell party held at the host school one day before departure to Japan. In preparation, the students practice songs and dances that they will perform at the party as a capstone for their international experience.

The actual two-week trip is really a six-month project and does not end when the students arrive back in Japan. On their return, all of the students use their multiple intelligences to debrief and share the trip with others. They make a collage of memorabilia of their stay in the host country, produce a publication entitled "Our Memory of the Sister School Exchange Program," and present what they learned through their experience with schoolmates who did not participate in the program.

The benefits of the program prove to be far reaching. Many of the students used their exchange experience as springboard research projects back at school in Japan. For example, one student learned how to teach Japanese and was able to do it at her sister school. Another student used her study of aging to visit a nursing home in her host country, thus giving a cross-cultural perspective to her research. Still another did environmental research in the host country and applied it to a more comprehensive research project. Their reflection sheets proved how this program has influenced their way of living and thinking, motivations, interests, and future life courses.

As a teacher at a model school, Keiko Ishiwata wrote about the efficacy of MI in a SELHi report (2003, 2004a, 2004b, 2005) and gave a presentation at the Kanto District English Teachers' Conference (2004a). Her hope is that MI will play a major role across the curriculum in education in Japan and guide them in the right direction.

AN MI SCIENCE PROJECT AT MIDORIMACHI JUNIOR HIGH SCHOOL

Another model award-winning school is the Midorimachi Junior High School in Chiba Prefecture. This school, honored as the Most Excellent Project Award in the Sony Science Education Program 2007 sponsored by Sony Foundation for Education, exhibits innovative MI applications. As a leading junior high school science teacher in this school, Naohiko Furuichi is particularly interested in the application of MI to his students' daily lives and to the way they respond to science education. He wants to provide them with multiple entry points to science that will stimulate their interest and curiosity. For example, in the photographs in Figure 7.1, he is explaining the waxing and waning of the moon, using the following haiku by Buson Yosa (in a translation by Gabi Greve, 2008):

> rapeseed flowers—
> the moon is in the east,
> the sun in the west

Furuichi's own interest in MI developed through his participation at the Project Zero Summer Institute as a member of the Sony Science Teachers Association (SSTA), a volunteer organization dedicated to fostering inquiry and appreciation of science in children. The SSTA currently works with approximately two thousand elementary and secondary school teachers and provides assistance in research and training activities. Since the first cohort of Project Zero graduates returned to Japan in 2003, the SSTA member graduates have been applying what they have learned to their own classes and have provided support to colleagues and useful feedback to the Harvard Graduate School of Education.

Furuichi has implemented a particularly successful MI science project in his school's science curriculum. This is a self-directed independent research project that middle school students complete primarily throughout their summer vacation. The project is a step-by-step introduction to science research and culminates in a written report of approximately forty pages. Students are asked to reflect on the following challenging questions:

1. How do I select my topic, and what should I research? [This is the most difficult step.]
2. How do I proceed with observation and experimentation?
3. How do I report my findings?

Because this project can be overwhelming to students, Furuichi designed three supporting projects, each corresponding to a step or research question.

First, students must clearly understand their viewpoints in the research questions they want to ask. They must write one hundred potential research questions, referred to as, "Whys?" These questions arise from questioning of a past lesson or experiment in science class, a question about another academic discipline that could be explored scientifically, a question raised by a newspaper article or

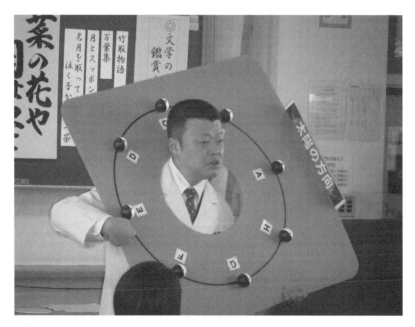

Figure 7.1 Waxing and Waning of the Moon Through Haiku

book, a question raised in daily life, including school life, or a question raised that addresses a local or seasonal issue. Students compile this list from May until the start of summer vacation in July, and when they have narrowed down one topic for study, they can begin their research.

In addition, an individual "dream box" is prepared for each student and is kept in the science classroom. This box contains various old toys, household utensils, stationery materials, and foods. Students must explain why each of the items is included in the box as a way of understanding order and logic in choosing and developing a research topic.

Finally, the science room and environs are set up to resemble a science theme park. The corridor and steps to the science room are decorated with science theme haiku and *senryu*, traditional Japanese humorous poems, printed on colorful cards and accented by seasonal flowers (accompanied by magnifying glasses to view them), seasonal art and literature, and science books. To add to the interactive display, reference books and materials from past studies and projects are available, and panel discussions are frequently held by students from previous years who have completed the project and by students currently undertaking the process.

Furuichi was very pleased with the higher quality of recent projects after the incorporation of MI and TfU frameworks. And indeed the success of this MI-based project is notable. In 2005, 67 percent of the students who participated in the project found the MI focus both supportive and stimulating. In 2006, 72 percent corroborated this finding.

Based on his experience and research, Furuichi has been able to share his work with colleagues through articles in periodicals that have appeared throughout Japan. His classroom was featured in the June 2007 edition of the popular Japanese magazine *President Family*. Information distribution in the science teaching community of Japan continues, and we hope it will come to be accepted as a part of all science curricula. As students begin to enter the workforce, they will take MI with them as a tool for developing a better world.

DEEP UNDERSTANDING IN COMMUNICATION: VISIONS FOR THE FUTURE

There is certainly no better time than the present for all of us as citizens of the world to recognize the importance of understanding one another beyond national borders, cultures, religions, and economic diversity. In the paragraphs that follow, one of us, Masao Kamijo, suggests ways by which we might change our lives by connecting cutting-edge technology with some selected frameworks to create a networked global society for the future. Frameworks of deeper understanding allow us to hone our own personal intelligence profiles for the purpose of deeper understanding and sharing our knowledge with others. Kamijo bases his work on innovations he has developed through his work with Sony. As he puts it:

> Well, what is deep or deeper understanding in communication? Suppose you gain new knowledge from a TV program or newspaper article. If that knowledge can enrich your previous knowledge web further, then that reinforced knowledge construction is now available for flexible use in a new environment of problem solving. As a result, it may lead to deep or deeper understanding that is different from that of basic *"Yes, I got it"* communication.

After having worked for the Sony Corporation as an engineer and chief manager of marketing in audio and video products, Masao Kamijo entered the in-house Products and Lifestyle Research Laboratory. Its goal is not to make forecasts for forecasting's sake but to understand the world within the flow of time, develop ideas for the future, and explore how to prepare for this. At the research laboratory, he encountered the provocative corporate aphorism, "If a medium is a system to transfer messages, Sony is a medium." (Karasawa, 1999) From then on he started to explore ways that would facilitate the development of human potential, which he hoped would contribute to better lives for the world's people. His quest led him to the study of the mechanisms of intelligence, knowledge, and understanding and to the work of Howard Gardner. In 1999 Kamijo knocked on Howard Gardner's door. He had heard about Gardner's work through his prior acquaintance with the notion of emotional intelligence. Kamijo was struck by a number of features of MI theory: that it offers a basic fair assessment of an individual's potential, and it makes an inventory, or profile of intelligences, possible; it allows the development of intelligences; it provides a way of monitoring this development; and it provides various entry points to concepts or topics. All of these elements, if they are in place, can be introduced to the network society. For example, the marketing of products in industry tends to emphasize the product or its specifications but not its users. In other words, it tends to neglect consideration for the humans who interact with the product. However, if cutting-edge technology, especially in industry, can apply MI frameworks, this may bring about a more organic focus on society than the current mechanistically oriented one.

Kamijo has been particular inspired by the teaching for understanding framework (TfU) proposed by Gardner and colleagues, which is closely woven with MI theory. Teaching for understanding entails the ability to think and act flexibly with what one knows. The TfU framework consists of generative topics, understanding goals, performances of understanding, and ongoing assessment. It thus opens a new window that allows us to see objects, processes, and concepts in a different and systematic way. Its potential is great, especially as a tool in planning and designing various new media. It is elegant and comprehensive, and the practical application of the framework is apparent.

But what are the qualities and depths of understanding? We need a specific definition to assess the way we will make progress toward achieving the understanding of goals. For this we can turn to Project Zero's dimensions of understanding framework—knowledge (K), methods (M), purposes (P), and forms (F) DoU (Gardner & Boix-Mansilla, 1998). If we teach just knowledge (the overemphasis of information or facts), we are trying to ride a one-legged horse. The key to performance of understanding emphasizes the dynamic relationships among all four—K, M, P, and F—in any discipline.

Consider broadband. Most of us now enjoy the use of broadband. It is at our disposal at all times (continuous connection), it is interactive, and increased bandwidth provides us with both explicit (such as text) and implicit (such as moving pictures) knowledge. If frameworks for understanding could be applied to this medium, ongoing assessment of information could exist within a network, and users could achieve better understanding of that information. In the future, global users with self-assessed, specific MI profiles could enter the network seeking a preassessed content profile from the network center.

As we consider the applications of Gardner's frameworks, it is the time to see their application beyond academe. Since 2003, Kamijo has been lecturing on deep understanding in communication to students of professional media studies in the Graduate School of Languages and Cultures at Nagoya University in Japan. Through his lectures, he wants his students to understand understanding and to seek being understood deeply in this century. He asks his students to use the TfU framework by applying each one to their own projects, generally their graduate thesis in media studies, but also documentaries and business case studies. Throughout their studies, students communicate through discussion, online course work, and written reflection. As Kamijo works with students in all these learning environments, Gardner's words echo in his brain: "You'll never understand the theory unless you apply it . . . and apply it again."

A caveat is essential here: intelligence and ethics must function together in a global society. As Ralph Waldo Emerson wrote, "Character is more important than intellect." Gardner, Csikszentmihalyi, and Damon (2001) seem to echo this in *Good Work: When Excellence and Ethics Meet*. The point is made particularly clear for the future media specialists in the chapter titled "Sources of Strength in Journalism." Besides honing our own intelligences, we have to figure out how intelligence and ethics can work together.

In his series of lectures on this topic, Kamijo has one overriding goal: that his students, future and current media specialists, can share the MI-TfU-DoU-GW

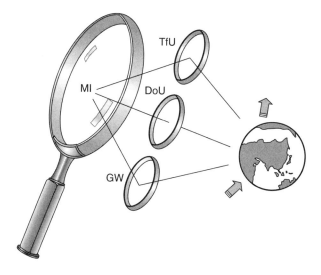

Figure 7.2 The World of Media Through the MI-TfU-DoU-GW Lens

Note: MI: multiple intelligences framework, TfU: teaching for understanding framework, DoU: dimensions of understanding framework, GW: good work framework.

© 2008 Massao Kamijo.

(Good Work) lens in their work. The lens, showed as a visual image in Figure 7.2, supports better understanding in today's global society.

CONCLUSION

The twenty-first century is here, and so are the frameworks that we will need for understanding ourselves and each other. Once the appropriate infra-structure is in place for a global network, we are all in business. But this is not about money; it can be achieved by the implementation of systems suggested above. As Howard Gardner said in his 2006 Tokyo lecture, "The world of tomorrow belongs to those who can understand and who help others to understand as well" (Kamijo, 2006).

From tea to technology, Japan continues to adapt to a changing world. Although changes come slowly, they are necessary, especially in the global community today. In Gardner's words, "Whatever one's business, one needs to be in touch with what else is going on and what else is being thought around the globe. That is how the content of one's mind becomes updated" 2004, p. 147). This is not to say that Japan has abandoned its own culture. On the contrary, new ideas in Japan are often embraced and incorporated within time-honored traditions. MI theory is no exception.

Table 7.1 Noteworthy MI Practitioners

Name	Academic Institution	Subject
Hideki Igari	Niwatuka Elementary School, Fukushima-Prefecture	Science
Kazuo Kobayashi	Ryuugasaki Junior High School	Science
Keiko Honda	Waseda University	Education
Kuniaki Sakai	Tayuhama Elementary School, Niigata Prefecture	English
Tsutomu Matsuyama	Temma Higashi Elementary School, Aomori Prefecture	Science
Setsuko Toyoma	Keiwa College	Humanities

Some pioneering MI practitioners find ways to use MI theory to complement and enhance learning of typically Japanese disciplines, providing students with fresh entry points and new frameworks for understanding. Tomoe Fujimoto teaches the use of the Japanese abacus (*soroban*) not only through logical-mathematical intelligence, but also through linguistic and kinesthetic intelligences. She conducts lessons in English, thus challenging her students to reframe their thinking about the subject in a different language, and they physically move in different ways to develop a sense of the characteristics of numbers. Satomi Watanabe is an elementary school teacher who advocates musical, kinesthetic, linguistic, logical-mathematical, and interpersonal and intrapersonal intelligences in the teaching of Chinese characters used in the Japanese language (*kanji*), providing a variety of entry points to attract students to the study of this subject, a vital component of all Japanese school curricula.

International schools in Japan have also begun to incorporate MI theory into their curricula to varying degrees. These English-medium schools are open to Japan's international community, and some globally minded Japanese parents find them a viable alternative to the Japanese educational system.

The network continues to grow (see Table 7.1) in Japan as information about the efficacy of MI reaches more practitioners, and as more practitioners begin to find ways to turn MI theory into practice. Collectively we welcome this as an opportunity for our minds to become updated.

References

Amagi, I. (1979). *Erito no daigaku, taisyu no daigaku. [Universities for elites, universities for non-elites]*. Tokyo: Simaru Shuppan.

Ezaki, R. (2007, January 29). My personal history. *Japan Economy, 40*.

Fujimoto, T. (2006). *MITAHYORON: The power of Japanese abacus.* Tokyo: Keio Gijuku University Press.

Gardner, H. (2004). *Changing minds.* Cambridge, MA: Harvard Business School Press.

Gardner, H., & Boix-Mansilla, V. (1998). What are the qualities of understanding? In M. Stone-Wiske (Ed.), *Teaching for understanding: Linking research with practice.* San Francisco: Jossey-Bass.

Gardner, H., Csikszentmihalyi, M., & Damon, W. (2001). *Good work: When excellence and ethics meet.* New York: Basic Books.

Greve, G. (2008). *Haiku topics.* Retrieved February 3, 2009, from http://wkdhaikutopics. blogspot.com/2008/05/four-directions.html.

Hirahara, H. (1993). *Kyoiku gyousei gaku. [Educational administration].* Tokyo: Tokyo University.

Ishiwata, K. (2003). *English camp: Super English language high school research report.* Yokohama: Kanagawa Prefectural Senior High School of Foreign Studies.

Ishiwata, K. (2004a). *English camp: The Fifteenth Anniversary National Conference of Eigo Jygyou Kenkyu conference report.* Tokyo: Eigo Jugyou Kenkyu Conference.

Ishiwata, K. (2004b). *Evaluation for performance-rubrics: Super English language high school research report.* Yokohama: Kanagawa Prefectural Senior High School of Foreign Studies.

Ishiwata, K. (2005). *Discussion & research: Super English language high school research report.* Yokohama: Kanagawa Prefectural Senior High School of Foreign Studies.

Ito, A. (2006). *Kan-min kakusa no karakuri. [Inequality between private company workers and public officers], 84*(11). Tokyo: Bungeisyunju.

Kamijo, M. (2006). *Why deep understanding should be central in all education.* http://www .japanmi.com/mifile/070118SummaryHGLectures2006withPersonalViews%5BWeb% 5D.htm.

Karasawa, H. (1999). *Quest for digital NICE age: New media lifestyle 1999–2010.* Tokyo: Products and Lifestyle Research Laboratory, Sony Corporation.

Katagiri, Y., & Kimura, Y. (2008). *Kyoiku kara miru nihon no shakai to rekishi. [Japanese society and history from a point of educational View].* Tokyo: Yachioyo Shuppan.

Kito, H. (2002). *Bunmei to site no Edo system. [Edo era system from a point of view of civilization].* Tokyo: Kodansha.

Kubo, Y. (2001). *Gendai kyoikusi jiten. [Modern educational history dictionary].* Tokyo: Tokyo Shoseki.

Lacey, J. (2003). *English camp handbook.* Kanagawa: Kanagawa Prefectural Senior High School of Foreign Studies.

Matsumoto, K. (2007, January 23). Kokoro no tamatebako. [My treasure]. *Japan Economy Evening Newspaper,* p. 20.

Meech-Pekarik, J. (1986). *The world of the Meiji print.* Tokyo: John Weatherhill.

Ministry of Education, Culture, Sports, Science, and Technology. (1997, January 24). *Program for educational reform* press release.

Ministry of Education, Culture, Sports, Science and Technology. (1999a). *Wagakuni no bunkyou shisaku. [Our country educational policy]*. Tokyo: Okura Sho Insatsu Kyoku.

Ministry of Education, Culture, Sports, Science and Technology. (1999b). *Gakusyu shido youryou. [Curriculum guidelines]*. Kyoto: Higashiyama Shobo.

Morishima, M. (1985). *Gakko, gakureki, jinsei. [School, academic record, and life]*. Tokyo: Iwanami.

Okabe, Y. et al. (2008). *Koko kyoiku [High school education]*, May. Tokyo: Gakujisya.

Okakura, T. (1906). *The book of tea*. Tokyo: Tuttle Publishing.

Osaka Bunka Center. (1996). *Kyoshi no tabouka to burn out. [Teachers' hectic life and burn-out syndrome]*. Tokyo: Hosei Shuppan.

Refusal to go to school. (2007, August 10). *Asahi Newspaper*, 1.

Sakamoto, N., & Sakamoto, S. (2006). *Polite fictions in collision*. Tokyo: Kinseido.

Sakata, T. (2007). *Gakkou kyoiku no kihon horei. [The basic regulations of school education]*. Tokyo: Gakuji.

Sen, S. (1981). *Ura senke sato no oshie. [Tea pedagogy by Ura-Sen–school]*. Tokyo: Dai Nihon Insatsu Co.

Tachibana, T. (2001). *Todaisei ha baka ni nattaka. [Is the academic level of Tokyo University students going down]*. Tokyo: Bungeishunju.

Ueno, C. (2002). *Sayonara gakkou ka shakai. [Goodbye, academically oriented society]*. Tokyo: TaroJiro Sha.

Wada, H. (2006, August). *Finland, sekai ichi no kyouiku taikoku. [Finland offers the best education]*, *84*(11). Tokyo: Bungeisyunju.

CHAPTER 8

The Integration of MI Theory in South Korean Educational Practice

Myung-Hee Kim
Kyung-Hee Cha

This chapter describes how Korea adopted MI theory into its education system and the theory's current influences in Korea. Korea's social, cultural, and educational realities have played a major role in why and how MI theory has been embraced. The desire of Koreans to find an alternative to their monolithic system of education geared for university admission facilitated the acceptance of MI theory. A bottom-up approach starting from the classroom, collaboration between researchers and practitioners, and early recognition by policymakers characterize Korea's adoption process. MI theory has influenced education philosophy, teaching methods, and assessment systems. It also has enhanced the quality of education in Korea and is part of the country's national education policy implementation through curriculum development. MI theory has firmly established itself as an independent field of academic research in Korea.

Through sustained commitment and collaborative activity over a ten-year period, MI theory has been integrated into South Korean educational practice. The successful adaptation of MI grew out of emerging cultural priorities and immediate educational needs. Through the application of MI theory, the quality of Korean education has improved. We discuss specific challenges and benefits discussed from the perspective of schools, teachers, and students and conclude with reflections on the universality and uniqueness of MI theory in relation to Korean experiences.

HISTORICAL, SOCIAL, AND CULTURAL CONTEXT

The Korean education system has been greatly affected by the quantitative measurement approach to education, a focus on the economic impact of education, and reduced parental support for schools.

A U.S. delegation, dispatched in 1948 to assist with the establishment of a modern Korean public school system, recommended a scientific approach to education. This approach emphasized quantitative measurement rather than qualitative evaluation of learning. Specifically, it promoted the use of standardized and psychological tests and was reinforced by educators' exposure to Skinner's behavioral psychology (Song, 2002).

The impact of the scientific approach remains strong in Korean schools today through a heavy dependence on multiple-choice assessments. This type of evaluation was justified by educators' claims that it was an appropriate means to scientifically understand student behavior (Lee, 1999). Evaluation was reduced to checking students' understanding of simple textbook facts through paper-and-pencil tests.

A political turn of events magnified the importance of quantitative measurement and multiple-choice assessment. In 1960, when a military regime was established, its top priority was economic development. Because education supports economic development, the regime put education under the control of the central government, which dictated all aspects of education: curriculum, textbooks, instructional methods, and teacher training.

Schooling was devoted to promoting students' university entrance. An education system focused on university entrance, however, aggravated an excessive zeal for educational measurement, resulting in a system obsessed with ranking students' individual achievement based on their scores on standardized tests.

This focus on test scores has influenced parents' views of the public schools. Parental support is the cornerstone of public education. Without it, neither students nor schools are likely to succeed. Yet parents are dissatisfied with Korean public education, and many send their children abroad or supplement their learning with private education.

Many Koreans want to send their children to English-speaking countries. Korean law first officially allowed students to go abroad for primary or secondary education in 1988. Currently, about forty thousand Korean students are estimated to be studying in primary or secondary school abroad (Gu, 2008).

The number of students leaving for the United States has increased twenty times during the past eleven years (Han, 2006; Park, 2007).

Of the students who stay in Korea, an increasing number pay for private education services to help them score higher on standardized tests. In 2003, Korea's private tutoring was 2.9 percent of gross domestic product, more than four times the average of member nations of the Organization for Economic Cooperation and Development (0.7 percent). Equally alarming, about 40 percent of all education-related spending in Korea is for privately hired education. The private education service market is growing an average rate of 17 percent a year and currently is estimated at $33 billion. Private education centers are becoming larger and employing systematic business operations.

Governmental and parental obsession with university entrance, the explosion of private tutoring, and the atrophy of public education have been escalating. These challenges led to the search for alternative education theories and methods.

ADAPTING AND ADOPTING MI THEORY

The adaptation and adoption of MI theory in South Korea has focused on efforts to translate the theory into strong educational practices that fit the country's unique social, cultural, and educational environment. The interaction of three factors have proved critical for spreading MI theory: a bottom-up approach to MI reform, the involvement of MI researchers, and the endorsement of policymakers.

Bottom-Up Approach to MI Reform

MI reform in South Korea began at the classroom level and moved from the bottom up. Previous attempts at South Korean education reform that used a top-down approach had failed. Reform had been imposed unilaterally through educational policy. Neither school administrators nor teachers were prepared to implement the mandated theory and practice. This lack of preparation disconnected theory from practice.

In contrast, MI education in South Korea started by applying the theory in the classroom. Researchers and teachers were present in MI classrooms, working on application and practice together. Such joint projects were unheard of in South Korea before MI's introduction. This new form of collaboration created a foundation for fundamental educational change by developing a network of education professionals who could share information and resources.

Involvement of MI Researchers

Multiple intelligences theory was formally introduced to South Korea in 1990 by scholars seeking education reform. Many South Korean MI researchers published articles to introduce the theory, which created a public discussion about this new perspective to teaching and learning. These articles drew many school administrators to support projects aimed at changing education using MI theory. Teacher workshops conducted at the Institute for Educational Research at Hanyang University addressed MI theory in relation to teaching-learning models, instructional methods, and MI naturalistic assessment approaches.

In 1995, field applications of MI theory began in South Korea, first at a private elementary school. Researchers on site participated in all MI classrooms to address questions or challenges immediately. This support proved to be highly effective in facilitating teacher understanding of MI theory. Evaluation of outcomes in these experimental schools showed that the MI approach improved not only academic achievement but also intellectual enthusiasm, curiosity, positive attitudes toward school, and voluntary participation in learning. Results of the initial field applications led to high positive acceptance of MI theory in South Korea as a feasible alternative to traditional methods.

In 2000, Branton Shearer, the chair of the MI Special Interest Group of the American Educational Research Association, spoke in South Korea. Later that year, Howard Gardner delivered a keynote speech for an international symposium held at Ewha Women's University. His personal appearance triggered a major wave of MI awareness in South Korea. From newspapers and mass media coverage to education companies claiming to follow MI principles, MI theory became widely known to teachers and parents.

With this media publicity and the positive results from field applications, MI theory integration more quickly propagated to various school settings (Shin & Kim, 2006). It enhanced the professionalism and empowerment of teachers, who became motivated to develop their own performance assessment tools and, eventually, their own curricula. Teachers in regular public schools requested support from the Institute for Education Research at Hanyang University, which led to the foundation of the South Korean Multiple Intelligences Education Association in 2001. Currently the organization has more than two thousand teacher members and has conducted dozens of training courses. Many teachers have become MI missionaries at teacher training courses and field researchers as well as practitioners.

Endorsement of Policymakers

Through symposia, workshops, and publications, educational policymakers began to recognize the possibilities of using MI theory to develop a new educational paradigm. In 2000, with the help of experimental school teachers, the Ministry of Education produced an MI classroom video for teachers that provides examples of appropriate ways to integrate MI theory into classroom practices.

The most powerful influence of the Ministry of Education on the integration of MI was to include the theory as an ideological and implementation framework for the South Korean Seventh National Curriculum, which pursues diversity and individuality. It seeks to provide customized education for individuals, changing education from teacher-centric to student-centric. It calls attention to respecting individual differences and adapting curriculum to differences among students. It proclaims "creativity, balance and ethics" as educational objectives (Korea Institute of Curriculum and Evaluation, 2005).

With this adoption into the national curriculum, MI theory use became systematic and widespread. Curriculum commentaries, teacher guides, and performance assessment guides helped teachers reinforce the role of theory. In the guidebook for the social sciences, for example, MI theory is held up as a theoretical foundation for desirable teaching-learning methods. The approach is also referenced in the teacher's guidebook for high school ethics and philosophy (Ministry of Education, 2003).

CHALLENGES TO MI RESEARCH AND PRACTICE

South Korean MI researchers encountered several challenges during the introduction of MI theory and the dissemination of MI practice. The most common problem in the beginning was insufficient or incorrect understanding of MI theory concepts. Initial misunderstandings often resulted from practitioners' directly applying MI in the classroom without engaging in an in-depth study of the theory. In particular, teachers, parents, and school administrators were concerned about how to evaluate the impact of MI practice on student learning outcomes. In addition, teachers faced concerns regarding whether there was a "right" way to implement MI practice, how to deal with the extra work required initially to bring MI into classrooms, and how to work through the bureaucratic system in South Korea.

MI Evaluation of Students

The most serious misconception was the incorrect notion that MI evaluation could be conducted by measuring each of the eight intelligences with intelligence tests. The results of each test were considered the score of the individual's level in each intelligence and were referenced in the formation of cooperative learning groups. Teachers failed to recognize, however, that MI evaluation starts with identifying the student's intelligence profile through extensive observation. The misconception grew from assimilating MI theory to the structure of traditional evaluation.

The conflict over student evaluation was one of the most contentious. In comparison to traditional assessment, which is quantitative and focuses on other people's evaluation of student work, evaluation in MI education is a qualitative system that includes the student as an evaluator. MI evaluation respects potential, diversity, flexibility, variability, and context. Through the use of alternative MI-based assessment methods and performance evaluation, researchers were able to document that each child is qualitatively different. Recognizing this difference was the first step toward the conviction that each student can express his or her own ability and that all students can be successful.

The multidimensional MI evaluations designed to gauge student levels of understanding were met with doubt at first. However, the new evaluation approaches gradually gained the confidence of practitioners by incorporating thorough and clear standards. Because evaluation methods allowed students to express their level of understanding in different ways, students became genuinely involved in the evaluation process. When students were involved in setting the criteria for rubrics, learning achievements measured at the end of the semester showed significant improvement. Many parents and students came to appreciate the multidimensional approach because it provided insight into students' characteristics and strengths that could be referenced in career decisions.

For example, in many MI classrooms, intrapersonal intelligence was fostered by encouraging students to keep a reflection journal at the end of the day describing the day's content of instruction and their understanding of it. Students also took quiet self-reflection times during the day and wrote about their thoughts. These activities helped students develop metacognitive thinking skills and see themselves as capable of evaluating their learning and progress. Previously most school evaluations were based on the perspective of another person, typically the teacher. In contrast, MI evaluation includes self-understanding and self-confirmation components. This gives students ownership in the evaluation process and the feedback it produces. The abilities to self-evaluate and self-direct are critical skills in a global society that values initiative and creativity.

Teachers, school administrators, and parents were concerned that MI theory–based education would lower students' academic achievement. This issue was especially important because university entrance was dependent on high levels of academic achievement. Various quantitative tests showed that MI education was not causing deterioration in academic achievement. MI education demonstrated positive influences in language and mathematic achievement, scientific research skills, creative art skills, and self-esteem. These achievements led to a higher level of student satisfaction with school, which contributed to stronger learning factors such as motivation and enthusiasm (Kim, Kim, Kim, Lee, & Jung, 1996).

Other Teacher Concerns

Initially teachers questioned whether their instructional design was correct. They wanted MI researchers or other practitioners to provide them with a specific model. Some were convinced that there must be a right answer in a lesson plan. Similar to the misunderstanding of MI evaluation, this confusion was the result of approaching MI theory with a traditional mind-set. Most of these misunderstandings about curriculum were resolved with the assistance of fellow teachers or by the teachers' use of video resources produced by the Ministry of Education.

A second concern was the additional work required of teachers. When MI theory was introduced to South Korean education, lessons revolved around textbooks based on the national curriculum. Teachers who were accustomed to teaching textbook knowledge found it challenging to develop curricula based on MI theory. As they were recast into the role of curriculum experts, they developed integrated curricula through analyzing and reconstructing textbooks based on MI theory. In addition, they shared ideas with other teachers and built an education network for continuous development.

A third concern was South Korea's centralized and uniform education system. When students were required to progress at a certain pace in all textbooks, teachers had difficulty finding time to provide instruction that leveraged all eight intelligences for every unit. This issue was resolved by selecting key themes from textbooks and reconstructing curriculum around them.

BENEFITS OF INTEGRATING MI THEORY

Despite these challenges, in just over a decade, MI theory has made a noticeable contribution to South Korean education. We present the benefits of MI theory integration in four areas: a broader scope of character education, new ways to assess student learning and development, enhanced teacher growth, and addressing underachievement. Since student success is the ultimate outcome of educational reform (Hoerr, 2000), we share the story of Ji-min and his turnaround from being an underachiever to a motivated learner.

Character Education

As one example, MI theory contributed to a return of meaningful character education. Historically, the strong influence of Confucianism in South Korean society and culture emphasized the importance of character education. South

Korean education includes the topic of ethics, but its significance was reduced in an educational system that directed student attention to memorizing facts for taking multiple-choice tests and achieving college entrance.

MI theory's identification of interpersonal and intrapersonal intelligences provided critical ideas for a new vision of ethics education that is designed to develop ethical behavior and practice, as well as intellectual knowledge and understanding. Furthermore, the integration of an intrapersonal perspective has created a more balanced approach to character education. In the past, character education emphasized relating to others, including consideration for others, understanding others, self-sacrifice, and devotion. While continuing to raise awareness of others and promote altruism, the curriculum now also helps students develop respect for their own perspective and relate to others based on a firm foundation of self-understanding.

Assessment

Traditionally most South Korean educational assessments were formal and focused on specific content, and they were administered to particular groups on set dates. These traditional assessments tended to emphasize outcomes rather than the process of learning. Students' academic achievement results were considered the teacher's responsibility. The possibility of students' low scores was a source of pressure that motivated teacher attention to the tests.

Influenced by the MI notion on multiple ways of learning and doing, many South Korean teachers have adopted alternative assessment tools to discover students' intelligence profiles and respect individual differences. Formal assessments involving pencil and paper and short answers are still used, but they now are complemented by informal assessments: peer reviews, observation logs, self-reflection journals, portfolios, rubric assessments, working style assessments, student interviews, and parent interviews.

Informal assessment generates feedback for students and teachers. For students, the results have become a source of pride since they can now observe and describe their own progress. They take more responsibility for their learning as the feedback helps them improve their performance. The use of a reflection journal, in particular, helped develop students' knowledge about self, self-regulation, and emotional control, which promoted their intrapersonal skills and contributed to their school behaviors and learning outcomes.

MI theory has helped teachers overcome the limitations of traditional formal assessments. Prior to the introduction of MI theory, teachers were frustrated with using evaluations that relied on rote knowledge of academic facts. MI theory put a halt to these practices and brought a fundamental change in teachers' understanding of students.

Teacher Growth

The integration of MI theory also helped advance the development of teachers. Teachers practicing MI education appreciate a theoretical framework that recognizes and understands the diversity of students' cognitive strengths. They welcome opportunities to understand students based on their individuality rather than according to a uniform standard.

MI provided a new paradigm for reconstructing what and how teachers taught. According to Cha (2005), practitioners who embraced MI theory became active leaders of classroom reform through self-motivation and self-reflection. Assuming responsibility for curriculum development enhanced teachers' identity as professionals in education.

Overcoming Underachievement

Underachievement was one of the most common problems in South Korean school education. A major contributing factor was the failure to provide appropriate early educational intervention before a child fell too far behind. In an educational system that did not make adjustments for individual differences, some students lost interest in learning. Because they did not acquire basic knowledge and skills, their insufficient learning in primary education was amplified when they faced the demands of secondary school. The root cause of underachievement was not the inability of students to learn, but rather the schools' failure to provide education that met the needs of individual students.

MI practice presented a way of breaking the cycle of underachievement. MI theory's belief in human potential and the need to identify and develop each individual's strengths helped teachers understand differences in students' learning pace (Chen, Krechevsky, Viens, & Isberg, 1998). Teachers regained respect for each student as a whole person.

In addition, MI theory provided the means to intervene in primary school. One of the main reasons that teachers continued the practice of MI education, despite the additional work of developing new curriculum and teacher-student materials, was that they witnessed changes in their students, especially in underachievers. To fully appreciate the significance of MI contribution to South Korean education, it is helpful to understand what the changes look like to a child. The following case study shows how MI integration turned around an underachieving student, Ji-min.

The Case of Ji-min

Ji-min was a kind-hearted, mild-tempered child who came from a financially challenged family. Due to her demanding work, Ji-min's mother assumed that she would not be able to provide to her son special educational privileges, such as private tutoring, so she decided to send her son to private school.

This decision is unusual for financially challenged parents, but Ji-min's parents expected everything from their son's education.

Unlike many of his peers, Ji-min started school with little prior educational preparation. At the start of third grade, he was still unable to follow teacher instructions and became an outsider in his peer group. He did not participate in cooperative learning activities and scored zero on his spelling tests for three months.

Ji-min's third-grade teacher, Ms. Han, began to observe his activity intensively. After three months of observation, she discovered that Ji-Min had a special interest in insects. He observed them, identified their characteristics, and classified them. This activity indicated a strong naturalistic intelligence.

Ms. Han learned that Ji-Min's parents had bought him a stag beetle as a pet. When Ji-min started to show an interest in insects, his father bought him several related books. Ms. Han began asking Ji-Min questions about insects to stimulate his linguistic abilities and asked him to keep an insect observation journal.

Offering a wide variety of insect-related learning activities to the class, Ms. Han provided stimulation to help Ji-Min overcome the obstacles that had blocked his learning. She observed that he now carried on long conversations with other children about insects. He demonstrated detailed knowledge of insect names, types, body lengths, and names of body parts. He impressed classmates by using expert terminology when describing insects. Ji-min experienced great pleasure in communicating his knowledge about insects to his teacher and his classmates.

Ji-min then began to actively participate in class. When the insect project was launched, he started to speak in front of the class and answered questions from classmates. In the second semester, seven students decided to join Ji-min's insect project as a part of their project learning. Responding to an opportunity to share his knowledge of insects, Ji-min, who had never before completed a homework assignment properly, surprised Ms. Han by putting great effort into completing the assignment. Over time, he improved in other areas as well, such as spelling.

Ms. Han said that recognizing a student's strength in front of his or her peers and parents was effective reinforcement. Ji-min had started the school year with a strong negative self-image. He had told his teacher, "I'm not smart and can't do anything." But he started to participate in cooperative activities and received recognition from friends for expressing his opinions. By the end of the year, he had demonstrated rapid academic progress and had caught up with his peers. He said that his dream was to become a zoologist.

An overall underachiever at school, Ji-min achieved a breakthrough when he participated in projects based on his area of interest. These projects made it possible for him to pursue his interests and develop his naturalistic intelligence, one of his intellectual strengths. By developing and leveraging his naturalistic intelligence, he was able to gradually strengthen linguistic, spatial, interpersonal, and intrapersonal intelligences and demonstrated growth in basic learning such as language and math. Equally important, he gained a positive attitude toward learning and a positive self-image.

Ms. Han explained that MI practice allows her to informally observe and recognize the abilities of individual students and to appreciate their value without having to distinguish between high and low achievers. Teacher recognition of student diversity helps students build confidence and self-esteem and maintain positive interactions with the teacher. Ms. Han explained:

> I'm so happy to see my students change. Children who used to bring stones to school or who wished schools did not exist or who came to school with no thought at all are now coming to class curious about what they will learn that day. An MI class refrains from making the classroom competitive. It makes learning interesting, not boring. Motivation is more about a student's internal sense of satisfaction than about any external influence or compensation.
> I think that is why MI practice makes such a difference for the underachievers.

Underachieving students often say, "I don't want to" or "I'm not interested," to refuse involvement and maintain a negative attitude toward learning. The example of Ji-min shows how teachers can break through this wall by suggesting activities that focus on the strengths of each child. In using their strengths and experiencing success, children recover their self-esteem and can begin to work on their areas of weakness.

INTO THE FUTURE

As South Korean practitioners continue to apply MI theory in classrooms, they encounter new challenges, including continuing concerns about student evaluation and the lack of an integrated MI approach across school levels. These challenges reflect the commitment of educators to apply MI theory at deeper levels in more schools.

Student Evaluation

It appears to be practically impossible to replace the traditional report card with a development evaluation card focusing on a student growth. In addition, unlike linguistic or logical-mathematical intelligences, which have relatively clear concepts and readily accessible evaluation schemes, evaluation tools for artistic ability or for interpersonal and naturalistic intelligences require development. For MI theory to be established as a firm, universal education theory, multidimensional evaluation for each intelligence is needed (Gardner, 2006). Alternative evaluation methods for intrapersonal intelligence are particularly critical.

Not only the content of student evaluation but also the approach is disputed. MI theory emphasizes authentic performance assessment. This method has been seen as less objective or reliable for evaluation in South Korea. Nevertheless, there are signs of this conflict being addressed. Many universities and testing companies are now placing more weight on interviews and essays to overcome the limitations of quantitative evaluation. Awareness of the need for qualitative evaluation to complement quantitative approaches is increasing.

This evaluation challenge exists in research also. Most of the MI theory–related master's theses in South Korea to date evaluate the teaching-learning effects of MI theory–based curricula. These curricula were developed by teachers who had studied exemplary classroom examples in other countries. However, the tools designed by these researchers to evaluate effectiveness bore little resemblance to the performance assessment recommended by MI theory. Observation, process evaluation, and portfolio work were not used. In many cases, the research projects used standardized aptitude test tools to study the MI teaching-learning process. Further research on evaluation systems must develop new qualitative tools compatible with MI theory.

Integration Across Primary and Secondary Education

Many South Korean primary teachers learn MI theory during pre-service education and student teaching. About 30 percent of the 160,000 primary school teachers in South Korea apply MI theory to at least some aspects of their curriculum or assessment (Korea Multiple Intelligences Educational Association, 2007). However, MI theory application remains quite limited at the secondary school level, where teachers and administrators in secondary schools feel much greater pressure to prepare students for university entrance. They struggle to cover the courses directly related to college entrance and are reluctant to take on additional responsibilities.

However, some high schools are using their creative discretionary activity time to conduct self-discovery activities that draw on intrapersonal intelligence. Creative discretionary activity time is part of the regular curriculum that addresses school-specific education needs or incorporates multidisciplinary learning or student self-regulated learning. In grades 1 to 10, two hours a week can be used according to school discretion (Rue, 2003). Integrating MI theory into the regular curriculum of secondary schools is a challenge, but now appears to be the right time to start discussing how to spread it to higher school levels.

UNIQUENESS AND UNIVERSALITY OF MI THEORY

The application of MI theory in South Korea has been based on its universal characteristics, as well as aspects of the country's social, cultural, and educational context. South Korean researchers and practitioners have discovered ways to apply MI theory in accordance with special South Korean circumstances. At the same time, we believe that MI theory's universal qualities can be leveraged anywhere in the world. In this final section, we share our insights about these distinctive aspects of our experience.

Application of MI Theory in South Korea

A voluntary network of teachers has been pivotal to MI theory application in South Korea. Although responsibility and authority regarding curriculum and instruction lie with individual teachers, a network of teachers is necessary to practice effectively in a given situation and to respond to student diversity. Teachers who have already practiced MI theory in the classroom strongly advocate the need for networking and are proposing strategic ideas on how to use such networks. MI theory is an American theory and cannot be applied in South Korea without modification. As one teacher said, "That's why you need to think about how to apply it case by case, and that's when a network of teachers would come in very handy."

Another special factor related to South Korea is that some intelligences are relatively less developed in South Korea due to their perceived weak link with careers. Both teachers and students have become more aware of the equal importance of all intelligences. Yet when it comes to career decisions or university entrance, valuing interpersonal intelligence and intrapersonal intelligence is still limited. No matter how outstanding a person's other intelligences are, it is difficult for him or her to select a career without going through evaluation of linguistic or logical-mathematical intelligences.

MI theory's contribution in helping schools to develop creative, balanced, and ethical members of society is aligned with a specific educational priority in South Korea. Because South Korea's social, cultural, and educational environment tends to place the group before the individual and equality before creativity, the need to develop creative people with skills for the information age has become a focus of social discourse. South Korean policymakers embraced MI theory because of its focus on discovering and developing areas of excellence in each individual. The application of MI theory not only helps individuals realize their potential; it also helps meet the educational needs of a society that demands excellence and creativity.

Theory Universality

MI theory originates from a social, cultural, and educational environment very different from that of South Korea. Nevertheless, it has been applied in South Korea with great success and has been accepted as a theoretical framework for educational reform. This firm and sincere acceptance demonstrates the universality of the theory. In every country where educational practitioners commit to apply it, MI theory can improve education by strengthening educational policy, advancing teacher development, and leading to new successes in student achievement. MI theory initiates this change process by offering a new way of looking at people. Through the lens of MI theory, teachers can understand how different students are. This understanding underpins the belief that there is an immediate need for education that respects individuals and addresses that individuality. Instead of applying a single yardstick to all students, MI theory supports an array of efforts to understand and evaluate students in terms of their own uniqueness.

Through empowering teachers, MI theory helps teachers become more professional. With better curriculum development skills, teachers take the initiative to develop performance evaluation tools and design more creative curricula. They gain confidence in their ability to plan instruction and can reconstruct curricula using the expertise they have developed. Changes in their understanding of curriculum and assessment reinforce changes in their perceptions of students.

Finally, MI theory contributes to career and vocational education. Many schools around the world focus on distinguishing high achievers from low achievers. An education based on MI theory shifts the focus to educating all individuals. No longer restricted to university entrance, the goal becomes optimal human resource positioning for the betterment of society. Intelligence profiles raise students' awareness of career possibilities based on their strengths and provide teachers with the information they need to align career guidance with the characteristics of individual students. While conventional career education typically addresses the introduction of different occupations and learning necessary skills, MI theory-based career education gives students more ownership to establish their own life goals.

CONCLUSION

The integration of MI theory has improved South Korea's quality of education and raised the level of educational achievement. The most obvious benefit is the change in perception regarding human capacities at the classroom and national policy levels.

Prior to the introduction of MI theory, South Korean schools were bureaucratically systematized and uniform. South Korean, English, and mathematics were the focus of curriculum and normative tests the dominant form of evaluation. Students were ranked according to their linguistic and logical-mathematical intelligences. Except for the few who earned the highest test scores, most students were classified as failures. In this educational context, MI educators argued that each student had a distinct profile of intelligences. The theory inspired student motivation to learn and restored student confidence in instruction. Stronger motivation brought about higher achievement levels.

MI theory also strengthened national education policy by helping educators respond to societal and cultural trends. To prepare students for participation in this global, knowledge-based century, schools need to foster the development of individuals with diverse abilities and qualities rather than require conformity to a singular understanding of intelligence and ideal performance. By integrating MI theory, educators began to respect the potential of multiple intelligences and develop talented individuals in a wider range of areas. Educational aims based on MI theory have broadened South Korea's definition of education to include academic ability as well as nontraditional learning areas such as art, social understanding, and self-understanding.

References

Cha, K. H. (2005). *A qualitative case study of the multiple intelligences into the elementary schools.* Unpublished doctoral dissertation, Hanyang University.

Chen, J. Q., Krechevsky, M., Viens, J., & Isberg, E. (1998). *Building on children's strengths: The experience of Project Spectrum.* New York: Teachers College Press.

Gardner, H. (2006). *Multiple intelligences: New horizons.* New York: Basic Books.

Gu, J. (2008, January 27). Study abroad syndrome. *Maekyung Newspaper.* Retrieved February 15, 2008, from http://newx.mk.co.kr/newsRead.php?sc=&year=2008&no=49883.

Han, J. (2006, November 28). College entrance examination provoking studying abroad. *Maekyung Newspaper.* Retrieved November 29, 2000, from http://joins.com/bryankang.

Hoerr, T. (2000). *Becoming a multiple intelligences school.* Alexandria, VA: American Society for Curriculum and Development.

Kim, M. H., Kim, Y. B., Kim, Y. C., Lee, K. H., & Jung, T. H. (1996). *Research an open education performance assessment base on MI theory.* Seoul: Subject Matter Research Institute, Korea National University of Education supported by Ministry of Education.

Korea Multiple Intelligences Educational Association. (2007, December 17). *Dissemination of MI theory in schools.* Retrieved December 18, 2007, from www.kmiea.net/mistudy/ms0.asp.

Korean Institute of Curriculum and Evaluation. (2005, December 7). *Major features of the Seventh National Curriculum.* Retrieved December 21, 2005, from http://www.kice.re.kr/kice/article/m301/view?searchtype=stored&hitadd=1&articleid=60420.

Lee, H. (1999). A difference of identifying variable skills assessment between performance and multiple choice items. *Journal of Science Education, 19*(1), 146–158.

Ministry of Education. (2003). *Guidebook for high school ethics and philosophy teachers.* Seoul: Gihaksa Press.

Park, S. (2007, October 30). Korean private tutoring expense, greatest among the OECD nations. *Segye Newspaper.* Retrieved January 21, 2008, from http://news .isegye.com/9754.

Rue, B. (2003). *Practical analysis and tasks of implementation of the Seventh Curriculum.* Seoul: Korea Education Development Institute.

Shin, W. S., & Kim, M. H. (2006). *Early childhood curriculum based on MI theory.* Seoul: Hakgisa Press.

Song, I. (2002). Developmental direction and problems of standardized psychological tests which have been made in Korea. *Journal of Educational Evaluation, 15*(2), 1–20.

CHAPTER 9

Multiple Intelligences Make a Difference

Mary Joy Canon-Abaquin

This chapter describes the vision, goal, and practices of the Multiple Intelligence International School in the Philippines. Offering an alternative learning experience, the school was designed to develop students' diverse intelligences and encourage students to use their intelligences to make a difference in the lives of others. Through its educational practices, the school advocates intelligence for all, reaching all students, teaching for understanding, and performance of understanding. Students in the school work together to develop the three big Cs: capacity, character, and community. That is, they build their intellectual capacity and good character, expressing both in their willingness to contribute to the betterment of the community.

In 1996, I founded the Multiple Intelligence International School in Manila, Philippines. It began as a preschool with sixty children. It now serves six hundred students from eighteen months to seventeen years old. As the name signifies, the school is founded on principles of MI theory. Bearing the name, many people assume that its goal is to achieve academic excellence or simply develop children's various intelligences. This idea appeals to Filipino parents who want their children to have a competitive edge and to maximize their academic success. We are a small private school composed of children from middle- to high-income families, a privileged sector of society, and have a mission to instill a sense of responsibility in our students so that they will want to contribute to making the world better. To achieve this larger goal, we need to present a paradigm for education other than the traditional school model. More than acquiring knowledge and developing intelligences, we at the MI School believe that the true goal of education should be the use of the knowledge and intelligences to make a difference. This advocacy to use multiple intelligences for good work—work that is excellent in quality, socially responsible, and meaningful to its practitioners (Gardner, Csikszentmihalyi, & Damon, 2001)—has elevated the role of the school as an educational institution. The MI School has become a tool for educational reform and nation building. This unique journey of applying MI as a means of providing multiple ways to make a difference is the lens through which our MI practice is shared in this chapter.

I first present four MI-based reform advocacies evident in our school: intelligences for all, reaching and teaching all students, teaching for understanding, and performance of understanding. Each of these advocacies will be contrasted with traditional Filipino practice to highlight its difference and significance. I then describe how our school integrates MI theory with the principles of good work to promote children's awareness of using their intelligences to make a difference in their world. Specifically, I highlight three big Cs of capacity, character, and community, the three cornerstones of our school, to take children beyond themselves toward thinking about their contribution to the community and society. The chapter concludes with a discussion of how a school can serve as an agent of change as the minds of future citizens are formed through curriculum and instructional practices.

REFORM ADVOCACIES BASED ON MI

Recently Secretary Jesli Lapus, the Department of Education chief in the Philippines, sounded an alarm that education should be a primary concern because it has sunk to its lowest level (Ubac, 2008). There are systemic problems—from unusually large class sizes to outdated teaching strategies. Most schools are rooted in a traditional system of teacher-centered education where the search for knowledge is reduced to memorizing a page from a textbook. The MI School advocates an alternative education—one that respects the individual learner and promotes learning and teaching for understanding.

Intelligences for All

A banner at the entrance to the MI School proclaims: "Where Every Child Is Smart." This presents a paradigm shift not only for teachers, but also for parents and children. Filipino parents hold education in high regard, believing that a good education offers the hope that a child will succeed and achieve his or her aspirations. However, this success is often associated with academic ranking in schools. Many Filipino parents push their children to be among the top 10 percent of students in their class, because anyone without this distinction is not considered intelligent. The parents' perception of success and intelligence no doubt affects the way their children think of themselves and their peers.

To alter the traditional view of one way of being smart, the MI School has created a culture of respect: all learners, from gifted children to alternative learners, are viewed as equally empowered to contribute their specific strengths to activities in the school community. This is especially important as a model that can influence future societal values. In the Philippines, the larger culture is just beginning to tolerate the idea of inclusion in school settings. Despite the many challenges of being counterculture, the MI School stands as a pioneering institution that embodies the inclusion of individual learner intelligences profiles. MI theory has served as a lever to allow more children to access information and be recognized for their strengths in diverse learning areas. Intelligence is seen as inclusive of everyone rather than exclusive to a few.

An MI-influenced school culture encourages collaboration instead of competition. Typically children focus on each other's weaknesses and do not hesitate to belittle each other, even calling each other names. In the MI School, mutual respect is evident. Children easily introduce their classmates by saying, "This is John; he is word smart" or "You take the lead because of your musical abilities, and I will compose the words." This is not simple labeling. Rather, it reflects the culture in which children learn at an early age to know and treasure each other's gifts. Intelligences are not a privilege for the elite, but for all. Chiara, a ten-year-old student at MI School, summarizes it well: "I like MI because I believe each of us is smart in our own way." And she is right. In the MI School, every child is smart in his or her own way and they can all do something to contribute to the betterment of the community.

To Reach and Teach All Students

In the Philippines, parents dream about their children earning degrees in medicine, law, or engineering, believing these degrees will pave a bright future for their children's career and therefore success. Arts and music are frowned on and referred to as hobbies rather than possible careers. Our national curriculum allocates very little time for music and the arts. Children's performance in music and arts is assessed predominantly through a paper-and-pencil quiz. This cultural belief system, accompanied by curricular practice, disregards the diverse intelligences that children possess and does not allow us to reach and teach all students.

Guided by MI theory, our school gives equal respect to a number of disciplines. We deliberately made a paradigm shift in music and arts education. Domain experts engage children in playing indigenous musical instruments and developing their own styles of painting after a careful study of art history. Furthermore, multiple intelligences serve as entry points to lessons in the classroom. For example, music, art, and movement are regularly incorporated as entry points for learning and understanding in traditional academic subjects. Teachers have at their fingertips a menu of strategies anchored in different intelligences to reach and teach all students. For example, a teacher may be teaching fractions, a math concept, and ask students to reenact a story, cook pizza, or go for a nature walk to better understand the lesson.

As the MI School offers broader curricula to students and incorporates multiple entry points in teaching, knowledge becomes more accessible to all learners regardless of their intellectual profiles. Consequently students have become aware of their diverse intellectual profiles and more willing to offer their strengths for group efforts. When asked to describe his group project on the environment, Stephen, a nine-year-old student, said, "Saving the environment is very possible. Kids can help by using their different intelligences. . . . Even if you are as young as me, don't think that you won't be able to help save nature because there is so much a kid can do!" Stephen's comment indicates that when the school curriculum reaches more students, students reach out to give more to the community and society.

Teaching for Understanding

The Department of Education of the Philippines, which is responsible for the national curriculum, designates a range of topics that need to be covered in schools. Often schools are forced to race through lessons, running the risk that learning becomes no more than rote memory and many students never understand the lessons entirely. This is made evident by the numerous tutoring services and after-school programs in the country that have mushroomed as a result of what children have not learned in their classrooms.

At the MI School, the goal of using multiple intelligences in the classroom is to gain understanding. Instead of teaching all lessons in eight ways, teachers and students are empowered to choose strategies that best match their way of learning. When understanding is a goal, we are very deliberate in choosing what is worth knowing, creating opportunities to encourage students to apply the knowledge they have gained, and incorporating meaningful learning projects that adhere to the national curriculum content.

One way to ensure teaching for understanding at the MI School is to develop schoolwide themes around which students are encouraged to solve problems using the knowledge they have acquired. For example, in the theme "Understanding Ourselves as Filipinos," children studied national heroes through reading, art, surveys, and interviews. Teachers then asked them how they can be heroes. Children were challenged to put their different intelligences to use in the real world. A group of second graders, after interacting with children in a nearby economically depressed area, experienced how different the living conditions of these children were from their own. Instead of enumerating "poverty" as an item in a test, children were encouraged to be part of the solution. Problem-solving as a class, they brought to school their old toys and clothes and held a white elephant sale to raise money for books for their less fortunate counterparts. Reflecting on the importance of teaching for understanding, Felicia, a thirteen-year-old student, commented, "I think it's important to always understand what you are being taught. Behind these four walls is a world where we put the things we learn to use. So memorizing the lessons will help you get through the tests they give you in school, but on the other hand, understanding the lessons you have learned in school will help you get through the tests in life." Students at the MI School are not only empowered by their understanding; they are also given the opportunity to find themselves and their purpose.

Performances of Understanding

Traditionally in the Philippines, children are expected to demonstrate understanding primarily through paper-and-pencil test performance. Teachers deliver knowledge, and students receive it. Whether children can make good use of the knowledge beyond classroom is not a question asked.

MI theory has helped our school use a wide range of assessment processes, from standardized tests to children's portfolios and opportunities, to perform understanding. One example is the Rainforest Café Project. After learning about the dwindling rain forest in the Philippines and the animals that live there, our five and six year olds wanted to help save the rain forest by planting trees. To raise funds to buy seedlings, the idea of Rainforest Café was conceptualized. Children demonstrated their understanding by cooking different kinds of food that resembled animals in the rain forest—such as beetle wings and worms in dirt mud pies. They wrote to their parents for help with the cost. They simulated a rain forest environment and put up fact posters around the campus about saving the animals. In addition to raising funds to buy seedlings for trees, the children also used the café to raise awareness about animals in the rainforest through the products and posters in the café. When they launched the Rainforest Café, they chose their roles depending on their interests and intellectual strengths—number smart as cashiers, people smart as sellers, and word smart as receipt writers. Children worked well together in the café and the whole school community served as their customers. No one could imagine the power of demonstrating understanding through performance when the Rainforest Café Project started. What began as a small initiative has now become a five-year commitment to help rehabilitate a distant mangrove area through proceeds from the café that the MI School has donated to a local environmental foundation. Children also trooped to the last urban rain forest with their parents and planted trees with the funds they had raised. Through activities like these, children can clearly articulate what they have learned about the subject matter. What is more, they showed the passion to make a difference for the environment through this project. To a teacher, these types of projects tell much more about each student, what she or he learned and understood, than a test can ever show.

USING MULTIPLE INTELLIGENCES TO DO GOOD WORK

John Dewey once said, "Education is not a preparation for life, education is life itself." We want the lives of students to be an experience of empowerment and their journey as learners to reflect their journey as citizens. Aligned with this vision, we marry MI theory with good work—work that is technically excellent, personally meaningful, and carried out in an ethical way (Gardner et al., 2001). When multiple intelligences and good work go hand-in-hand, MI becomes a tool to maximize human potential and empowers individuals to use their strengths to make a difference. If we dare to dream that we can bring up future leaders, then it is possible to think of a future in which every politician, journalist, businessperson, and professional uses what he or she knows and his or her intelligences to make a difference in the lives of others. We would be living in a world free of corruption, injustice, and poverty. Every good thing starts with a vision and a first step. How do we operationalize this in our daily life as a school? What are the prerequisites in using multiple intelligences to do good work? At the MI School, we build on three cornerstones—capacity, character, and community—to help us in promoting the development of children who will become productive, engaged, and responsible citizens in the future.

Building the Capacity to Make a Difference

In the MI School, we understand that knowledge and skills are tools to be used for a meaningful purpose. Children need to know how to write in order to articulate their cause to the public, and they need the tools of mathematics to be responsible businesspersons. The approach to teaching from multiple entry points for understanding helps all of our children become academically competent. Understanding also empowers children to seek higher purposes for learning and to dare to ask themselves, "Now that I know, so what? What can I do?" Gardner (1993) made clear the relationship between knowledge building and the ability to use it when he proposed a vision of MI education: to "foster students' deep understanding in several core disciplines and encourage students' use of that knowledge to solve problems and complete tasks that they may confront in the wider community" (p. 75). Our MI School has made a serious effort to bridge academic excellence to societal usefulness. Our efforts are evident in children's learning and what they do with their knowledge and skills.

A group of second graders became actively involved when they learned that only 6 percent of the Philippine rain forest is left. To them, this was not a fact to be memorized for a quiz, but a fact that needed to be acted on. They asked numerous questions about the fate of the animals if they lost their homes. "What will happen when we grow up? There'll be no more rainforests," they asked as they graphed and made projections about what would remain of the Philippine rain forest in the future. Representatives of Haribon, an environmental foundation, and the World Wildlife Fund were invited to talk about species endemic to the Philippines. Through collaboration and with mentoring, these second graders subsequently published an original picture book entitled, *Where Are the Animals in the Forest?* To us at the MI School, this is a snapshot of authentic learning: the lessons are no longer obligatory but instead meaningful. This is what MI-inspired education can do: children are not only equipped with competence and excellence in skills but are also motivated to learn and use them purposefully.

Building Character to Make a Difference

Building students' character involves the development of their personal intelligences and self-awareness. Our advocacy, "Use Your Intelligences to Make a Difference!" stands counter to the popular message from the media and society in general. The popular message is to use one's intelligences to become rich and powerful. We knew that our voice as a school would fall on deaf ears unless it was entrenched in the character formation of children.

Confucius reminds us that "to put the world right in order, we must first put our nation in order; to put our nation in order, we must first put the family in order; to put the family in order, we must first cultivate our personal life; we must first set our hearts right." As the founder, I give children a "value for the week," such as respect or responsibility, that they need to consciously live out. I believe that academic excellence and intelligence—if not deliberately nurtured in an ethical environment—can be abused and used for personal gain. Teachers support this character campaign by asking children to document in their journals that they have practiced the value. Group discussions, class incentives, and visual reminders are often used to promote good character behaviors. In our school, everybody works together to reinforce the values. Instead of scolding a child, for example, a teacher could simply say, "Self-control, please" or "Respect, please," to signal a common understanding. It is one of our deepest convictions that to build leaders for our nation, we must prepare children to be moral, ethical, and caring, as well as educate their minds through academic rigor.

Alongside the value-of-the-week activity, we also launched the MI Kids Can! movement to demonstrate to the nation that children are capable of making a difference in the lives of other children. The movement has brought our children from the halls of Congress as they campaigned for the clean energy bill on behalf of Filipino children to the remaining urban rain forest of the Philippines. They have published books and used their artwork to raise funds for indigent paraplegic children. They helped build houses for the poor, launched a recycling campaign, and used their entrepreneurial skills to hold the first Kids' Bazaar in the country, produced and operated by children for the benefit of other children. Annually the graduating elementary students run a Smart for All camp for one hundred underprivileged children to help them learn that despite their poverty, they too are smart. In addition to opportunities to make a difference as a class, every child in the MI School keeps a personal commitment to make a difference through their own Kids Can! project that they work on with the support of their families. This schoolwide campaign to participate in making the world a better place has made it second nature for children to make their intelligences matter.

Caring About the Community to Make a Difference

Filipino parents often tell their children that as students, their "job" is to study. The only goal for typical Filipino students is academic competence. In the Philippines, it is a child's obligation to do well to eventually repay parents and take care of them in old age. Having been under Spanish rule for almost four hundred years and the Americans for fifty years, the Filipinos' colonial experience discouraged them from working together as a community. Those in control discouraged it out of fear of an uprising. Love for family far supersedes love for country. In the MI School, we value the family, but we also believe that it is critical to give children an awareness of being part of a community with shared responsibility for it.

We open the door of the MI School to real-world learning by bringing children out into the world and by bringing mentors (community leaders, teachers, and parents) into our school. We call this an MI learning community. All members in this community share their resources, time, and talents with the children. To raise awareness about the validity of MI theory in education, we organized a national conference in 2005 to advocate for better practice and invited Howard Gardner to give a keynote speech. Over twenty-five hundred educators, parents, and other stakeholders throughout the Philippine archipelago attended the conference, where the Multiple Intelligence Awards were launched to honor individuals who have used their intelligences in their life's work to make a difference. Among the recipients of the MI Awards were President Corazon Aquino, for using her interpersonal intelligence to successfully lead the peaceful People Power, and Von Hernandez, for using his naturalist intelligence to help pass legislation banning waste incinerators (making the Philippines the first country to do so). Through the MI Awards, the campaign for our leaders to use their intelligences for the good of others has been brought to national awareness as we continue to seek Filipino role models for our youth.

At the MI School, we have also partnered with the media, politicians, businesspeople, and corporations to make education everybody's business. Recently the children have taken the forefront again in another campaign for the environment. A national telecommunications giant partnered with the children to produce a calendar, "12 SMART Ways to Save the Environment," featuring the children's artwork. The school has also worked hand-in-hand with the local government to help uplift educational practice through teacher training in public schools and day care (see Chapter Ten).

To connect children's life to the community, the MI School pioneered entrepreneurship, starting at the elementary level and extending to high school in 2007. We were the first school in the country with a specific initiative for entrepreneurship and leadership. Gardner's definition of intelligence as the ability to problem-solve and create products valued in a cultural setting (Gardner, 1993) is the lens we refer to in laying the foundations of an "entrepreneurial mind." Business leaders mentor our teens as they propose their own business concepts aligned with their strengths. For example, some students who are strong in logical-mathematical intelligence set up a fundraising company, People Organizing Outstanding Fundraisers. Their tagline is, "Helping People Help Themselves." In MI School, everyone is encouraged to have an entrepreneurial mind-set, whether the student goes into medicine, politics, architecture, or some other field.

A distinguishing feature of our thrust for entrepreneurship is that we have deliberately built a culture for "entrepreneurs with hearts." Annually our students test their business plans in the market by holding the MI Kids Can! bazaar to benefit indigent children. After one of the bazaars, a third grader commented, "Business is not about making money; it is about helping others." Here lies the foundation for social entrepreneurship, which again anchors us to our advocacy to use our individual intelligences to make a difference.

CONCLUSION

The Philippine national hero Jose Rizal, who sacrificed his life for the nation's freedom, once said that the "youth are the hope of the nation." To be the hope of the nation, our children need to develop skills and competence as well as the willingness to use what they learn to make a difference in the community, the nation, and the world. The direction of a country lies in its leadership. The MI School shares many educational tenets with other MI-inspired schools. Our unique cultural context as a developing nation has allowed us to see MI theory not only for its value in pursuing individual competence and knowledge, but also for its importance in understanding the practice of intelligences in society.

When we were speaking of possible careers children would like to pursue, a little girl said that she would like to plant trees to help save the environment when she grows up. The teacher questioned her about thinking of a loftier goal, such as that of being president, so she could do even more. In horror, the little girl exclaimed, "I don't want to be president because I don't want to steal money." There is a need to restore integrity in leadership. There is no point in developing intelligent leaders who will use their brilliant minds only for corruption and exploitation. Our MI School culture systematically helps children learn through the development of competence, character, and a sense of community that prepares multiple intelligences to do good work.

It may sound most improbable, if not impossible, to live out a vision of creating a school that will purposefully help children discover their strengths, use them to make a difference, and ultimately become the hope of the nation. But this is the journey that the Multiple Intelligence International School has chosen to take as a pioneering MI institution in the country. We are a small school with big dreams. As our journey continues, this school will keep growing—in our own ways and always choosing to make a difference.

References

Gardner, H. (1993). *Multiple Intelligences: The theory in practice*. New York: Basic Books.

Gardner, H., Csikszentmihalyi, M., & Damon, W. (2001). *Good work: When excellence and ethics meet*. New York: Basic Books.

Ubac, M. (2008, January 3). DepEd chief: RP education has sunk to its lowest level. *Philippine Daily Inquirer*.

CHAPTER 10

Multiple Intelligences Theory and Day Care Center Reform in Tagbilaran City

Carissa Gatmaitan-Bernardo

This chapter describes a collaborative effort between the Multiple Intelligences International School and Tagbilaran City, Bohol, the Philippines, to stimulate day care center reform in the city. Six aspects of this concerted effort are described: reality assessment, professional development, learning environment building, curricular change, community involvement, and local leadership development. Challenges and creative solutions are presented to illustrate the process of the reform effort and its impact on teachers, children, families, and the community at large.

It was hot. The temperature in Tagbilaran City, Bohol, is always high. Inside a day care center in the city, it was even hotter. The classroom was cramped with forty children ages three to six. Standing in front of these children, a teacher was "teaching." She wrote a capital U on the blackboard and asked the children to write it down twenty times on their paper. With no template and minimal supervision, most children were busy with their own frivolities. Few accomplished anything. The large number of restless and unfocused children did not seem to bother the teacher, who did not respond even as two boys in front of her starting to get out of hand. It was not that she did not care about the classroom situation. Rather, her resigned look implied that there was nothing she could do about it. A similar scenario greeted us in each of the thirty-three day care centers when we first visited the city. These centers serve approximately two thousand children from indigent families in Tagbilaran.

Recognizing the inadequacies of our child care system, the national government has made a great effort to improve early childhood programs in the Philippines. A law, popularly known as the new ECCD Act, requires the establishment and institutionalization of a national system for early childhood care and development. Designed to be comprehensive, integrative, and sustainable, the system should involve the collaboration of multisectors and interagency groups at both national and local levels. Under the act, greater attention has been given to training day care workers in proper monitoring of children's nutrition and in parent education. An English version of the *Revised Day Care Workers Manual* was drafted by the Bureau of Child and Youth Welfare to guide day care workers in their everyday teaching (Bureau of Child and Youth Welfare and Department of Social Services and Development, 1992). The local government has assumed more responsibilities for the care of child care centers.

One of the cities that took to heart this responsibility is Tagbilaran, the capital of the island province of Bohol. In May 2004, the Philippine local elections brought Tagbilaran a new breed of local governance headed by Mayor Dan Neri Lim and Vice Mayor Nuevas T. Montes. The city, serving a population of approximately 94,137, takes pride in calling itself "The Little City with Big Dreams." With the new local government unit (LGU), the city was determined to create a better quality of life for its people and to help its citizens join the top achievers and performers in the country. One of the priorities for the city is a sound educational program, especially an early childhood education program for low-income families. According to Mayor Lim, one of the issues was the deterioration of public school education, marked by poorly prepared teachers, substandard center facilities, and neglected children.

Envisioning a brighter future and supported by the political will to make it happen, the new administrators in Tagbilaran City sought the help of the Multiple Intelligence International School in Manila to help reach their vision. In February 2006, the MI Smart Start Comprehensive School Reform Program (MI-CSR) was launched. As the city's first formal action to prove its commitment to the program, it passed ordinance C-192, known as the Multiple Intelligence School Reform Program in the Public Day Care Centers of Tagbilaran City (Republic of the Philippines, 2006). The purpose of this ordinance is to approve implementation of the MI-CSR Program approach in all of the public day care centers in the city.

The MI-CSR Program addressed a range of elements critical in school reform, such as the classroom environment, curriculum and management, day care worker performance, administrative support, and student achievement, to name a few. The program set eight objectives:

1. Recognize every child as an able learner with his or her own unique intelligence profile.
2. Use MI as a framework for curriculum and instruction in early childhood programs.

3. Design learning environments to support the development of multiple intelligences in young children.

4. Provide learning materials that enhance the development of children's multiple intelligences.

5. Equip day care workers with appropriate classroom and behavioral management strategies.

6. Increase home-school-community partnerships and communication.

7. Assess children's development in intelligence-fair ways.

8. Support teacher's implementation of MI theory in the classroom to improve school achievement.

To reach these goals, the MI-CSR Program engaged in six phases of work in all day care centers in Tagbilaran: reality assessment, professional development, learning environment building, curricular change, community involvement, and local leadership development. Although identified as phases, the last four do not follow a linear time sequence; often they take place simultaneously. In this sense, they differ from the first two aspects of the MI-CSR program. Each aspect of the program influences others and is influenced by others. Working in tandem, they promote the betterment of school learning environments and education for children in Tagbilaran City.

PHASE I: REALITY ASSESSMENT

Phase I of the MI-CSR concentrated on reality assessment. The primary purpose of the assessment was to learn about day care center conditions and identify the needs and goals of the stakeholders in the project: day care workers, parents, administrators, coordinators of the City Social Welfare and Development Office, and representatives of the local government unit. The MI Team, which was composed of day care workers, parent representatives, private businesspeople, and city officials including the mayor and the vice mayor, observed current practice in day care centers, evaluated curriculum plans, and conducted an environmental survey. The assessment results were disheartening.

Overall, day care center workers seemed to have adapted to a culture of mendicancy. They simply waited for handouts from the government and other institutions, and if they were not given supplies or training, they resigned themselves to doing nothing. Many of them stopped being resourceful and accepted that their classroom would be mismanaged and unequipped. Because many centers concentrated on feeding malnourished children, workers were hired to facilitate and monitor the child nutrition in the community. A high school diploma was the only requirement for these positions. Only recently have the centers been encouraged to teach curriculum and provide instruction. Many teachers feel unprepared because they do not hold an education degree, let alone a teaching license. A handful have not finished college. Although it is ideal to recruit licensed teachers, or at least college graduates from related fields, it is not the reality of those hired permanently and those who continue to apply for the position of day care worker. Imagine a small, humid classroom where day care workers are responsible for handling an average of eighty children each. Some centers have no running water or electricity, and workers are paid minimum wage of less than five dollars per working day. These were not inviting conditions for those who have earned a college degree in education.

Our assessment results also showed that although a few day care workers had had some training, translating what they had learned into classroom practice was a challenge. Each day care worker taught in the way he or she knew best. If one day care worker knew a little bit of math, then she taught those skills, and if another day care worker wanted to concentrate on arts and crafts, then that dominated the classroom. The discrepancies across different centers were both apparent and large. Yet no one seemed to take notice, and even if they did, no action was taken.

PHASE II: PROFESSIONAL DEVELOPMENT

Based on the results of the reality assessment of day care centers in Tagbilaran and a focus group with day care workers and members of the community, the MI-CSR went into phase II of the project: an intensive two-week professional development and capability building workshop. On the first day, the day care workers were asked to complete a multiple intelligence profile. In addition to expanding the day care workers' view of "intelligence," this also gave us the opportunity to get to know the group better. It was a revelation to find out that none of the thirty-three participants indicated they were strong in linguistic intelligence. In fact, most of them viewed this as their weakest intelligence. It was no wonder that the *Revised Day Care Manual* was gathering dust in the centers and previous trainings were merely a faint memory. If our day care workers were not strong in linguistic intelligence, we could not expect them to read and refer to a manual, especially one that is not written in their native dialect and uses a language they are not fluent in. For our part, we made some adjustments in our training, focusing less on talk and more on action. We made training very hands-on, and we created many materials such as classroom schedules, calendars, attendance charts, math and literacy manipulatives for teachers to take back to classrooms. In our training, the MI–CSR Program focused on the empowerment of day care workers as providers of learning. Belief in one's self is one of the most powerful gifts of MI theory.

Before focusing on any teaching strategy, we worked with day care workers to help them develop the perception that they are intelligent, whatever their educational background or economic standing may be. Developing this perception greatly influenced the way they value themselves. As the training continued, we began to notice a difference in their attitude. According to one day care worker, the premise that they too are intelligent is a new concept for them, and this renewed concept gave a big boost to their confidence. This spark of self-worth was translated into classroom practice as they began to see each child's potential, and thus the life of children and the community were affected. In addition, the day care workers felt that for the first time, their local government valued them since time and resources were being spent on their training.

The grueling two-week training was only the tip of the iceberg. Originally the MI-CSR Program was designed to include quarterly visits to monitor the progress of the day care workers. Between visits, day care workers would use the training manual to self-monitor their teaching practice. Having learned that most of our day care workers are stronger in nonlinguistic learning, we realized that the training manual was not likely to be the most effective approach to sustaining the training effects. In order to build a bridge between the two-week training and classroom practice, we implemented a monthly mentorship program to replace quarterly visits.

During the monthly visits, we observed classroom practices and provided support and supervision to teachers. We sat down with teachers and discussed different strategies with them immediately after our observation. We worked collaboratively in planning curriculum, solving problems, and addressing issues they needed help with. At the end of each visit, we once again held a general meeting for the whole group, discussing common issues across the center. In the beginning, the task seemed insurmountable. Some veteran teachers showed no signs of classroom management skills. In terms of curriculum planning, the old practice of paper-and-pencil tasks and memory exercises prevailed despite our efforts to introduce the idea of multiple entry points to learning. But as the months passed, the pace began to pick up, especially with new hiring and contractual workers. Resemblances to a rich MI environment began to surface.

PHASE III: BUILDING LEARNING ENVIRONMENTS

Before the MI-CSR Program, there were very few learning materials in the day care centers around Tagbilaran City. All eighty children in a center would share the same small puzzle, for example. The day care worker, fearing its wear and tear, sometimes wrapped the puzzle with plastic, and children were allowed only to look at it. There were few, if any, children's books. Many children had never handled markers, paint, or glue, and a fresh box of crayons was a rare commodity in classrooms. The MI Smart Start Group solicited donations from the parents of the MI School in Manila, from Tagbilaranons who reside abroad and from foundations and organizations. Gradually the empty shelves started to fill up with age-appropriate educational toys, books, and supplies. To maximize the use of educational resources, some items were rotated among the classrooms and centers.

As part of the agreement of the MI-CSR Program, the LGU was to be responsible for any physical repair needed in the centers, such as running water, electricity, and roof repair. Although this promise was not fulfilled by the end of the school year, the LGU did supply teachers with basic instructional materials such as chalk, paper, and glue. In the past, day care workers had to use their own pocket money to purchase these materials. The basic supplies from the LGU not only provided a basis for teaching but sent a message that the local government was working to improve early education.

The cheapest and yet the most wonderful addition to the classroom environments was the increase of teacher-made materials, such as puzzles, game boards, and math manipulatives made of recycled materials. To build learning environments, teachers were called on to work with what they had and to use their talents to create resources for learning. Over time, teachers also realized that children's work should be part of the learning environment. They started displaying children's writing samples, art work, and other activities done in school.

PHASE IV: CURRICULUM CHANGE

At the beginning of the MI-CSR Program, many classroom activities did not meet the standards of developmentally appropriate practice. Due to lack of age-appropriate music, for example, many classrooms used the latest tunes on adult television shows for children's music or dancing activities. Most lessons were rote memory exercises and did not encourage higher-order thinking skills. Children were frequently unfocused and showed no interest in classroom learning.

The MI-CSR suggested setting common goals for all centers. We sat down with the day care workers, identifying developmental goals and skills that are age appropriate and should be taught throughout the school year. Teachers were mentored to plan developmentally appropriate activities using the eight intelligences as entry points for their lesson plans and projects. Through this process, teachers became more aware of and gave value to a wide range of intelligences. For example, various art forms, which are highly valued in Bohol, became part of the curriculum. Development of the interpersonal and intrapersonal intelligences was also evident as the day care workers tried to respect individual differences by encouraging self-reflection activities and creating group work.

It would have been much easier for the MI-CSR team to provide ready-made session plans for the day care workers to follow. This approach, however, would not help to create thinking teachers, that is, teachers who can come up with their own lesson plan and implement it. As tough as it was to walk day care workers through the process of planning, in the end the hard work paid off. The best lesson plans and the best learning activities were those that the day care workers thought of independently and those relevant to their community. One day care worker commented on this curriculum change experience in one of the interviews: "You [the MI Project] gave us back the dignity of our job. People now look up to us and respect us more" (J. Zamora, personal interview, June 2006).

Curriculum change resulted in an increase in student achievement in the centers. Teachers noticed that children seemed to be more engaged in their work. Even during recess, they talk about "fair sharing" as introduced in a theme on fractions. When we compared the results of entrance and exit assessments, we found that children had higher self-esteem and seemed to enjoy school more toward the end of the year. In terms of academic learning, children showed an average increase of 30 percent in literacy skills and a 15 to 20 percent increase in mathematics skills when their performance from the beginning to the end of school year was compared.

PHASE V: COMMUNITY INVOLVEMENT

One of the challenges posed by the MI-CSR for the day care workers was to involve the community in the education of their children. According to the results of our assessment, community involvement was minimal in almost all of the centers. Day care workers tried to do everything: they prepared materials for the classroom, made snacks, cleaned the classroom, and helped take some children home after school, to name a few of their tasks. If a day care worker had to create a worksheet, she typically replicated it by writing it out manually. Depending on the number of students in the center, this task might be repeated as many as eighty times.

After attending parent meetings and conducting interviews, we also learned that parents were not aware of the importance of early childhood education. Day care was often seen as a child-sitting service, not a path for learning. In addition, they had no idea what they could possibly contribute because most of them are uneducated and see themselves as underprivileged. This was another "changing minds" moment for the MI-CSR Program.

A community meeting held by the MI team aimed to acquaint the members of the community with the changes taking place in the centers, introduce them to Howard Gardner's MI theory, and emphasize that everyone can contribute. In addition, they were asked to help out in the centers.

The Parents Share Program was adopted by the centers. Parents were invited to get involved in the day care centers in different ways: donating to the parent councils, helping day care workers create materials and reproduce learning sheets for the children, assisting with making snacks, cleaning the classrooms, helping repair broken facilities, serving as guards in the center to prevent stealing, tending the garden, helping raise funds to hire an assistant in the classroom, and serving as resource speakers in the classroom. Resource speakers are those valued by the community, such as drivers of public utility transportation, peddlers who sell produce on the streets, and parents who are skilled with crafts. A classic example is Tatay Timoy who drives a tricycle, one of the main modes of transportation in the city. He was invited to talk about his tricycle to children. Never did he imagine that the children could learn a lot just by counting the wheels on his tricycle or that he was important to the children. Parent involvement in the schools significantly increased throughout the year as a result of these activities, and they took an active role in helping to solve center-related problems. More important, through involvement, they became increasingly aware of the importance of early childhood education.

Community involvement was also evident in the recycling program the day care centers initiated, *Naa'y Kwarta sa Basura* (There's Money in Trash). The city's waste management team created a special route and setup for the collection of recyclables in the centers. With a simple text message from the day care worker, partner recycling centers would come to the center to collect and purchase recyclable materials. Funds from the recycling program go to the centers' activities. The workers and their parent councils collaborate in decision making about how to use the funds. Moreover, through the concerted efforts of the centers, we have seen more and more donations from local companies. The government in Tagbilaran intends to create an "adopt-a-day-care" program for private companies in the city as part of their corporate responsibility. The future will tell the importance of such an endeavor.

It is important to point out that parent involvement does not function in isolation. To a great extent, it depends on the day care workers' ability to build rapport with the parents and members of the local community. Some workers still would opt to work alone or complain their parents are unresponsive or uncooperative. Moreover, the start of every school year is difficult because there are new sets of parents who need to be oriented about MI, the language they use with their children, and their view of intelligence. Despite these challenges, the MI-CSR Program affirms that the school-home-community partnership is critical to ensure that good practices take place in centers and that they are valued and exercised beyond the centers to have a true impact on children's lives.

PHASE VI: DEVELOPMENT OF LOCAL LEADERSHIP

The sustainability of good practice is a top priority for the MI-CSR Program in Tagbilaran City. To accomplish this goal, we established a monitoring and sustainability program within the program to develop school leadership teams. The day care workers are divided into small groups called smart learning groups. Each group has seven to eight day care workers based on the proximity of centers. Each group identifies a team leader, who receives additional training at the beginning of each month and assists the consultants with the monthly training of the rest of the group. These groups sit with the consultant once a month for updating practice, curriculum planning, and problem solving related to issues in the center.

The MI-CSR Program has had a great impact on the teaching and learning processes in the Tagbilarn day care centers and is proving to be a sustainable and feasible program with a promising future. Nevertheless, the program faces further challenges. The goal of the program is not only to introduce MI theory to teachers, but also to affect their practice and influence the entire community. Without center-based leadership, we will not be able to accomplish such grand goals. Through center-based leadership, we are able to better address the needs and issues of the low-income community. The program is also more creative and resourceful in meeting a range of challenges to ensure the program's sustainability.

The MI-CSR Program is now under the Special Projects of the Mayor of Tagbilaran City and has drawn positive attention from the community. At the same time, it has been subjected to criticism from political opponents. To an outsider, the centers may not seem to have changed much. The lack of age-appropriate materials and dilapidated facilities are still evident. However, the physical structure does not reflect the internal changes the MI-CSR Program has created. To his detractors, the mayor responds, "It is true that Tagbilaran does not have the resources to turn things around quickly. But we also cannot allow time to pass without doing anything, so we are taking our chances with what we have" (D. Lim, personal interview, October 1, 2007). We work with the center-based leadership team and all day care workers in Tagbilaran to take every chance we have to make whatever positive changes we can.

CONCLUSION

The partnership of the MI-CSR Program and the local government of Tagbilaran is an outstanding example of how much can be achieved through hard work and collaborative efforts. The initiative and participation of the local officials, the day care workers' perseverance, the community's receptiveness, the private sector's support, and the MI Schools' commitment all work together to benefit the children who are the future of Tagbilaran and of the Philippines. The project affected not only the children currently enrolled in the day care centers and their families; it also changed day care workers in the city of Tagbilarn. Through these day care workers, the centers now offer more meaningful curriculum and instruction, have enriched learning environments, and built stronger home-school-community partnerships. These changes will continue to benefit many generations to come.

Underprivileged children in the day care centers are given a chance to develop and hone their intelligences during the most critical period of their lives. What better gift can underprivileged children receive than a "smart start" in life? Through developing their multiple intelligences, the children of Tagbilaran will be prepared to meet the demands of this century. The MI-CSR Program leaves the legacy of a strong foundation in early childhood education for the children of Tagbilaran, and we hope it will serve as a model for other cities around the country. A lot of work remains, but the seeds of progressive reform have been planted in this city that dares to dream big.

References

Bureau of Child and Youth Welfare and Department of Social Services and Development. (1992). *Self-instructional handbook for day care workers* (2nd ed.). Quezon City: Author.

Republic of the Philippines. Office of the Sangguniang Panlungsod. (2006). *The Multiple Intelligence School Reform Program in the public day care centers of Tagbilaran.* Tagbilaran City: Author.

CHAPTER 11

Dinosaurs and Taxis

Educating Learners with Diverse Needs

Wilma Vialle

This chapter focuses on the influence of MI theory in special and gifted education in Australia. In both contexts, the MI impact is evident in changes of teachers' attitudes and practices toward these students. In gifted education, MI has provided a means to more broadly define and identify giftedness in students across all economic and cultural groups. It has also influenced the design of curriculum materials for gifted students. In special education, MI teachers have transcended a deficit approach; they have become more positive toward students and recognize a wider range of learning potentials. Through the framework provided by MI theory, teachers have learned to genuinely value and appropriately respond to the diversity of learners in integrated Australian classrooms.

On a bitterly cold, rainy day on the northwest coast of Tasmania, an island south of mainland Australia, the drama teacher consults her timetable and sighs audibly, contemplating the thirty eighth-grade students who wait for her outside the drama classroom. Her thoughts turn to one student, Peter—whether he will be there and what she can do to ensure that the lesson progresses without anyone ending in tears. Peter is an enigma to her. He is obviously very bright, and she is constantly impressed by his creativity, his improvisational skills, and his stage presence. The other students are drawn to him. But he can also be contemptuous of others and cruel in his comments to them. He is one of the most promising students she has ever taught, but he is failing every subject at school and is regularly sent to the principal's office because of his behavior. Because it is so difficult for him to follow rules, the other teachers predict that he will leave school early and be habitually unemployed or possibly end up in jail. The drama teacher wonders what the key is to unlock Peter's potential and to steer him onto a more positive pathway.

Several years later in a primary school in regional New South Wales, a teacher is conducting a literacy lesson with her class of six year olds. She holds up a flash card on which is written "Thursday" and draws the children's attention to the "*ur*" sound. She asks the twenty-four children if there are other days of the week that also have the *ur* sound. "Friday," one child responds; another enthusiastically guesses, "Monday." After further deliberations, the answer of "Saturday" is finally given. The teacher congratulates the student and turns to the next flash card when one of the children, James, says, "Turtle has the *ur* sound too." The teacher nods at the child and returns to the flash cards when James again interrupts, stating, "And dinosaur. That ends with *ur*." The teacher dismisses his observation by sharply retorting, "Yes, but dinosaur doesn't make the *ur* sound, does it?" and then continues with her lesson. Later in the staff room, the teacher comments, "James is *too* smart. He gets us off task all the time."

Richard, a five year old, is with his family on a trip to the beach. As they leave the parking lot at the end of the day, the following exchange occurs:

Richard (pointing to the exit sign): Look! *Exit* has the same letters as *taxi*! [There was no taxi in sight]

Dad: Where do you see *exit*?

Richard: On that sign up there.

Dad: How do you spell *exit* then?

Richard: E-X-I-T.

Dad: Good job! So where's the taxi?

Richard: I just remembered that . . . There must be one around here somewhere."

Dad: So how do you spell *taxi*?

Richard: T-A . . . uh . . . X-I. It's got an A. Oh, well, they're almost the same.

Dad: Pretty smart observation there, kiddo.

These three scenarios are actual examples that encapsulate my experience with MI theory over a twenty-year period. I was the drama teacher who grappled with the challenge of trying to motivate Peter to apply himself to his schoolwork. The other two incidents are extracts from my field notes, made several years later and after I had completed a doctorate using MI theory as a framework. The three boys were quite different in how they presented in classrooms: Peter was perceived as a severe behavioral problem with little to redeem him, James was seen as verbally precocious but a time waster with learning problems, and Richard was welcomed as an intelligent and compliant student. Though different, they had at least one characteristic in common: all were gifted.

In Australia, giftedness is defined as inborn potential. Up to 10 percent of the student population can be identified as gifted across a number of domains (Gagné, 2003). Under this definition, potential develops into talented performance as a result of catalysts, including appropriate educational interventions. Although the incidents involving Peter, James, and Richard were separated by time, they exemplify the different ways gifted students can be perceived and treated.

When I was struggling to get through to Peter, I was completing a thesis on gifted students for a master of education degree. It occurred to me that Peter might be an underachieving gifted student and I needed to find some way to reverse that underachievement. But I was alone among Peter's teachers in thinking that he had some identifiable talents. After completing my thesis, I was no closer to understanding what made Peter tick and decided I needed to investigate further.

That decision inevitably led to my traveling to Florida, where I studied gifted education. As part of that process, I observed several gifted programs. I was concerned by the underrepresentation of culturally diverse children in these programs, which were made up largely of white middle-class students identified through their performance on IQ tests. Consequently, my burning question shifted from, "How do I get through to an underachieving gifted kid?" to "How do we identify giftedness in kids who don't score high on IQ tests?" Searching for an alternative to traditional IQ testing to identify giftedness, I soon encountered MI theory. My doctoral dissertation used MI as a framework to structure observations of preschoolers living in low-socioeconomic circumstances. Through the adoption of a dynamic assessment approach based on Project Spectrum, a project that applied MI theory to early childhood education and assessment (Krechevsky, 1991), I gained insights into how children learned from the prompts and scaffolds provided by teachers. Armed with these insights, I returned to Australia to apply what I had learned to some of the educational issues we faced there.

SCHOOLING IN AUSTRALIA

In 2007, there were more than 3.4 million students in 9,612 schools across Australia, with just over 270,000 teaching staff. Education is largely the responsibility of the states and territories, with funding, policy, and curricula determined by state governments. Schooling commences at kindergarten, which children enter at about age five. It is compulsory for all students up to the age of fifteen or sixteen. About 75 percent of students continue into eleventh and twelfth grades to complete a higher school certificate. Primary schools encompass kindergarten to sixth grade in most states and seventh grade in others. Secondary schools go up to twelfth grade. Approximately two-thirds of students attend government schools, with the other third attending Catholic schools and independent private schools.

The Australian education system, like many others around the world, has been engaged in a seemingly constant process of restructuring over the past two decades. In the 1990s, there was a move toward adopting National Curriculum Statements with clearly specified learning outcomes for students. These National Curriculum Statements divide the curriculum into eight key learning areas: English; mathematics; human society and its environment; science; technology; the arts; languages other than English; and personal development, health, and physical education. Each state has the responsibility to translate these statements into curricula and assessment practices within its own state.

Historically, children with special needs due to intellectual, learning, or physical disabilities were educated separately in special schools or self-contained units within regular schools. Because its administration was relatively quick and economical, the IQ test was, and still is, used to identify students who require special educational services. The worldwide trend of integrating special and regular education has been adopted in Australia over the past two decades. A large proportion of students with special needs are being enrolled in mainstream classrooms. Some segregated settings remain for students with severe intellectual disabilities; for autistic, deaf, or blind students; and for students with extreme behavioral problems.

Under the philosophy of integration, compulsory units on students with special needs are included in all teacher training programs. Additional financial resources are provided to schools with identified special needs students. Consequently there is a compelling financial incentive for schools to identify students with intellectual, learning, and physical disabilities, as it enables the hiring of support teachers in the school. Nevertheless, many teachers feel ill equipped to cope with the range of needs in their classrooms.

The educational needs of gifted students have not been given the same level of attention as other special needs in Australian schools. There is no additional funding for gifted students, and very few teacher training programs include more than a single hour-long lecture on the educational needs of such students. The number of school counselors is minimal in Australia, and they spend most of their time testing and working with children who have learning difficulties. They are rarely called on to identify gifted students or provide programs for them. The philosophy of integration has also translated into a strong belief on the part of most teacher unions that gifted students should be educated in mainstream classrooms and neighborhood schools. Nevertheless, most states do offer some separate classes and schools for identified gifted students. New South Wales, the largest Australian state, has the most extensive provision, with Opportunity Classes for gifted students in fifth and sixth grades in some primary schools, and selective high schools for gifted secondary students. Entry into these programs is gained by taking a test similar to an IQ test, again because of ease of administration.

In addition to the demands of implementing new curricula based on National Curriculum Statements and responding to a wide range of student needs that may include students who are gifted as well as those with special needs, teachers are constantly bombarded with increasing demands to improve their teaching practices. Newspaper reports frequently excoriate the shortcomings of the schools, and state governments regularly restructure their departments of education to increase economic efficiencies. In turn, the departments of education constantly evaluate curricula and teacher quality (see, for example, Ministerial Advisory Council on the Quality of Teaching, 1998; New South Wales Department of Education and Training, 2003; Ramsey, 2000; Vinson, 2002). That these increasing demands are rarely accompanied by the resources needed to effect change exacerbates the situation.

It was in this educational climate of escalating demands and diminishing resources that I returned from the United States and accepted a position as an academic at a university in New South Wales. For the ensuing fifteen years, I have taught preservice teachers, contributed to the professional development of in-service teachers, and continued my research in the field of gifted education. During this time, I have seen firsthand how MI has captured the imaginations and commitment of a number of Australian teachers and schools. Elsewhere I have reviewed ways that MI has been applied in Australia, ranging from a television series to workplace training programs (see, for example, Vialle, 1997). In this chapter, I focus on how MI has influenced the practices of gifted education and special education in Australia.

GIFTED EDUCATION PRACTICES

MI has affected gifted education practices in Australia in two significant ways. First, in broadening the scope of intelligence, it has provided a more inclusive model of gifted education, which hitherto had been associated with elitism and narrow IQ-based thinking. Second, MI has been used by teachers to plan curricula that support a range of abilities in their classrooms, and through this planning, they have become more aware of the diversity of gifted students.

To understand how MI has influenced the adoption of a more inclusive approach to gifted education, some background on the educational context in Australia is needed. Gifted education has always been in a somewhat precarious position in Australia. Despite two federal inquiries acknowledging the need for special provisions for gifted students (Senate Employment, Workplace Relations, Small Business and Education References Committee, 2001; Senate

Select Committee, 1988), the delivery of appropriate programs has not been systematized in any way and occurs only with the will and efforts of committed educators and parents. Australia prides itself on the motto of the "Fair Go," and anything that seems inequitable is frowned on. This sentiment was most apparent in the 1970s when the federal government focused on funding educational programs aimed at overcoming disadvantage, which turned attention away from the needs of gifted learners. In response, a number of Australian educators argued that gifted students were also disadvantaged because the lack of appropriate educational programs prevented them from developing their full potential (Braggett, 1985). Nevertheless, many educators remained unconvinced and equated gifted education with elitism. The challenge, then, was to convince educators that nurturing gifted students was a matter of equity. MI became important in attaining this aim.

I was initially drawn to MI theory because it offers a broader conceptualization of intelligence that I thought could be useful for identifying giftedness in children who did not perform well on a standard IQ test. However, a conservative element in gifted education in Australia has remained resistant to any move away from narrow definitions and assessments of giftedness. MI theory was perceived as a threat to gifted education because it challenged the conception of intelligence as IQ. My critics believed this equaled saying that every child was gifted. By contrast, I argued that MI theory was consistent with the international shift to more inclusive and broadened notions of giftedness (Gallagher, 2003; Shore, Cornell, Robinson, & Ward, 1991) and countered the claims that gifted programs were elitist by identifying students across all cultural and economic strata.

My research has demonstrated that MI is an effective framework for identifying giftedness in students from disadvantaged groups (Vialle, 1991, 1994a, 1995) and results in broader representation of indigenous, low-socioeconomic-status, and English-as-a-second-language students in gifted programs. As in other countries, the educational attainments of indigenous Australians fall significantly below those of the general population. Relatively few Aboriginal children are selected for gifted programs. If the term *gifted* is applied to an Aboriginal child, the assumption will be that the child is good at sport, usually football. Seeing Aboriginal children through an MI lens has permitted educators to look beyond the stereotype of sporting ability to discover the spatial, oral language, and interpersonal strengths exhibited by many Aboriginal children and to use these in designing educational programs to encourage the development of their talents (Gibson & Vialle, 2007). MI thus provided a more authentic means for assessing giftedness in children from diverse backgrounds. To illustrate this, I return to Peter, James, and Richard.

Peter was Aboriginal and came from a low-socioeconomic background. His everyday language was peppered with grammatical errors. His writing was poor, and he struggled with mathematical tasks. At the age of fourteen, he had a long history of school failure and had developed a negative attitude toward school. In my drama classroom, he was able to think on his feet, revealing his ability to feel and communicate powerful emotions through drama improvisations. Although I was not aware of it at the time, Peter had particular strengths in the personal intelligences and in spatial intelligence that often came to the fore in drama lessons. He was a natural leader who was not permitted to lead because of his general behavior. Peter's interactions with teachers were colored by their focus on his deficits and their perception that he lacked intelligence.

James was born in Papua New Guinea and had moved to Australia when he was five. The observation recounted at the beginning of this chapter occurred after James had been in Australia for one year. His first-grade teacher recognized his verbal ability but often failed to capitalize on learning opportunities for him because she thought he was off task. She indicated to me that he was easily distracted and not achieving at grade level in writing and mathematics. Many of her interactions with him were negative as she instructed him to attend to the specific task she had set.

Richard, by contrast, was a white middle-class child whose positive interactions with his father, as indicated at the beginning of the chapter, were echoed at school. His precociousness was recognized and valued by his teachers, and he was later identified for inclusion in a gifted program.

While traditional assessment procedures identified Richard as gifted, they did not identify Peter and James. Furthermore, it is unlikely that either Peter or James would have been recommended by their teachers for a gifted program because of the disruptive behavior they sometimes exhibited in the classroom. I have argued that gifted education entails the delivery of an appropriate education that recognizes and responds to the individual differences of all students and can identify the potential in Peter and James as readily as in Richard. In working with teachers, I have used MI as a framework to encourage them to think more broadly about giftedness and the need to respond appropriately to the diverse students they teach.

In the process of designing learning activities for gifted students, a popular approach in Australia is to combine MI with Bloom's taxonomy. Widely used for gifted students in regular Australian classrooms, Bloom's taxonomy was originally created as a hierarchical list of educational objectives ranging from knowledge to evaluation. In gifted education, it has been used to encourage teachers to include sufficient higher-order thinking tasks (analysis, synthesis, and evaluation) for gifted students. According to recent Australian education documents (see, for example, New South Wales Department of Education and Training, 2003; Ramsey, 2000), quality teachers are those who possess sound knowledge of the interests, abilities, skills, and learning behaviors of the individual students in their class and are able to adapt their programs and teaching styles to suit those students. In order to do this effectively, teachers need to be able to observe students closely across a range of endeavors. One of the strengths of MI theory is that it provides a manageable framework to guide teachers in this process. By looking at each of the eight intelligences in relation to the six levels of Bloom's taxonomy, for example, teachers can provide a range of activities for the diverse interests and abilities of the students. The teachers who embrace this approach report that they observe their students more closely and look for strengths rather than responding automatically to deficits.

SPECIAL EDUCATION PRACTICES

MI has also influenced the practice of special education in Australia, again largely through encouraging attitudinal change in teachers. This has entailed looking differently at students with special needs by constructing individual profiles that depict relative strengths and weaknesses rather than simply focusing on deficits. Historically, special education practices have been dominated by a remedial approach where deficits become the driving force for the students' programs. MI theory appeals to special education teachers because it has helped them shift from a deficit view to an understanding that children with learning problems may also possess intellectual strengths (Vialle, 1994b). This has had a liberating effect on their curricula. Teachers are casting aside their remediation techniques in favor of designing activities that both capitalize on the strengths and interests of students and build up students' weaknesses. But the most important part of this shift is not the curriculum but the attitudinal changes in teachers.

Before learning about MI theory, many special education teachers had expressed reservations about an educational system that too readily tests, compares, and labels children. For these teachers, MI theory has reaffirmed their beliefs that children cannot be so easily categorized and that some children are misdiagnosed because of the limited forms of testing used to assess them. The ways in which special education teachers have taken up MI are as varied as one would expect in a country the size of Australia. There is no single approach to using MI in special education contexts. Those I have observed have used the pluralism of the theory to look beyond their students' limitations in linguistic and logical-mathematical activities. Rather than narrowing the curriculum, these teachers have enriched it through providing engaging tasks across all the intelligences. To illustrate this point, I will outline the work of Lorna Parker, the principal of a school for students with special needs. She has successfully used MI to educate teachers, students, and community members about the learning potential of the special needs students in her school.

Influenced by MI theory, Parker developed a new model for educating special needs children that requires teachers to observe students closely as they undertake activities related to diverse intelligences rather than literacy and numeracy only. In particular, they were asked to identify the intelligences that were relative strengths or interests for each of the children. The teachers also collected anecdotal information from parents and other teachers. It is mandated special education practice in Australia that all children have an Individual Education Plan tailored to meet their needs. Under Parker's model, this plan started with a statement of what the child could do rather than what he or she could not do. The focus on strengths then permeated the educational programs devised for the special needs students. The students engaged in enriching experiences in all the key learning areas rather than just drill routines limited to literacy and numeracy.

Drawing on the principles underpinning MI of developing all of the intelligences, Parker's model also helped the students better understand their own profiles of intelligences. The students were asked to think of their brain as a computer with integrated software that Parker dubbed Brainworks. For example, linguistic intelligence was the word processor; logical-mathematical intelligence was a spreadsheet; spatial intelligence was a drawing program; musical intelligence was a synthesizer; bodily-kinesthetic intelligence was the typing program; interpersonal intelligence was the network; intrapersonal intelligence was a PC; and naturalist intelligence was the graphic design elements (Vialle & Perry, 2002). Prior to any class activity, the students would be prompted to "load" that particular piece of software. For example, if students were about to write a story, they would be instructed to turn on their linguistic intelligence software (Vialle & Perry, 2002). In this way, Parker used the MI framework to communicate to students that they could learn, even if they were not good at everything at school.

Lorna Parker's approach to the education of special needs students is a clear example of how MI theory has been used to modify special education practices in Australia. The focus of her work with special students has been to regard them in a positive light, encourage their development across all intelligences, and use their strengths and interests to motivate them in learning. Her approach uses MI as a framework to recognize the diversity in children and encourage teachers to hold higher expectations of the intellectual capacities of their special needs students.

CONCLUSION

Educational fads come and go; teachers enthusiastically embrace new ideas and then move on. MI theory, however, has stood the test of time with many Australian teachers. From my observations, it has endured because it fits well with what good teachers do: it provides a structure to value and appropriately responds to the diversity of learners in integrated Australian classrooms.

In the context of gifted education practices in Australia, MI has had two impacts. The first is the design of curriculum materials for gifted students in regular classroom settings. The second is providing a means to more broadly define and identify giftedness in students across all economic and cultural groups.

In special education settings, MI theory has allowed teachers to move away from focusing on children's deficits and instead look for their relative strengths. Primarily this has entailed their understanding that children's intellectual profiles are uneven. As a result, special education teachers with an MI philosophy are more positive toward their students and have higher expectations of their capacity to learn.

My enthusiasm for MI has not diminished over the twenty years that I have been working with it, but obviously it cannot resolve all the issues confronting educators. In Australia, it has clearly made a small but significant difference to educational practice. Twenty years ago, very few educators had heard of the theory; today the majority recognize its name. More important, a small percentage of schools and teachers think about and interact differently with children in a way that respects and responds to their diversity.

References

Braggett, E. J. (1985). *Education of gifted and talented children: Australian provision.* Canberra: Commonwealth Schools Commission.

Gagné, F. (2003). Transforming gifts into talents: The DMGT as a developmental theory. In N. Colangelo & G. A. Davis (Eds.), *Handbook of gifted education* (3rd ed., pp. 60–74). Needham Heights, MA: Allyn & Bacon.

Gallagher, J. J. (2003). Issues and challenges in the education of gifted students. In N. Colangelo & G. A. Davis (Eds.), *Handbook of gifted education* (3rd ed., pp. 11–23). Needham Heights, MA: Allyn & Bacon.

Gibson, K., & Vialle, W. (2007). The Australian Aboriginal view of giftedness. In S. Phillipson & M. McCann (Eds.), *Conceptions of giftedness: Socio-cultural perspectives* (pp. 193–220). Mahwah, NJ: Erlbaum.

Krechevsky, M. (1991). Project Spectrum: An innovative assessment alternative. *Educational Leadership, 48*(5), 43–48.

Ministerial Advisory Council on the Quality of Teaching. (1998). *Teacher preparation for student management: Responses and directions.* In *Report by Ministerial Advisory Council on the Quality of Teaching, October, 1998.* Sydney: New South Wales Department of Education and Training.

New South Wales Department of Education and Training. (2003). *Quality teaching in NSW public schools.* Sydney: Author.

Ramsey, G. (2000). *Quality matters. Revitalising teaching: Critical times, critical choices*. Sydney: New South Wales Department of Education.

Senate Employment, Workplace Relations, Small Business and Education References Committee. (2001). *The education of gifted children*. Canberra: Commonwealth of Australia.

Senate Select Committee. (1988). *The education of gifted and talented children*. Canberra: Australian Government Publishing Service.

Shore, B., Cornell, D., Robinson, A., & Ward, V. (1991). *Recommended practices in gifted education: A critical analysis*. New York: Teachers College Press.

Vialle, W. (1991). *Tuesday's children: A study of five children using multiple intelligences theory as a framework*. Unpublished doctoral dissertation, University of South Florida.

Vialle, W. (1994a, November). *Racism in the classroom*. Paper presented at the Annual Conference of the Australian Association for Research in Education, Newcastle.

Vialle, W. (1994b). Identifying children's diverse strengths: A broader framework for cognitive assessment. In P. Long (Ed.), *Quality outcomes for all learners* (pp. 90–100). Clifton Hill, Victoria: Australian Association of Special Education.

Vialle, W. (1995). Giftedness in culturally diverse groups: The MI perspective. *Australasian Journal of Gifted Education*, 4(1), 5–11.

Vialle, W. (1997). Multiple intelligences in multiple settings. *Educational Leadership*, 55(1), 65–69.

Vialle, W., & Perry, J. (2002). *Teaching through the eight intelligences*. Melbourne: Hawker Brownlow Education.

Vinson, T. (2002). *An inquiry into the provision of education in New South Wales*. Retrieved July 30, 2002, from http://www.pub-ed-inquiry.org.

PART THREE

EUROPE

Throughout Europe, new educational structures, pedagogies, and teacher training programs enable innovative MI applications. Translating theory to practice, several contributors describe integrating MI with approaches such as teaching for understanding and "flow" theory. Successful MI applications are as diverse as the educational contexts. Novel learning environments support the development of multiple intelligences. A cave in a classroom, flow activity centers, and a science theme park transcend the limits of traditional notions about where and how children learn. Inclusive educational policies, restructured teacher training, and achievement in reading are among the positive results reported by contributors. These chapters offer a powerful portrait of teachers as change agents. A bottom-up approach can be a powerful strategy in educational reform.

CHAPTER 12

Multiple Intelligences in Norway

Mia Keinänen

Education in Norway emphasizes values similar to MI: it promotes multimodal inquiry, strives for individually adjusted education, and rejects narrow measures of students' performance. Indeed, from the late 1990s, educators in Norway have used MI theory in their practice, and today at least seventy-one schools and kindergartens implement MI-theory. In a country of four million people, this is surprisingly many.

In this chapter, I postulate three reasons for the current wave of MI-inspired schools in Norway: it is a tool for egalitarian education, it complements the core values of Norwegian education, and it is a tool for individual education. I also discuss the recent trend toward greater quantification in education in Norway. The poor performance by Norwegian students in the Programme for International Student Assessment study has prompted a new school reform that may dilute MI-inspired and other progressive education.

Few other countries come closer than Norway to having a national educational system that reflects the core values of multiple intelligences: it emphasizes the multiplicity of human activity, strives for individually adjusted education, and rejects narrow measures of students' performance. Furthermore, with at least seventy-one schools and day care centers throughout the country incorporating multiple intelligences in their curriculums to some degree, the theory has a visible presence within the Norwegian educational system.

I thank the staff and the students at Apeltun school, Gjerpen school, Grønli school, and Torvmyrane school, as well as the staff at Porsgrunn and Skien municipalities, for generously sharing their experiences with MI with me. Jorunn Spord Borgen provided me key contacts and helped me to understand the complex case of Norwegian educational system. Ola Erstad offered important background information. I also thank Gudmund Hernes for his invaluable insights on education in Norway. I gratefully acknowledge the financial support from the Academy of Finland.

VALUES IN EDUCATION IN NORWAY

In Norway, education has always been free for everyone. Today school is mandatory for all children between the ages of six and sixteen. All children are also entitled to attend a three-year free upper secondary program. Most schools are public schools. Providing equal rights for education has been fundamental to the Norwegian social-democratic welfare state and is connected to the egalitarian ideal in Norwegian society in general. Historically Norway was a poor country ruled by Danish or Swedish monarchs, whose population was distributed in geographically distant rural communities. The inhabitants of the villages developed fairly independent means of survival and governance based on democratic cooperation. Absence of aristocracy and strong local communities fostered populist values such as defense of small communities, emphasis on democratic values, and rejection of market forces (Welle-Strand, Tjeldvoll, & Thune, 2004).

Today Norway is the world's third largest oil exporter and one of the richest countries in the world. Nevertheless, its welfare policies continue to reflect traditional populist values. Each citizen is guaranteed free access to health care and education, as well as unrestricted participation in democratic decision making regardless of gender or ethnicity. Such efforts have established Norway as an impressively egalitarian country that for six years has topped the World Human Development Index that measures general well-being in countries worldwide.

Embedded in the egalitarian ideals is also another implicit law commonly known in Norway as the Jante Law. Introduced by Norwegian-Danish author Aksel Sandemose in his 1933 novel about a small village in Denmark, the law has ten rules, each a version of "don't think you're anyone special or that you are better than us." In other words, while striving for perfect equality, there is cultural pressure to stay within the norm and not to excel, or at least keep quiet and remain modest about accomplishments. Claus Magnus, a teacher in Gjerpen school, explains: "Social democracy is so present. You are not allowed to be good at something, almost. Everybody is supposed to be equal."

At the same time, Norwegian education has emphasized personal growth as the most important aim (Welle-Strand et al., 2004). This emphasis has been reflected in the Norwegian curriculum by placing a high importance on play, group inquiry, and individually motivated activities as tools for learning. The focus has been solidified through various educational reforms. The Reform of 1994, for example, introduced a core curriculum that summarizes the purpose of education.

The core curriculum, written mainly by the minister of education at the time, Gudmund Hernes, a Johns Hopkins–educated sociologist, lists six dimensions education should foster: the spiritual human being, the creative human being, the working human being, the liberally educated human being, the social human being, and the environmentally aware human being. The seventh dimension, the integrated human being, is an integration of the previous six. The categories were derived from the statement of goals (*formålparagrafs*) in the national laws for primary, secondary, and higher education. Furthermore, Gudmund was inspired by American theorists James Coleman (1972) and the cultural literacy movement by E. D. Hirsch (1988). "It is a foundation document of the whole education system in Norway," explained Hernes in an interview for this chapter. "The interesting thing is that it is not just the standard knowledge, it is not just the three Rs the core curriculum specifies; it also talks about the social skills, the capacity to exert oneself in order to achieve new knowledge, leadership skills, and so on."

Indeed, although Hernes was not aware of multiple intelligences when creating the document, it specifies a broad-based education similar to the perspective of MI. The core curriculum was not changed in subsequent reforms in 1997 and 2006. The Reform of 1997 also requires schools to use project-based learning, the Education Law of 1998 provides for schools to adjust their teaching to the needs of each individual child, and the Reform of 2006 (knowledge promotion) continues the focus on individual learning and introduces goals for students for each year.

STATUS OF MI THEORY IN NORWAY

When MI theory was published in 1983, it received some attention in Norway. However, the early reception was mainly critical. Ola Erstad, an associate professor of education at Oslo University, explains that this is because the theory was discussed only among academics in pedagogy at universities and not among broader circles of educators. According to Erstad, the Norwegian academic climate of the 1980s was strongly characterized by egalitarian views of learning and social learning theories that were less concerned with intelligence. The MI view was thus regarded as elitist and interpreted as a method of looking for talent and giftedness.

Jorunn Spord Borgen, a research professor at the Norwegian Institute for Studies in Innovation, Research, and Education, explains that MI theory was then somewhat overlooked for the next fifteen years. In the late 1990s, it was picked up by educators who were drawn to it because it resonated with their experience in schools. In fact, currently there is an active effort by many schools in Norway to integrate MI into their curriculums.

Norwegian schools were introduced to MI principally through media or visiting educators from Denmark, where MI has been implemented for longer. Of the schools implementing MI in Norway, I consider four places closely: Torvmyrane

School in Florø and Apeltun School in Rådal as well as Grønli and Gjerpen schools in the municipalities of Porsgrunn and Skien, respectively, where all teachers receive basic training on MI and are required to find ways of implementing it in their teaching.

Torvmyrane School is a public primary school of 220 students between the ages of six and twelve, as well as a child care facility for 80 children between the ages of one and six. It is located in the picturesque small town of Florø on the west coast of Norway, north of Bergen. Built in 1998, Torvmyrane school uses the MI perspective and philosophy for children as tools for learning and teaching.

Apeltun School is a public primary school of 270 students in Rådal near Bergen on the west coast of Norway. Established in 2003, it too has a focus on MI for children. The school has an open architecture plan: students work in groups within one large open space, not in separate classrooms. Apeltun won the Queen Sonja Prize for 2007, awarded to a school that offers a rich, multifaceted, and inclusive learning environment.

Porsgrunn and Skien municipalities are located in southeast Norway in the region of Telemark. There are seventeen schools in Porsgrunn and twenty-nine schools and twenty-two day care centers in Skien that are all required to use MI as a part of their teaching. All schools and day care centers are public. In Porsgrunn, I visited Grønli primary school of 290 students and in Skien the Gjerpen lower secondary school of 348 students. Porsgrunn implements a flexible learning strategy that includes MI and Dunn and Dunn's (1992) learning styles. Although educators often combine learning styles with an MI approach, these two are fundamentally different psychological constructs; learning styles refers to way in which individuals usually like to learn, and intelligences refers to the computational power of the mental system. Since August 2006, all schools in the municipality have been required to use MI and learning styles in their teaching. In Skien, the municipality implemented MI, learning styles, and learning strategies (referred to as the MILL project) from 2003 to 2007. Learning strategies is a collection of cognitive strategies including Carol Santa's learning-to-learn theory. The goal of these cognitive strategies is to enhance the students' metacognition, their understanding of their own learning. The three approaches in the MILL project are about complementary but different constructs; MI is about our biopsychological potential to process information in different ways, learning styles are about our customary ways of learning, and learning strategies are about our awareness of our learning.

Considering the large number of schools and day care centers in Norway that incorporate MI theory in their curriculum, one could talk about a wave of MI in the country. Apart from the fact that MI strongly resonates with educators' practical experience in schools in Norway, as it does elsewhere in the world, I postulate four reasons for MI's popularity in Norway: (1) some educators have been very active and organized in promoting MI theory, (2) it is seen as a tool for egalitarian education, (3) it fits the aim of educating the seven sides of human beings specified in the core curriculum, and (4) it helps educators address the demand for individual education. I look at each of these points more closely.

A Top-Down Implementation Approach

The municipalities of Porsgrunn and Skien employed a top-down approach to implementing MI in schools and day care centers. They organized information sessions on MI and the other approaches that were mandatory for all teachers in the municipality. All teachers were required to use the theories in their teaching, although they were free to choose how and to what extent to do this.

The MILL project in Skien was remarkably well organized. It was led through a central management team that consisted of the board, project leaders, and a project group of five consultants. Each school had a few teachers who acted to spread MILL theories to the other teachers. After the first year of the project, the MILL team adjusted the plan according to the needs of the schools, thus making the process reciprocal. Skien also organized two conferences in 2005 and 2007 on the theme. Six hundred and four hundred participants, respectively, from all over Norway took part.

Egalitarianism

Unlike the early interpretation of MI theory in the 1980s, MI is now seen as contributing to the cultural ideal of equality and inclusion in Norway. As Øivin Monsen and Tone Aasrud, the headmaster and the superintendent, respectively, of Torvmyrane School, state: "MI is emancipating in every way. No elitism." The plurality of MI highlights the fact that everybody is good at something, as Kristi Odeèn, headmaster of Apeltun School, attests: "MI theory has been important for our teachers in terms of recognizing that everybody has strengths." The educators also feel the MI perspective democratizes their relationships with students' parents. In Torvmyrane, teacher-parent discussions are based on children's strengths, weaknesses, and preferences in the different intelligences rather than their performance in math, geography, physical education, and so forth. Øivin explains: "That is also emancipating because when you talk about subjects, the teacher says your child does well there but not there. But when you talk about intelligences, you are on an equal footing; the parents know more about their child than the teacher does. The parent-teacher talk becomes more of a conversation than a lecture."

Indeed, many educators mentioned that viewing students through the lens of MI builds overall mutual acceptance. Understanding that everybody has individual strengths lessens the discrimination of students who may be less conventional. Øivin points out how this understanding fosters a feeling of inclusion within the school community: "Also in terms of school dropouts, you drop out or you rebel when you feel you have nothing to lose. If there is nothing for them, what is there to lose? Multiple intelligences gives the students a feeling of their own worth that conventional schools are not capable of giving because they are so narrow-minded or mathematical-logical or linguistic." Thus, MI creates an atmosphere where all students can thrive, complying with the ideal of providing equal opportunities for all in the Norwegian society.

Educating the Core Curriculum Values

According to the core curriculum, education should foster seven qualities. The MI perspective fits these aims and also extends them. Since the core curriculum is a binding guiding document for implementing educational policies in Norway, it establishes an implicit value system that contributes to the current wave of MI-inspired schools in Norway. When I asked the author of the core curriculum, Gudmund Hernes, whether he feels that his work has set the stage for MI, he answered: "Absolutely. Because there are the same basic ideas underlying much of the core curriculum and the multiple intelligences."

Thus, the core curriculum has created an aptitude for broad-based education. MI has helped educators concretize the core curriculum values. "It has something to do with how you look at pupils. The core curriculum makes teachers notice that students are different. Together with multiple intelligences, it makes a whole. They fit together," explains Ellen Cathrine Rødnes, a teacher at Grønli School.

As an example, Apeltun School implements and integrates core curriculum and MI on two levels. On the top level, Apeltun organizes the school year thematically into eleven sections, each focusing on one or more intelligences or core curriculum values. For example, in May the theme is the core curriculum value "The Environmentally Aware Human Being: Nature," during which the focus is on naturistic intelligence. During this time, the students make outdoor field trips, work on their school yard planting new plants, and work on themes related to nature in most subject areas.

MI is also applied in the organization of students in the open architecture space in Apeltun. Music teacher Inger Lien Røe developed a method she calls the "musical elements," a series of brief musical elements that teachers use to get students' attention rather than shouting, which is disturbing in a shared space. These rhythms and tonal intervals are done by an instrument or by singing or just body language with punctuated silence. All teachers use the method. Inger explains: "It is integrated music education. The kid doesn't know it, but it is. While conducting the school choir, I have noticed that the students are much more ready to learn new melodies because of musical elements. They are more conscious of different sounds and can better repeat tones." Thus, musical elements, which grew out of a practical need, is a method that contributes to musical intelligence in multiple contexts. In its simplicity, it is an elegant example of how an MI-inspired approach can be used to fit local needs, as well as to promote creative and integrated human beings.

Individually Adjusted Education

A law passed in 1998 requires schools to adjust teaching to the individual needs of every child. However, the law does not state how to implement this requirement. MI offers teachers concrete ideas of how to offer individually adjusted teaching. "We have to know what to do when each child has to have education adjusted to them. MI is helpful for that," explains Kristi Odeèn, headmaster of Apeltun School. Bjørg Haugen, pedagogic leader of Torvmyrane day care center, continues, "The MI perspective gives a clear framework and new ideas for how to explore a theme." For example Åse Saunes, a sixth-grade teacher at Torvmyrane School, designs activities that span all intelligences for each topic she is teaching, which gives her more breadth to meet the needs of individual students. Sometimes the students get to work with their preferred intelligence, and sometimes they are challenged to take up an intelligence they are less comfortable with. Thus, MI enables Åse and other MI teachers to find ways to organize activities to meet individual needs.

Some schools also challenge students to build an intellectual profile for themselves using MI. At Torvmyrane School, in order to start the process of thinking in terms of intelligences rather than conventional school smarts, the parents, together with their child, fill in an MI questionnaire that maps the child's intelligence profile in preparation for first grade. According to the teachers, better understanding of their strengths and weaknesses better equips students to self-adjust their learning in subjects, further helping the teachers with the goal of individual learning plans.

CHALLENGES

Schools implementing MI have also faced challenges. The two main challenges mentioned were the lack of knowledge of how to implement the theory in practice and how to balance MI against other developments in Norwegian education.

Lack of Knowledge About MI

The teachers at the schools I visited were introduced to the MI approach through an active headmaster or administrator who found MI theory compatible with their vision. However, when trying to inspire the teachers to follow their lead, they often face some resistance. "The staff is in doubt. Are we doing it right or not?" asks Øivin from Torvmyrane School. Teacher Ellen Cathrine from Grønli school tells of her experience: "The intelligences, they were confusing to me actually. We felt that the intelligences were pushed down on us, and nobody knew how to use them. It was very confusing."

All of the teachers I talked to care deeply about their teaching practice and take their responsibility as educators seriously. They want to implement MI with integrity. However, because of the lack of clear, authorized guidelines, teachers are largely responsible for finding ways to implement MI by themselves. This requires time, effort, and know-how, and teachers do not have a lot of any of these. Therefore, it is understandable that questions and uncertainties arise.

In Skien and Porsgrunn municipalities, where MI is coupled with learning styles and learning strategies, the focus had shifted more toward learning styles because the teachers find them easier to implement. Furthermore, the educators there do not see multiple intelligence and learning styles as separate entities but rather different expressions of the same idea. This is problematic since Howard Gardner has repeatedly and explicitly disassociated the two theories, pointing out that some of the methods learning styles advocate are questionable and may promote superficial rather than deeper application of MI.

The superficial application of MI has its strengths, however. Providing multimodal activities can be entertaining and may be more effective at engaging students with learning difficulties. However, a deeper application of MI challenges both the low- and high-performing students to probe questions more profoundly. This is especially important in Norway, where, in connection with the implicit Jante Law, it is emotionally easier for teachers to help students with problems than those who are talented. An illustrative example is a conversation I had with one of the MI teachers about the national standardized tests that were recently reintroduced. The teacher worried about the low-performing students because of the anxiety they felt about performing poorly on the tests. When I asked what should be done about this, the teacher answered that the tests should be made easier so that everybody would feel good about doing them. Merete Jølstad, an educational advisor from Porsgrunn commune, explains, "It is very hard for Norwegian teachers to put somebody above others; they would much rather concern themselves with helping the low-achieving students."

With a lack of information about MI, teachers are more likely to implement it superficially or turn to other similar but more codified approaches. This may exacerbate the deeper cultural bias for keeping everybody equal and not providing enough challenge for more advanced students.

Recent Developments: The Programme for International Student Assessment Study and the Knowledge Promotion

The results of the Programme for International Student Assessment (PISA) study, a multinational comparative study of mathematical, scientific, and reading skills of fifteen year olds in the more than sixty Organization for Economic Cooperation and Development (OECD) and collaborative countries, has prompted many countries to reassess their educational systems and its efficacy. This is the case for Norway. Used to topping international rankings such as the Human Development Index and Global Peace Index, Norway has been shocked by its mediocre performance on PISA. In the most recent study, published in December 2007, Norway hit an all-time low in the rankings, scoring well below the OECD average.

The results of the first PISA study in 2000 were published at a time when Norway was already concerned about its standard of education and the lack of attention to fostering a knowledge society. This reflected a fear that the enormous oil revenues had become a cushion that inhibited improvements in key areas of society such as business and education. PISA confirmed that when measuring quantitatively, Norwegian schools and universities were mediocre, despite Norway's spending more money on education than any other country in the world. The conservative government that came to power in 2001, and in particular the new minister of education, Kristin Clemet, set out to address this problem by launching a sizable effort to build the Norwegian knowledge society.

As part of this effort, a new school reform, Knowledge Promotion, was drafted and implemented in the fall of 2006, introducing fundamental changes to the national curriculum at all school levels. National multiple-choice testing was reintroduced for grades 5 and 8. The reform specifies what students are expected to learn each year in each subject and identifies five basic skills that should be cultivated through all subject matter: the ability to express oneself orally, the ability to read, the ability to do arithmetic, the ability to express oneself in writing, and the ability to make use of information and communication technology.

The basic skills identified by the reform are precisely the skills the PISA tests for. Indeed, although educators using MI in Norway unanimously welcome the clearer goals for teaching and learning, they also expressed concern about the implicit value system ingrained in the reform. "The main problem about it is that the public debate about it is very reactionary, a very conservative, a very right-wing way of thinking school" explains Øivin. Also, the resemblance of the new reform and the PISA study did not go unnoticed. "I think our recent reform is greatly inspired by the PISA test and other international tests," explains Jens Petter Berg, an educational advisor in the Porsgrunn municipality. In terms of the MI perspective, the new reform seems to have different goals. "I think of them as opposites," Øivin explains and continues: "The thinking about the reform is contrary to multiple intelligences. But I don't think they have to be opposite because the use of multiple intelligences may help in reaching these goals."

In fact, the staff at Gjerpen School in the Skien municipality believe that because of their MILL project, they are actually ahead in implementing the reform of 2006. An important goal of the MILL project, as well as the new reform, was to increase metacognition, the students' self-understanding of their learning, which Gjerpen achieved in part through MI. This puts Gjerpen one step ahead of others in terms of reaching the goals of the new reform, as teacher Claus Magnus notes.

However, the new reform interferes with teaching through MI in at least two ways. First, implementing the new reform takes up teachers' time and energy, reducing time spent on MI. Second, yet another reform may make the teachers think of MI as a passing trend. Nevertheless, the teachers and headmasters I talked to feel strongly about retaining the MI perspective when implementing the new reform. "Every time we talk about Knowledge Promotion, we remind the teachers we are still thinking in terms of MI and learning styles. We think it is important," explains Bjørn Kronstad, the headmaster of Grønli School.

Indeed, although the reform specifies clear goals for what should be learned at different levels, it retains teachers' freedom to teach those goals whichever way they see fit. Thus, there is still room for an MI perspective or other alternative approaches.

CONCLUSION

Much of what MI promotes already exists in Norwegian education. It helps educators make more vaguely defined educational ideals concrete and expand their teaching practice. However, local implementations may vary drastically because putting MI in practice is not codified. The local variation is both a strength, because it enables educators to address vastly different problems, and a weakness, because it may leave some teachers unsure what to do, which may lead to reduced quality or quantity of implementation. Furthermore, alarmed by its PISA results, Norway introduced the Knowledge Promotion reform that focuses on the key areas the PISA tests for. There is a danger that Norway's remarkably broad educational focus will narrow.

With sensitivity to MI, Knowledge Promotion could escape its seeming pitfall of teaching for the test, not for life, and be the clarification and quality control the Norwegian education system needs while retaining its progressive focus. The results of this union will not be immediate. Indeed, most of the schools implementing MI in Norway adopted this approach only a few years ago. If it takes hold, the schools implementing MI may experience some impressive results in terms of improvement in student learning.

References

Coleman, J. S. (1972). How do the young become adults? *Review of Educational Research, 42*(4), 431–439.

Dunn, R., & Dunn, K. (1992). *Teaching elementary students through their individual learning styles: Practical approaches for grades 3–6.* Boston: Allyn & Bacon.

Hirsch, E. D., & Trefil, J. S. (1988). *Cultural literacy: What every American needs to know.* Boston: Houghton Mifflin.

Welle-Strand, A., Tjeldvoll, A., & Thune, T. (2004). Norway moving away from populist education? *Acta Paedagogica Vilnensia, 12.* http://www.leidykla.vu.lt/inetleid/acta_pae/12/straipsniai/str10.pdf.

CHAPTER 13

The Application of MI Theory
in Danish Education

Hans Henrik Knoop

Following a brief survey of Denmark's educational history, I share two cases of how the application of MI has played out in Danish education. These cases highlight how MI has informed teaching, what opportunities have thereby been made available, and what problems have occurred. The first case regards a municipal comprehensive school where a group of very dedicated teachers have combined the theory of multiple intelligences (Gardner, 1993, 1999) with the theory of flow (Csikszentmihalyi, 1990). The second case is about a successful television program that was aired on national television for six consecutive weeks in spring 2007. As portrayed on the program, individualized teaching created results that had been deemed impossible after eight years of reading failure in ordinary school.

While not without controversy, the idea of respecting individuals and individual differences in particular has a long tradition in Danish education. A few historical notes leading up to Danish education today may help to explain why Howard Gardner's theory of multiple intelligences (MI) has had wide inspirational impact in this country.

According to legend, a French Benedictine monk, Ansgar, was the first missionary to visit Denmark around 822 A.D. He freed twelve male thralls (slaves) so that they could be educated in the first school in Denmark, at Hedeby in Schleswig. This liberation of slaves some twelve hundred years ago could be regarded as an emblematic precursor to current battles of progressive education in Denmark: that is, the struggles to find a path somewhere between the overstandardized and understandardized in education. In the meantime, many smaller steps toward human liberation and greater acknowledgment of individual differences, the hallmark of MI theory, were taken. Here are a few of the most notable.

From about 1100 A.D., religious houses arose all over Denmark. In their cloisters, boys from surrounding villages, as well as girls now and then, were instructed in elementary math and in dogma; soon after, the trades and crafts called for more practical schools. Some four hundred years later, when the Lutheran Reformation came to Denmark in 1536, Protestants broke up the Catholic school system and reorganized education under the crown and the estate. The Church Law of 1539 was Denmark's first educational legislation mandating formal schools in all provincial boroughs. An important step in the direction of general education was taken in 1721 when King Frederick IV established 240 schoolhouses bearing the royal insignia. He named them "cavalry schools" due to a division of the country into military districts at the time. Through pressure to prepare children in literacy prior to religious confirmation, initial steps toward compulsory educations were then taken.

Yet only after the so-called philanthropic movement, an educational school of thought especially inspired by the French philosopher Jean Jacques Rousseau (1712–1778) in the second half of the eighteenth century, did Denmark succeed in creating a school for ordinary people that was open to all children. Rousseau is famous for his assumption that human beings are basically noble savages, corrupted by the chains of culture, leading further to the assumption that children need very little discipline in order to thrive since they are inherently "good." However, modern science does not give much credence to this one-sided notion, as humans appear to have had an extremely violent history (Pinker, 2002; Wrangham & Peterson, 1996). But Rousseau was highly influential at the time, and the idea of being able to live peacefully without power structures was of obvious appeal to many groups in society.

State-planned training of teachers was developed in parsonages and training colleges. In 1814, two education acts were adopted to introduce better municipal primary schools and independent schools for children in even the most distant rural areas of Denmark. With the Napoleonic wars and a severe agricultural crisis threatening to cripple educational reform, the government temporarily resorted to the mechanical Bell-Lancaster method of education. By this method, formulated in the industrial north of England, the cost for teachers was reduced drastically by simplifying the curriculum and giving each teacher very large numbers of pupils. Understandably this method generated substantial opposition, not the least from parents who demanded something better for their children.

The opposition received strong support from poet-clergyman Nikolai Frederik Severin Grundtvig (1783–1872), who has ever since had a strong influence on Danish education. For one thing, Grundtvig wanted to reduce the literacy mandate of the school to make room for more natural, liberal, and individualized ways of learning, both in and out of school. Another important contribution from him was the foundation of so-called folk high schools: these were "open schools" for adolescents and adults, especially in distant rural areas, who would otherwise have no chance of "enlightenment."

Strongly inspired by Grundtvig, the teacher Christen Kold (1816–1870) brought the ideas powerfully into practice by laying the foundation for a distinctively Danish parent-controlled school known as the free school, an alternative to state-sponsored education. In 1894 and 1900, new acts of education promoted significant upgrades in teacher training and expanded the curriculum to reflect the societal need following modernization and urbanization of the Danish society. The so-called middle school was essential in this reform. Two streams emerged: an exam stream to bridge elementary school and gymnasium and a free stream to lead toward more practical work. With further acts of education in 1937, 1958, and 1975, Danish education was steadily changing to ever more egalitarian, gender-equal, informal, and, many will say, more humane educational forms. Thus, from 1975, all general streaming of children was abolished, and in legislation in 1994, it became mandatory that a pupil be nurtured to develop "all-around," that is, develop a multitude of talents and aspects of personal being in a comprehensive school. More specifically, at the methodological level, for the first time in twelve hundred years of Danish education, it had become mandatory to teach in differentiated ways so as to accommodate the needs of different pupils facing the same curriculum.

Given this historical perspective, it would seem rather surprising if MI theory did not catch on in Denmark. And it did. The 1994 act was arguably the single most important factor indirectly promoting widespread popularity of MI in the following years. The first paragraph of the act's general aim stated, "The Folkeskole shall—in cooperation with the parents—further the pupils' acquisition of knowledge, skills, working methods and ways of expressing themselves and thus contribute to the all-around personal development of the individual pupil" (Ministry of Education, 1994).

Later, from around 2003, this aim was specified into three topics, termed "many ways to learn, desire to learn and learning together" (Ministry of Education, 2003). These three ideals were to be seen as ranking above and across all other curricular, and more disciplinary, demands, in direct recognition of the importance of individual differences, the joy of learning, and social inclusion. Moreover, a number of personal skills were stipulated so as to promote pupils' chances of experiencing this ensemble of goals.

To give a few impressions of how the application of MI has played out in the Danish context of education, I present two cases about how MI has informed teaching, which opportunities have thereby been made available, and what problems have arisen. I believe these two cases capture a significant portion of the esprit guiding much MI-inspired teaching in Denmark, and both highlight strengths, weaknesses, opportunities, and threats. To be sure, in Denmark MI has been applied by teachers and psychologists to a broad range of children, from those with severe learning disabilities, to pupils with minor or specific learning difficulties, to more general settings. But it seems quite generally to have been done with the same aspiration of improving the quality of teaching through increased respect for individual differences displayed in these cases.

As a note of caution, it has been argued that many of the Danish MI approaches have been carried out more in hope than by empirically supported professional rigor. Yet whether this is the case or not, the stories that follow show how much can be gained by adopting educational technology that is also sensitive and respectful to individual differences.

ROSENLUND MUNICIPAL SCHOOL, BALLERUP

The municipal Rosenlund School (RS; www.rosenlundskolen.dk), situated in Skovlunde, a suburb fourteen kilometers outside the center of Copenhagen, has 920 pupils, employs approximately a hundred teachers, and is led by a principal and three vice principals. It spans kindergarten to tenth grade, ages six to sixteen years. Two to 4 percent of the pupils have ethnic backgrounds other than Danish, and families in the area have average to lower incomes.

Susanne Aabrandt has been a teacher at RS for twenty-two years. She knows she is doing well when her pupils do not want to leave school in the afternoon. And she knows why she has come to do such good work: combining play, immersion, and learning in her teaching and involving herself with equally committed colleagues. Here we enter their world.

Playful Talents

The third graders are going to have their play hour. After a brief introduction, the pupils engage in different activities. There are games, tasks, computer programs, homework, and plays to start with, and after a few minutes everyone is working. There are two adults in the room and in the surrounding flow centers where special opportunities for full immersion are provided by hermetic glass walls and more secluded corners to work in. One helps in opening cabinets and closets, starting computers, and instructing games and tasks. The other one observes: What do the children choose when we do not choose for them? What goes well, flow-like, for the individual child once on the task? And which children become so immersed in their activities that they find it difficult to obey the teachers and stop when the school day is over? The play hour is a gold mine of information about the individual child's ways of learning and a key for teachers and pupils alike to uncover each child's strengths.

The experiential understanding gained in the play hour can be used later when new and difficult material is to be introduced or when the pupil must work with topics that are in other ways problematic for her or him. The play hour is but one element in the ambitious three-year introductory project at RS.

Three individuals conceived the school introduction project: Gitte Rasmussen, vice head teacher at RS; Sussi Maale, school introduction consultant in the municipality of Ballerup; and Susanne Aabrandt, who besides her teaching assignments is a writer and a sought-after public speaker focusing on MI teaching. After study and work in 1995 in the United States, Aabrandt introduced MI theories and tools (Armstrong, 1999; Gardner, 1993, 1999) and flow (Csikszentmihalyi, 1990) to RS. She drew on the principles in her own class with a wish to share and disseminate the ideas to the school. As vice head teacher, Rasmussen had a dream of creating a new and exciting introductory school environment at RS, and Maale had a strong wish as a consultant to be able to support a more integrated school day for the children and a more coherent way of thinking across the different professional groups working with the children. Thus, a fine mix of personal ambitions and visions for a new school culture became the inspiration and the driver in this project that in several ways turned out to be ground breaking.

Difficult Pedagogical Problems Seeking New Solutions

The Danish comprehensive school has proved inadequate in a number of ways. There are still, and unfortunately often on a daily basis, pupils who are bored during class, pupils who do not think that school has much to do with their life, and pupils who within only a few years have had their self-esteem crushed so badly that their overall development is threatened. Educators and politicians have not been paying sufficient attention; they have failed to appreciate the harm done to children when they do not have proper learning conditions and when the content of the school is not relevant for the individual child.

At RS, teachers find themselves in a mine field. On one side they are up against formal demands, time pressures, and the multitude of tasks inherent in the job; on the other side, they wish to do the best possible for the individual child and meet each child where he or she is, and they seek to improve the school system from within. It will always be the art of the possible. Nobody can get everything right all the time, but much can be done much of the time. And according to RS, much is already being done, and more is under way.

In the theories of MI and flow, Aabrandt and her colleagues saw tools that could help individual children develop their full potential. The inspiration for combining these two theories came from the well-known American Key School in Indianapolis, one of the pioneers in the field. When Aabrandt visited there in 1995, teachers were already combining MI and flow theory as crucial parts of the foundation for their pedagogy (see Chapter Twenty-Four, this volume). Aabrandt saw this combination as potent. MI allowed finer distinctions between pedagogical content and methods, while flow theory illuminated the dynamics of psychological and social processes.

The application of MI and flow theory at RS differs from the original model created by the Key School in several elaborate ways. The centers at RS are fully accessible for pupils throughout the school day. They are used for play hour, specific MI activities used to draw MI profiles, and free play in the afternoon. Thus, contrary to the Key School, where specific "flow teachers" are assigned, all teachers and pedagogues at RS make use of the centers, and part of ordinary teaching is placed in the centers, thereby functioning as material and resource areas at RS. At the Key School, they do it the other way around: experience made in the flow center is used later to strengthen ordinary teaching.

An Idea Brought to Life

In 2002, the whole school was more or less turned upside down: young pupils moved to the section where the older pupils usually were, and vice versa. The common areas of what before was an open-plan building were decorated with intelligence-specific flow workshops and places. Materials and activities were now organized in ways very different from what had gone before. All existing materials were distributed according to which intelligence they most directly related, and new materials for bringing the different intelligences in play were acquired. New and old furniture was placed in ways so that every "intelligence area" or "activity area" had a number of workplaces. In addition, a collection of materials that in part supported and in part challenged the individual intelligence was gathered. In this way the areas could be used for more intense immersion and as resource centers at the same time, covering each intelligence.

Four months of hard work passed between the conception of the idea and the time that the new premises were fully functional. Today improvements continue to come about through the spirited engagement of teachers and pedagogues. The vision was to create a learning environment that provided professional integrity and coherence, could be used for formal and informal purposes, and first and foremost made sense and was authentically meaningful to everyone involved. For the individual child, the aim was to work in ways that provided experience-based, that is, firsthand, understanding of one's own strengths and learning resources, something of benefit throughout life.

In the initial physical setting, an open-plan complex housed both central areas and the classrooms. Today glass walls and doors have been mounted at the individual rooms to lower the noise level. The central room is still one large area, though visually divided in two, surrounding a multipurpose hall in the middle that can be locked. The two parts of the central room house the intelligence-specific flow centers. Included are work spaces, exhibitions, individual pupil storage, secure storage for materials for the teachers, and a wagon that can be pulled into the classroom as needed. The central rooms also make up a convenient transit route for the approximately 250 pupils up to third grade.

The furniture is coded so that each intelligence has its own color. One picks up nonverbal information about which primary intelligence is at work at a given time; clean-up is much easier since it can be accomplished by even the smallest children. In the work space for linguistic intelligence, which children called the "word-smart-space," there are reading and writing materials but also costumes for dramatizing, tape recorders, and numerous word and letter games. The work space for bodily-kinesthetic intelligence houses a small theater, props, costumes, tactile materials, and various light sport facilities and tools. The work space for intrapersonal intelligence is fully equipped with a cave for solitary recluse and reflection, puzzles, study boxes, and ways to keep a diary or create a portfolio along with a tape recorder and a personal audiocassette player for meditation and relaxation. The work space for logical-mathematical intelligence holds games for math but also equipment for measurement, weights, dice, and logical puzzles. The computer room, with ten monitors, is located near the work space in a separate glassed-in area.

Noise and other disturbances will always be an issue in large spaces. This has been partly accommodated by visual screening with closets and book shelves and by placing "intelligences" that do not "interfere auditorily" with one another in close proximity. In other parts of the central room, noisier intelligence-based work spaces are located. Here is the musical intelligence area, with musical instruments, songbooks, and a karaoke system with mirror and costumes. Also featured is the spatial intelligence work space, with materials for visual art, easels, and washing facilities. The work space for interpersonal intelligence holds many games and collaborative challenges, along with an office-like spot for writing letters to friends and family. Finally the work space for the naturalistic intelligence has general tools and materials for studying nature and technology including field trips; it houses a turtle and a little weather station.

The work spaces are used in a multitude of ways. Sometimes they are used to dive into an individual intelligence through intense immersion, at other times they are used for planning activities, and at still other times for developing new competencies within a certain area. After a year and a half of work in the work spaces, all children are familiar with the basic understanding of MI, they know the flow concept, and they have a good sense of their own profile. According to Aabrandt and Rasmussen, the mutual understanding of the strength of diversity within the group of pupils is significantly reflected in their self-esteem, enthusiasm, and the clear absence of bullying and other bad behavior. Indeed, behavioral problems in this hub of 250 pupils are almost nonexistent.

Often we see pupils in the traditional classroom environments rank each other hierarchically according to intellectual skill, physical agility, or some other perceptible parameter. And mostly the individual pupil knows her or his rank, as well as that of the others, rather precisely. It goes without saying that many pupils must feel intimidated and uneasy over such a clear, if informal, hierarchy. This dynamic is well known at RS, but Aabrandt, Rasmussen, and their colleagues are countering it effectively by bringing many different talents and skills into play at the same time. It becomes clear to everyone that there are many ways to be good and successful and that each child is unique in his or her personal combination of strengths. According to Aabrandt and Rasmussen, the binding motto at RS is, "Others can do things that I cannot; I can do things no one else can; and together we can do much more than we can alone." In other words, RS has worked consciously with individual strengths as a platform for personal development but also as levers for work in their weaker areas, and all immersed in a social atmosphere of mutual respect and recognition.

The mutual understandings that have emerged are described as "almost getting a third teacher" in the classroom. In the individual classrooms, there are words on everything—signs, posters, and many books in support of linguistic intelligence. There are watches, tables, and charts, and a principle of putting everything in its right place, which appeals to logical-mathematical intelligence. There are all kinds of art around, spanning art by professionals to art made by children, and the rooms are made visually stimulating with colors and lights. There are tents and smaller spaces with carpets for quiet time and quiet motor activity. There is conscious use of music, from Mozart to New Age. There are plants, birdhouses, and small gardens, and clear signs, from adults to children, regarding the frames for quality and mutual respect. And all this sits within a purpose of letting the children sense that they are at the right place at the right time—in flow, in their process of life—letting them experience (rather than telling them) that it is of utmost importance for them to show up every day and letting them know that it is not only a good life they live at school, it is the preparation for everything that will follow. Aabrandt sums up:

> Since MI theory was not originally conceived as an educational theory, and since Gardner himself is not giving very precise ideas for implementation of MI, there will always be a large room for interpretation. My suggestion for educational practice has been an attempt at bringing as many of the intelligences in play on

a daily basis as possible: Including methods for conveying difficult content, principles for interior decoration, design of projects and as tools for more authentic and intelligence-fair evaluation. . . . It seems to me that the often rather dubious business of marketing has really taken the theory in, and I have gathered much inspiration from them here. Any well-done TV commercial contains spoken and written language, facts, strong visual and bodily-kinesthetic elements, people acting and interacting and background music that often has hit quality. Education can definitely learn something about affecting communication from these people, just as they may be able to learn something from us, should they have the time.

Thus, the work at Rosenlund Municipal School exemplifies how much can be done when committed practitioners are at work. It shows that the application of MI theory, though certainly also debated in Denmark on theoretical and methodological grounds, is not only possible but also pragmatically defendable—and especially when in the hands of professionals like Susanne Aabrandt and Gitte Rasmussen.

ADVANCED PEDAGOGY ON NATIONAL TELEVISION

The second story about the application of MI and flow theory, here in combination with learning-style and reading-style theories, may be even more extraordinary than the story of RS. It is the story of how the largest television station in Denmark, TV2, became interested in effective teaching.

I was asked whether I would take on the role of responsible expert in a documentary series focusing on what good teachers can do for challenging students. Could something be done in an area in which the school had failed according to the Programme for International Student Assessment (PISA) scores? Could different ways of teaching help eighth graders who had never learned to read properly through the traditional means at school? Could we make a difference in the reading, spelling, and grammar skills if we got the children for ourselves for three weeks in an isolated camp? More than 400,000 Danes suffer more or less from functional illiteracy, with, arguably, spelling the most serious problem in Danish education today. The leaders at TV2 had made it one of their top priorities to make more meaningful reality shows than were seen in the past.

Initially, based in part on my doubts stemming from earlier viewings of such entertainment-slanted programs, I passed the offer. But after understanding how seriously committed the core staff were, I felt honored to accept the role of overall responsible educational expert in the program. Rather than being a top-down approach where theory was brought from the university to the public in the form of a prefabricated program, Plan B, as it was known, soon evolved. The result was a fully collaborative effort in which responsibility for aims, theory, practice, and tools was shared.

Our first task was to base the methodology firmly on scientific grounds. Basically we mapped out a model of ideal circumstances for effective learning drawn from the literature and from experience; worked out a graphic and a verbal version of this; and started training ourselves and the relevant staff. Three levels of expertise were employed: (1) general psychology about learning and well-being (Csikszentmihalyi, 1990; Knoop, 2002, 2006; Knoop & Lyhne, 2005; Schmidt & Aabrandt, 2005) (2) a theory of human strengths: MI (Gardner, 1993, 1999); and (3) theory about learning styles (Dunn, 2003) including reading styles (Carbo, 2007; Schmidt & Aabrandt, 2005). Gardner's distinction between intelligences and learning styles was adopted in that we defined an intelligence as "a way of understanding the world" and a learning style as "a way of learning about the world."

From different regions of Denmark, nine eighth-grade pupils with severe learning challenges were selected on the basis of several criteria: serious, but not hopeless, reading difficulties; no serious mental or behavioral problems; and no serious family problems. The plan that was eventually effectuated spanned six weeks, including downtime during which the cameras ran almost nonstop. The program unfolded as follows.

The nine pupils met with teacher Per for one weekend at a remote camp at the northern coast of Zealand. Here Per assessed the strengths of each pupil, that is, the initial circumstances covering these areas for the pupils:

- Reading, spelling, and grammar skills acquired by means of paper-and-pencil tests and online surveys
- Perceived positive emotions, engagement, and meaning acquired by the online test www.godskole.dk
- Perceived effectiveness of pedagogical methodology
- MI profiles acquired by means of observation, self-reports during interviews, and specially tailored intelligence-fair tests
- Learning-style and reading-style profiles by means of observation, self-reports during interviews, and specially tailored style-fair tests

Everything was filmed, and everyone in the team was there to support Per as necessary.

Based on the results from the camp, Per had one week for preparing the a three-week course. During this week the pupils went to their home school as usual.

Then the three-week course was conducted at another remote camp on the southern Danish island of Møn. Here the pupils were alone with Per and the film crew, with our team in the background from morning until 3:00 P.M.

Then two pedagogues took over the nurture of the pupils, instructed not to interfere with what Per had done earlier and not to try to teach the pupils anything in particular related to reading, spelling, or grammar. The pupils spent the two intermediate weekends at home with their parents. The most important elements explaining the success of the project were a combination:

- A meaningful institutional setting with committed professionals and parents supporting the pupils and each other all the way
- A focus on individual strength profiles (combining MI, learning styles, and reading styles) as levers for improvement in weaker areas (reading, spelling, and grammar)
- A stimulating and joyful atmosphere for immersed learning based on key insights from general psychology and, especially, flow theory

At the end of the three weeks, a formal examination was held in which the progress in the areas of reading, spelling, and grammar was assessed. Special tests were designed in order to match the standardized tests regarding level of difficulty but also to accommodate the content of the three weeks of learning and make reliable comparison with the initial tests possible.

As a final follow-up training, all students were given the task of teaching second graders a lesson on reading at Per's own school two weeks after finishing the course on Møn.

The results of the project were astonishing. Within a month, one teacher, having no exceptional skills in teaching reading or employing MI-related tools, learning styles, or reading styles (though obviously he had a natural teaching talent and strong social skills), was able to raise the academic level of these children about three years on average in reading quality, spelling, and grammatical understanding. More than 600,000 Danes (12 percent of the entire 5 million Danes) watched the program, many for its entire six consecutive weeks. The first episode was even nominated for the Golden Rose, a highly prestigious television award given annually at the Festival Rose d'Or in Montreux, Switzerland. And since the airing, many Danish politicians, including government representatives, have expressed clear wishes to do something along the lines laid out in the plan. Indeed most share an ambition of including it in ordinary practice.

To be sure, the political interest may in part have economical reasons because pupils with these kind of difficulties have typically cost the state around $50,000 each in special intervention alone, for which the state has acquired a load of unhappy teenagers, plus often tiring frustration among teachers. Yet most politicians seem fascinated on the grounds of purely educational and humane motives, often referring to how moved they were by following Plan B and pupils' struggle upward to a much more skilled and optimistic outlook on life.

When asked directly in a follow-up debate program on television, many of the pupils and their parents described what happened as a "miracle." Yet clearly no particular educational wizardry was involved here. We merely used the best theory, methods, and tools we knew of in a consistent manner—something that is in principle an option for everyone. When interviewed later about this achievement by the main professional journal for teachers in Denmark, *Folkeskolen* (Becher Trier, 2007), Per Havgaard summarized his experience: "The most important thing for me is that people understand that Plan B was nothing more than an experiment, if in primetime TV. . . . It is by no means a direct critique of what goes on in schools today, but it is a demonstration of what we are capable of doing if we use what we have at our command today. I am first and foremost a teacher, and I will remain a teacher . . . [but I wish I was better educated]. [At college] we study didactics and pedagogy but we don't learn it."

CONCLUSION

In contrast to what is described in several other chapters in this volume, the focus on individually designed education has deep historical roots in Denmark. Perhaps Denmark's extremely high level of interpersonal trust can be traced back to the Vikings, who very much depended on each other while conquering large countries in small boats. Whether this speculation can be justified, the two cases from Rosenlund Municipal School and Plan B, if not exactly statistically representative for what is going on in Denmark, in many ways capture important basic sentiments and cultural inclinations support-ive of the idea of multiple intelligences. And they clearly show how many Danes are eagerly seeking ways to understand and treat people in more humane and fairer ways. Surely people are not born with equal opportuni-ties in any absolute sense. But the two cases show how we, with intelligent education, based on respect for individual differences and the need for social cohesion, may render absolute differences between pupils less and less impor-tant in the future.

References

Armstrong, H. (1999). *Mange intelligenser i klasseværelset*. København: Adlandia.

Becher Trier, M. (2007). *Det store skoleeksperiment*. København: Fagbladet Folkeskolen.

Carbo, M. (2007). *Hvad enhver lærer og skoleleder bør vide om god læseundervisning*. København: Adlandia.

Csikszentmihalyi, M. (1990). *Flow: The psychology of optimal experience*. New York: HarperCollins.

Dunn, R. (2003). *Fleksible læringsmiljøer*. Fredrikshavn: Dafolo.

Gardner, H. (1993). *Frames of mind*. New York: Fontana Press.

Gardner, H. (1999). *Intelligence reframed*. New York: Basic Books.

Knoop, H. H. (2002). *Leg, læring og kreativitet—hvorfor glade børn lærer mere*. København: Aschehoug.

Knoop, H. H. (2004). *Plan B for talentudvikling*. København: Kognition og Pædagogik 17.

Knoop, H. H. (2006). Når lysten til at lære overlever mødet med skolen. In J. Hejgaard et al. (Eds.), *Mit barn skal I skole*. København: Mejeriforeningen, Rådet for Større Færdselssikkerhed og Skole & Samfund.

Knoop, H. H., & Lyhne, J. (Eds.) (2005). *Et nyt læringslandskab: Flow, Intelligens og det gode læringsmiljø*. København: Dansk Psykologisk Forlag.

Ministry of Education. (1994). Lov om Folkeskolen. Copenhagen.

Ministry of Education. (2003). *Fælles Mål: Elevens alsidige personlige udvikling*. Copenhagen: Author.

Pinker, S. (2002). *The blank slate: The modern denial of human nature*. London: BCA.

Schmidt, S. E., & Aabrandt, S. (2005). *Mange intelligenser i praksis*. Fredrikshavn: Dafolo.

Wrangham, R., & Peterson, D. (1996). *Demonic males*. Boston: Houghton Mifflin.

CHAPTER 14

The Explorama

Multiple Intelligences in the Science Park, Danfoss Universe

Charlotte Sahl-Madsen, with Patricia Kyed

As an important element for strengthening the knowledge base for the activities at Danfoss Universe, a unique theme park in south-west Denmark, Howard Gardner's theory of multiple intelligences has been employed. Gardner's ideas have been drawn on in both the facility design processes and the shape of an entire exhibition, the Explorama, where visitors can learn about multiple intelligences firsthand. The theory has proven inspirational in work at the science park. This chapter explores the larger enterprise, Danfoss Universe, and its various components, manifestations, and interactions. This complex undertaking has as its fundamental aim the improvement of science, technological, and engineering skills among young people in Denmark and elsewhere. The chapter shows that a project stimulated by a particular educational need has broader implications for the development of youth as a whole and may prove useful as well to teachers, businesspersons, and indeed, anyone else who maintains a curiosity about self, other persons, and the wider world.

Figure 14.1 is a drawing of the Explorama, an interactive exhibition, with multiple intelligence installations on the first and second floors in a refurbished building. Visitors to the Explorama can get an understanding of what the different intelligences imply, how they are experienced, and how they are used in everyday life. A principal goal of Danfoss Universe, a science theme park, is to communicate science clearly to visitors. The MI perspective of the Explorama is a valuable tool for this goal.

Virtuelt kort

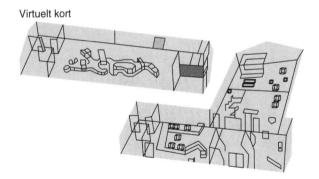

Figure 14.1 The Explorama

In Explorama, it is also possible for visitors to go one step further and map their own intelligence profile based on how well the different challenges are met. For the latter purpose, a small test was developed in collaboration with Howard Gardner. The test is used individually by the students who come to the park to show their own MI profile and also by teachers who want to have a profile of their entire class. Recently businesses have shown considerable interest in a version designed for managers.

Mapping one's own intelligence profile begins with children from seventh grade up using a personal digital assistant (PDA) to answer thirty questions relating to different intelligences. On completion, the user receives a graphic profile of his or her preferred way to learn. The children are then sent to the Explorama, and by using a PDA, they complete practical tests—at least two or three for each intelligence. The class reconvenes to discuss the findings and compare their scores to the profile of the entire class or previous visitors. This comparison is the basis for a discussion of what intelligence is, how we are different, and which jobs need which skills, among many others. Moreover, the PDA provides a valuable opportunity to reflect on one's own intrapersonal intelligence: How precisely can a user predict how he or she will do on the various games and tasks at the Explorama?

This game is also used by adults as part of the workshops, seminars, and other business-related activities that the Danfoss Universe organization offers to companies and organizations. The same thirty profile questions can also be tried by any Danfoss Universe visitor using three PC-based kiosks installed in the Explorama. Their results are then added to our statistics and used for comparisons. As the visitors have fun while learning, they probably do not realize that the activities in the Explorama all relate to multiple intelligence theory. We do, however, want to offer school classes and business visitors the opportunity to understand the theory as well as their own preferred ways to learn.

During the introduction and the discussions in the teaching facility, we stress that the test is meant to be an inspirational and fun way to experience individually preferred ways to learn and that everyone's profiles will be quite different in that respect. We use no numbers to quantify results, only a graphic indication of the profile.

This set of experiences should be seen as a complete learning package: the initial explanation in the teaching facility, the first test using a PDA, the practical tests in the exhibit, and the comparisons and discussions regarding intelligence and abilities back in the teaching facility. Both users and teachers find this test interesting, and it raises awareness of the variety of human capacities and how they can be observed in oneself and assessed by others.

TWO EXAMPLES OF EXPLORAMA ATTRACTIONS

In the "Emotions" exhibit visitors can explore how adept they are at reading other persons' "frames of mind" by examining their facial expressions. A picture of a face fades in on a computer screen, and the visitor must choose one of the three possible frames of mind that best describes the facial expression: "Is the person happy?" "Is the person having fun?" "Is the person concentrating?" When the visitor has chosen which mood best describes the face, a new face appears on the screen, along with three more choices.

After the eight different faces (different ages and sexes) have been shown and classified, the visitor's performance is evaluated. The visitor has the opportunity to see how all of the visitors who have already taken the test have evaluated the different facial expressions, and the visitor can see how he or she evaluated the faces as compared to the others who have done so. There is no official correct answer, simply the consensus—and, perhaps, the wisdom of the crowd. The visitors who have taken the test earlier form the basis for evaluation. Assuming that they have done their best, one gets an impression of whether he or she evaluates facial expressions in the same way as the other persons.

In the "Find the Tune" exhibit visitors try to separate the pieces of music with two different rhythms that play across one another. On the screen, eight sliding buttons adjust the volume. Four of the buttons represent instruments from the one piece of music, and the other four represent instruments from the other piece of music.

The task is to adjust the buttons so that the music sounds harmonious to the user. As it turns out, visitors have very different approaches to the task. Some let all eight soundtracks play at the same time and move the buttons more or less randomly up and down as if playing by ear. Others have a more analytical approach. They close all of the soundtracks and then open them again, one at a time. In this respect, it is much easier to hear which soundtracks have the same pulse. We might say that in the latter case, the visitors are applying logical analysis to a musical task.

The designers of and visitors to the Explorama agree on one thing: it is not possible to give a completely satisfactory verbal description of the Explorama; it must be experienced firsthand. Nonetheless, I will try to convey a sense of the facility. Here are examples of the short tasks and questions that stimulate visitors to solve the challenges posed by the Explorama's diverse attractions:

Logical-Mathematical Intelligence

- *Treasure or tiger:* Read the text and think carefully about it. Which door hides the treasure? Be careful not to let the tiger out!

- *Rush hour:* Can you move the cars around so the red car is able to park on the right-hand side of the street? (See Figure 14.2.)

- *Pottering:* Twelve stones must be placed on the squares with two stones in each row and column and no more than two stones across. Eighteen stones must be placed on the squares with three stones in each row and column and no more than three stones across.

- *Magic square:* Can you move the plates with numbers around so they give the sum of thirty when you add up the rows and columns? If so, all the lamps will light up! (See Figure 14.3.)

Figure 14.2 Rush Hour: Using Logical-Mathematical Intelligence

Linguistic Intelligence

- *Fountain of words:* Turn the wheel. Which word comes up? Change a letter and make a new word. How many words can you come up with before the sand runs through the hourglass?

- *Speak Chinese:* Listen to a sentence spoken in Chinese or Arabic. Can you repeat the sentence so it sounds almost the same?

- *Plain language:* Build a figure behind a screen, making sure your partner cannot see it. Explain how your partner should build a similar figure without peeking.

- *Figure it out:* Sit opposite each other and read the first sentence aloud: "I am a building." How many sentences do you have to read before your partner can guess what you are talking about?

Spatial Intelligence

- *Soma cube:* Can you build a Soma cube by using all the cubes?

- *Pyramid puzzle:* Can you build a pyramid from three pieces?

- *Chinese puzzle:* There are six pieces. You can build a square and you can make all the figures illustrated on the table. Sometimes you think a piece is missing, but it is always possible with the available pieces.

Figure 14.3 Magic Square: Using Logical-Mathematical Intelligence

- *Labyrinth game:* Can you find your way around inside a labyrinth once you have consulted the site map? Can you find your way from where you are now?

- *Memory game:* How many of the thirty images can you remember whether you have seen?

- *Packing problems:* The cupboard is filled with all kinds of geometrically shaped bricks. If you take them all out, can you then put them all back into the cupboard using all the bricks?

Bodily-Kinesthetic Intelligence

- *Obstacle course:* Press the button and hurry through the track with the strings without touching the strings. Press the button on the other side when you finish the course. (See Figure 14.4.)

- *Steady hand:* Grab the handle with the ring at the end of it. Can you lead the ring through the track without letting it touch the metal pole? If you touch the pole, you will set off a loud beep. If you continue to touch the pole, the sound also continues.

- *Shake and quiver:* Can you move the ball from one cup to another when the small cup is positioned at the end of a long, movable stick?

Figure 14.4 Obstacle Course: Using Bodily-Kinesthetic Intelligence

- *Climbing mountains:* The camera and the image behind it turn the horizontal axis into vertical. Can you crawl or make your way across the uneven, horizontal "rock" so it looks as if you are climbing a vertical wall?

Musical Intelligence

- *Find the tune:* In a sea of sounds, some rhythms and tunes can be detected. Can you distinguish the sounds from each other and find the tune?
- *Theremin:* The sound machine, which is sensitive to your movements, constructs light and deep sounds depending on your proximity to the rod at the right-hand side. The strap at the left-hand side controls the volume: come close, and it is completely silent; move farther away, and the Theremin increases its volume. (See Figure 14.5.)
- *Sampler:* The sampler records sounds, which you can then use for composing a piece of music.
- *Hit the note:* Two notes will be played. Listen carefully. Which one is the higher?

Figure 14.5 Theremin: Using Musical Intelligence

Interpersonal Intelligence

- *Teambot:* Two or four persons need to work together to control the robot. Pick up a brick, and place it on the orange circle.
- *Seesaw cooperation:* When you are standing on a seesaw, you constantly feel the presence of the other person. Can you work together at the seesaw by stepping up and down on the seesaw?
- *Emotions:* Look closely at the images. Which emotion do you think the face expresses?
- *Team labyrinth:* Step onto the board and move around so the ball runs from one end of the curved track to the other. Make sure you don't fall off!

Intrapersonal Intelligence

- *Angry dog:* Do you have the guts to put your hand inside the cage and press the button below the dog? The dog's tongue moves while the arrow shifts from normal to brave. It starts drooling and finally it barks. The arrow has then reached "recklessness."
- *Shaky tower:* How tall do you dare to build your tower? It should be able to endure the vibrations. It makes a terrific noise when it all comes tumbling down.
- *Reversed glasses:* How good are you at adjusting? Grab the glasses, take hold of the sticks, and combine two circles in the same color. You will hear a loud beep.
- *Beneath the rock:* Do you have the nerve to lie down beneath the rock? Perhaps you are feeling a bit uncomfortable? Perhaps you are completely confident that the rock will stay there and no harm will come to you.
- *The fakir's bed:* Lie down on the board and press the button. The board slips down and you are now lying on top of "nails." (It makes a bit of noise when the board is moving.)
- *Fakir test:* Put a balloon on top of the nails and lower the board onto the balloon. How many kilos can the balloon endure before it bursts?

DANFOSS UNIVERSE: A SCIENCE PARK BRINGING THEORY AND PRACTICE BACK TOGETHER

A dream came true in May 2005 when Jørgen Mads Clausen, president of Danfoss until October 2008 and currently chairman of the board of directors at Danfoss, and his wife, Anette Clausen, chairman of the board of directors at

Danfoss Universe, inaugurated the Danfoss Universe experience park. They were the driving forces behind the creation of this experience park, which is funded by the Bitten and Mads Clausen Foundation (headed by Peter Mads Clausen, also son of the Danfoss founder).

With some nostalgia, Jørgen Mads Clausen looks back on his childhood when it was possible to take an alarm clock apart and see how it works. It was an eye-opening experience that he still remembers. Today, it is impossible to see how common technology tools work. Clausen believes that being unable to observe how technology functions is a real problem and one of the reasons why too few young people turn to engineering studies. The park is meant to visualize technology and give young people lots of eye-popping experiences. This unusual set of experiences enables them to learn and understand. In the best instance, a visit may shape their lives, and perhaps, one of these young people will be inventive or start a successful enterprise.

When asked whether the park is for the geniuses and geeks, Clausen passionately replied that it is for everyone—boys and girls of all ages. The park emphasizes hands-on experiences that do not require reading explanatory signs to understand. The idea is to entice young people to continue exploring when they get home or back at school. Through school programs, classes can solve specific tasks while in the park. The centrality of the experience is enhanced by preparation before they arrive and follow-up when they are back at school. In addition, the park hopes to nurture development and tourism in the local community and southern Jutland. Clausen also hopes to brand Danfoss by showing that we care about generating interest in science as few other industrial enterprises in the world have done before.

Asked why it is important to generate interest in science, Jørgen Mads Clausen says that we all want to have a society that takes care of our most pressing needs: this cannot happen unless we have flourishing industries that produce new products and engineers and scientists to create the products necessary for us to survive and thrive.

From the very first day, we have been cautious, even humble, with respect to the important job of inspiring young people to be interested in technology. It must be done in the best possible way. We must have access to both scientists and practitioners.

The Universe Foundation

In a targeted attempt to strengthen the knowledge base for the activities at Danfoss Universe as well as for the entire formal and informal learning environment such as science centers, museums, and businesses, the board of Danfoss Universe decided to establish the Universe Foundation. On invitation, Howard Gardner, along with Svein Sjøberg of the University of Oslo, and Charlotte Rønhof, chief of research policy for Danish Industry, accepted an invitation to serve. The board is headed by Anette Clausen. I am the president of the Universe Foundation as well as CEO of Danfoss Universe.

Teaching Facility of the Future

The first task of the Universe Foundation is a project entitled Teaching Facility of the Future, which, as the name implies, will submit proposals for teaching and classrooms of the future. Research has already been done in this field, but little has been converted into practical applications. This project addresses the practical goal in close collaboration with Danfoss Universe and its many science exhibits and attractions. The project will be managed by the foundation, but the actual work will be performed jointly with a vast number of experts from Denmark and abroad. The knowledge gathered and practical examples produced by the foundation will subsequently be made available to the general public.

Universe Research Lab

In a recent initiative, the Universe Foundation established the Universe Research Lab, a scientific research center located in a newly constructed university compound on the waterfront in the city of Soenderborg, about twenty minutes from Danfoss Universe. Headed by Hans Henrik Knoop of the University of Aarhus, a long-time collaborator in Howard Gardner and colleagues' GoodWork Project, the center conducts basic research on learning, creativity, teaching, and innovation in interaction with developers and practitioners in the educational system in general and at Danfoss Universe in particular. An important task for Universe Research Lab is to ensure the research required for further development of the Explorama and related exhibitions is carried out.

As in so many other developmentally dynamic enterprises, we have had to "build the airplane while we were flying." During the establishment of Danfoss Universe and Explorama, we did not have everything we needed to know in place. Therefore, continuing development and optimization is a very natural thing for us. We become wiser and more experienced every day.

WHO DEVELOPED EXPLORAMA? HOW DID THE IDEA ARISE?

It would be convincing, and perhaps for others inspiring, if I could describe a disciplined development process, where clients initially formulated a brief and hired consultants for the task, who then implemented the attractions. Unfortunately, this was not the case. In fact, in retrospect, it can be difficult to answer precisely how Explorama came to be.

The board and group of owners had no doubt that learning would weigh heavily at Danfoss Universe in general and Explorama in particular. Many ideas and proposals for communicating learning and many learning philosophy approaches were studied. As in every other development process, some ideas were rejected along the way. Some ideas were rejected because they were not inspiring enough. Others called for too little user involvement. Some had an old-fashioned scholastic approach and some were much too expensive.

From the discussions, Explorama, as we know it today, gradually emerged. No one person can take credit for the Explorama idea alone. It was the result of the cooperation among the board, international learning and development experts, pragmatic teachers, parents (who had had good and not-so-good experiences with their children's education), as well as a team of designers and architects. Diversity has always been a strength of our development projects. After a slow start and many unusable ideas, the actual concept for Explorama was developed in a few months and construction of the many installations took another few months.

It is a job that we will never finish. We learn continuously and see new possibilities for improvement all the time. We are continually inspired by students, teachers, researchers, colleagues, and others. The Explorama we see today will not be the same tomorrow.

Why Multiple Intelligences?

Howard Gardner asked me once why using MI as a conceptual framework was appropriate in designing a science park. My answer was simple: it is the most convincing way to ensure that optimal learning takes place and is fun. Our ambition is not just to entertain, of course. At Danfoss Universe, one becomes wiser and more curious. We are convinced that this happens best when learning through play. Thanks to Gardner's theory, we are now aware of the importance of communicating scientific knowledge in several ways at the same time. Our ambition is to activate several intelligences. This means that visitors at Danfoss Universe can gain knowledge through reading; listening to instructions, film, and sound sequences; becoming physically involved (as on the ice slide); having sensual experiences (with glacier fissure and the volcano); and solving tasks alone or as a team.

The Challenge

In Denmark (as in most other countries), it is a challenge to inspire school students about science and technology. Over the decades, many have tried, but convincing results are absent. (International studies show this, but this is also the impression we get from the network of teachers who contact Danfoss Universe for guidance.) The will to optimize teaching is there, but the challenge remains: "What should the teachers do differently?"

I suggest that Gardner's research on multiple intelligences be synthesized with Gardner's thoughts on five minds—in particular, his ideas about acquiring discipline, synthesizing knowledge from different spheres, and engaging in innovative, creative thinking (Gardner, 2007). This combination has proven extremely inspirational for Danfoss Universe. It has been an increasingly challenging task to interest pupils in science and technology even though humans have been preoccupied with creating tools since the dawn of human history. The major reason, we believe, is that education has been structured in ways that are neither stimulating nor engaging. So much of education, even today, consists of regurgitating facts and figures rather than engagement in active problem solving and problem finding. At Danfoss Universe, we are trying to combat this. By employing multiple intelligences in the design of facilities and educational processes, we believe we are reaching more children and adults than we would otherwise be able to. The fact that people tend to gain a deeper understanding of things when they are represented in different ways, as allowed for with multiple intelligences, corroborates our assumption.

Knowledge Is Necessary

Too few teachers have a major—or even a deep—interest in science. The few who do have the proper education to teach science are often strongest in subject knowledge but lack pedagogical insight. One requirement is content—the subject of science—but how instruction can be orchestrated is something completely different. This state of affairs was acknowledged early in the concept development of Danfoss Universe. As a consequence, we have initiated partnerships and networks with both scientists and experts in pedagogy. Nevertheless, it was difficult to find experts who were fluent in both areas.

We feel we have a unique park that clearly inspires many young people to develop an interest in science. If anyone should think that we could have done the entire concept development phase differently, I would like to point out the importance of:

- Ensuring that both subject knowledge and pedagogy are taken into consideration from the beginning. It does not help to perceive these as two separate disciplines.

- Mastering the art of making science a relevant part of students' daily lives. In other words, we must start with the situations that young people know from their everyday life.

- Increasing the physical involvement in attractions. Hands-on is not enough. The entire body needs to be involved (we don't have any buttons that can be passively pushed and we never will have).

During Danfoss Universe's development, we had great success in involving young people in the development of the attractions. We have a "test school" agreement with a local school and have established a so-called young ministry.

One might assume that the greatest challenge during the development phase was getting Howard Gardner's theory converted to practice. This was not the case. When the development team and our committed network of teachers (both Danish and German) started, they generated many good ideas for concrete tasks that students should solve in Explorama. Once the content and the purpose of the tasks were clearly defined (and here the teachers carried the greatest load), the developers and designers could make the prototypes fairly easily. They were refined and improved before the final version of floor or table installations could be produced. In some cases, we started with the already developed attractions and made small adjustments.

Our predominant success regarding the development of Explorama, the park's other attractions, and our ambitious future plans have been the inspirational cooperation we have had with international researchers. Together with them, we have been able to translate our research into knowledge for exciting new attractions. They have been (and continue to be) a true and necessary source of inspiration. No one can take on the task of communicating science (or other subjects) without acquiring an understanding of the fundamentals. This is ensured by our network of researchers, among others.

It has not been easy or straightforward. Many things were discussed and considered from many different angles and interests. However, our work together has always been characterized by mutual respect and a joint wish to find the best solutions for the benefit of all students, who are our future. It is a job that merits great effort.

THE IMPORTANT BRIDGE

At Danfoss Universe, we are organized so that we ensure a bridge between Universe Research Lab and our network of researchers and development department. Because many of the researchers also have a considerable interest in seeing our knowledge converted to practical learning processes and new attractions, we continually challenge ourselves with respect to the theory of the many intelligences. At the same time, our accumulated knowledge affects the optimization of existing and all new attractions at Danfoss Universe. The development takes place within a team, where researchers and practitioners work side by side. Students are often involved too so that relevance can be ensured.

EXPLORAMA: AN IMPORTANT CHALLENGE

During the development of Explorama, the many intelligences have been the starting point. The task was to increase consciousness of the different intelligences, and especially to inspire different ways of working with the intelligences by finding out which profile one has and considering the deployment of other intelligences and methods in order to acquire knowledge. Explorama should be inspirational for students, teachers, and the many families with children that visit Danfoss Universe. Today, with the benefit of hindsight, we can see that it would have been optimal if the Explorama was the first attraction inside the park. Insight into which methods are best to acquire knowledge would be an optimal start for a visit to a science park. It is also the first thing that should happen in the cooperation between teacher and students.

We are in the process of developing educational material so that by practicing MI, one can inspire teachers and school management to further spread MI. An example is our cooperation with Universe Research Lab regarding a new knowledge base that converts key facets of the theory of MI to practice, among other things.

Since the opening of Danfoss Universe in 2005, we have had many experiences with MI. There is no doubt that the combination of MI and Five Minds (Gardner, 2007) will be part of the groundwork when we implement the park's next phase. Young people must have their interest in science stimulated and they must have their creativity encouraged. We believe Gardner's ideas are fundamental in achieving these goals.

WHAT WE HAVE LEARNED

The reception that the Explorama has received from its many visitors and the media convinces us that we are on the right track with this complex facility. This being said, however, we are in the process of upgrading and fine-tuning many of the installations. In collaboration with researchers and developers, we are analyzing each installation to ensure that we do as much as we can to make the respective intelligences come across clearly to users. Our goal is that the intelligences function synergistically in the Explorama and that what is learned there can be used subsequently both inside and outside the park. In other words, everyone can learn about his or her own ways of thinking, understanding, and acting, and everyone has the option of learning about others by observing them interact in the Explorama.

Although Howard Gardner was not personally involved in the development of Explorama, he has visited Danfoss Universe several times, and we are pleased that we can discuss our development initiatives with him. On occasion, Gardner himself has expressed admiration for the Explorama, as in this statement from a debate in a Danish journal:

Perhaps the most important contemporary demonstration of MI can be found in Denmark. I am referring to the Explorama at Danfoss Universe, which opened in May 2005. The Explorama features dozens of games, exercises and challenges that draw on different intelligences or combinations of intelligences. These exhibits can be used by children as well as adults of all ages. While the Explorama is not a formal learning environment, individuals can learn a great deal about their own profile of intelligences (intrapersonal intelligence) should they spend some time at the site. Moreover, practice in the various skills should enhance the intelligences in question [Gardner, 2007].

Reference

Gardner, H. (2007). *Five minds for the future.* Boston: Harvard Business School Press.

CHAPTER 15

An English Translation?

Multiple Intelligences in England

Anna Craft

Education in England at the national and local policy levels increasingly emphasizes personalized learning for all young people. This chapter explores current approaches to education futures in England and considers examples of how Howard Gardner's multiple intelligences (MI) theory has influenced teachers and schools seeking to widen participation in learning. Some difficulties inherent in associating MI theory with other approaches—such as learning styles, varied modalities and neurolinguistic programming—are discussed. The chapter closes by exploring reasons why, despite challenges, MI may remain of interest to teachers in England for some time to come.

Howard Gardner's multiple intelligences (MI) theory (1983, 1993) has influenced classroom practitioners in England over a number of years. Initially it appealed especially to those working with lower-achieving students. It has become one of a large number of strategies that enable teachers to address an increasingly demanding vision of education. To understand why classroom practitioners in England find MI theory useful, it is important to understand the significant changes that have occurred in educational policy and practice in the quarter of a century since MI theory was first published. Teachers and schools experienced a squeeze in the late 1980s and early 1990s to teach to the test. This squeeze gradually relaxed to the point where, by the mid-2000s, there are two parallel and interlocked agendas supporting teaching and learning: a culture focused on student and school performance measured by tests, often referred to as a performative culture, and a culture focused on creativity (Troman, Jeffrey, & Raggl, 2007; Craft & Jeffrey, 2008).

EDUCATIONAL REFORM SINCE 1988

In 1988, the Education Reform Act (Department for Education and Science, 1988) presaged huge change in the English education system. Following twenty years that perhaps had focused more on pedagogy and learning than on curriculum, assessment, and school governance, the government introduced in 1989 (Department for Education and Science, 1988), the national curriculum, which would guide the content and assessment of learning for children from ages five to sixteen. It was seen as an entitlement curriculum, in other words, a curriculum that would even out what children might encounter regardless of where they were at school. This curriculum was significant because it recognized both a broad curriculum but also each child's right to have access to the whole span.

The introduction of the national curriculum was accompanied by other changes. Schools were given greater powers to control their financial and other governance. Parents were given greater choice about where to send their children to school. The role of the local education authorities (LEAs) which had, from the 1960s in particular, supported, inspected, and funded schools, was significantly reduced as the spotlight turned to the schools themselves.

This shift of attention to curriculum and assessment was directed at the national level. Combined with a school-based focus for resource and delivery, it offered sharp contrast with the former structure of educational administration. The previous Education Act in 1944 had given LEAs, together with higher education institutions (HEIs) including universities, a powerful role in supporting schools. The new regime gave the secretary of state for education and the civil servants in the Department of Education and Science additional directive powers in relation to curriculum, assessment, and governance. The new regime also increased the rights and responsibilities of schools, diminishing the influence of LEAs and HEIs. This change has been interpreted as a market forces model where resources are distributed based on supply and demand rather than need. This market forces model was, consonant with the values of the then Conservative government, led by Prime Minister Margaret Thatcher, who believed in the market as all powerful in leading and determining social change.

The new regime accordingly increased the influence of the consumers of education (parents and pupils) by introducing market principles into education. This influence encouraged competition among schools based on perceived value-added measures made visible primarily, initially at least, through public release of outcomes from statutory testing at the ages of seven, eleven, fourteen, and sixteen. It was a period that recognized the need for structure and sequence and focused on content and delivery. Government officials responsible for evaluating progress in schools took less account of how teachers nurtured learning while "coverage" and "getting results" took over. A powerful accountability culture that involved regular school inspection and a process of appraisal and performance management within schools emerged. Schools, which now had the power to employ staff, took on less experienced, more malleable, and less expensive staff. Older, more experienced, more expensive staff retired early or moved out of the profession.

The period of change in education from 1989 to 1997 can be seen as reflecting a neoliberal perspective, which placed high value on the capitalist marketplace in distributing resources and opportunities. Neoliberalism has been critiqued by many, including Harvey (2005), who considers it to be a form of hegemonic "creative destruction" on a global basis. To the extent that education policies are harnessed to a Western capitalist, inexorable consumption and development model (Craft, 2005), the ends of education were, it could be argued, during the first years of the national curriculum rather disconnected from the overall project of social and economic prosperity (Craft, 2008a, 2008b).

Yet researchers have documented ways in which teachers resisted this culture of performativity (Woods & Jeffrey, 1996; Woods, Jeffrey, Troman, & Boyle, 1997). Teachers whose creative and resistant practice Woods and Jeffrey documented were committed to enabling access for all learners in making personal meaning from a curriculum. This focus is also a feature of MI when applied to learning in schools. These principles of access and meaning making were to be much more fully developed at the policy level from the late 1990s onward.

THE LATE 1990S: A POLITICAL AND POLICY SWING?

Following the landslide election of a Labour government in 1997 and the succession of Tony Blair as prime minister, the later 1990s saw further change, framed in the context of what became known as New Labour's policies. At the time of writing this chapter (June 2008), Labour is still the ruling party, and Prime Minister Gordon Brown has been in power for twelve months.

New Labour represented the modernization of Labour to reflect a mix of socialist and free market principles. This mix became known in common parlance as the Third Way. While critics (Osler, 2002) argue that the Labour party is no longer the party of socialist principles, New Labour's policies in education nevertheless have sought to bring together social justice and socialist concerns with an expectation to deliver high student achievement in a global knowledge economy.

Along with continued reorganization of government and other centralized policy organizations, the past ten years have been characterized by deeper policy engagement education with a much more radical twenty-first-century futures agenda (Craft, Chappell, & Twining, 2008; Daanen & Facer, 2007; Qualifications and Curriculum Authority, 2008). In part, this radical turn was triggered by the Every Child Matters agenda initiated following the tragic death in 2000 of an eight-year-old child, Victoria Climbie. Her death resulted from a series of failures by the education, health, and welfare systems to identify accurately the neglect she was suffering.

Every Child Matters unleashed a massive and transformational program (discussed further in Chapter Sixteen, this volume). Close attention has since been paid to the early years of education and care, as well as primary, secondary, special, further, and higher education sectors. The futures debate also spans workforce, structures, provision, and governance, as well as curriculum, assessment, pedagogy, and learning. Rapid social, economic, technological, ecological, and political change has affected the governance of education at the national level.

As a consequence, many opportunities have arisen since the late 1990s for schools and other educators to develop pedagogy and learning with less emphasis on content-heavy curriculum and assessment practices focused on accountability to the government. One aspect of change in education has been the introduction of specialist schools and academies. These schools offer expertise in specific aspects of the curriculum. They primarily are funded by the state but with additional contributions from the private sector. White (2008) has argued that this move toward specializing is a reflection of an MI approach to education. These schools provide a range of (to a degree, selective) specialized curricula catering to a wide breadth of intelligences rather than a small number of schools for students with high scores on IQ tests. For example, they make possible the public valuing of bodily-kinesthetic or musical strengths in a way not previously feasible.

PUPIL ENGAGEMENT AND VOICE IN IMPROVEMENT AND TRANSFORMATION

MI theory provides a positive, constructive approach that supports schools and local education authorities in enabling all learners by understanding their talents. There is also growing concern among analysts (Craft, 2008b; Thomson, 2007) about high levels of disengagement and failure among many school students. Schools constructed and enacted using a nineteenth-century model of education are unlikely to meet the needs of students whose lives may span the twenty-first century. Some educators seek to transform the existing school systems (Craft et al., 2008; Futurelab, 2008; Twining, 2007a, 2007b), which can be thought of as "radical" or transformational solutions. Others seek to "personalize" the experience of young people in schools such that learning is more accessible and compelling for more students. But they do not necessarily aim to transform the school system itself; these might be thought of as "improvement" perspectives.

At the radical end, we see arguments for deschooling, or for versions of "not school, not home: schome" (Twining, 2007a, 2007b). These ideas promote ways of providing education other than through school. Such broadening of horizons for schools can be seen as a global phenomenon (Craft, Cremin, & Burnard, 2008; Craft, Gardner, & Claxton, 2008).

At the improvement end, a major concern is consulting and involving young people. The General Teaching Council (2007) for England has emphasized the importance of encouraging students to take an active part in their learning, evident, for example, in the Every Child Matters policy (Department for Education and Skills, 2003) and the "common core" of capabilities necessary for those who work with children (Department for Education and Skills, 2005). Analysts interpret this commitment to student voice as active participation in improvement and transformation (Davies, Williams, Yamashita, & Ko Man-Hing, 2006; Frost & Holden, 2008; Hargreaves, 2004). Another concern is recognizing students as rounded learners.

MI AND ACCESS TO LEARNING FOR ALL STUDENTS

MI theory is one of a raft of approaches some teachers and schools have adopted to increase access to learning within classrooms. Recognizing multiple capabilities has been attractive to teachers who seek to recognize more than the traditional logical-mathematical aspects of learning and thus to widen participation. The theory has been used by teachers to encompass learners considered hard to reach, as well as those considered gifted and talented. Schools and sometimes LEAs have devised diagnostic tests for children and teachers to determine the unique mix of intelligences exhibited by particular individuals. These tests include the Web-based questionnaire situated in the Birmingham Grid for Learning (2008). Based on self-report to forty MI questions, this grid leads each learner to generate a personalized circular graph suggesting a personal profile of intelligences. Other test examples include both spreadsheet-based and do-it-yourself multiple intelligence profile calculators such as the one developed by Chislett and Chapman (2005).

MI COMMUNICATES TO STUDENTS "MANY WAYS OF BEING SMART"

As Fleetham shows in Chapter Sixteen, many schools use MI to help students celebrate the ways in which everyone can be smart. Use of self-assessment checklists with learners is widespread, enabling them to generate their own developing profile of intelligences. Students' perspectives often are compared with teachers' evaluations. This comparison should, in theory, generate a more sensitive profile of approaches to learning for each student.

One school that conducts such assessments and uses an MI approach is Queen Elizabeth's Community College (QECC) in Crediton, Devon, for students aged eleven to eighteen. This school's learning strategy focuses on anticipating and developing appropriate twenty-first-century learning. As Tommy Evans and Bryan Smith, teachers at the school, write, "The Learning Strategy is an attempt to shift the balance more towards the 'how to' rather than the 'what' and is effectively a model of factors influencing learning such as motivation and emotional climate" (personal communication, 2008).

The staff view their entire learning strategy as having "MI running through it" (Smith, personal communication, 2008), and all new staff participate in an induction process that addresses the school's approaches to learning. The school has introduced the concept of teacher as learning consultant rather than pedagogue, with the emphasis on nurturing the capabilities of all pupils by reflecting on their preferences, strengths, and weaknesses in learning. Students are viewed as more self-directed. QECC regularly challenges students to make judgments about their own learning. Evans and Smith emphasize the way that older students are involved in MI approaches: "Within the post-sixteen curriculum, Learning Conference days are organized around the idea of smart skills for a more advanced learning environment. Students are exposed to much of the theory around learning and are given practical techniques for developing and assessing their own learning in response to this." Students use what they call a "self-smart" assessment, which invites them to evaluate what mix of learning styles they adopted and determine how they might extend this repertoire.

QECC recognizes that to enable such learner engagement in multiple ways of being smart, novel means of pedagogy are necessary. This program includes a number of sessions on MI theory and opportunities for staff to discuss the theory and its application in the classroom. While the QECC model is certainly informed by MI theory, it is also perhaps typical of initiatives in English schools to be informed by other approaches, such as accelerated learning and the 21st Century Learning Initiative.

MULTIPLE INTELLIGENCES AND GIFTED AND TALENTED CHILDREN

In general, MI has been embraced as representing and encouraging an inclusive and democratic approach to learning. But it has also been used extensively in England to help identify and support students in the top 5 to 10 percent achievement of all learners. MI theory challenges a view that effectively places English and mathematics (and occasionally the sciences) as more significant than other curriculum areas. Without MI, particularly in primary education, gifted and talented children may be identified only through their achievement in these subjects. One school for children aged three to eleven that has used MI since 2005 to identify children who are excelling is St. Leonard's Primary School in Exeter in the southwest of England. Jenny Perry, the coordinator responsible for provision for gifted and talented children in the school, says:

> We have found the categories based on the multiple intelligence principle very useful, not only as a vehicle for identification but as a practical starting point for implementing gifted and talented provision both within and beyond the classroom. Class teachers are all aware of the categories on a day-to-day basis, and our list of children is constantly being amended. Some children display an intelligence in one particular area and others may be listed under a variety of categories.

The school uses a range of informal and formal evidence from the classroom to identify gifted and talented children. This evidence includes discussion with teachers, children, parents, and specialists outside school; a national profile for children aged five; and national curriculum tests for children from the ages of seven to eleven. MI is a vital part of this battery of approaches to link teaching with the assessment of need.

Providing multiple ways for able children to learn is a concern for many schools in England. Churston Ferrers Grammar School in South Devon selects only the highest-achieving students to become pupils. It uses MI theory to encourage students and their parents to value the many entry points to learning. The school seeks to extend pupils out of their preferences in learning, arguing that "preference is not an excuse" (Churston Ferrers Grammar School, 2008, p. 20). Even the most able students can benefit from expanding their repertoire of abilities.

CHALLENGES FOR SCHOOLS USING MI IN ENGLAND

The use of MI theory to determine which students are gifted and talented and how they are gifted has been critiqued (McShane, 2006). Such critics argue that these assessments use a quantitative methodology to calculate a qualitative phenomenon. Using MI theory to identify the top students may also appear counter to its intention of embracing democratic values. Yet these challenges highlight the enormous strength of MI in acting as a chameleon theory, capable of adaptation to diverse educational ends. It enables those who struggle as well as those who excel. It reaches from the traditionally narrow academic curriculum to a broader one.

Perhaps the greatest challenge faced by MI proponents in education is the overlap with other enabling and pupil-centered approaches, including neurolinguistic programming (NLP); work on visual, auditory, kinesthetic, and tactile modalities (Walsh, 2005); and learning styles (Coffield, Moseley, Hall, & Ecclestone, 2004). Teachers and schools must distinguish MI from similar but distinct approaches when there is a paucity of evidence on the efficacy of thinking styles theories (Coffield et al., 2004).

NLP emphasizes representations (Bandler & Grinder, 1979; Dilts, Grinder, Bandler, & DeLozier, 1980). But Druckman and Swets (1988) note that there is little empirical basis for the claims made by NLP. Akin to the evaluations of NLP, recent research suggests that pedagogical approaches based on supposed differences in visual, auditory, and kinesthetic modes of learning were actually wasted effort (Kratzig & Arbuthnott, 2006). Indeed, it is claimed there is no neuroscientific basis for these theories (Goswami & Bryant, 2007).

Distinguishing MI and learning styles is a particularly taxing task, as the differences between them are not clear at the level of classroom and school practice. Schools frequently refer to MI as "learning styles" (for example, Churston Ferrers, 2008). The possible complexities are vast. Coffield et al. (2004) identify five families of learning styles reflecting distinctive underlying conceptualizations of what gives rise to differences in approaches to learning:

- Family 1: Learning styles as primarily genetically derived (Gregorc, 1982; Dunn & Dunn, 1992)

- Family 2: Learning styles as reflecting deep-seated features of cognitive structure, including patterns of capability (Riding, 2002)

- Family 3: Learning styles as a component of a relatively stable personality type, such as the Myers-Briggs Type Indicator (Myers & McCaulley, 1988, 1995)

- Family 4: Learning styles as flexibly stable preferences for learning (Kolb, 1984, 1999; Honey & Mumford, 1992, 2000)

- Family 5: Learning styles as pragmatic approaches, strategies, orientations (Entwistle, 1988; Sternberg, 1999)

MI theory, qua theory, could be seen as offering a typology of learning styles and may often be presented by practitioners as a family 1, family 2, or family 4 approach. As a theory with application to the classroom, MI is frequently understood as belonging to family 5. But while MI may inform the development of multiple entry points to learning, which responds to pupils' unique constellations of preferred learning styles, it is not itself a theory of learning style. Yet practitioners frequently perceive it to be offering such practical insights, with any combination of the family types implicit in these perceptions. This mix of MI theory with learning style, combined with varied perceptions about MI's potency depending on the assumptions about family type, means that MI theory may in practice be interpreted multiply (as the QECC and Churston Ferrers examples earlier in the chapter illustrate).

A further challenge is raised by English philosopher of education John White (1998, 2006). He claims the theory confuses culturally derived values around specific intellectual activity and biologically based fixed aptitudes or characteristics. He thinks the theory produces its own version of rigidity in assessing intelligence, and he suggests that the distinctiveness of individual intelligences may be questionable. Fundamentally, White argues, the theory needs to be empirically tested. Without empirically based criteria, such testing is not possible. Therefore, the only validity that can be achieved is a priori, which he suggests is insufficient (White, 2006). While teachers may be little aware of White's critique, the government, through the Teacher Development Agency, has made White's key challenges available to student teachers through a teacher-friendly Web site of resources (Teacher Training Resource Bank, http://www.ttrb.ac.uk/viewarticle2.aspx?contentId=12738).

POTENTIAL FOR MI IN ENGLISH EDUCATION

Despite these challenges and critiques, MI theory remains of great interest to teachers and schools in England for several reasons. First, it implies equal value allocated to each area of the curriculum. This equality counters the government stance that positions English, mathematics, and science as the core of the curriculum. Second, MI connects learning modes with types of knowledge. This connection opens up many entry points in terms of pedagogy. Third, MI may lay a foundation for learning and teaching (and working) that demands a wider, more imaginative, and perhaps more responsible repertoire that Gardner (2006) argues for. Together, these reasons afford a means by which teachers may appropriate creative engagement as professionals and enable the generative potential of their students within the context of a performative discourse in education.

MI is an optimistic theory that recognizes rich patterns of competence and expertise in each learner. As England's teachers and policymakers stretch toward radical, flexible, and personalized models of learning, it seems likely that MI will continue to provide a philosophical and practical guide with a strong focus on the learner as a unique member of a community. But it will not be enough on its own. The neoliberal, economy-driven model of education may, unchecked, result in reductive, ecologically, ethically, and spiritually unsustainable outcomes (Claxton, Craft, & Gardner, 2008). What the current era demands of educators is wisdom in developing imaginative responses to the issues faced by all in this century. Monitoring the wise educator's response to the opportunities MI theory offers, in an increasingly receptive policy and practice context, will be a task for the coming years.

References

Bandler, R., & Grinder, J. (1979). *Frogs into princes: Neuro linguistic programming.* Moab, UT: Real People Press.

Birmingham Grid for Learning. (2008). *Multiple intelligences.* http://www.bgfl.org/ bgfl/custom/resources_ftp/client_ftp Retrieved March 3, 2008, from 8/ks3/ict/ multiple_int/what.cfm.

Chislett, M.S.C., & Chapman, A. (2005). *Multiple intelligences: Based on Howard Gardner's Multiple Intelligences Model.* Retrieved June 6, 2008, from www.businessballs.com.

Churston Ferrers Grammar School. (2008). *Powerpoint—preferred learning styles: From the ideas of Howard Gardner.* Retrieved July 9, 2008, from http://www .churstongrammar.com/learningstyles.htm.

Claxton, G., Craft, A., & Gardner, H. (2008). Education for wise creativity. In A. Craft, H. Gardner, & G. Claxton (Eds.), *Creativity, wisdom, and trusteeship: Exploring the role of education.* Thousand Oaks, CA: Corwin Press.

Coffield, F., Moseley, D., Hall, E., & Ecclestone, K. (2004). *Learning styles and pedagogy in post-16 learning: A systematic and critical review.* London: Learning and Skills Research Centre.

Craft, A. (2005). *Creativity in schools: Tensions and dilemmas.* London: Routledge.

Craft, A. (2008a). Tensions in creativity and education: Enter wisdom and trusteeship? In A. Craft, H. Gardner, & G. Claxton (Eds.), *Creativity, wisdom and trusteeship: Exploring the role of education.* Thousand Oaks, CA: Corwin Press.

Craft, A. (2008b, Feb. 27). *Leading creative learning: Running the creative school.* Keynote address presented at Café Royal, London.

Craft, A., Chappell, K., & Twining, P. (2008). Aspiring to transform education? Young learners aspiring toward creative education futures. *Innovations in Education & Teaching International, 45*(3), 235–245.

Craft, A., Cremin, T., & Burnard, P. (2008). Creative learning: An emergent concept. In A. Craft, T. Cremin, & P. Burnard (Eds.), *Creative learning 3–11 and how we document it.* Stoke-on-Trent: Trentham Books.

Craft, A., Gardner, H., & Claxton, G. (2008). Nurturing Creativity: Wisdom and trusteeship in education: A collective debate. In A. Craft, H. Gardner, & G. Claxton (Eds.), *Creativity, wisdom and trusteeship: Exploring the role of education.* Thousand Oaks, CA: Corwin Press.

Craft, A., & Jeffrey, B. (2008, October). Creativity and performativity in teaching and learning: Tensions, dilemmas, constraints, accommodations and synthesis. *British Educational Research Journal, 34*(5), 577–584.

Daanen, H., & Facer, K. (2007). *2020 and beyond.* Retrieved March 3, 2008, from http://www.futurelab.org.uk/resources/publications_reports_articles/opening_education_reports/Opening_Education_Report663.

Davies, L., Williams, C., Yamashita, H., & Ko Man-Hing, A. (2006, March). *Inspiring schools: Impact and outcomes.* Carnegie Young People Initiative/Esmee Fairbairn Foundation.

Department for Education and Science. (1988). *The Education Reform Act.* London: HMSO.

Department for Education and Skills. (2003). *Every Child Matters.* London: HMSO. Retrieved March 3, 2008, from http://www.dfes.gov.uk/consultations/downloadable Docs/EveryChildMatters.pdf.

Department for Education and Skills. (2005). *The common core of skills and knowledge for the children's workforce.* London: HMSO.

Dilts, R. B., Grinder, J., Bandler, R., & DeLozier, J. A. (1980). *Neuro-linguistic programming, Vol. 1: The study of the structure of subjective experience.* Capitola, CA: Meta Publications.

Druckman, D., & Swets, J. A. (1988). *Enhancing human performance: Issues, theories, and techniques.* Washington, DC: National Academy Press.

Dunn, R., & Dunn, K. (1992). *Teaching secondary students through their individual learning styles.* Needham Heights, MA: Allyn & Bacon.

Entwistle, N. (1988). *Styles of learning and teaching.* London: David Fulton.

Frost, R., & Holden, G. (2008). Student voice and future schools: Building partnership for student participation. *Improving Schools, 11*(1), 83–95.

Futurelab. (2008). *e-resources.* Retrieved March 3, 2008, from http://www.futurelab.org.uk/resources#.

Gardner, H. (1983). *Frames of mind: The theory of multiple intelligences.* New York: Basic Books.

Gardner, H. (1993). *Multiple intelligences: The theory in practice.* New York: Basic Books.

Gardner, H. (2006). *Five minds for the future.* Boston: Harvard Business School Press

General Teaching Council. (2007). *The voice, role and participation of children and young people: summary of existing research.* London: GTC. Retrieved June 6, 2008, from http://www.gtce.org.uk/shared/contentlibs/126815/211152/Pupil_voice_research.pdf.

Goswami, U., & Bryant, P. (2007). *Children's cognitive development and learning.* Cambridge: Cambridge University.

Gregorc A. F. (1982). *Gregorc Style Delineator: Development, technical and administration manual.* Columbia, CT: Gregorc Associates.

Hargreaves, D. (2004, October). *Personalised learning: Next steps in working laterally.* iNet and Specialist Schools and Academies Trust.

Harvey, D. (2005). *A brief history of neoliberalism.* New York: Oxford University Press.

Honey, P., & Mumford, A. (1992). *The manual of learning styles.* Maidenhead: Peter Honey Publications.

Honey, P., & Mumford, A. (2000). *The learning styles helper's guide.* Maidenhead: Peter Honey Publications.

Kolb, D. A. (1984). *Experiential learning: Experience as the source of learning and development.* Upper Saddle River, NJ: Prentice Hall.

Kolb, D. A. (1999). *The Kolb Learning Style Inventory, Version 3.* Boston: Hay Group.

Kratzig, G. P., & Arbuthnott, K. D. (2006). Perceptual learning style and learning proficiency: A test of the hypothesis. *Journal of Educational Psychology, 98*(1), 238–246.

McShane, J. (2006, October). Learning curve: Multiple intelligences and G&T. *Gifted & Talented Update.* Retrieved February 29, 2008, from http://www.teachingexpertise .com/articles/learning-curve-multiple-intelligences-and-g-t-1320.

Myers, I. B., & McCaulley, M. H. (1985). *Manual: A guide to the development and use of the Myers-Briggs Type Indicator.* Palo Alto, CA: Consulting Psychologists Press.

Myers, I. B., & McCaulley, M. H. (1998). *Manual: A guide to the development and use of the Myers-Briggs Type Indicator.* Palo Alto, CA: Consulting Psychologists Press.

Osler, D. (2002). *Labour Party plc: New Labour as a party of business.* New York: Oxford University Press.

Qualifications and Curriculum Authority. (2008). *What is futures?* Retrieved March 3, 2008, from http://www.qca.org.uk/qca_6073.aspx.

Riding, R. (2002). *School learning and cognitive style.* London: David Fulton.

Sternberg, R. J. (1999). *Thinking styles.* Cambridge: Cambridge University Press.

Thomson, P. (2007). *Whole school change: A review of the literature.* London: Arts Council England.

Troman, G., Jeffrey, B., & Raggl, A. (2007). Creativity and performativity policies in primary school cultures. *Journal of Education Policy, 22,* 549–572.

Twining, P. (2007a, May 25). *Using Teen Second Life to explore visions of schome.* Paper presented at the Second Life Best Practices in Education Conference, Second Life Main Grid. Retrieved July 28, 2007, from http://schome.open.ac.uk/ wikiworks/index.php/Second_Life_Best_Practices_in_Education.

Twining, P. (2007b, March 22). *Developing visions of schome.* Paper presented at the Massively Multi-Learner conference, University of Paisley. Retrieved June 22, 2007, from http://www.ics.heacademy.ac.uk/events/displayevent.php?id=142.

Walsh, B. E. (2005). *Unleashing your brilliance.* Victoria, BC: Walsh Seminars.

White, J. P. (1998). *Do Howard Gardner's multiple intelligences add up? Perspectives on education policy.* London: Institute of Education, University of London.

White, J. P. (2006). Multiple invalidities. In J. A. Schaler (Ed.), *Howard Gardner under fire: The rebel psychologist faces his critics.* Peru, IL: Open Court.

White, J. P. (2008). *Howard Gardner : The myth of multiple intelligence?* Teacher Training Resource Bank, Teacher Development Agency. Retrieved March 3, 2008, from http://www.ttrb.ac.uk/viewarticle2.aspx?contentId=12738.

Woods, P., & Jeffrey, R. J. (1996). *Teachable moments: The art of teaching in primary schools.* Buckingham: Open University Press.

Woods, P., Jeffrey, B., Troman, G., & Boyle, M. (1997). *Restructuring schools, reconstructing teachers: Responding to change in the primary school.* Buckingham: Open University Press.

CHAPTER 16

Does Every Child Matter in England?

Mike Fleetham

This chapter continues the themes described in Chapter Fifteen with three reflections of MI-infused learning from my personal perspectives as educational consultant and father. I describe England's Every Child Matters (ECM) educational strategy and ten-year Children's Plan. I suggest there is a genuine political intention for every child in England to really matter, but the current educational assessment system makes some children matter more than others. An adoption of MI-inspired thinking and classroom practice is necessary to fully meet national aims. I present three examples. I showcase the work of an infant school teacher who uses MI puppets to enrich the concept of intelligence for the very youngest learners. I detail my own work helping teachers develop their classroom practice. Finally, I describe my experience as a father of a son currently struggling in school yet succeeding in the scouting movement.

On February, 25, 2000, eight-year-old Victoria Climbié died from a combination of hypothermia, malnutrition, and sustained physical abuse. The pathologist who examined her body counted 128 individual injuries and scars. Victoria slipped through a net held by the many education, health, social, and legal professionals who should have saved her. Her horrific death shocked the nation. The subsequent inquiry (Department for Education and Skills, 2003) discovered a catastrophic breakdown of communication and the systemic failure of child care organizations to work together effectively. There was no joined-up thinking and no coherent action.

The Government's Every Child Matters (ECM) strategy (Department for Education and Skills, 2003) was the phoenix that rose from the ashes of this tragic set of blunders. Agencies responsible for various aspects of child care (including schools) are now required to communicate and cooperate on the implementation of ECM's five requirements: "The Government's aim is for every child (from 0-19), whatever their background or their circumstances, to have the support they need to: Be healthy, Stay safe, Enjoy and achieve, Make a positive contribution, Achieve economic well-being."

ECM takes shape in schools through curriculum redesign, extension of provision, and greater community involvement. It emphasizes the concept of personalized learning (PL) (Hargreaves, 2006), which recognizes that each pupil learns in a different way and that teaching and schools must evolve to meet diverse learning needs and changing social and cultural contexts. It has five strands:

- Assessment for learning
- Effective teaching and learning
- Curriculum entitlement and choice
- Organizing the school
- Beyond the classroom

There is a pedagogical link between PL and multiple intelligences (MI) theory, though this connection is not made explicit in national policy. Schools interpret PL in their own ways, but some do make use of MI theory.

THE CHILDREN'S PLAN

In response to a six-month consultation with members of the public and experts from various fields, the government launched the Children's Plan (Department for Children, Schools and Families, 2007), a ten-year strategy for education, welfare, and play. The hope expressed by Ed Balls, the minister of education, is that implementation of the plan will make "our country the best place in the world to grow up." It places families at its heart because young people spend only one-fifth of their time at school. The plan links effective learning to high-quality experiences in the remaining four-fifths of young people's time, including support from the family, encouragement, and purposeful activities outside the standard school day. The Children's Plan is an expansion of the ECM agenda to encompass all aspects of a child's life.

THE ASSESSMENT PARADOX

Three core aims of the Children's Plan demonstrate the varying criteria by which children are assessed—and therefore valued—as they grow up. At age five, success is measured in the six diverse areas of the foundation stage (ages three to five) profile: personal, social, and emotional development; communication, language, and literacy; mathematical development; knowledge and understanding of the world; physical development; and creative development. By age eleven, although a broad curriculum is still on offer, the achievement measure has narrowed to just literacy and numeracy. Standards in these two skills are decided by written tests and teacher assessment. At age sixteen, assessment is through the public written examination, the General Certificate of Secondary Education, currently available in sixteen subjects.

Every Child Matters and the Children's Plan are worthy attempts to meet the educational, social, and economic requirements of the twenty-first century by addressing the needs of all children. However, the value measures above are inconsistent across age groups and, after the Foundation Stage, favor only children with linguistic and logical strengths and those who perform well on exams. One result is a system that aims to value every child yet forces on teachers a classroom culture that values passing tests instead of deep, meaningful personalized learning. Why might there be such a paradox?

THE ENGLISH PERSPECTIVE ON INTELLIGENCE

One answer could be the English view of intelligence. Two aspects of the conventional wisdom about intelligence in the English context operate against an MI conception. First, there is a suspicion of breadth, particularly breadth that might extend to the arts, salesmanship, or well-roundedness. Second, there is a very narrow sense of what is termed "clever"—largely, the capacity to produce factual knowledge quickly on demand.

The English are suspicious of intellectuals, especially the broad-minded, and prefer to maintain a restrictive definition of success. This perspective is hinted at by the comments of two well-respected English commentators. Journalist and political commentator Andrew Marr proposed, "Is there part of the English character that can't quite cope with the all rounder? This country is still deeply suspicious of people who can do too many things." Professor of Naval History Andrew Lambert concurred: "There is a profound suspicion of intellectuals. Those who are able to span across various disciplines are, as the classic English expression has it, 'Too clever by half.'"

Furthermore, the English reveal their view of intelligence as regurgitation of facts by the intellectual skills valued in television game shows. Contestants are usually asked to recall facts or perform simple numerical or linguistic tasks. For example, *University Challenge* pits the so-called cleverest students from English universities against one another in several quick-fire rounds. Those who answer fastest get the points, and the team with the most points at the end of the show wins. Implicitly this equates intelligence to volume of knowledge and speed of recall. Other shows set the members of different professions against each other. Accountants may take on hairdressers, or builders compete with doctors. But again, recall of facts, rather than the assessment of any career-specific skills, decides the winner.

IN ENGLISH CLASSROOMS

These media highlights imply a school system that values memory, literacy, and numeracy. Indeed, the national assessment of all eleven year olds, in the final year at primary school, takes the form of written tests in math, English, and science. Other subjects, skills, and personal qualities are not tested or publicly valued in the same manner. This paves the way for the overt success of the handful of children who perform well on these tests.

Schools feel pressure to meet performance targets that are set for them nationally. Research has discovered that schools therefore teach to the test (Select Committee on Children, Schools and Families, 2008), an emphasis that causes teachers to resort to traditional pedagogies that are "good enough." They stay safe in their classroom practice, unwilling to take teaching and learning risks for fear of failing to meet their targets. Such attitudes affect the type of learning activities that take place.

THE POTENTIAL OF MI

These three issues of intelligence, assessment, and classroom learning activity can be addressed through MI. MI theory offers a more diverse and inclusive definition of intelligence, suggests many alternative methods of assessment, and presents numerous options for learning activities. Here follow three examples that show what is possible with MI.

Puppets Change Perceptions of What Intelligence Is

Lynne Williams originally developed her use of MI with three and four year olds in a less-than-sympathetic environment. She was once told, "You can't make children more intelligent. . . . You just need to work with those who have already got high intelligence." Lynne wanted to overturn a restrictive definition of intelligence, believing that learning would then be improved. On her discovery of MI, she said, "I suppose, on reflection, that my involvement in multiple intelligences started from just a feeling, an intuition about what worked. I didn't have any real knowledge about it when I started teaching, only an understanding that I had learned best when working in certain conditions and when I could show my learning through ways that didn't involve a timed examination."

Lynne has a management role in her school and has been able to include MI in many aspects of school life: parents' meetings and workshops, training for other staff, and performance targets inspired by MI. By infusing MI, she is implicitly and explicitly altering what it means to be clever. Her real challenge, though, was to ensure that her children developed a far richer definition of intelligence than is commonly expressed by three and four year olds.

First, she helped them to create their own MI language. For example, musical intelligence is "la la la smart," and bodily-kinesthetic intelligence is "wiggly smart." But the real impact came through the introduction of MI puppets. Each puppet was made from a wooden spoon and decorated with characteristics matched to an intelligence. The spoons were the same size to imply equality of intelligence. Lynne developed an approach to help the children understand and respond to the puppets. It began with introductions:

> In a circle time session, I told the children that I had brought some friends to meet them. But the friends were very shy. One child responded with, "We will be their friends. . . . We will look after them!" One by one, the spoon puppets emerged, and I had them whisper to me. I whispered back and then told the children what they were saying, for example, "Number Smart says you look friendly. He likes your smile." Another child asked, "If we are careful, would they like to come around our circle so we can say hello to them?" I said that we would need to make them feel safe, and then, as I sent the first puppet around the circle, a child said, "What's his name?" "Let's ask him," I replied. "I'm Friend Smart," said the puppet in a whisper to me. As each child held the puppet, he or she whispered, "Hello, Friend Smart," to him. When this first puppet had completed his welcome circuit, I asked the children, "What do you think he is smart at doing then?" "Being a friend" came the reply. I then questioned them further, and we worked out what a good friend would look like and sound like. Each puppet was introduced in this way, and by the end of the session, we had eight new members of the class! We now use the puppets to stimulate and extend learning experiences and as alter egos for the children to use when they want to express themselves in alternative MI-inspired ways.

The puppets are used in class to help with learning and assessment and to give all of the children (regardless of skill or talent) an alter ego with which to identify. The puppets stay in the room and are always present as a constant reminder that intelligence is more than literacy and numeracy.

Modeling MI Enriches Learning Activities

Good teachers use MI intuitively or would if they had the ideas and permission to do so. More often than not, a focus on achievement in a narrow area restricts adoption of MI. By modeling MI use, I hope to inspire others to develop their classroom practice. I have been training teachers and delivering MI demonstration lessons for over six years after ten years as a full-time classroom teacher.

I have noticed a shift in attitude toward MI. In 2001, I would ask an audience to choose who, from a list of celebrities, they felt to be the cleverest. They would debate, discuss, and argue, then come to a final single answer. In 2008, the same question elicits a range of answers, and few people will commit to a single one: "They're all clever in their own way." To investigate this change further, I set up a poll on my Web site (http://www.thinkingclassroom.co.uk). A majority of the 159 respondents believed that MI was beneficial to learning and was possible to implement. The poll's major findings were that MI:

Enriches learning and is easy to do	64.8 percent
Enriches learning but is difficult to do	18.9 percent
Is just another trendy method	6.9 percent
Hinders learning	1.3 percent

Another 8.2 percent did not know what MI was. However this poll must be seen in context. I get asked to work only with schools that use or want to use MI. My Web site is generally visited by teachers who are already embracing nontraditional methods.

Schools are usually after two things. They want to know about MI theory, or they want to find out how to use MI in the classroom to deliver their curricula. Some schools already understand the basics. Others use the terms "learning styles" and "multiple intelligences" interchangeably and seek a practical clarification of the differences. A growing number ask for demonstration lessons. After I have provided such demonstrations, teachers tell me that they have gained tacit approval and implicit permission to do the same type of lessons for themselves. It is only in the past few years that these same teachers have been released from the content-driven restrictions of the national curriculum with its prescriptive literacy and numeracy strategies. After many years of being told what to teach and how to teach it, teachers are understandably hesitant to take creative risks. Even now they are asked to produce exam results over and above ensuring learning.

Teacher training sessions are well received. I make a point of using MI in the design of all my workshops. For example, in one session, I have sixty minutes to inspire thirty teachers to try MI in their classrooms. With no time for a thorough elucidation of the theory, we jump to an MI song: the eight and a half intelligences described in actions, words, and a tune. We take three minutes to learn the song; then I ask them to recall the words. Each person does it in a different way: some write; some talk; a few work alone; most work in pairs. Others hum the tune, many use the actions, and some doodle. They all have fun, and they all remember. I hope I have made a point here. I could have provided a handout and asked them to read it, or maybe even have them copy the information. Instead, I let everyone play to their strengths and allow their preferences to reveal themselves.

In six years, I have worked with thousands of people, and I can recall only three who were vocal in their criticism of MI. One participant walked out of the session described above when I got people singing an MI song: "This is all very well, but I simply haven't got time for all this singing and getting out of your seat and stuff. I have a curriculum to teach you know!" Someone else stated plainly and loudly, "It's just stupid to even consider that everyone can be clever." A third critic typified what a very small and silent minority probably think during my MI sessions: that MI is only another initiative and there just is not time to do it.

The vast majority of teachers engage with these workshops. They realize that MI is providing them with effective classroom tools and a philosophy that values every child for who he or she is and could become. Moreover, teachers now have eight possible entry points to the same content and eight potential areas through which to assess strengths.

The Scouting Movement Addresses Intelligence and Assessment

I suspected that my son, from age two, had severe language difficulties and particular cognitive strengths. Specifically, I thought he had well above average visual-spatial and logical intelligences yet a significantly degraded verbal-linguistic one. "Leaky bucket" was and is an apt metaphor for his learning. He struggles to retain vocabulary and the rules of language. He also has to work extremely hard to decode the written word. However, he can build physical structures and solve real-life problems in a manner consistent with someone many years his senior.

For his first few years at school, he was labeled "happy" yet "a little slow" and "just a boy." Formal assessment of his difficulties was not deemed necessary, and recognition of his strengths was not consistent with school policy and priorities. I eventually had my son assessed by a language expert outside the school system who discovered an enormous discrepancy between various aspects of his learning profile and abilities. Most notably, my son had a visual IQ score of 139 (standardized) alongside a reading fluency of 78 (standardized). His basic literacy skills were well below chronological age, and the gap between these and his advanced processing skills was widening daily. Severe dyslexic tendencies were described for which daily intervention by a specialist teacher was recommended.

Such an intervention, however, was not forthcoming. The fight for extra support (together with a celebration of his strengths) began, a battle that is still being fought for him in 2009. The difficulty lies in the criteria for provision of language support. His needs are not severe enough to justify additional spending. However, what does not feature in the calculation is the gap between his needs and his potential.

Furthermore, this potential remains under the radar when his school looks for gifted students. Criteria for giftedness are linked to subjects on the school curriculum and not the more generic skills of problem solving and visual thinking. If his school were to look through an MI lens, they would find a boy with a very skewed profile. But they would have a framework for recognizing his weaknesses and celebrating his strengths.

There is one organization in which my son does thrive, and it does not yet realize how well it is implementing MI theory: the scouting movement. One evening at the end of his weekly session, I watched with pride as my son completed a PowerPoint presentation to the rest of his pack about model making for his hobby badge. For once, he succeeded and was publicly valued for his unique skills and talents.

At all age levels in this organization, boys and girls can work for a variety of badges at increasing levels of challenge. The badges are external indicators of achievement in various domains, which can be mapped readily onto combinations of all the intelligences. For example, the global conservation badge calls on the naturalist intelligence, navigator requires visual-spatial skills, and the communicator badge makes use of verbal-linguistic and interpersonal intelligences. The hobby badge allows any interest, and therefore any intelligence, to be celebrated. Whereas school focuses on specific areas within a much narrower curriculum, scouting values competences equally in a large number of areas: artists alongside astronomers, scientists with skaters. On this evidence, a gifted and dyslexic learner is served better by scouting than school.

CONCLUSION

English national educational policy has the child at its heart. A political will is present that truly wants every child to matter, to be valued, and to succeed. Unfortunately, some aspects of the same education system are not congruent with these aims. There exist internal contradictions that pull the child and teacher in different directions. On the one hand, the child is supposed to matter. On the other hand, the child can matter only if he or she has certain skills and can pass exams.

I believe that these and other paradoxes are caused in part by a belief that intelligence is specific and fixed in nature. I argue that MI-inspired learning can address the contradictions, and I cite three examples where this is happening: Lynne Williams's use of MI puppets has drastically altered children's perceptions of what it means to be clever. My training of teachers embodies MI in its style, and through practical demonstration, it gives teachers the tools and permission to enrich their classroom practice. The scouting movement values a vast range of domains equally and allows its members to demonstrate their achievements in diverse ways. It offers a model that simultaneously addresses the issues of intelligence definition and assessment. These examples suggest that an adoption of MI-inspired thinking at the national level and the use of MI-infused learning in classrooms are compatible with the publicly stated aims of Every Child Matters and the Children's Plan.

References

Department for Children, Schools and Families. (2007). *The children's plan: Building brighter futures.* London: The Stationary Office Ltd.

Department for Education and Skills. (2003). *Every child matters green paper.* London: The Stationary Office Ltd.

Hargreaves, D. (2006). *Personalised learning.* London: Specialist Schools and Academies Trust.

Laming, W. H. (2003). *The Victoria Climbié inquiry.* London: Her Majesty's Stationery Office.

Select Committee on Children, Schools and Families. (2008). *Third report.* London: The Stationary Office Ltd.

CHAPTER 17

Multiple Intelligences in Ireland

Áine Hyland
Marian McCarthy

In Ireland, Howard Gardner's theory of multiple intelligences was the right theory in the right place at the right time. In the past decade, Ireland's population has changed from being largely monolithic in terms of language, culture, ethnic background, and religion to being multicultural and diverse. New education laws in Ireland in the late 1990s required the education system at all levels to be inclusive and to facilitate and respect the diversity of learners in the system. Multiple intelligences theory provided an ideal framework for curriculum reform and delivery from early childhood to third level. This chapter describes how a research and development project on multiple intelligences, curriculum, and assessment, which started in University College Cork in 1996, influenced a growing number of educational policymakers, teacher educators, educational leaders, school principals, teachers, and students at all levels of the Irish educational system.

In the 1990s, Ireland's population changed from being largely monolithic in terms of language, culture, ethnic background, and religion, to being multicultural and diverse, with significant implications for the Irish educational system. Until the 1990s, the population of Ireland, in comparison to other European countries and to the United States, was relatively homogeneous. Ireland had virtually never experienced immigration but was all too familiar with emigration. However, the scene changed dramatically in the 1990s when Ireland experienced an unprecedented economic boom and became known as the Celtic Tiger. As a result of this boom, Ireland began to attract immigrants from many countries, especially from Eastern Europe, Africa, and Asia. From being a largely monolithic society in terms of race, color, language, and religion, Ireland became a much more diverse country almost overnight with an eclectic mix of people of various cultural, ethnic, religious, and linguistic backgrounds.

Although this was an exciting and welcome development, it created a challenge for an education system that had little experience catering to a diverse school population. Irish schoolchildren had traditionally attended separate schools depending on their religious background. Since the early nineteenth century, schools in Ireland had been run by the churches, though with significant state aid. Over 98 percent of primary schools are owned and managed by the Roman Catholic church. And almost all of the remainder are run by other churches, such as the Church of Ireland and the Presbyterian church. Less than 0.5 percent are multidenominational, that is, attended by children of all religious backgrounds or children with no religious affiliation. There are no primary schools owned or run by the state or by public authorities. The majority of second-level schools (those for pupils aged twelve to eighteen) are also run by churches. They traditionally have been academically selective, although the introduction of free second-level education in the late 1960s began to erode the elitist tradition of second-level education.

NEW EDUCATION LEGISLATION IN THE LATE 1990S

The Education Act of 1998 recognized for the first time the diverse nature of the Irish population. The act explicitly required the education system to provide "for the education of every person in the State, including any person with a disability or who has other special educational needs" and "to respect the diversity of values, beliefs, languages and traditions in Irish society." Similarly the University Act of 1997 required the universities to develop a policy on equality, highlighting "access to the university and to university education by economically or socially disadvantaged people, by people who have a disability and by people from sections of society significantly under-represented in the student body."

The new education legislation of the 1990s therefore challenged schools at all levels to provide an education that respected all children and young people equally, regardless of their abilities or disabilities or their cultural, social, linguistic, ethnic, or religious background. The theory of multiple intelligences could contribute to a pedagogical framework through which schools could implement an inclusive ethos.

It would be wrong, however, to suggest that Irish society or the Irish school system had traditionally been unsympathetic to those who were different or did not conform to a traditional view of intelligence. In *Frames of Mind*, Gardner (1983) pointed out that the definition of intelligence varies from culture to culture and that different communities value different forms of intelligence.

THE WORD *INTELLIGENT* IN THE IRISH LANGUAGE

There is no one word for intelligence in the Irish language. The English word *intelligent* can be translated into a number of different words depending on the context in which the word is being used. The Irish words *éirim aigne* and *éirimiuil* are probably the words that most closely approximate the English word *intelligence* or *intelligent*. But these words are not often used, and rarely within a schooling context.

The word *cliste* is probably most often used to denote intelligence or cleverness. *Duine cliste* is a clever person (clever with positive connotations), but *cliste* is not confined to academic learning. It can encompass creativity, talent, and skills in a wide range of areas. *Duine glic* is also a clever person, but he or she is usually intelligent in pursuit of his or her own interests. That intelligence might be manifest in the evasion of payment of tax or debts or in escaping from deserved punishment.

Duine críonna is a wise or sagacious person, worldly wise from the experience of many years. In ancient Irish myths and legends, such a person was often depicted as an elder of the community, a reflective old man or woman looked up to by neighbors and called on to settle ancient disputes. Yet another word that infers intelligence in the Irish language is *stuama. Duine stuama* means solid, reliable, and sensible, an important form of intelligence in certain situations. In addition, modern dictionary translations of the word *intelligent* include the words *intleachtúil* derived from the English word "intellectual," and *tuisceanach,* which translated directly means "understanding."

The variety of descriptions of intelligence in the Irish language explains to some extent why IQ tests such as the Stanford/Binet test, which focus largely on linguistic and logical-mathematical intelligence and were popular in many other countries throughout the twentieth century, have not been part of the Irish educational landscape. Although the notion of intelligence testing found some favor among Irish educational academics in the 1930s and 1940s, IQ tests were not generally used in Ireland, as is attested to by the fact that no Irish-language version of IQ tests ever existed. Not until recent decades did IQ testing enter the Irish educational scene, and their use is confined largely to identifying children with special educational needs to ensure that the required additional learning resources are provided for them.

THE CURRICULUM IN IRISH PRIMARY SCHOOLS

Since the early 1970s, there has been no national examination or national testing of primary school children in Ireland. This fact makes it easier for primary teachers to adopt a multiple intelligences approach to teaching and learning. In 1971, following the introduction of free second-level education, a new primary school curriculum was introduced in Ireland. A child-centered curriculum was introduced, the national examination at the end of primary schooling was abolished, and an individual record card of the pupil's progress and achievements was introduced.

The pedagogical approach in primary schools changed from didactic class-based teaching to a guided discovery approach. The teacher was to be a facilitator of learning, and children would play a more active role in their own education. The prescriptive, narrow, subject-focused curriculum of the early years of Irish independence was replaced by national curriculum guidelines that included a broader range of subjects, encouraged subject integration, and provided flexibility and choice for schools and teachers. The current national primary school curriculum in Ireland, which was further revised and refined in 1999, explicitly recognizes that children have different styles of learning and different intelligence strengths. This curriculum lends itself to an MI approach to teaching and learning.

In spite of (or maybe because of) the fact that there is no national testing in primary schools in Ireland, pupil literacy and numeracy levels are high. In the most recent international pupil achievement study carried out by the Organization for Economic Cooperation and Development (2006), the PISA study, Irish pupils were the second highest achievers in the European Union in terms of literacy. Only 11 percent of fifteen year olds in Ireland are classified as low achievers compared to a mean of almost 19.8 percent in participating countries. However, literacy and numeracy rates are considerably lower among pupils from less advantaged than from more advantaged backgrounds, and young people from advantaged backgrounds are four times more likely to enroll in higher education than their less advantaged peers.

Primary teaching in Ireland is a highly sought-after profession, attracting the top 15 percent of high school academic achievers. Primary teachers are well educated to honors degree level, with sound theoretical and practical training. These teachers are open to adopting new and innovative pedagogies; they expect these to be soundly based in theory and to be relevant and appropriate to the curriculum they are teaching.

THE CURRICULUM IN IRISH SECOND-LEVEL SCHOOLS

The pedagogical approach in second-level schools tends to be more traditional than in primary schools. It places a greater emphasis on subject-based teaching and textbook-based learning. While there have been significant changes in the second-level curriculum in recent years to cater to the learning needs of a diverse population of learners, the junior certificate and leaving certificate examinations continue to have a major influence on teaching and learning in second level schools.

The leaving certificate, in particular, is a high-stakes examination, since results for this exam determine access to higher education. Irish universities rely solely on leaving certificate results to allocate scarce places, with the more prestigious courses such as law, medicine, and dentistry requiring very high levels of achievement. Students can choose from over thirty subjects at different levels (foundation, common, and higher levels) for the leaving certificate, and many of the curricula are innovative and creative. But examination requirements dominate teaching in second-level schools, especially in the third and final years, in preparation for the junior certificate and leaving certificate exams.

There is, however, one year of a student's second-level schooling where students are encouraged to explore their multiple intelligences and to undertake projects that reflect their individual interests and abilities: the transition year, which takes place in the year after students have completed the junior certificate examination—usually around fifteen years of age. According to national guidelines, the transition year "provides a bridge to help pupils make the transition from a highly-structured environment to one where they will take greater responsibility for their own learning and decision-making. Pupils will participate in learning strategies which are active and experiential and which help them to develop a range of transferable critical thinking and creative problem-solving skills" (National Council for Curriculum and Assessment, 2004).

MULTIPLE INTELLIGENCES IN IRELAND

Kathleen Lynch, director of the Centre for Equality Studies at University College Dublin, was the first person in Ireland to write about Gardner's theory of multiple intelligences and to discuss its potential for Irish education. In 1989, she referred to the theory in her book, *The Hidden Curriculum* (Lynch, 1989). In a later book, *Schools and Society in Ireland* (Drudy & Lynch, 1993), she devoted a full chapter to the topic of intelligence, the curriculum, and education. She argued that the definition of *intelligence* is crucial, since "what is defined as intelligence or ability has a profound effect on what is defined as legitimate knowledge in schools" (Drudy & Lynch, 1993).

In January 1995, Lynch invited Gardner to University College Dublin, where he spoke to a public audience and facilitated a workshop for senior policymakers and teacher educators. As a result of this lecture and workshop, we decided to initiate an action research project, to be funded by the Atlantic Philanthropies, on multiple intelligences, curriculum and assessment in University College Cork (UCC), where the two of us were faculty members. The key research question addressed by the project focused on whether MI theory could be applied to and enhance aspects of curriculum and assessment at the primary and second levels in Ireland. The project involved educators from all levels and sectors, and it included an action research component, which involved over thirty teachers from schools in the Cork region.

During the first year of the project, the emphasis was on MI theory and developing pedagogic approaches using multiple entry points. This approach was easily understood and readily adopted by most participants in primary and second-level schools. A primary teacher (now an assistant chief inspector with the national Ministry of Education) wrote about his use of MI theory:

> My fifth class and I have been learning through MI over the last few months. As a teacher, I was attracted to the theory because of the very broad view of intelligence it promotes. MI gives schools an educational theory which genuinely values *all* the talents which children possess. It is a positive philosophy of education which looks for strengths in people and really values them. All the talents which children bring to school are developed and valued. In the MI classroom, we use these strengths as doorways into learning. Teaching with MI means reaching for a story, a poem, a drawing, a song, a quiz or a dance. In short, anything which will help a child connect with a concept or new skill.
>
> . . . How does MI teaching and learning go down in the classroom? In a word—brilliant! The children really love the group-work, the sharing, the swapping, the singing, drawing, calculating, storytelling, planning, deciding—whatever. But I am sure that their greatest satisfaction comes from having their own interests valued as a central part of the learning process. Learning isn't presented as the same diet for all.
>
> An important part of our classwork is learning that we all have different interests and talents. The [pupils] in my classroom have each made out their personal MI Passport—reflecting their particular blend of interests and abilities. We are learning that when we come across something new, certain avenues of learning will work very well for us [O Donnchadha, 1997].

As they began to engage more deeply with curriculum planning and integrating content, pedagogy and assessment, many teachers in the MI project found that MI theory alone was not enough. As one teacher, who appreciated the value of an awareness by teachers of MI theory, asked: "What do you do with that awareness? Foster it? Apply it to teaching methods? Where do you go from awareness?"

TEACHING FOR UNDERSTANDING

The answer for many of the teachers was to adopt a teaching for understanding (TfU) approach. The TfU framework, developed at Harvard Project Zero under the guidance of Gardner, David Perkins, and Vito Perrone, is based on a particular view of understanding, terming it "a performance view" (Blythe, 1998; Stone-Wiske, 1997). The performance perspective says, in brief, "that understanding is a matter of being able to do a variety of thought-provoking things with a topic, such as explaining, finding evidence and examples, generalizing, applying, analogizing, and representing the topic in new ways" (Blythe, 1998, p. 12). The framework contains four key ideas: generative topics, understanding goals, performances of understanding, and ongoing assessment. Good performances of understanding allow students to build and demonstrate understanding in a variety of ways. A teacher can design performances with a view to supporting pupils' multiple intelligences and building on their intelligence strengths. The Cork project found that the TfU framework is ideal for use in conjunction with an inclusive MI approach to curriculum design, implementation, and assessment.

The overall findings of the MI project in UCC confirmed that MI theory was consistent with the prevailing philosophy of education in Irish primary schools, which encourages a child-centered approach to education (Hyland, 2000). In second-level schools, the dominance of an examination-driven approach to teaching and learning militated against the implementation of MI theory. But good examples of MI approaches were evident in some subject areas, particularly in first- and second-year classes and in the transition year.

Overall, teachers involved in the project acknowledged that MI theory provided them with a new lens through which to view their students' potential. This was particularly true with pupils whose academic performance was poor and where teacher expectations had traditionally been limited. MI theory was especially welcomed by teachers in schools in socially disadvantaged areas. This finding confirmed the view of the project leaders that further work with such schools would be worthwhile and that any new supportive initiative should be on a whole-school basis rather than simply involving individual teachers.

In 2001, a further university-school partnership project, Bridging the Gap, was set up with forty participating primary and second-level schools in socially disadvantaged areas of Cork city. The aim of the project was to bridge the gap between pupils in schools in socially disadvantaged areas and their more advantaged peers. While the focus of the project was not specifically on MI, an MI philosophy was adopted from the start, and the arts played a major role in helping to enhance the educational opportunities of the pupils involved. Researchers from Harvard Project Zero came to Cork on a number of occasions to lead workshops and seminars and to enhance and critique the work of the project. The cascade and osmotic effects of these activities on the educational culture of Cork were significant. While engagement with and application of MI theory and associated practices differed from individual to individual and from school to school, the language of MI became common currency in Cork. MI theory became increasingly accepted in Ireland.

MULTIPLE INTELLIGENCES AND TEACHING FOR UNDERSTANDING IN TEACHER EDUCATION

A one-year postgraduate diploma in education is a prerequisite for registration as a second-level teacher in Ireland. Almost two thousand student teachers who completed this diploma in UCC between 1997 and 2007 were introduced to MI theory and the TfU framework and encouraged to use these approaches in their teaching. An extract from the teaching portfolios of one of these student teachers gives a flavor of how MI theory influenced these teachers' thinking and classroom pedagogies during their teaching practice:

> In terms of teaching and learning, MI theory concentrates our mind on the fact that we need to address the plurality of the child's intellect. . . . Group discussion provides an opportunity for the child to make a valuable input. . . . The fact that each individual group member has their own strong points serves to make the group stronger because they each need the other. . . . If we truly accept and value the theory of MI, we must search for and develop methodologies that will allow all intelligences to shine in the learning experience. It means that we cannot go back to the hierarchical structure of teaching. Rather, we must grasp the notion of constructivism with both hands and give the students the freedom to explore and construct knowledge and understanding beginning with their own strengths.

MULTIPLE INTELLIGENCES AND THE BROADER EDUCATIONAL COMMUNITY IN IRELAND

The MI project in UCC also sought to influence attitudes among educational policymakers nationally. This was done through a series of strategies, including lectures, workshops, and seminars for various interest groups and individuals; involvement on national curriculum committees and advisory bodies; and one-to-one meetings with key influential policymakers. Many of these strategies proved effective over time. National educational policy documents and guidelines during the past ten years increasingly make reference to MI theory and its relevance to teaching and learning.

A recent search of the Web site of the National Council for Curriculum and Assessment (NCCA), the statutory body that advises the Irish government on curriculum and assessment at preschool, primary, and second levels, identified numerous references to MI theory in NCCA documentation. The "New Understandings of Child Development" section in the guidelines on early childhood education, *A Framework for Early Learning* (2007a), includes Gardner's theory of MI. This theory is acknowledged to "give rise to the principles underpinning the NCCA Consultative Document 2004 and ultimately the May 2007 Framework for Early Learning."

Another recently published NCCA document, *Exceptionally Able Students: Draft Guidelines for Teachers* (2007b), explicitly takes account of MI theory in describing exceptional ability and suggesting checklists for identifying children with exceptional ability. (This is the first joint document issued by Ireland's NCCA and Northern Ireland's CEA and may well mark the beginning of a new era of cooperation on educational matters between the north and south of the island, following the signing of the Northern Ireland agreement by the Irish and British governments and the installation of a power-sharing government in Northern Ireland in 2006.) This publication includes a chapter entitled "Other Ways of Thinking About Teaching and Learning," which highlights MI theory and gives examples of teaching strategies based on the various intelligences. Explicit references to MI theory also can be found in national documents relating to the arts at the primary level; social, personal, and health education; an evaluation of the primary curriculum; civic, social, and political education at the second level; and approaches to teaching and learning in the transition year.

MULTIPLE INTELLIGENCES THEORY AND TEACHING FOR UNDERSTANDING IN UNIVERSITY TEACHING AND LEARNING

From the late 1990s onward, targeted funding became available from the national higher education funding body, the Higher Education Authority, for enhancing teaching and learning in universities and for improving access for groups that had traditionally been underrepresented. These groups include students from lower socioeconomic groups, students with disabilities, and mature students. Universities were encouraged to expand their teaching approaches to develop a more inclusive learning environment that recognized the diversity of learners.

Among the projects funded in UCC under the targeted initiatives were A Multiple Intelligences Approach to Teaching and Learning and Teaching for Understanding in a University Context. These projects and professional development courses for faculty provided a new opportunity to apply MI theory and the TfU framework, this time in a university-teaching context. As well as being influenced by the work of Harvard Project Zero, the courses drew on the findings of research carried out by the Carnegie Foundation for the Advancement of Teaching, in particular the work of the Carnegie Academy for the Scholarship of Teaching and Learning in Higher Education. These studies included Boyer's seminal work, *Scholarship Reconsidered* (1990), and its sequel, *Scholarship Re-Assessed* (Glassick, Huber, & Maeroff, 1997), as well as Pat Hutchings's (1996, 1998) various publications on teaching and course portfolios, the work on disciplinary approaches to teaching and learning by Mary Huber (Huber, 2004; Huber & Hutchings, 2005; Huber & Morreale, 2002), and Lee Shulman's (2004) work on signature pedagogies. The complementarity of the work of scholars and researchers in the Carnegie Foundation and that of Project Zero was particularly relevant for university teachers in UCC (Hyland, McCarthy, & Higgs, 2007).

In its strategic plans, UCC has explicitly committed itself to equality; social, cultural, and ethnic inclusiveness; and facilitating students with disabilities. An MI approach to teaching and learning is a visible manifestation of this commitment and has been adopted by many faculty members. Some comments from faculty who attended courses, seminars, and workshops in UCC on MI theory and the TfU framework show how their approach to teaching in a university context changed as a result of engaging with these theories. Laurence Dooley in the Department of Management and Marketing embraces MI theory because it scaffolds him in his belief that good teaching can enhance student intelligence and performance and can make a difference:

> Gardner's work offers hope to all educators by emphasizing that teachers have the ability to nurture the intelligence level of their students by better instruction and resources that traverse the multiple intelligences. Thus, students can improve their intelligence capability in certain intelligence types, and all students can learn. It is only through adequately embracing MI theory through both a constructivist and teaching for understanding perspective, that all students can have equal opportunity to succeed and fulfill their potential.

André Toulouse in the Department of Anatomy discusses the implications of Gardner's MI theory for his teaching:

> While some aspects might be debatable, one can only recognize the variety and uniqueness of combinations of "intelligences." It is very important to offer learners a broad variety of learning opportunities to maximize the learning experience.

He concludes that this theory is "probably the closest reflection of the true nature of human intelligence that is available at the moment."

At a national level, faculty at other universities and higher education institutions have also adopted an MI approach to teaching and learning. At Waterford Institute of Technology, faculty in engineering construction are involved in a research-teaching project to create a multiple intelligences instructional design framework for virtual classes. This project includes partners from other European Union (EU) countries, including Turkey, the U.K., Cyprus, and France. It is part of an EU-funded research project under the Socrates Minerva Action.

Also at Waterford, staff of the School of Nursing are using Ellen Weber's multiple intelligences teaching approach to deliver the nursing curriculum. Preliminary research indicates that student groups using this approach are outperforming control groups not using these approaches in nursing practice exam results. A summary of this work has been published in the annual report of the (Irish) National Academy for the Integration of Research and Teaching and Learning (2007).

CONCLUSION

Teachers in elementary schools, high schools, and at the university level who have been associated with the MI movement in Cork and throughout Ireland have found MI theory enables them to plan and deliver the curriculum in a way that more effectively engages students and creates an inclusive environment for student learning. This has proved to be particularly the case where students felt excluded in the past, the examination failure rate was high, and many students had been failed by an unduly academically focused system.

While the various MI research and development projects undertaken in UCC do not provide conclusive evidence that increased academic success is necessarily associated with the application of MI theory, there is compelling evidence that MI-focused teaching and learning has led to greater involvement by students in their own learning, increased motivation on the part of students and teachers, and a more inclusive learning environment.

In our experience, MI theory has acted like an injection of enthusiasm for sometimes jaded teachers. It has given them a renewed faith in their role as teachers and in the potential of their students. They now believe that their students can achieve and that they as teachers can play an important role in that achievement. Nevertheless, the UCC projects confirm the view that MI theory alone will not sustain improved teaching and learning. MI strategies need to be grounded in a rigorous curriculum planning and delivery framework. For the UCC researchers and practitioners, the TfU framework proved to be the ideal delivery vehicle.

It will no doubt be argued that any sustained professional development program will help teachers to engage more effectively with their teaching. However, the same cannot be said about students and their learning. It is not often that a professional development program brings about visible and sustained improvement in student involvement in the way that introducing an MI approach does. Between us, we, the authors of this chapter, have over half a century of experience delivering initial and continuing education courses for teachers. We have experienced a greater sense of excitement among teachers and students when they are introduced to MI theory than to any other learning theory. Understanding the basis of MI theory and its potential for improved teaching and learning takes time and effort, but it is time and effort well spent. Implementing and sustaining MI through a TfU framework takes more sustained effort and persistence, but we believe it is an educational tool that really leads to improvement.

In the book *Good Work,* Gardner, Csikszentmihalyi, and Damon (2001) make the point that "doing good work *feels* good. Few things in life are as enjoyable as when we concentrate on a difficult task, using all our skills, knowing what has to be done." That sentence aptly summarizes our own views: MI theory and the sustained work of many good school principals, teachers, students, and faculty not only make teachers and learners "feel good," but it results in a more inclusive learning environment and improves the lives and the achievements of students.

References

Blythe, T. (Ed.). (1998). *The teaching for understanding guide.* San Francisco: Jossey-Bass.

Boyer, E. (1990). *Scholarship reconsidered: Priorities of the professoriate.* Princeton, NJ: Carnegie Foundation for the Advancement of Teaching.

Drudy, S., & Lynch, K. (1993). *Schools and society in Ireland.* Dublin: Gill and Macmillan.

Gardner, H. (1983). *Frames of mind: The theory of multiple intelligences.* New York: Basic Books.

Gardner, H., Csikszentmihalyi, M., & Damon, W. (2001). *Good work: When excellence and ethics meet.* New York: Basic Books.

Glassick, C. E., Huber, M. T., & Maeroff, G. I. (1997). *Scholarship assessed: Evaluation of the professoriate.* San Francisco: Jossey-Bass.

Huber, M. T. (2004). *Balancing acts: The scholarship of teaching and learning in academic careers.* Washington, DC: American Association for Higher Education and Accreditation and the Carnegie Foundation.

Huber, M. T., & Hutchings, P. (2005). *The advancement of learning.* Jossey-Bass.

Huber, M. T., & Morreale, S. P. (Eds.). (2002). *Disciplinary styles in the scholarship of teaching and learning: Exploring common ground.* Washington, DC: American Association for Higher Education and Accreditation and the Carnegie Foundation.

Hutchings, P. (Ed.). (1996). *Making teaching community property: A menu for peer collaboration and peer review.* Washington, DC: American Association for Higher Education and Accreditation and the Carnegie Foundation.

Hutchings, P. (Ed.). (1998). *The course portfolio: How faculty can examine their teaching to advance practice and improve student learning.* Washington, DC: American Association for Higher Education and Accreditation.

Hyland Á. (2000). *Multiple intelligences, curriculum and assessment.* Cork: University College Cork.

Hyland, Á., McCarthy, M., & Higgs, B. (2007). Fostering, recognising and rewarding scholarly teaching in University College Cork: Three perspectives. In C. O'Farrell (Ed.), *Teaching portfolio practice in Ireland: A handbook.* Dublin: Centre for Academic Practice and Student Learning, Trinity College.

Lynch, K. (1989). *The hidden curriculum: Reproduction in education. A reappraisal.* Lewes: Falmer Press.

McCarthy, M., & Higgs, B. (2005). The scholarship of teaching and its implications for practice. In G. O'Neill, S. Moore, & B. McMullin (Eds.), *Emerging issues in the practice of university learning and teaching.* Dublin: All Ireland Society for Higher Education.

National Academy for the Integration of Research and Teaching and Learning. (2007). *Annual report.* Cork: Author.

National Council for Curriculum and Assessment. (2004). *Transition year guidelines.* Dublin: Author.

National Council for Curriculum and Assessment. (2007a). *A framework for early learning.* Dublin: Author.

National Council for Curriculum and Assessment. (2007b). *Exceptionally able students: Draft guidelines for teachers.* Dublin: Author.

O Donnchadha, G. (1997, Summer). MI in our classrooms. *MI Bulletin.*

Organization for Economic Cooperation and Development. (2006). *PISA report: Assessing scientific, reading and mathematical literacy: A framework for PISA.* http://www.pisa.oecd.org/document/.

Shulman, L. (2004). *The wisdom of practice: Essays on teaching and learning, and learning to teach.* San Francisco: Jossey-Bass.

Stone-Wiske, M. (Ed.). (1997). *Teaching for understanding: Linking research with practice.* San Francisco: Jossey-Bass.

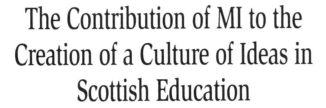

CHAPTER 18

The Contribution of MI to the Creation of a Culture of Ideas in Scottish Education

Brian Boyd

Stands Scotland where it did?
—Macbeth, IV. iii. 164

Full many a gem of purest ray serene,
The dark unfathom'd caves of ocean bear;
Full many a flower is born to blush unseen.
And waste its sweetness on the desert air.

Some village-Hampden, that with dauntless breast
The little tyrant of his fields withstood;
Some mute, inglorious Milton here may rest,
Some Cromwell guiltless of his country's blood.
—Thomas Gray, "Elegy Written in a Country Churchyard"

This chapter focuses on the growth of more inclusive models of education in Scotland over the last hundred years through the lenses of family history and national policy. The chapter describes policy changes that have reduced the role of intelligence testing and traditional conceptions of intelligence on access to secondary school, even as streaming, or tracking, within schools can still be problematic. In 2004, I participated in a ministerial review group that argued that curriculum should enable young people to become successful learners, confident individuals, effective contributors, and responsible citizens. The use of Gardner's theory is consistent with these aims. In 2007, I conducted a survey of the use of MI theory. The data from the survey give an indication of the extent to which MI has had an impact on teachers' professional practice. The data are presented here in the form of case studies and in the words of the teachers themselves.

⌒

This chapter looks at the impact of MI on schools in Scotland. It begins with a personal-historical account of schooling in Scotland over the past hundred years, looking at the role played by the traditional concept of intelligence. It then looks at recent curriculum reform within the Scottish school system and provides an account of a survey of Scottish schools undertaken in 2007 on the current understandings of MI and its roles within the learning and teaching process. Finally, it offers some pointers to future developments around MI in Scotland are offered.

THREE GENERATIONS OF SCOTTISH EDUCATION: A PERSONAL JOURNEY

On August 29, 1932, Margaret McDowall was awarded a day school certificate (lower) from the Advanced Division of St. Patrick's Primary School in Glasgow. At the age of fourteen, she left school with the following summary report:

Studies	Fairly Good
Character and Conduct	Excellent

What is important to note here is that she left from the advanced division of a primary school; she did not get to go to a secondary (high) school because she was not deemed to be academic. She did not study math or science or modern languages; instead she did cooking and housewifery.

It is difficult to comprehend that in a country proud of its claim, since the sixteenth century, to have provided a school in every parish with an aim to achieving universal literacy, there should be young people in the 1930s who had no right to a secondary education. The long-term effect of Margaret's experience in the advanced division was that she simply accepted that she was not very bright, yet in every aspect of her role as wife and mother, she demonstrated her excellent character and conduct—and her intelligences.

Secondary schooling became universal and compulsory in Scotland after World War II, but selection was the norm. The criteria were a mix of standardized tests of curriculum content (the qualifying exam) and IQ testing (under-taken across the whole population at ages eight and eleven). Senior secondary schools followed a traditional academic curriculum, with the classics, modern languages, sciences, history, geography, art, music, and physical education all in evidence. Junior secondary schools offered a similar range of subjects to the former advanced divisions. Modern languages, for example, did not appear in the junior secondary curriculum. But throughout the 1950s and early 1960s, junior secondary schools began to offer more academic courses.

The pressure for change in the structure of secondary education was building throughout the 1950s. Selection at age eleven or twelve was increasingly difficult to justify, with the growing realization that many pupils in junior secondary schools deserved an opportunity to achieve national certification on the same basis as their senior secondary counterparts.

In 1960, I attended a selective senior secondary school in the center of Glasgow. My secondary education represents what for many of my generation is regarded as some kind of golden age. Yet the reality was quite different. Streaming, that is, internal selection on the basis of general ability, ensured that of the six boys who went to the senior secondary from my primary school, only three made it beyond the school-leaving age of fifteen. This waste of talent was built into the system. My achievements at the end of my time there were modest, though enough to get me into Glasgow University, the first of my extended family to experience higher education.

My son, Christopher, was born in 1986. By then, all secondary schools in Scotland (with the exception of the small private school sector which takes around 4 percent of the school-age population, nationally) had become non-selective comprehensive schools. But while selection for secondary schooling had disappeared, internal selection was alive and well. At the end of his first year in secondary school, he was put into sets in English, math, and French: tracked classes based on measures of prior attainment subject by subject.

SCOTTISH EDUCATION IN THE EARLY TWENTY-FIRST CENTURY

Scottish education has been improving steadily over the past one hundred years. My education was better than that of my parents; my son's was better than mine. But intelligence remains the final frontier. Intellectually, MI, along with the work of others, including Reuven Feuerstein, has won the argument, but culturally, the psychometric notion of a single, fixed, predictable intelligence is difficult to shift from people's commonsense view of the world.

The ability to benefit from the school system is believed by many to revolve around concepts of intelligence, motivation, and behavior, and the research, from early intervention studies to secondary school examination results, consistently confirms that middle-class pupils in Scotland derive more benefit from schooling, are six times more likely to go on to university, and are seven times less likely to end up in prison. So if intelligence is not correlated with social class or race, if motivation is a complex mix of internal and external factors, and if behavior is context bound, then it suggests there may be something in the way schools are structured that is contributing to underachievement among some pupils.

In 2004, a ministerial review group on the curriculum, of which I was a member, produced *A Curriculum for Excellence* (Scottish Executive Education Department, 2004). This report provided a framework for the curriculum from ages three to eighteen, setting out aims, purposes, values, and principles. In essence, the curriculum, which includes the *how* as well as the *what* (pedagogy as well as content), should enable all young people to become successful learners, confident individuals, effective contributors, and responsible citizens.

The review group based its recommendations on Scottish publications such as *Teaching for Effective Learning* (Consultative Council on the Curriculum, 1996) which had reviewed the literature on intelligence, thinking, creativity, and teaching for understanding. It took as one of its starting points Howard Gardner's theory of multiple intelligences, which challenged many long-held assumptions and changed forever the way we speak about intelligence. The suggestion that the question, "How smart are you?" is no longer relevant, that the only legitimate question is, "How are you smart?" underpinned the report's belief that all young people are capable of being successful learners, "given a courteous translation."

In 2008, Jerome Bruner, in anticipation of speaking at the Learning and Teaching . . . and All That Jazz conference in Glasgow, wrote: "I've just received and read *A Curriculum for Excellence* of the Scottish Curriculum Review Group. All I can say is that Scotland can thank its lucky stars . . . a brilliant and ambitious document and a bold and creative one."

For the first time in a generation, Scottish education's school curriculum was being influenced directly by big ideas such as MI.

MULTIPLE INTELLIGENCES IN THE TWENTY-FIRST CENTURY: A SURVEY OF SCOTTISH SCHOOLS

There are, at the time of this writing, around three thousand schools within the publicly funded system in Scotland, some three hundred secondary schools, and the rest primary, additional support needs, and nursery. They are administered within thirty-two local authorities, ranging in size from Glasgow, the largest, with some thirty secondary schools, to Clackmannanshire, with three. The system is, in theory, nationally governed but locally administered. In reality, the local authorities have a strategic function and can implement their own policy initiatives, for example, to achieve national priorities in education. Within authorities, schools have some freedom to adopt pedagogical initiatives to enable them to improve the quality of learning among their students. Thus, until now, ideas such as MI were more likely to be adopted at a local authority or school level than nationally. There is no centralized, statutory, imposed pedagogy.

In 2007, a survey was undertaken to explore how Scottish educators understand and implement MI. All thirty-two local authorities were asked for permission for an electronic questionnaire to be sent to each of their schools, to be completed by whomever the school felt was most appropriate. In the event, we received 790 completed questionnaires, representing around 20 percent of the schools in the country and 83 percent of the LEAs. Of the respondents, 643 were teachers, classroom assistants, or school managers, and 36 indicated that they had teaching support roles such as behavior and learning support. A further 56 respondents indicated that they had nonteaching support roles, for example, librarians, technicians, and office staff, and 55 did not indicate what their role was.

The breakdown by sector was interesting, with some 66 percent coming from secondary schools, which represent only around 10 percent of the total number of schools. This was surprising since primary schools in Scotland have a reputation of being more innovative and creative than secondaries. Perhaps, as we shall see, problems of motivating learners in an increasingly examination-driven system may well have been the catalyst for secondary schools to see MI as part of a perceived solution.

Multiple Intelligences: A New Idea?

There is a perception, widely held in Scottish education, that MI and certain other educational ideas, such as philosophy for children (Lipman, 2003), instrumental enrichment (Feuerstein & Jensen, 1980), and teaching for understanding (Perkins, 1995), are of relatively recent origin. Some Scottish teachers, conservative by nature, still see them as "new-fangled" and "progressive." This was partly borne out by the survey, with the percentage of respondents saying they had heard of MI within the past five years being 60 percent. Indeed, if we extend the period to ten years, some 91 percent of all respondents had heard of MI within that time frame. It suggests, perhaps, a time lag in the transfer of ideas, both geographically and theoretically.

Sources of Information

The answers to the question, "Where did you first come across the idea of MI?" partly explain the relatively high percentage of respondents who had only fairly recently heard of MI. Initial teacher education (ITE) emerged as the most likely source of information on MI (28 percent), with continuing professional development (CPD) coming a close second (23 percent). Reading of books or articles represented some 34 percent of the source of information. It is not possible to tell from the data, but it is reasonable to assume that those who learned of MI from ITE were fairly recently qualified, while those whose source was CPD are likely to have encountered MI recently also, since issues of thinking skills and metacognition have become widely discussed among Scottish school teachers only within the past ten to fifteen years.

Perceived Benefits of MI

According to the data, teachers in Scotland regard the benefits, real or potential, of MI as including these:

- Teachers can address a pupil's learning failure by approaching it from a different intelligence (65 percent).
- People have more than one kind of intelligence (58 percent).
- Everyone is intelligent in some way (49 percent).
- We can develop and improve our intelligences (55 percent).
- Intelligences represent entry points into children's learning (41 percent).
- Pupils should be made aware of this understanding of intelligences (43 percent).
- The conventional notions of IQ are challenged (35 percent).

Some of these responses are perhaps more predictable than others. The idea that some children simply do not respond to the heavily linguistic and logical approaches to academic learning but may be successful learners if others of their intelligences were engaged is a view commonly held by teachers in Scotland. They see the notion of Gardner's intelligences as being entry points into learning as attractive. What is less expected is the view that learners should be "made aware of this understanding of intelligences." Historically Scottish pupils, especially in secondary schools, have not been allowed to engage with such meta-issues in the way, for instance, that Carole Dweck has argued in *Self-Theories* (1999).

It is clear that teachers see the concept of MI as something that gives them insight into why it is that some young people seem unable to learn at certain points in their education. The fixed mind-set (Dweck, 1999) exists in teachers as well as learners, but once MI is understood, it opens up possibilities for teachers to mediate learning for the child. It offers an optimistic perspective that sees intelligence as a multidimensional concept, and each of the intelligences can act as an entry point for the child to help them to achieve understanding.

Multiple Intelligences and Student Learning

When asked to indicate the extent to which MI helped with certain aspects of the learning process, the most popular response was in the affective domain, while most of the others were cognitive. Engagement (89 percent of respondents) was the main area in which respondents felt MI could help learners; in the cognitive domain, understanding (86 percent) and creative thinking (76 percent) emerged as the most important. It would appear that Scottish teachers believe that the concept of MI helps motivate children who might otherwise conclude that their initial failure to learn was some reflection on their lack of intelligence.

The Stories Behind the Data

The survey asked respondents to write comments on the issues. The comments were extensive, running to a total of 104 pages. No attempt has been made at this stage to present a systematic analysis of the themes and subthemes. Instead, I have tried to allow the teachers' words to speak for themselves and to present some of the stories that emerge. The following sections are organized by school sector.

Additional Support Needs

In Scotland until very recently, young people deemed unable to benefit from a mainstream education attended a special school. In the 1970s and into the 1980s, these schools were organized by classification of special need—for example, moderate learning difficulties, emotional and behavioral difficulties, and severe and complex needs. Terminology was crude, and even one of the most enlightened educational documents of the 1960s, The Primary Memorandum (Scottish Education Department, 1965), which introduced the theories of Piaget to Scottish primary schools, contained the sentence, "Backwardness cannot be cured." The "dull and backward" were seen to be a distinct subcategory of pupils until the 1970s. By the 1980s, the terminology had changed to reflect the changing focus, and *special educational needs* (SEN) replaced the various subcategories. More recently in Scotland, the term has become *additional support needs* (ASN), and for every child there is now a presumption of mainstream schooling. The number of separate schools has fallen; inclusion is the aim, but some separate ASN schools still exist.

Ladywell School is in Glasgow. Staff within the school have reflected on their practice, have considered MI, and are trying to apply the principles to learning and teaching. Their comments were by far the most extensive of any school in the survey, suggesting a commitment to and an enthusiasm for the concept of MI. The school was under no external pressure to engage with MI; it was a professional response to the phenomenon of young people with additional support needs, whose educational potential might easily be perceived as being limited by their ASN label.

The Ladywell curriculum places an emphasis on what they call "social and emotional learning":

> *Intrapersonal* learning enables us to know and understand ourselves, to recognise and identify our feelings, to know our strengths and weaknesses, our preferences, beliefs and values, what motivates us and how we learn best, and to apply this self-knowledge to our choices and actions. It is this intrapersonal learning that underpins our ability to manage our feelings and to become internally motivated, self-directed individuals, able to take responsibility for our own behaviour and learning and to demonstrate persistence and resilience in the face of setbacks, failure or disappointment.

In an ASN setting, it is not surprising to find an emphasis on relationships and social interaction. The Ladywell response argued:

> Learning within the social domain—*interpersonal* learning—enables us to form social relationships, to co-operate with others, to resolve disagreements, solve problems and to celebrate and respect the similarities and differences between us. The fundamental skill for social learning is empathy—the ability to understand others. This social and emotional learning can broadly be described as the development of emotional literacy.

Ladywell's curriculum also has a number of specific foci within MI. In the school, "background music plays an important role in learning and pupils are encouraged to reflect on the effects of different kinds of music on their mood, attention and motivation (*musical-rhythmic* intelligence)." The school is aware of the need for literacy to be developed and claim that "*verbal-linguistic* intelligence is developed through person-to-person interactions and written reflection." Visual-spatial intelligence "is developed through our dedicated Art Curriculum and in many Personal and Social Education and Drama activities." *Bodily-kinesthetic* intelligence is developed "in our dedicated Drama and Art Curricula and in PSE activities." In the wider context of well-being, pupils are "encouraged to look after their mental health and gain more from life by appreciating nature and engaging with their environment (*naturalist* intelligence)." And finally, "some of our thinking and problem-solving activities in PSE will enhance *logical-mathematical* intelligence."

It cannot be argued that such a thoughtful and thorough application of MI to the curriculum in a school for young people with ASN is typical, but responses from other similar schools indicate that those in the ASN sector, perhaps because of the nature of the challenges, are likely to be better able to link their practice more directly to theory than other sectors.

Echoing Jerome Bruner (1962), another respondent from an ASN school argued: "Taken to its extreme conclusion, every child should be able to learn anything using the appropriate 'intelligence' as an entry to this learning." Another respondent suggested: "I think it [MI] is vital to our children and they should all be aware of their intelligences and how they are building them. It is a tragedy if this is not being taught!"

Primary Schools

No individual school in the primary school sector stood out in quite the way Ladywell did, but a consistent picture emerged, presented here as a composite.

Primary teachers are generalists; they teach the whole curriculum. For this reason, they are more likely to believe that "not everyone is the same, and people can be gifted in one area, while seeming apparently lacking in other areas." In recent years—since the Thatcherite drive toward account-ability of a narrow, quantitative type—they have been subjected to an ever more restrictive testing regime, and they resent it: "For too long, achievement has been measured by how well you can learn facts. However, this does not necessarily make a well-rounded citizen." They are aware of the importance of their role; they are with their class all day, five days per week for thirty-eight weeks of the year and they are acutely aware of individual differences: "I believe that if teachers are aware of different types of intelligences and how they can be transfered to practice then more children will achieve their potential." Primary teachers talk of looking to the "other intelligences, such as music or naturalistic," to provide opportunities for pupils to learn when the going gets tough. One teacher spoke of "working with a group of reluc-tant readers" and using a "reciprocal reading" format. The children help each other to question, clarify, predict, and summarize while engaged in reading. This resulted in a group of boys who were motivated to read and were stimu-lated by being asked to predict, question, and engage with the text in other ways. The teacher believed that she had "tapped in to their interpersonal and creative intelligences."

In recent years, Howard Gardner has visited Scotland on a number of occasions to take part in conferences and workshops offered by Tapestry, a nonprofit organization established in 2000 to provide educators with longer-term engagement with seminal educational ideas. His personal charisma has had an effect on teachers (thirteen hundred of them turned up to hear him speak on one occasion). One primary teacher recalled: "When I first heard Professor Gardner speaking about multiple intelligences, I was enthused by his words and my mind raced with the possibilities for children. . . . Learning and teaching should be about addressing each individual child's potential."

For primary schools, MI is an antidote to the more didactic, target-driven reforms. It represents the philosophy that underpinned their creative practice in the 1960s and 1970s. The child as an individual, with strengths and developmental needs, able to be led to understanding by teachers willing to approach learning from different perspectives, is at the heart of Scottish primary school thinking, and MI has struck a chord with teachers.

Secondary Schools: Conflicting Pressures—Academic Attainment or Wider Achievements?

The comments made by respondents from secondary schools ran to sixty-five pages, reflecting, in quantity and in the focus of their concerns, the tension in Scotland between measures of success, at individual student and whole-school level, based on national academic examinations and a concern, expressed by many teachers, that many pupils continue to underachieve because their intelligences are not recognized: "I have always believed that some people were not given enough credit for things they could do if they did not fit in with the traditional academic groupings and am pleased to be able to encourage them with the intelligences they have."

The practice of setting is widespread in Scottish secondary schools, but not all teachers are comfortable with it: "I think it is important for both teachers and pupils to see that intelligence is NOT fixed, that there is not a predetermined ceiling of development or potential. I think it is important for the pupil to be at the centre of the learning."

The pressure of high-stakes examinations is often cited as a barrier to the implementation of MI: "Learning through multiple intelligence will have limited value if the exam system only assesses on words/mathematical terms. In my view there is little point in learning through MI only to regress because you are assessed in a way in which you are not 'competent.'" Another noted: "We also don't yet have an examination system which recognises MI. We are working under a huge exam constraint and will have to display much more imagination in how we recognise, cultivate and reward achievment."

Yet the survey data from secondary schools are heartening. It appears that the most heavily exam-dominated part of the Scottish school system is emerging from the narrow, instrumental vision of education and is looking at the needs of the learners in all of their complexity. MI has provided a challenge to the status quo, a challenge to which, it would appear, teachers are responding in a positive, thoughtful manner.

THE FUTURE?

MI has had only a limited impact on the practice of the Scottish school system as a whole. Developments have been piecemeal, patchy, and largely due to enthusiastic individuals. However, the landscape is changing. Organizations such as Tapestry are engaging teachers in a consideration of big ideas like teaching for understanding and MI. *A Curriculum for Excellence* (Scottish Executive Education Department, 1965), with its emphasis on deep learning, pedagogy, and educating the whole child, building on the culture of ideas developing among Scottish teachers, may soon enable MI to make the kind of impact it should have made on young people's ability to become successful learners. What we want is to enable teachers to create *The Learning Classroom* (Boyd, 2008), a place where MI is at the heart of pedagogy and where thinking, understanding, and creativity are the hallmarks of teaching.

Now, at the beginning of the twenty-first century, ideas are back in fashion. Powerful pedagogies are emerging from all over the world, and the professional development of teachers is benefiting from the confluence of theory, research, and practice. The way is open now for ideas such as MI to find their rightful place in an education process that aims to produce successful learners, confident individuals, effective contributors, and responsible citizens.

References

Boyd, B. (2008). *The learning classroom.* Paisley: Hodder Gibson.

Bruner, J. S. (1962). *The process of education.* Cambridge, MA: Harvard University Press.

Consultative Council on the Curriculum. (1996). *Teaching for effective learning.* Dundee: Author.

Dweck, C. S. (1999). *Self-theories: Their role in motivation, personality and development.* Philadelphia: Psychology Press.

Feuerstein, R., & Jensen, M. R. (1980). *Instrumental enrichment: An intervention programme for cognitive modifiability.* Baltimore, MD: University Park Press.

Lipman, M. (2003). *Thinking in education* (2nd ed.). Cambridge: Cambridge University Press.

Perkins, D. (1995). *Smart schools: Better thinking and learning for every child.* New York: Free Press.

Scottish Education Department. (1965). *Primary education in Scotland (The Primary Memorandum).* Edinburgh: HMSO.

Scottish Executive Education Department. (2004). *A curriculum for excellence.* Edinburgh: Author.

CHAPTER 19

Curriculum Reframed

Multiple Intelligences and New Routes to Teaching and Learning in Romanian Universities

Florence Mihaela Singer
Ligia Sarivan

This chapter looks at how to use MI in order to renew teacher training programs. The curricular design we implemented highlights deep understanding and aims at bridging the traditional gap between domain-related and teaching competence. We devise a multirepresentational model as a starting point for a methodological approach that supports student teachers' learning and transfers into classroom settings. We provide a number of examples from the curriculum implementation and discuss the new developments that originate in the classroom interactions.

ONCE UPON A TIME IN EASTERN EUROPE: A CONFLICTING HERITAGE

Once upon a time there was a beautiful land ("a mouth of heaven," a ballad would say): high mountains with breathtaking views over valleys, lakes, and forests; gentle hills with orchards, vineyards, and oil wells; rich fields (so rich that some historians called the land "the barn of Europe"). Its capital was posh and fun and referred to as "the little Paris." Its inhabitants proudly called themselves "Romanians" in order to show their honorable ancestry derived from the famous, rich, powerful Roman Empire. It was like a Latin oasis among mostly Slavic speakers, so it was quoted as the most Eastern Latin country.

Unfortunately, the riveting land was not spared of ugliness, lie, and evil. A big war came, and at the end of it, a red army occupied Romania and forced it behind the iron curtain. That is how the beautiful land moved into darkness and became a very sad country. Living in a police state, people were no longer proud, and they turned fearful: anybody could be arrested and sent to a reeducation center, mental hospital, forced labor building site, or prison.

People forgot to smile and forgot to love one another: anybody could be an informer. A propaganda system attempted to infuse the collective mind with the benefits of the communist regime: *Everything is thoroughly programmed by the party. If you obey, you are given what you need.* "What you need" was not an individual option but a mandatory package. People started to look the same: men and women lived in gray blocks, wore gray, walked on gray roads, under a gray sky. Big Brother wanted an easy-to-lead, uniform, and obedient society.

The result was a profoundly schizoid society: individuals never said what they thought, always wore a mask in public, declared all official "truths" if asked to, never trusted anyone, and shut down to all the meanings the propaganda wanted to convey. And probably the worst of all possible human responses to a hard-line regime, mothers would risk death in an illegal abortion rather than give birth to the centrally planned six children for every family.

Schools shared the conflicting features of the Romanian culture. The party tried to program school performance the way it programmed economic growth. At first sight, the propaganda mainly attacked the humanities in terms of curricular selection and standard discourse. History became *official history*; ideology restructured the list of compulsory authors. Nevertheless, the obsessive programming reproduced the authoritarian approach in all school subjects. The teacher informed, explained, and concluded. The students listened, took notes, and memorized the single view of the single textbook. Later students reproduced the material for the information-based test. Students had to be obedient, silent, and sit in rows, never facing one another. Collaborative work was nonsense, suspected of subversive behavior and fun. School had to deal only with serious matters. Instruction must be difficult and never enjoyable.

The schizoid reaction manifested in education too. As a means of escape, math and science teachers overtheorized their approach, and humanities teachers chose to mime the canon. Stuck between abstract theory and mimicry, the educational system was unofficially confronted by a huge tuition industry. This aimed at what the school was unable (or not allowed) to do: effectively train students individually or in small groups.

During the fifty years of dictatorship, the communist leadership boasted the remarkable results of the only progressive society and declared record industrial production, amazing crops, the largest building in Europe, the best leader, the most learned first lady, and, last but not least, the smartest students, who won prizes at the international competitions. This attitude was another instance of the big lie that communism brought about.

Society was far from being egalitarian, the economy was hardly competitive, and the standard of living was among the lowest in Europe. The leader and his wife were illiterate, and the clever students who did win the international prizes were the product of the tuition system and defected for better education and lives on the other side of the iron curtain. The overwhelming majority of the graduates of the praised "school for all" had a superficial factual understanding of school subjects and, happily enough, missed the conformity to the communist uniform that the system tried to inculcate. These very graduates were in the front lines of the surprising uprising that abolished the last iron curtain in 1989. Have they lived happily ever after?

NEVER-ENDING REFORM STORY: OLD WAYS, NEW WAYS, AND MI IN THE MELTING POT

The violent separation from communism brought unrest. Everybody wanted change. The intention for school reform was genuine and shared by teachers, students, decision makers, and parents. Yet these actors did not have a common vision for how the change could take place. Many were groping in need of direction. Others were exploring innovative ways to shape a student-centered school. All found out quite fast that political freedom had been far easier to get than a true liberation of old habits.

A new view of education was constantly blurred by the phantoms of the past. Theory and mimicry, the omniscient and authoritarian teacher, the neutral student, the stress on quantity, the rigid curricular tradition, the standard examples, and lots of methodological clichés still haunted Romanian education in the 1990s. For most of the decade, educational policies fluctuated with the seasons. Ministers of education came in and went off the political stage, each carrying his or her own old baggage and trying to reshape the predecessor's strategy (if any). Such an approach left no room for coherent development in the long run. Top-down reforms were declared and started anew at the beginning of every school year. Their outcome led to eroded hope and frustration for parents, students, teachers, and principals alike. A bottom-up perspective was virtually unknown.

Despite the constant stumbling of the reform, modern approaches permeated the newly opened borders and refueled the need for change. MI entered the Romanian school system by several routes. During the mid-1990s, small-scale experiments were carried out in one school (Sarivan, 1996, 1999), but the limited scope of the project was not sufficient to turn MI into a force for change.

In the late 1990s, differentiated instruction and MI were part of a cascade-based in-service teacher training program. The cascade is a top-down pattern in harmony with our centralist tradition, and thus MI received official endorsement. Geographically it brought extended impact. The implementation of the program went from the national to the regional level, then from regional to county, and finally from county to school level. The dilution that is inherent to retelling the story at various levels did not allow teachers to reach deep understanding.

By the end of the twentieth century, MI had also entered the curriculum of many academic initial teacher training programs. Being a theory, MI qualified as a trustworthy body of knowledge, and it was descriptively packed along with other theories. Prospective teachers had to study it. Although they memorized the intelligences, they barely understood the idea of an individual cognitive profile, and they did not understand how to implement MI in the classroom. When asked how they recognize the smart children in a school, the prospective teachers' answer revealed the traditional bias: "The smartest are those who perform well in math and science."

MI had become a fashionable trend by the beginning of the new millennium. Nevertheless, like all fashion, it remained very much at the surface. It did not reshape teachers' mind-sets and rarely changed anything in their students' minds. The habit of mimicry made teachers use MI circumstantially. Tasks that value various talents were a guarantee of innovation in front of the inspector. Whether the tasks were correctly stated or had any meaning for students was inconsequential. What was absent in this superficial implementation was the student-centered goals. Despite the potential of the theory, the main characters in the educational plot remained untouched.

If we are to give a sound cause for the failures of MI fashion, we must look to the roots of the teacher training system in Romania. As part of academic education, initial teacher training displays a number of clichés. One is that extended knowledge is valued, whereas deep knowledge is less of a focus. It is more important what the graduates know than what they do with their acquisition. Another is the focus on theory. The more abstract the theory, the more praised the result and the graduates who reach it. Last but not least, academic assessment is decontextualized and evanescent. The authority of the professor is the single standard for assessing student performance.

What are the consequences for prospective teachers? The theory they learn has very little to do with their future classroom practice. The role played by the theorist teacher trainer is hardly a model to consider for prospective teachers' future careers. The uniform pattern of academic instruction and assessment replicates the uniform view of their own undergraduate experience. Thus, the pattern of ineffective school results is reproduced with every generation of new teachers and is multiplied, rather like repeating a story with an unhappy ending. The power of this academic tradition rearranges every innovation according to its old standards. MI theory opposes the mere idea of uniform (uniform intelligence, uniform school, uniform curriculum), yet when it was absorbed into the pattern, it became part of the uniform approach. Despite the cracks in its walls, the school is buttressed by its old ways.

For a successful implementation of educational reforms, we should aim to better train prospective and graduate teachers. Their learning must be so good that they should be able to transfer domain-related knowledge in the specific context of a variety of classes. In the next sections, we discuss MI application within a teacher training program, present a multirepresentational model, and describe an example that was effectively implemented in both academic and school settings.

MULTIPLE INTELLIGENCES RELOADED: A STARTING POINT FOR TEACHER TRAINING RENEWAL

We believe MI can be used as a conceptual tool for reshaping the academic curriculum and teacher training that will have an impact in schools. In this respect, we highlight MI theory as a model for curriculum development for at least three reasons. It describes the human mind in terms of a multiplicity of abilities expressed by means of symbolic codes and specific procedures. It explains the epistemological identity of the various domains of study as specific representational codes and procedures that organize knowledge and allow problem solving in the real world. And it provides a context that values the trained individual who is able to respond to a variety of challenges in a given culture (Gardner 2000, 2006).

As a result, teacher training could split from a burdensome tradition and target new horizons. In this context, we made an attempt to restructure teacher training programs by highlighting competence in curricular design and by offering multiperspectives in its implementation. We designed the curriculum with a focus on individuals' talents and previous experiences. Thus, we developed a curricular framework as a generator for specific domain-related strands in which prospective teachers enroll (Singer & Sarivan, 2006). According to this framework, the graduates' competences are to be structured along four main stages.

First, prospective teachers should identify and overcome misrepresentations on learning in a given domain. The students in teacher training programs come with their own ideas about how learning occurs. Most of the time, these are personal theories or generalizations the students derive from their own schooling, including higher education. Basically these teachers-to-be enter the training programs with schooled minds evolving from the uniform pattern of education. That is why our first goal is to support students become aware of their false representations and help them deconstruct harmful learning and teaching clichés.

Second, prospective teachers should observe and analyze their students' learning difficulties in the context of those students' individual cognitive profiles. They must overcome the habit of looking at a class as a group of smart and less smart students. When asked why some students encounter difficulty in learning, these teachers explain that some youngsters are more able or gifted than others. They fail to recognize that there are varied abilities with strong points and weak points in every student. Therefore our teacher training program supports prospective teachers in finding out more about their students and their learning difficulties.

Third, prospective teachers should develop a set of competences that contributes to their students' understanding of the domain. We provide contexts for teachers to structure and restructure their own learning in terms of educational issues, theories, personal observations, and cognitive experiences. Within this process, our students obtain multiple representations on their domain of expertise and the school subject they will teach.

A specific teaching profile develops along the three stages presented above. History teachers, art teachers, technology teachers, and all the others share a number of teaching activities, but they learn and perform them differently. Regardless of their domain-related expertise, all teachers plan, organize, assess, and reflect: these are broad categories of teaching competence. But beyond abstractions and generalizations, teaching competence manifests in the subject taught. Math teachers and language teachers, for example, do not plan in the same way, do not lead a group discussion similarly and do not even decode the curricular provision in the same way. These differences develop not only because the teachers are individually different, but also because their training within a subject area gives them specific perspectives on how to deal with a problem. By no means are these domain-related lenses a handicap in teaching. On the contrary, when well used, they promote students' deep understanding of the subject matter. This is why future language teachers, for example, learn how to structure the language learning of their more or less linguistically able pupils if they activate philological knowledge, such as text analysis and plural interpretation, point of view, *Erwartungshorizont (horizon of expectations)* and so on (Sarivan, 2005). Similarly, mathematics students will become effective mathematics teachers if they learn, among other things, how to plan meaningful problem solving by making use of their strategic thinking.

Finally, prospective teachers should develop a reflective attitude as well as teamwork and partnerships to improve their own learning and teaching. Our aim is to provide learning contexts that challenge students to structure metacognitive competences in themselves and their students, as well as to open them to integrated approaches and networking in school and in the community.

In order to reach such goals, a new methodology is needed. We attempted a shift toward a genuine learning partnership between the trainer and trainees. That is, the unique voice of the teacher provides space for the multiple voices of the students. Instead of the *magister dixi* traditional pattern, we have tried to develop a polyphonic story of success.

BEYOND THE ACADEMIC OMNISCIENT POINT OF VIEW: A METHODOLOGICAL INNOVATION

If we are to involve our students in writing their own meaningful learning stories, we have to deal with the variety of talents and areas of expertise. At this point, it is important to ask: What would stimulate, for example, mathematics students' interest in MI theory? Throughout the course, a stress on some numerical characteristics of the brain (for example, the human neonate has approximately 2.5×10^8 synapses per 100 mm^3 of gray matter [Huttenlocher, 2002]) has proved to be a good entry point with this group. Alternatively, graduate language students were introduced to MI by being told the story of how Gardner developed his theory.

To support their understanding of the intelligence profile, students were reminded of a famous Romanian poem entitled *Lake.* Recall of the poem allowed a comparison that helped deep understanding. The individual profile is like an image of the water. The pupil's intelligence profile is a collection of intelligences with strengths and weaknesses similar to a lake glittering in the sun. Some parts are shining gold, some are twinkling between shade and light, and some are dark. Philologists were thrilled with the image and took the challenge of trying something similar for their own students. So did the mathematicians after being exposed to numerical and logical experiences. They all looked for introductions, metaphors, and analogies to the concepts they were to teach during the coming weeks. In these approaches, the entry point and the meaningful metaphor represent both MI concepts and procedural frames that facilitate an understanding of teaching and learning.

Our methodological option is suggested with a model that presents a spiral path to understanding concepts (see Figure 19.1). We call this approach *multirepresentational training* (MRT). The model is based on two directions of action: providing a variety of representations as powerful tools in various disciplines and developing representational models to stimulate abstraction and synthesis (Singer, 2007, 2009). Our major challenge was to overcome the superficial implementation of MI as well as the academic cliché of "highly theoretical and extended knowledge."

How could we facilitate the prospective teachers' understanding of the theory beyond the reciting of the eight plus intelligences list? Moreover, how could we strengthen their commitment to use the theory in their teaching career? The answer lies in the use of MI concepts that have procedural impact. At the level of course planning, we translate the declarative knowledge into procedures. These procedures are used in a variety of learning contexts to mobilize content and methodological understanding.

Following the learning paths in Figure 19.1, we note that the teacher trainer selects a concept (entry point), transfers it into a procedure (designing meaningful introductions), then develops and uses it in various learning contexts (for example, MI theory, curricular planning, interactive methods, grading schemes). The teacher trainer supports students to explore, reflect on, synthesize, and apply various elements of the contexts by means of the entry point procedure, which works as a vehicle for understanding. In the debriefing sections of the course, students are challenged to reflect on the teaching procedures they were exposed to. They review the stories and songs they listened to, the images and schemes they looked at, the role plays they acted in. Throughout this process, students internalize the entry point. They can define and explain the use of it. They can even invent some of their own in order to introduce various topics

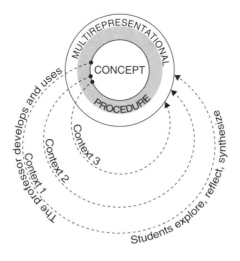

Figure 19.1 A Visual Model for Multirepresentational Training

of the curriculum to their students. Ultimately we expect the entry point to become a multirepresentational concept: a well-learned concept and procedure ready to be applied in a variety of classroom contexts.

Our experience with the implementation of the competence-based teacher training program shows that the MRT leads to successful learning transferable to successful teaching. The contextualized learning paths developed through the MRT help students reach a depth of understanding that enables them to reiterate their learning acquisition in the different and complex problem-solving context of teaching in a planned or real situation.

The MRT in Figure 19.1 applies to the partnership of the teacher trainer and the prospective teacher. But it also applies to the teacher-student partnership within a successful class. Of course, the concepts used and their level of complexity are different, but the mechanism of developing deep understanding is the same. Thus, Figure 19.2 replicates Figure 19.1 in the classroom setting, where the former student has become a teacher and facilitates the learning of his or her own students. The teaching and learning contexts support both the teacher in going deeper in his or her own personal understanding and the student in internalizing new concepts.

The stories in the next section detail two examples of MI teaching and learning in actual school settings. These represent an instance of the MRT implementation with evidence of the transfers that put a different perspective on students' understanding.

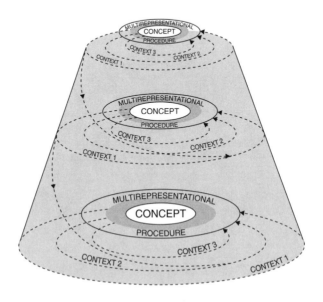

Figure 19.2 Implementing MRT: A Developmental Model

MULTIREPRESENTATIONAL TRAINING STORIES: FROM THE CURRICULAR MODEL TO REAL LIFE EXPERIENCES

During the past five years, we developed our model within teacher training programs for both graduate and undergraduate students. We discuss in this section the main issues of a course in mathematics education for prospective teachers in kindergarten and primary school. Results from mass competitions and national assessments show that number and geometry concepts, as well as basic mathematics operations, are rather poorly understood by young children. The reason is the decontextualized drill-based learning that originates in the routine of primary teachers.

The need for deep understanding of math concepts led to the following hypothesis: if young learners are involved in transdisciplinary projects connected to real-life situations, they will better acquire both the concepts and problem-solving strategies within a joyful context. To put it plainly, if we use the MRT model, the quality of classroom practice will improve, and our students' pupils will gain deeper understanding of the main concepts.

The students were first confronted with the Reggio Emilia early education example by reading the relevant chapter in *The Disciplined Mind* (Gardner, 2000). They applied critical thinking techniques for a meaningful reading of the excerpt. A group discussion followed individual analysis. Next, they were challenged to role-play and reflect. The professor played the role of primary teacher, and the students played the children who got the chance to learn contextualized math. Thus, they went through number, measures, geometry, and problem-solving project work. The prospective teachers then reflected on each role play. They were able to experience and see the benefits of the approach from their future pupils' perspective: fun and motivation, meaning for learning, construction of the concept.

Then the students were asked to develop a teaching plan for an instructional unit. The topic, grade, and age of the children to work with were the students' choice. On completion, they presented the plans, which were reviewed by the professor and, if needed, improved. The students implemented their plans and shared their results, conclusions, and artifacts from the classroom implementation at the final exam. For a more vivid demonstration of their teaching skill, they enacted a sequence of activities from the teaching plan in a role play where their colleagues took the part of the children. Thus, the exam turned into a rather enjoyable event, and the prospective teachers could experience both the fun and the rigor of assessment. Nevertheless, the most spectacular result was the children's response to our students' approach. We briefly describe one of the artifacts developed during the project work in classroom setting.

At the beginning of the term, the children in the class discussed their recent summer holiday and made a list of their favorite locations. Starting from this list, students were grouped to develop a display in which they integrated their personal memories with revised geometry and correspondence. They also learned to add and subtract. Figure 19.3 shows one of these displays, which presents a grandparents' village. We describe below the sequence of tasks that led to this outcome. Pupils played with geometric plastic shapes, by means of which they built a road thus separating the village into two parts. Using patterns provided by the teacher, they cut flowers and butterflies from colored paper. According to their imaginations, children decorated the artifacts with smaller pieces of paper of various shapes and color.

The next task was to associate the elements of the two parts of the display in a one-to-one correspondence. After this part of the display was done, pupils analyzed it from an aesthetic point of view and decorated it accordingly. On the other side of the "road," the children built houses made of cubes and pyramids from colored cards cut by the teacher and then applied by the pupils. Children associated a cube with a pyramid, glued them together, and added other shapes to mark windows and doors. The church was built by the teacher and decorated by the students while making use of geometrical shapes. A pond made of small marbles was a good way to bring "thirsty"

Figure 19.3 Student-Created Grandparents' Village

animals into the display, which helped pupils learn how to add and subtract. Because children remembered a modern village where there are cars on the main road, they placed toy cars next to the pond. The result is a playful image of "thirsty" cars coming to drink as animals do. Nevertheless, the teacher used this representation to speak of a parking lot by the pond and redesigned the context for some extra practice of addition and subtraction.

REREADING THE STORIES: WEAKNESSES AND STRENGTHS

Not everything looks bright in our teacher training experiences. Mainly in the earlier phases, during the first three or four weeks of the course, many responses are superficial. Thrilled by the appearance of fun in the activities and testing the new theory, a number of students are tempted to consider every song, picture, or anecdote as a genuine MI application, whether it is connected or not to the topic of discussion, whether it fits or does not fit the profile of actual children. They focus on using a variety of codes to better fit a standard representation in a textbook. The students miss the essence of the contextualized and individualized learning promoted by MI and reproduce the essence of the uniform school under a mask of innovation.

Another tradition-biased perspective takes place when students design their instructional units. As they plan assignments to meet the requirements of multiple representations, two types of mistakes blend with correct interpretations at the group level. Some students' tasks focus on learning the facts instead of learning the concepts. This is again an instance of how to make children buy the norm of the "famous quote–famous example–famous author–best comment–drill problem" without aiming at the deep understanding of concepts that will support future transfers.

Other students design multiple tasks that focus on different things and fail to target a clear objective. In this case, the focus is on giving multiple tasks that are irrelevant to the curriculum objectives for the sake of multiplicity, which actually causes the multiple perspective to be lost in translation. All of these clumsy approaches show us that effective MI-based approaches are not easy to implement in our culture. Despite declarations about education reform, the Romanian school is still marked by methodological prejudices so deeply rooted in the teachers' and students' minds that they can barely identify them.

Beyond the superficial use of MI, MRT-based courses have brought a new perspective to teacher training programs. Our students have been enthusiastic about MI application, whether this involved a personal learning experience or the design of an MI task and consequent implementation in the classroom. Enthusiasm as a positive attitude toward MI works as a catalyst in learning how to teach and in actual teaching.

MRT is important to understanding in both learning and teaching. After drafting several plans for instructional unit projects, students are able to design opportunities that help their students understand concepts and procedures. These projects give scope to the students' prior experiences as well as to their cognitive profiles. They aim to multiply the possible response in more than just one symbolic code. Accordingly, pupils give the best of their talent and efforts, and we observe spectacularly creative results coming from classrooms.

Another positive result of our courses is a category of products developed by teachers, or their pupils, or the teachers and pupils in partnership. These products are valuable learning resources for future activities. Consider the example of the Math Castle in Figure 19.4.

This artifact is not just pretty, it also has a tremendous learning potential. The teacher is the architect of a math castle. Students cut and color shapes to bring the blueprint to life. This is how a rectangle becomes a cylinder as the main

Figure 19.4 Students' Math Castle Guarded by Soldiers

part of the building. A cut circle becomes a cone and then the roof. A rectangle stuck to a half circle made a door to be attached to the main tower. The building process combines the two dimensional and the three dimensional. Once completed, the castle is guarded by soldiers. These let only those who can provide a password, which is a good answer to a math question, enter the castle. Children are thus motivated to look for the right answer because access to the castle will allow them to participate in a live fairytale. Questions are set out in progress on the staircase of the castle in order to help all children enter. Support questions, hints, and clues are provided by the soldiers to enable everyone to find the right password. When the whole group can give a password, the children step into the magic of the castle (Figure 19.5). They continue to play games in the castle.

With adequate methodology, a stargate is open to the realm of knowledge, and from there any instructional story can start. "Once upon a time there were

Figure 19.5 Everyone Is Inside (the Story)

some mountains, some forests, and a big lake guarded by a . . ." "Once upon a time there was a Roman emperor that went to war against . . ." "Once upon a time there was a thermometer shivering with cold . . ." And they hopefully learned effectively ever after.

ACKNOWLEDGMENTS

We thank student teachers from the University of Ploiesti and graduate students from the University of Bucharest who enthusiastically participated in the experimental programs.

References

Gardner, H. (2000). *The disciplined mind: Beyond facts and standardized tests, the K–12 education that every child deserves.* New York: Penguin Books.

Gardner, H. (2006). *Multiple intelligences: New horizons.* New York: Basic Books.

Huttenlocher, P. R. (2002). *Neural plasticity: The effects of environment on the development of the cerebral cortex.* Cambridge, MA: Harvard University Press.

Sarivan, L. (1996). Multiple intelligences: A theory for classroom practice. *Învăţământul primar (Primary Education Journal), 3,* 63–67. (In Romanian).

Sarivan, L. (1999). Multiple intelligences: New steps towards classroom practice. *Învăţământul primar* [Primary education journal], *3–4, 49–54.* (In Romanian).

Sarivan, L. (2005). Multiple intelligences and teacher training: The story of an experience. *Limba şi literatura română. Perspective didactice* [Romanian language and literature: Didactic perspectives] (pp. 127–134). Bucharest: Editura Universăţii din Bucureşti. (In Romanian).

Singer, F. M. (2007). Beyond conceptual change: Using representations to integrate domain-specific structural models in learning mathematics. *Mind, Brain, and Education, 1*(2), 84–97.

Singer, F. M. (2009). The dynamic infrastructure of mind—A hypothesis and some of its applications. *New Ideas in Psychology, 27,* 48–74.

Singer, M., & Sarivan, L. (coord.). (2006). *Quo vadis, academia? Landmarks for a comprehensive reform of higher education.* Bucharest: Sigma. (In Romanian, with an abstract in English).

CHAPTER 20

Multiple Intelligences Practices in Turkey

Osman Nafiz Kaya
Ziya Selçuk

After the Turkish Republic was established by Atatürk in 1923, many radical revolutions, including within the Turkish education system, were made in order for Turkey to reach the level of contemporary civilizations. However, as an extension of traditional intelligence theories, the Turkish education system has been based on mathematics and verbal skills. In the past two decades, multiple intelligences (MI) theory has been an important instrument for improving all learners' cognitive, affective, and behavioral development. The first studies about MI theory were made after the mid-1990s. This chapter examines the initial efforts to use MI theory as an organizing principle for several private schools; shares how MI-oriented methods courses for preservice teachers in education faculties were structured; and focuses on the impact of MI theory on the education reform developed by the Turkish Ministry of National Education in 2005.

The Turkish Republic was established by Mustafa Kemal Atatürk in 1923 after the abolition of the Ottoman Empire. Life in Turkey is a rich variety of cultures and traditions, some which can be traced back to 5,000 B.C., and others of more recent heritage. People of many different cultures and religions lived during the time of the Ottoman Empire, and this diversity has been preserved in Turkey. Although 99 percent of the population is Muslim, religion is considered strictly a private matter. Turkey has a long-running democracy and a secular legal system that separates religion and state affairs. Today there are approximately 250 churches and 35 synagogues open for worship. Istanbul is one of the few places in the world where you can see churches, synagogues, and mosques built within a short distance of each other. Hospitality is a cornerstone of Turkish culture, and Turks believe that visitors should be treated as guests of God. Most Turks welcome the opportunity to meet foreign visitors and learn about different cultures.

Education in Turkey consists of compulsory primary education, with eight years of elementary and middle school education (ages seven to fifteen). Secondary education lasts four years (ages fifteen to nineteen) and covers general, vocational, and technical high schools. All schools are expected to use the curricula developed by the National Ministry of Education. Students take a nationwide university entrance examination for admittance to higher education programs. Higher education is provided by sixty-seven state universities and thirty private universities. The universities—generally two- and four-year undergraduate programs—are under the supervision of the Turkish Higher Education Council. In the universities, the medium of instruction is Turkish; however, English also is used in a few universities.

The history of Turkish education is closely related to Turkey's cultural values and pedagogical insights. As an extension of traditional intelligence theories, the Turkish education system is based on the study of mathematics and language. Indeed, the examinations for admittance to higher education have a mathematical and a verbal part. Engineering, mathematics, and the pure sciences have always been popular in Turkey. Other occupations have been regarded as secondary fields. To have an occupation related to music, painting, sports, literature, law, and nature is preferred when there is no opportunity for scientific occupations.

Turkey has an education system in which input is highly appreciated, but there is no assessment infrastructure. For example, the following inputs are considered so important in Turkey: portion of the budget allocation for education, number of new teachers for each year, and number of new computers purchased for schools. However, there is no effort or infrastructure to assess the quality of the outputs. The goal of education is to prepare students for examinations. The high school and university entrance examinations allow only 10 percent of students to pass. Among forty-one member countries of the Organization for Economic Cooperation and Development, Turkey has the greatest disparity between schools with the most and fewest opportunities for students. Unless the inequalities among schools are ended, some schools will always attract more students, and the exam pressure will continue. In such an atmosphere, parents and sensitive educators are trying to find alternatives.

The customary pedagogical approach at schools is didactic and based on the transmission of knowledge. Students who memorize most of the information are regarded as the most successful. One of the most important criticisms made about the Turkish education system is that pedagogy is not tailored to students' individual interests and abilities. There is no economic or educational infrastructure for orienting students and no policies of employment to cater to these interests and abilities. How the interests and the abilities of students will be classified and the demand for an intelligence theory to support such a classification has become a serious subject for discussion. Parents and teachers hope that abilities outside the mathematical-verbal discourse will be considered. Multiple intelligences (MI) theory has been used as evidence of such considerations.

RECOGNIZING MI THEORY IN TURKEY

The first studies in Turkey about MI theory, which appeared during the second half of the 1990s, were translations of material about studies done abroad. Simple models transferred from the United States clarified the theory. In addition, speakers invited from various countries gave lectures to a limited number of educators. The question, "What is MI?" was emphasized, and the focus was on the definition and explanation of multiple intelligences.

After 1997, a different, question, "Why MI?" came to the fore. In other words, what was wrong with the existing system that made a new perspective necessary? Why would MI theory improve the Turkish education system? Such questions were asked by both academicians and innovative teachers at seminars and conferences. Concerned academicians received invitations from government officials, business, and public schools to introduce the theory. Teachers in cities had opportunities for the first time to learn about the theory through nationwide seminars. Although a group of teachers talked about MI theory in great admiration, the majority argued that they already practiced MI.

During the third stage, the question of "How?" became popular. How can teachers apply MI theory in the classroom? Extensive workshops, seminars, and conferences held at public and private schools allowed feedback from practitioners to draw the connection between theory and practice. Finally, a new story of a Turkey-specific development pathway for MI theory appeared.

MULTIPLE INTELLIGENCES AS AN ORGANIZING PRINCIPLE FOR SCHOOLS IN TURKEY

The initial efforts to implement MI theory in the Turkish education system began in the Enka private schools in Istanbul toward the end of the 1990s. The schools organized their classrooms based on MI, and students from a number of countries attended. The Enka schools published the Turkish version of Gardner's *Multiple Intelligences: Interviews and Essays* (1999), the first Turkish version of a book published on multiple intelligences. A few educators interested in how to arrange a school based on MI visited Enka schools and tried to conduct similar practices in their schools.

The theory was initially seen as a new fashion in education, and few university scholars took interest in it. However, as the scientific basis of the theory was elaborated, the number of academicians interested in it increased. For example, Ziya Selçuk of the Gazi University of Ankara, the capital of Turkey, analyzed schools in the United States that used MI and synthesized observations and ideas. In 1998, he opened the first institute of education where MI theory was combined with the Turkish education system and existing curricula.

As a result of the studies made in the Practice School of Gazi University, *Multiple Intelligences Practices* was published (Selçuk, Kayılı, & Okut, 2002). The book adapted MI theory to the Turkish education system and set out the principles of multiple intelligences and how those principles can be put into practice in classrooms. In Private Gazi Elementary School, as well as in public schools oriented toward MI practices, three effects of MI implementation became evident: interdisciplinary cooperation, broader ways of defining how students were smart, and a switch from measurement to evaluation.

Interdisciplinary cooperation became necessary among teachers. Whereas before, teachers of the same discipline used to work together, teachers of different disciplines began to meet after MI was introduced. As a school principal said, "The directors began to go out of their rooms after MI practices." The principal of Cay Primary School of Rize, a small province in Turkey, said, "After MI practices, we learned how to be a company, and it is not only us who represents the school. All the personnel began to represent the school. The reason was that the projects were common to everyone." Thus, a horizontal organization developed out of the traditional vertical organization.

After the introduction of MI, teachers perceived students differently. A teacher from Private Gazi Elementary School said, "Previously I used to consider the students who were good only in mathematical and verbal skills as successful. The students from other fields were less intelligent to me. However, I now am aware that I define the popular field as intelligence, and I am sorry for the students for whom I have had prejudices. . . . I had a garden of eight square meters, but I had watered only two square meters of it."

Before the application of MI, teachers used to pay attention to measurement but neglected evaluation. Now they have begun to pay more attention to the evaluation process rather than limit learning achievement to a few test scores. For example, a classroom teacher, speaking of one of his students from Private Maya Elementary School, said, "When I measured, he failed; but when I evaluated, he passed. The reason was that the student was not very good with regard to the result but was positive and a good participator in the process."

To show how these changes were manifested and to illustrate the value of MI theory's contribution to the Turkish education system, we present the opinions of one of the first Turkish MI teachers, Hussein, and a case study of a student, Mehmet.

Hussein, the Changed Teacher

Hussein had graduated from the Teacher Training College, the most important institute educating teachers in Turkey. He began to teach at age eighteen and continued for twenty-five years at public schools. Then he worked at Private Gazi Elementary School and now teaches at Private Maya Elementary School.

He contributed to the MI training of thousands of teachers, focusing on the question: "What has changed in your professional life after learning MI?" His own response to this question revealed how he had changed his view of both his students and his own teaching methods:

> Until I understood MI, I was a self-centered teacher. I used to think that students cannot teach each other or perform some instructional contribution because they were not teachers. After I began using MI, my opinions of making students active totally changed.

> I noticed that I did all my teaching in a mathematical-logical style. I had a tendency to regard the students who followed my style as more successful. I used to worry that group work could lead to empty classroom hours. I began to use activities based on the interpersonal development of students more than ever before. I could not imagine that peer learning could contribute to personal development to a great extent.

> However, mathematical, linguistic, and visual fields of intelligence were more important for me. The questions in international examinations were concerned with these fields. But later I changed my point of view totally when I realized that even musical activities can contribute to understanding mathematical and linguistic subjects.

> The positive feedback of kinesthetic activities in understanding mathematical and geometrical subjects was unbelievable.

> A sample of one hundred intelligence activities gave us a variety of ways of instruction. Puzzles, museums, streets, business offices, posters, telephone diaries, and newspapers became course materials or appropriate places for lessons.

> Another advantage of MI was that it gave us an opportunity to know our students better. For example, until I understood MI, I used to think that students with high intrapersonal intelligence were asocial. I used to require them to spend some time with others in the same environment. But then I understood that they are more productive working alone. When they want to, they spend time in a more social environment.

Another example is related to kinesthetic students. I used to have the general opinion that they could not be successful in mathematics and geometry. But I was shocked when one of my students answered the question on his exam sheet about the field of a triangle located on a circle by holding a pair of scissors and cutting out a triangle. Following this, I paid more attention to developing some mathematical activities for kinesthetic learners.

In the course of my seminars, I became more enthusiastic when I heard that thousands of teachers said they became more active after they had learned about MI. I am of the opinion that it is too late for students who have taken one-sided instruction. For students today, there is still much of a chance.

Mehmet, the "Unsuccessful-Successful" Student

Mehmet is a fourth grader who has very low grades. But everyone loves him, and he takes part in most social activities at school. He is a strong leader. He is active and runs a lot, and he is a leading soccer player. He writes letters to various companies about the problems his school faces.

His teachers claim that Mehmet has a high capacity for learning. But his mathematics, science, and language achievements are weak. The yearly reports in these subjects are very important to schools, so in this respect, he is unsuccessful. Mehmet's self-confidence is very high in some subjects but very low in others. Therefore, Mehmet describes himself as "unsuccessful-successful."

After Mehmet's school decided to apply MI principles, many things changed. Mehmet is pleased with the situation: "Previously, there were both games and lessons, but now there are gamelike lessons." Mehmet overcame his math anxiety by using MI practices and scored a very high score on a national secondary education placement test.

PRESERVICE TEACHERS GAIN ACCESS TO MI THEORY

Multiple intelligences theory was introduced into Turkish higher education in the 2000s. The positive results obtained from graduate studies of the theory (Başbay, 2000; Bümen, 2001; Çakir, 2003; Dilli, 2003; Doğan, 2000; Göğebakan, 2003; Kaptan & Korkmaz, 2001; Kaya, 2002; Sezginer, 2000; Talu, 1999; Tarman, 1999) attracted the attention of faculties of education.

As a result, teacher candidates began to analyze MI theory in their general education courses (learning and teaching, educational psychology). These courses now include the fundamental principles of MI theory, the definitions and characteristics of multiple intelligences, the differences between MI theory and traditional teaching, and the innovations MI theory has brought to the learning environment. Because of the positive attitudes of teacher candidates toward MI theory and their adoption of the theory, a number of books related to teacher education now include a chapter on MI (Demirel, 2000).

The transfer of MI from theory into practice at faculties of education gained momentum through courses on teaching methods in mathematics, science, social studies, and elementary teacher education. Some courses also included other methods of teaching, such as problem-based learning and cooperative learning, but others focused only on MI theory.

For instance, Kaya has taught the science methods courses taken by elementary and science teacher candidates completely in terms of MI theory since 2003. From the start of this course, he has not been the source of information; rather, the teacher candidates are actively involved. After a general introduction to education theories in the first two weeks of class, Kaya introduces MI theory, its basic principles, and how the intelligences affect science education. Students analyze science textbooks from the perspective of MI theory, examine what MI theory contributes to the process of evaluating children's learning, and investigate criticisms about the theory. Most teacher candidates understand the definitions of multiple intelligences, which individuals are strong in which intelligences, and which instructional activities address which intelligences.

A common problem that arises is misunderstandings and superficial knowledge about the fundamental principles of MI theory and how the theory was developed. Many preservice teachers think that Gardner developed the theory after long years of observation or just sitting at a table without doing any research on how the human mind functions. Accordingly, small groups of teacher candidates analyze parts of Gardner's (1983) book, *Frames of Mind: The Theory of Multiple Intelligences,* to help them better understand the nature of the theory. Then they present their results. For instance, one group reviewed how Gardner identified multiple intelligences and represented the eight specific criteria that he used to qualify each candidate intelligence from multidisciplinary perspectives.

Next, teacher candidates learn how MI theory can be practiced in the classroom to realize the goals of science education. Most teacher candidates have some difficulty in designing a science lesson based on the principles of MI theory. One elementary teacher candidate explained this challenge: "When I prepared my MI science lesson plan to teach the concept of matter to fifth-grade students in a forty-minute lesson period, I was not sure what kinds of teaching activities were more appropriate for one of the intelligences than for others for the effective teaching of science and how I could go forward from one activity to another." Teacher candidates interview a teacher who has applied MI theory in elementary science courses and observe this person's lessons.

After teacher candidates share their observations, Kaya presents practical ideas from published sources for how MI theory-based science lessons could be planned (Armstrong, 2000; Campbell, Campbell, & Dickinson, 1996; Kaya &

Ebenezer, 2003; Lazear, 1992). Most teacher candidates tend to use a modified version of Armstrong's (1994) seven-step procedure for creating an MI lesson sequence (Kaya & Ebenezer, 2003). However, a few prefer to use the model of Campbell et al. (1996). Teacher candidates choose a subject from the elementary science curriculum and develop a lesson plan for it according to MI theory. Each plan is evaluated by the teacher, his or her peers, and the professor.

One common myth among teacher candidates is that each learning objective or knowledge structure should be taught through all multiple intelligences or they may not reach all students. They believe that each student should learn using only his or her strengths, not weaknesses. They ignore the MI principle of developing students' underused intelligences to a reasonable level. Accordingly, teacher candidates are asked to include teaching activities based on students' underused intelligences and to note what happens during class.

As a result of intensive face-to-face and online discussions of their experiences and observations in the classroom, these teacher candidates realize there are four important factors affecting how MI science lessons are planned and carried out in a forty-minute session: (1) identifying individual students' multiple intelligence strengths using a reliable and valid tool, (2) paying attention to the scholarly findings related to students' difficulties in learning the relevant science topic, (3) considering the nature of the knowledge structure that students are supposed to learn with respect to MI, and (4) examining a teacher's ability to manage MI activity. Finally, they decide that there is no need to address all intelligences in every objective or lesson, but each lesson should be reasonably allotted to implement approximately three to five intelligences.

Teacher candidates implement their lesson plans in elementary school classrooms and observe their peers implementing their own lesson plans. Kaya observes the practice of many of the teacher candidates. Most of the implementations are videotaped. Both observer reports and video recordings are discussed afterward.

Most teacher candidates significantly benefit from their experiences with MI practices in authentic classrooms. One teacher candidate said:

> I heard about MI theory a lot before taking this course. But I never believed that all students can learn school subjects, especially science, because science was always boring and a hard subject for me. In particular, after my teaching experience with MI theory, I realized that each student is unique, and he or she should use his or her own strengths while learning the subjects. . . . I saw how MI works very well in real classrooms. For example, most students wanted to continue their sequential science lessons without a break. This kind of behavior, especially in the elementary years, is an important piece of evidence indicating the positive effects of the implementation of MI theory on students' interest in learning, school, and science.

An online communication group supports teacher candidates throughout the course. Although class time is limited to three hours a week, the online module makes it possible for the professor and teacher candidates to interact regularly. Almost all teacher candidates describe their online communication as an interesting way of sharing information about MI theory and practices. They believe that their electronic discourse has made their theoretical and practical knowledge about MI theory more meaningful and permanent, and it has a positive effect on their attitudes toward the use of MI theory in the classroom. One teacher candidate said, "Online communications related to the criticisms about the theory and Gardner's responses to them helped me to better understand what the theory is and how the theory was developed. . . . Intensive discussions over the Web on the observer reports gained from real classrooms helped me a lot to understand the value of MI practices in elementary classrooms."

Another significant gain from the online communication was an awareness by many teacher candidates that there is not a single instructional approach based on MI theory. They saw how their peers interpreted MI theory in classrooms. Most of the teacher candidates, who are now teachers working in the eastern and southeastern cities of Turkey, state that they certainly want to use the MI theory in their classrooms.

THE ROLE OF MI THEORY IN THE REFORM OF NATIONAL EDUCATION

By 2003, Selçuk, the founder of the Practice School of Gazi University, was appointed the head of the board of education in Turkey. MI theory was inserted systematically into public schools. The curriculum, which had not been radically revised since 1968, was overhauled by Selçuk and his company. This change stemmed from the technological and scientific developments in the world, adaptation to European Union criteria, and national requirements. The cornerstones of this educational transformation were the progressive approach in philosophy, a cognitive-constructive approach in theory, and MI theory as a pedagogical model.

MI theory was introduced to academicians and teachers working to make a paradigmatic change in instruction programs. Workshops for the different disciplines taught how MI theory could be inserted in curriculum design. Seminars were held for publishers about how MI-based practices could be incorporated in textbooks.

This round of training sought to correct some misunderstandings from the past. For example, some teachers were focused on MI theory rather than the curriculum itself. Similarly, some mistakes had been made in inserting MI-based practices in textbooks. For example, it used to be suggested that teachers classify students according to their particular intelligence strengths and then conduct lessons only toward those intelligences. Instead, teachers were given instruction on how to integrate many intelligences within a lesson. To cite an example, in teaching the fraction ½ to first graders, a teacher suggested the following practice to draw on the bodily-kinesthetic intelligence to increase the logical-mathematical intelligence: "All students in the class stand up and hold their arms out level with their shoulders; the arms thus become the line of the fraction. The head represents 1, the legs represent 2, and in this way, the fraction ½ can be taught bodily-kinesthetically."

The principles for preparing daily lesson plans in all schools throughout Turkey were published in the form of a regulation, and daily lesson plan standards based on MI were shaped. MI theory and samples of its application began to be inserted in textbooks. The new curriculum aligned with constructivist theory, but it was not referred to as an MI theory curriculum. Teacher books and student workbooks were added to the textbooks. Thought was given to how teachers can benefit from MI theory in preparing a daily plan, implementing it, organizing materials like worksheets, using books in the practice period, and testing and evaluation. These changes in curriculum in Turkey have been influential on the books, periodicals, and materials of the private sector. Since 2003, the label "appropriate for multiple intelligences" has been affixed to thousands of reference books, periodicals, and educational instruments in Turkey.

Today the practices in Turkish schools have been compared to schools abroad. Turkish educators are sharing their experiences with MI with each other and with educators abroad at regional and international academic seminars. In symposia on best practices in Turkey, teachers and academicians from every part of the country are presenting examples that might be implemented at schools all over the world.

References

Armstrong, T. (2000). *Multiple intelligences in the classroom* (2nd ed.). Alexandria, VA: Association for Supervision and Curriculum Development.

Başbay, A. (2000). *An analysis of curriculum and classroom activities according to multiple intelligences theory.* Unpublished master's thesis, Hacettepe University, Ankara, Turkey.

Bümen, N. (2001). *The effects of implementation of the multiple intelligences theory supported by reviewing strategies on student's achievement, attitude and retention.* Unpublished doctoral dissertation, Hacettepe University, Ankara, Turkey.

Çakir, İ. (2003). *Designing supplementary activities for the sixth grade English course through the multiple intelligences theory.* Unpublished doctoral dissertation, Hacettepe University, Ankara, Turkey.

Campbell, L., Campbell, B., & Dickinson, D. (1996). *Teaching and learning through multiple intelligences.* New York: Basic Books.

Demirel, Ö. (2000). *Curriculum development: Theory to practice.* Ankara: Pegem A Publication.

Dilli, R. (2003). *To use multiple intelligence theory on art education courses.* Unpublished master's thesis, Gazi University, Ankara, Turkey.

Doğan, Ö. (2000). *The effect of the teaching activities based upon multiple intelligences theory on grade-4 students achievement and retention in mathematics.* Unpublished master's thesis, Gazi University, Ankara, Turkey.

Gardner, H. (1983). *Frames of mind: The theory of multiple intelligences.* New York: Basic Books.

Göğebakan, D. (2003). *How students' multiple intelligences differ in terms of grade level and gender.* Unpublished master's thesis, Middle East Technical University, Ankara, Turkey.

Kaptan, F., & Korkmaz, H. (2001). The effect of science teaching using multiple intelligences theory on students' achievement and attitude. In *IV. National Science Education Conference* (pp. 169–174). Ankara, Turkey: Turkish Ministry of National Education.

Kaya, O. N. (2002). *The effect of the multiple intelligences theory on grade-7 students' achievement, retention of their knowledge, attitude and perceptions in the topic of atom and atomic structure.* Unpublished master's thesis, Gazi University, Ankara, Turkey.

Kaya, O. N., & Ebenezer, J. (2003, April). *The effects of implementation of the multiple intelligences theory on grade-7 students' attitudes and perceptions toward science.* Paper presented at the annual meeting of the American Educational Research Association, Chicago.

Lazear, D. (1992). *Teaching for multiple intelligences.* Bloomington, IN: Phi Delta Kappan Educational Foundation.

Selçuk, Z., Kayılı, H., & Okut, L. (2002). *Multiple intelligences practices.* Ankara, Turkey: Nobel Publication.

Sezginer, Y. O. (2000). *Effect of multiple intelligence activities on expository essay writing performance.* Unpublished master's thesis, Middle East Technical University, Ankara, Turkey.

Talu, N. (1999). Multiple intelligences theory and its reflections on education. *Hacettepe University Journal of Faculty of Education, 15,* 164–172.

Tarman, S. (1999). *The theory of multiple intelligences in curriculum development process.* Unpublished master's thesis, Hacettepe University, Ankara, Turkey.

PART FOUR

SOUTH AMERICA

P ersonal intelligences, the possibility of a new intelligence, and pursuit of education for all are focal points for contributors from South America. Representing countries with a history of poverty and violence, authors work to create innovative schools and educational systems in Argentina and Colombia. Barrera and León-Agustí focus on developing interpersonal and intrapersonal intelligences to help students solve problems productively and peacefully. Battro documents growing importance of digital intelligence. With the digital revolution, new skills and new ways of thinking are required. All the authors stipulate the need for schools that are inclusive.

CHAPTER 21

Multiple Intelligences Theory in Argentina

A Conceptual Framework That Favors an Education for All

Paula Pogré
Marcela Rogé

This chapter describes the work of L@titud, the Latin American Initiative toward Understanding and Development, and other initiatives developed by some of its members. The specific focus is the work to introduce and implement MI theory to promote an education for all in Argentina. Contextualized in Argentina's long tradition of public education and the ongoing debate about pedagogy, the chapter highlights specific principles and strategies that L@titud developed to guide the implementation of MI in Argentina's schools. Using specific examples, the chapter illustrates how MI can help schools reach all children regardless of their prior experience and educational background. In 1996, a group of educational researchers and practitioners from different Latin American countries attended the Summer Institute of Project Zero at Harvard University in Cambridge, Massachusetts. Along with in-depth studies of MI theory and the teaching for understanding framework, the participants engaged in a series of discussions about how to develop what we had learned in the cultural context of our home countries. To promote dialogue and advance educational innovations in Latin America, in 2001 we partnered with Project Zero to launch the Latin

We would like to thank Universidad Nacional de General Sarmiento, PROYART Project, Universidad de San Andrés, L@titud Nodo Sur, Fundación Acindar, Fundación Ford, and all the teachers and students involved for their collaboration and support.

American Initiative Toward Understanding and Development (L@titud). The L@titud network connects professionals and educators in Latin America and supports local initiatives geared toward promoting student understanding of the social, cultural, and natural worlds they inhabit.

⌒

This chapter describes the work of L@titud in Argentina and other initiatives led by its members, focusing on the use of MI theory as a conceptual framework to promote an education for all. We begin by reviewing the historical context of challenges confronting Argentinean educators and the dominant pedagogical ideas when MI theory was first disseminated in Argentina. Next, we describe how the L@titud network in Argentina applies MI theory, adapting it for use in local contexts. Using specific examples, we illustrate current challenges in Argentinean schools and how we support our work with MI to meet these challenges. The chapter concludes with a discussion of how MI can help us reach all children regardless of their prior experience and educational background.

HISTORICAL BACKGROUND: A CONTINUUM OF PARADOX AND TENSION

Argentina has a long tradition of free public education. More than 70 percent of students attend public schools today. In the latter part of the nineteenth century, a large number of European immigrants came to Argentina. This so-called La Generación del 80 (The 1880s Generation) laid the foundation for Argentina's free public education system, which at the time referred to compulsory primary education that taught citizens to speak the same language and to respect order and discipline. Unlike primary education, secondary school was reserved for the elite, designed essentially to educate future political decision makers and serve as the pathway to university education.

In the early twentieth century, the provision of basic education expanded to the secondary level. The aim was to turn the tradition of educating a select few into a comprehensive system that provided equal access to knowledge for all. Though well intentioned, the movement did not achieve its goals. Students who were different or unprepared were rejected by the system. Teachers were unequipped to deal with the range of student learning abilities found in the same classroom. Contrary to the expectation of equal access and equal opportunity, the expansion process was characterized by high rates of failure for the impoverished and the underprivileged.

In 1976, a deadly junta seized power and assumed control of the country, including educational institutions. The ideology of this military government clashed with widespread "liberation pedagogy" in the field of education (Freire, 1972). Introduced in the early 1970s, liberation pedagogy emphasized dialogical or conversational instructional methods. Too much education, Freire argued, involved "banking," that is, educators attempting to make "deposits" in the students. According to Freire (1972), education should not involve one person acting *on* another; rather, it should be based on people working *with* each other.

In 1983, after seven years of authoritarian military government, Argentina returned to a democratic political organization, and its new leaders began to address the priority needs of the educational system and life at schools. We were faced with a paradox. On the one hand, we benefited from a long and productive tradition of a public educational system. On the other hand, our immediate reality was an educational structure and process that had been unsuccessful in accommodating socioeconomic, cognitive, and ethnic diversity.

In the 1990s, Argentina supported the objectives of equity in access to quality education as declared at the Jontiem Conference (1990) and in the Salamanca Accord (1994). In 1993, the Ley Federal de Educación (Federal Education Law), in an attempt to align with the principles of education for all, extended the provision of compulsory education to include kindergarten (five years of age) to ninth grade (fourteen years of age). The law also attempted to ensure the right of all citizens to gain access to quality education. Although the success of the law in terms of its impact is disputed, it did succeed in engaging Argentinean educators in interesting debates. Great attention was paid to issues such as inclusive learning contexts at school, the relationship between knowledge inquiry and a democratic classroom environment, and an education for all regardless of background.

Contemporaneous with the expansion of public education was the growth of private schools. Like public education, private education has a long history in Argentina. Some schools were founded more than a hundred years ago. Some of them were bilingual and served children from elite groups. During the 1970s, the spectrum of private education increased as the segmentation of society continued. Between democratic and authoritarian periods of governance, middle-class families fostered and supported the creation of private schools to ensure more democratic learning environments for their children. In this process, some private schools became pioneers for pedagogical innovation, which furthered a privileged level of education and fueled segmentation of the system.

In the midst of these challenges and debates, MI theory arrived in Argentina in the 1990s. A group of educational researchers and practitioners saw the potential of the theory to help transform the educational system, making it more democratic and inclusive. Argentinean educators also envisioned using MI as a framework to help achieve the goal of an education for all.

PEDAGOGICAL BACKGROUND: FROM TEACHER CENTERED TO STUDENT CENTERED

Teacher-centered pedagogies, a product of the modern age, had become the foundation of the Argentinean education system by the end of the nineteenth century. In schools, teachers delivered lessons, and all students were expected to learn at the same pace. This pedagogy generated learning matrices-internal schemes by which individuals confront reality and connect with the external world that is socially determined (Quiroga, 1991). Dominated by such learning matrices, students were not encouraged to think or act differently from what teachers taught. These learning matrices were based on the long-held assumptions that schools were not for everyone and that not everyone could learn, assumptions that led to the exclusion of students deemed to be culturally different and intellectually unfit.

In the 1970s, along with Freire's liberation pedagogy, the Argentinean academic field of education was also influenced by the work of Jean Piaget and Lev Vygotsky. These thinkers described a process of learning in which students played an active role in constructing their knowledge. This view of learning suggested a student-centered pedagogy that would reform the idea and practice of exclusion. Unfortunately, despite their strong influence on the academic field, the theories did not reach beyond the ivory towers to teachers' practices.

The arrival of MI theory in the 1990s brought a new perspective to the debate about student-centered pedagogy. If we all process information differently, how could a one-size-fits-all system be effective for all students' learning processes? MI theory challenged us to welcome diversity in the classroom, and it reinforced the notion of including, rather than excluding, students of different abilities. Moreover, MI theory seemed to be readily understood and easily accepted by Argentinean teachers. The concepts are transparent and support many of their beliefs and practices.

L@TITUD'S OPERATIONAL PRINCIPLES FOR MI IMPLEMENTATION

Initially MI suffered a number of misinterpretations. Some people considered the theory a set of labels for students, and others believed that the theory could automatically turn into a didactic proposal. In response to these misconceptions and based on the lessons learned from our experiences, the core group of L@titud in Argentina generated four operational principles for MI implementation.

First is to apply a grassroots approach to MI infusion. We understood that real change cannot be imposed through a top-down system; it has to take place within schools. To support grassroots change, L@titud networked professionals who promoted regional dialogue and local initiatives. We take full advantage of local expertise for professional training as well as for disseminating research and educational resources in Spanish.

Second is to understand the school's culture. Each school has its own unique culture. Working within that culture implies focusing on where the school is and determining its level of readiness for the new initiatives. When introducing new ideas or practices, we pay great attention to the needs and concerns of teachers and the circumstances of the school in which they work. We involve all of the stakeholders as active participants in the learning and change process.

The third is to bridge the gap between theory and practice. MI theory is powerful, and it requires concerted effort to apply it to classroom practice in appropriate ways. L@titud integrated Project Zero's teaching for understanding framework with MI theory to promote better teaching practices. Specifically, we helped teachers understand that MI practice is not about superficially imposing different intelligences on subject learning. Rather, MI practice encourages students to engage in a variety of "performances" concerning the topic, to think and act flexibly with knowledge (Stone-Wiske, 1998).

The fourth principle that the Argentinean L@titud network follows when implementing MI is to connect content areas of learning with the MI and teaching for understanding theoretical framework. To meet this challenge, L@titud in Argentina recruited content experts to join its team and assist with the work at schools. The group members, consisting of researchers, practitioners, and specialists in the disciplines of mathematics, Spanish, science, and arts, work with teachers from different grade levels and in different subject areas to help them reflect on their own teaching practices.

These four operational principles work in tandem to ensure the success of MI implementation by focusing on professional networking, school culture, theory into practice, and disciplinary knowledge. Guided by these principles, the L@titud network undertook several projects to improve teaching practices and disseminate MI work.

L@TITUD'S MI-RELATED PROJECTS

Since its inception in 2001, the L@titud network in Argentina has collaborated with many universities and corporations across the country to help implement MI theory in schools. Many of L@titud's MI-related projects were based in low-income neighborhoods or districts. Due to prejudice, many teachers hold low expectations of their students. They tend to teach less to these students and express less content in their teaching situation. Our focus on these disadvantaged districts aimed to reduce the inequality of our educational system and move one step closer to the goal of an education for all. A number of strategies, which we explore in the following section, were used in these MI-related projects.

Pedagogical Trios

A pedagogical trio is a team of three members: a school teacher, a teacher trainer, and a university researcher. In a project directed by the Universidad Nacional de General Sarmiento, we had as many as thirty pedagogical trios working in secondary schools for one project. The team worked together in planning lessons and delivering them. They used a dialogical approach when interacting with students. The trio met and discussed the development of the students' learning process after each lesson and also involved students in reflecting on their own learning achievements. The trios also created ways to make learning visible through documentation of the work everyone was doing: teachers, students, teacher trainers, and researchers. Pedagogical trios based on MI principles engaged everyone in movement along multiple pathways to knowledge acquisition and understanding.

Teacher Networks

Another successful strategy was formation of teacher and school networks. First, we formed the institutional network, connecting teachers within and across school departments. Through this network, teachers helped each other with discipline questions when planning projects or innovative lessons. They also discussed issues and challenges as they emerged. The network within institutions created a safety net for teachers, encouraging them to take risks and explore new practices. Once the institutional networks were established, we connected them to form a district network. In one project, we had forty schools interconnected through one network. The network enabled teachers and administrators to go beyond their own classrooms and schools to learn more about broader issues such as diversity of learning. Information sharing about MI approaches and the teaching for understanding framework formed the backbone of district network meetings.

Reflective Practice

Central to teacher change is establishing a habit of continually engaging in reflective practice. In all of our workshops, we helped teachers reflect on their learning process as well as their teaching practices, using MI theory as a guiding framework. Too often teachers were enthusiastic about the new ideas during the workshop. Back at school, however, they reverted to their old practices. The pedagogical trios and institutional networks helped teachers continue exploring the ideas they learned through workshops.

Public-Private Partnership

Due to their greater resources, some private schools were among the first to gain access to MI theory through workshops and English print materials, and they quickly implemented MI-related classroom practices. Given the high level of segmentation that existed in our education system, the introduction of MI only in elite schools could have widened the learning and teaching gaps between private and public schools even further. To prevent this negative outcome, L@titud invited the neighborhood public schools to the workshops offered to private schools to promote a public-private partnership. These workshops let educators see that teaching entails facing challenges, no matter the context in which they teach. They realized that diversity was not a question for private or public education; all teachers had diverse students in their classrooms. By working together, private and public school teachers started to see students as capable of learning, regardless of their social, economic, or cultural background. Some of the innovative private schools started sharing their knowledge and best practices with public schools during the MI workshops and other collaborative projects.

Focus on Student Strengths

The work of L@titud on MI-related projects has been fruitful. Teacher practices have changed, as have their expectations of students. For example, when a Spanish teacher was preparing a unit titled, "What are poems made of?" she used an MI framework to guide her lesson planning instead of delivering a typical lesson where students read and analyze poems and then move on. In this unit, students read classic and modern styles of poetry writing. They then engaged in discussions, dramatized the poems, and even created their own book of poems. The teacher was surprised to see how passionate the students' response was to this new type of learning experience. In her words, "I'm impressed to see students in a technical school get so passionate about poetry. They even shared their poems with their families." Through this lesson, the teacher gained a better understanding of how MI can help her reach more students and foster their deep understanding of the subject matter.

As teachers changed their practices, they began to view children differently. They became increasingly more aware of different kinds of talents and diverse learning approaches among their students, a change in perception that significantly affected teachers' expectations of their students. For example, some teachers had believed that it was not worth teaching certain content to underprivileged students because they were not likely to go to university. Now these same teachers started to include quality literature in their planning. After involving students in reading Kafka's work, one teacher commented, "I did not expect my students would enjoy reading Kafka."

Students' enjoyment of reading Kafka is only one of many examples. Many teachers noticed that when they stopped labeling students and realized that all students can learn, the children started producing many kinds of text and reading major works of literature.

Another example of this change of perspective is one experience led by the Universidad Nacional de General Sarmiento. The students compiled an anthology, which they called "Stories for Us." They chose short stories to include, justified their selection, and wrote the prologue and biographical notes about authors. Some students went to the library to look for information, others stayed to write papers, and still others read their productions to peers to check on the impact of their writing. Finally, the book was assembled and published. It became their literature textbook for the remainder of the school term.

In mathematics, most students and teachers at disadvantaged schools used to say, "Math is just for the brainy ones." With the changing view of children, a district network team organized problem-solving meetings in which a variety of mathematics problems were presented and all children were welcome to participate. Approximately a hundred students participated the first year the meetings were held. Some students from different classes and even different schools formed working groups. Members discussed the problems presented and worked together to solve them. At the conclusion of the meetings, groups chose the problem they enjoyed solving the most and presented it in an atypical way, such as acting it out or presenting it in poster form. One student said, "It was fun to design the poster and the concrete elements that would represent the solution. It was fun, because you learned new things on the way. I think that with our project. we added a little fun to math." The meetings engaged the interest of students to such an extent that the following year, almost a thousand students participated. Some of the newcomers said, "If so-and-so participated last year, so can I." At the final meeting for one of our projects, a student summarized well what learning meant to him: "Learning implies thinking, reasoning, analyzing, and questioning." Another student said, "When I learn, I can feel it in my body."

CONCLUSION

MI theory has had an impact on both pedagogical thinking and educational practices in Argentina. Schooling, public and private, is gradually changing. Instead of having all students sitting in rows facing the blackboard and listening to the teacher deliver a lesson, now there are more classrooms buzzing with meaningful work. Teachers' views of children, particularly those from low socioeconomic backgrounds, are changing. In schools where changes are ongoing, teachers enjoy teaching more, and students enjoy learning more.

On the national level, an important kickoff to spread MI principles was when the Ministry of Education in the 1990s realized that MI theory supported the tenets of an education for all and that its dissemination was politically and educationally important. It is worth mentioning that the following initiatives were a big plus for the work of the L@titud network. The Ministry of Education was promoting MI theory in seminars and workshops. The office also encouraged

MI-related language and practice through the distribution of its national magazine (*Zona Educativa*). And thanks to Paidós Publishers, Spanish versions of books on MI theory are available in Argentina.

Argentina has a long history of valuing basic education for all. MI theory contributed to our understanding that every student has the right to quality education. In a country where the education system also has a history of segmentation, MI-related educational practices are particularly relevant. MI theory, in dialogue with other progressive ideas and our own pedagogical traditions, has enabled us to focus on the learning capabilities of all individuals and opened new pathways to quality education. In Argentina, applications of MI theory have brought us ever closer to our goal of an education for all.

References

Freire, P. (1972). *Pedagogy of the oppressed*. Harmondsworth: Penguin.

Quiroga, A. (1991). *Matrices de aprendizaje. Constitución del sujeto en el proceso de conocimiento*. Buenos Aires: Edic. Cinco. Colección Apuntes.

Stone-Wiske, M. (1998). *Teaching for understanding: Linking research with practice*. San Francisco: Jossey-Bass.

CHAPTER 22

Personal Intelligences and a Colombian Experience

María Ximena Barrera
Patricia León-Agustí

This chapter explores the potential of the personal intelligences as a means to achieve the educational goal of developing autonomous individuals. We share our experience of promoting the personal intelligences in Colombia. We describe the challenges we faced when starting a school for disadvantaged children, developing curriculum relevant to these students' lives, and designing a discipline for empowerment program to affect students' behavior. Examples in the chapter illustrate how MI empowers teachers and students to become agents of change and growth. The chapter concludes with a discussion of the critical importance of personal intelligences for solving problems in productive and nonviolent ways.

In this chapter, we share the experience of a group of educators who took on the challenge of starting a school for disadvantaged children from the slums of Bogotá, Colombia. Central to our effort was finding ways to make formal education relevant to students who live in an environment characterized by cycles of poverty, hopelessness, and violence. For these children, we believed that the most important educational goal is to help them become agents of change in their own lives, as well as in the lives of those around them.

In the search for a meaningful educational model for disadvantaged children, we found Gardner's MI theory to be quite compelling as a guiding framework.

We thank the following individuals whose time and skills contributed greatly to this chapter: Rosario Jaramillo, Constanza Hazelwood, and Oscar Trujillo. We are especially grateful to Marcela Vásquez-León for her comments and editorial assistance.

In particular, we saw the relevance of his notion of personal intelligences (intra- and interpersonal intelligences) for our context. Personal intelligences emphasize self-knowledge and understanding of others. We see both as critical for the development of the intellectual, moral, and social autonomy of students. This autonomy is a precursor of the "capacity to govern one's self taking into consideration the points of view of those around him or her" (Kamii, 1984, p. 410). To us, personal intelligences, autonomy, and agents of change are interrelated. For example, it is difficult, if not impossible, to talk about autonomy if there is no appropriation and appreciation of oneself—one's feelings, thoughts, and actions. Likewise, it is this sense of autonomy that allows an individual to go beyond himself or herself to understand others: how they think, feel, and act. Following Gardner, we see personal intelligences as specific competences and skills that allow human beings to discover themselves and transform their reality to make the world a better place. Based on this conviction, our work focused on developing students' capacity to better understand not only specific subjects of study, but also themselves, the people with whom they interact, and the world they share.

We begin by providing a brief contextual background on education in Colombia. We describe the socioeconomic conditions of the students in Bogotá and some of the behavioral challenges educators encounter daily. We go on to tell the story of how our project started and our study group formed. The group was a key resource in addressing the challenges we faced. We provide examples of how our inquiry into the personal intelligences supported curriculum development and behavioral changes. Finally, we offer concluding remarks about how a deepening understanding of personal intelligences can support educators who are committed to students' autonomy and their development as agents of change.

OUR PROJECT AND ITS CONTEXT

In the mid-1980s, following the publication of a body of literature on liberation theology, the impact of the writings of Pablo Freire, and the launching of literacy initiatives in Central America, a group of Colombian educators turned their attention to the urgent need to offer an education that would allow students to develop their own voice—to pronounce themselves as people and not just to pronounce words. As part of this group, we founded a school in Bogotá, a city of more than 7 million residents where only a small percentage of children have access to good educational opportunities. Our school served students living in a community made up of several poor neighborhoods, or barrios. In this community, a potential student population of over 2,500 children had access to only one elementary school that was designed to serve 150 students.

In 1985, we started our school, Colegio Del Barrio (the low-income neighborhood school). Initially it was a primary school with 80 students. By 1995, it graduated its first high school class. Currently the school serves over 400 students. The growth in grade levels and number of students served is one sign of the school's success, particularly since we have received no government funds. The school's growth has been a long and hard, and ultimately rewarding, process. We have faced challenges from the society, community, and the children we serve.

Societal and Educational Challenges

From its colonial past to the present day, Colombia has remained highly dependent on Europe and the United States. Extending far beyond the economic and geopolitical realms, this dependence also has an impact on the country's intellectual, cultural, and human development. Our society's deep sense of intellectual and cultural dependence has resulted in a corresponding sense of insecurity. Unsure of ourselves, we are hesitant to seek ways of creating our own standards and developing our own lifestyles.

Colombian education, a mirror of society, upholds existing social structures: the traditional family, state bureaucracies, old political parties and economic elites, and a class-based society marked by wide socioeconomic inequalities. As social institutions, schools have been designed to create citizens who behave in ways that guarantee continuation of the status quo. The role of teachers is to transmit knowledge to students. Their actions are conditioned by authority and heteronomous principles. Students schooled within this educational system grow up to sustain the societal model of dependency.

The model of dependency is also evident in the lack of useful knowledge available to teachers when they try to solve pedagogical problems in the classroom. University training is not geared toward helping teachers understand either how to translate theory into practice or how to create theory from their own experience and reflection. Teachers seldom share their experience and knowledge through methodologies such as collaborative planning, collective reflection, mutual feedback on teaching methods, or classroom observation.

Thirty years of experience as educators in Colombia made us aware of the need to promote an educational system that moves society beyond this sense of dependency, deference to authority, and heteronomy. Our school offered this alternative. We set out to help more children develop both citizenship and autonomy. Because their access to education was severely limited, our priority was to serve children from low-income communities. In this effort, we also explored ways to support teachers' professional development.

Challenges from the Community

In addition to societal and educational challenges, we faced many obstacles in the community we served in our effort to start schools. The first was gaining the trust of parents. Although the idea of creating a new school in a low-income neighborhood appealed to parents, many feared that instead of serving the community, we would use their situation of marginality to our own advantage. In the past, this group of parents and their children had been subjects in a number of studies and research projects. Often researchers studied problems but contributed nothing specifically to the betterment of the community. Given these experiences, we found parents to be reticent and distrustful at the beginning of our project.

A second obstacle for us was the lack of a physical space in the barrio to build the school. We had no choice but to use Colegio St. Frances, an all-girls private Catholic school, as our initial site. A couple of miles away from the barrio, this location for the school was problematic. Parents were reluctant to send their children to a school located outside their community, fearing that their children could be kidnapped and sold—well-founded fears given that kidnappings in Bogotá were a daily occurrence at that time. To assure parents of their children's safety, we appointed teachers to ride in the school bus with students for the entire first year.

Another factor that hindered our work was the relationship between the community and the owners of Colegio St. Frances school. The building belonged to a North American religious community whose values were rejected by one potential barrio partner. This barrio was led by communists who opposed religious education and North American influence. Initially this ideological confrontation limited our reach to some of the neediest barrios. Over the years, through our constant communication and evidence of the school's success, the situation changed, and we were able to reach barrios that had greater needs.

Domestic Violence and Children's Behavioral Issues

Living in poverty and being illiterate, many parents use corporal punishment to discipline their children. Domestic violence is unfortunately so common that it is rarely reported. We will never forget the day that a nine-year-old girl came to class with a burned hand. When we asked her what had happened, she told us, "I am in charge of preparing the rice at home, and yesterday I burned it by mistake. My mother, as a way to punish me and to make sure that it would not happen again, put my hand on the burner." As she was telling her story, tears were rolling down her cheeks. Her physical and emotional pain was evident.

Many of our students also faced sexual abuse at home. One eleven-year-old girl was frequently observed by the teachers as sad, lonely, and fearful. As the school counselor began working with her, the girl was finally able to tell us that her two uncles raped her every Tuesday and Thursday, days they knew she was home alone. Sadly, this was not an isolated case.

In response to the harsh living conditions, many of our students treated one another with a great deal of aggression. They tended to address problems through violent confrontation, acting as if the law of the strongest were the only way to resolve conflict. Seldom would we see them engaging in dialogue or negotiating with one another. Frequently we found them carrying knives, screw drivers, or switchblades, which they described as "defense" or "personal attack weapons." These children were bringing to the school behaviors that were critical for their survival in the streets.

Too often students demonstrated a complete disregard for authority and school rules. Vandalism was common on the school campus. For example, the students repeatedly destroyed the plants and flowers in the carefully arranged flower garden on the school grounds, despite warnings that there would be consequences. This destructive behavior was also displayed in other places, such as classrooms and the dining room. Bathrooms were constantly littered.

Because our previous experience was with students from a high socioeconomic background, we lacked the contextual knowledge needed to understand the sociocultural circumstances of low-income students. As we started working with them, it became evident that in order to be effective, we must become familiar with their social context and recognize the individual differences that characterize their learning processes. Instead of blaming students, we needed to approach some of their behavioral challenges by examining the context in which they originated. These violent behaviors often are the only tools students have to defend themselves and survive on the streets. At the same time, we also must help students understand that school is different. It is a place where teachers have their best interest in mind, they are protected, and their behaviors have consequences. A fundamental challenge was to find ways to reduce the conflicts that arise from these colliding realities, for students and for teachers. Meeting this challenge has been a struggle throughout our project.

MEETING CHALLENGES AND MOVING FORWARD

The challenges and problems we encountered were not only many; they were also severe and required collective efforts. In this section, we describe how we addressed the challenges described above, including the formation of a study group of educators. We also discuss how our inquiry into the personal intelligences influenced the development of new forms of curriculum and led to the use of effective approaches to promote student empowerment.

Forming the Study Group

Along with the establishment of Colegio Del Barrio, we formed a study group consisting of teachers, the principal, the academic coordinators, and a psychologist. The purposes of the group were several: to systematically reflect on difficult situations as they emerged, study theories that informed our reflection, and put into practice the recommendations reached through our collaborative work. The group's greatest asset was each member's deep commitment to children's education. We started to read theories and study concepts, including the concept of autonomy, MI theory, and Project Zero's teaching for understanding framework. We met every Saturday morning for four hours to analyze and reflect on individual cases and situations that demanded action.

At the beginning of the study group's work, we also reflected on the importance of understanding our individual strengths and weaknesses and knowing how to use them to create an environment of trust and openness to learning. Studying personal intelligences reaffirmed our belief that a critical factor in improving the school was strengthening relationships and communication among administrators, teachers, students, and community members. We saw development of the personal intelligences as the driving force for change. When we started studying and developing materials and models among ourselves, one of the greatest sources of satisfaction was the recognition of our own personal growth. This sense of fulfillment led us to make an even greater commitment. We all felt part of the endeavor and were willing to take responsible risks to improve our practices in the classroom and the school.

MI theory helped us discover our strengths and use them to solve problems creatively and work collaboratively. As we continued our joint study and work, it became even more evident that applying MI theory empowered us to be more tolerant with people who were different from ourselves and to truly understand that not everyone processes information in the same way. Identifying our own strengths gave us the confidence and security to face our own weaknesses. Little by little, we created a trusting environment that allowed us to share with one another our greatest accomplishments and most difficult obstacles in trying to implement new ideas in the classroom and the entire school.

As a trusting relationship formed among the members, this study group began to play a leadership role in developing curriculum and solving everyday behavioral problems creatively. Our new curriculum was more engaging and relevant to the needs of our students and the community. Our discipline for empowerment program fostered students' skills in interpersonal negotiation and nonviolent problem solving.

Revamping Curriculum to Increase Relevance for Students' Lives

Because of their prior experiences in an impoverished and violent sociocultural context, our students receive and process information in unique ways. For example, compared to students who attend Colegio St. Frances, our students had greater difficulty solving textbook problems when operations had the mathematical symbols of "plus" or "minus." However, our students were much quicker at using mathematical operations when solving day-to-day practical problems, such as buying rice and bread and bringing back home the correct change. These children were comfortable working with mathematical concepts in the real world but encountered difficulty with abstract problems.

This example was one of many that made evident the importance of bringing the students' world into the classroom and making what they learned in the classroom relevant to their world outside school. This kind of curriculum, we thought, would bring new ways to interact with our students. To develop this curriculum, we needed to acknowledge the community as a source of learning and use that realization in formal school learning. It took us about four years to feel that we were bringing down the walls of the school and getting closer to meeting the challenge of combining school curriculum with the students' lives outside school.

One example of how curriculum changed to meet this goal was a project developed by fourth graders. They were studying plants and had planted a small garden to grow vegetables. One child said his father had worked on a potato farm and was now driving his truck to bring potatoes to small markets around the city. We invited him to the school several times, sharing with the children everything he knew about growing and shipping potatoes. The children then visited one of the small stores he delivered to and interviewed the owner about selling potatoes. The project, which started as a science activity, ultimately involved mathematics, language, and economics. It also gave the students a better understanding of the world around them as it related community activities to what they were learning in school.

Another example of connecting curriculum to students' lives comes from a computer technology class. In the early years, when we used the Colegio St. Frances building for our school site, our junior and senior students had access to the computer lab once a week for a three-hour period. The students were required to complete a number of assignments, including reports on the history of computer technology and its current importance, as well as written responses to questions in prescribed guides regarding technical aspects of computer use. Both the students and the teacher found this content disengaging, resulting in frequent disciplinary problems. The study group, which included the technology teacher, decided to rewrite the curriculum.

Developing a new computer technology course became a truly collaborative initiative among all participants, which resulted in the idea of having students use the computer lab to research and design an interdisciplinary project for graduation. The students had their senior year to choose a topic, develop the project, and complete it under the guidance of an adult mentor-advisor. The project had to reflect the interests and needs of the individual student and the community, provide the student with an intellectual challenge, and take into consideration his or her abilities, talents, and goals. Students used the computers to gather information, tabulate data, produce graphics, write the report, and present their final project. In the process, they learned how to use computers in a practical way. The teacher created a climate in the classroom that allowed students to learn at their own pace. Students who were quicker at acquiring computer competency helped those who were less advanced.

The students were clearly motivated. Despite the constraints of time and resources, they were able to produce final projects of impressive quality. At the same time, disciplinary problems almost disappeared. Many of the students found the use of computers to be of great help in their school-to-work program. This program for high school students allowed them to work in the mornings and study in the afternoons, thus offering them the opportunity to gain practical experience. For some of them, computer use became a source of income. After graduation, a good number of students continued the study of computer technology.

Our experience with MI theory had led us to see our students in a new light and helped us understand that all children, whatever their socioeconomic status, are intelligent in different ways, with distinctive abilities and talents. MI does not offer a prescribed curriculum or specific instructional strategies. Rather, it offered us an opportunity to think about possibilities for engaging our students in learning relevant to the contexts of their families and neighborhoods. In the examples, we incorporated multiple entry and exit points in our curriculum units. Gardner (1991) describes entry points as different ways a teacher can approach a topic. These different ways help all students find a way to engage in learning. To make the meaning more concrete, think of school topics as rooms. Entry points are different doorways through which students may enter the room. They may involve the use of narrative, logical-quantitative, existential/foundational, aesthetic, hands-on/experiential, or interpersonal. We also used exit points in our curriculum units, offering students different ways to express their understanding. We experimented with nontraditional forms, such as a poem, a sculpture, dramatization, and a brochure that students produced to show their understanding of a specific subject. We discovered that allowing students to express their understandings using their strengths helped them gain a better sense of who they are and what they do best. The process of expressing their understanding improved their self-esteem and self-confidence—the two qualities deemed essential for the development of students' autonomy.

EMPOWERING STUDENTS TO MAKE BEHAVIORAL CHANGES

Another area of concern where MI theory has been particularly useful is the development of better social interactions among students, family, and community. Specifically, we used the development of personal intelligences to promote changes in students' school conduct. We designed a "discipline for empowerment" program that aimed to foster students' ability to function as agents of their own change and growth.

Early in our work as a study group, we decided to move away from traditional school disciplinary procedures. In that model, the discipline coordinator was in charge of dealing with all student disciplinary matters. When a behavior problem arose, the teacher, instead of resolving it with the individuals involved, had to report to the discipline coordinator, who took responsibility for solving the problem and deciding on a punishment. In addition to being bureaucratic and inefficient, the punishment, such as no recess or staying after school, almost never related to the student's transgression. Furthermore, such disciplinary procedures reflected a level of heteronomy on the part of the adult. Students had no voice and took no interest in solving the problem. The study group tried many different strategies and failed many times. Eventually we identified a series of steps, called "discipline for empowerment," that proved to be effective.

1. When an act of aggression occurred between two or more students, each student was given the opportunity to tell his or her own version of what had happened. Sometimes the students were questioned individually and sometimes together. In most cases, we obtained very different versions of the same incident. The common tendency was to blame the other.

2. In some cases, especially with older students, they were asked to individually write down, as faithfully as possible, their version of the incident. Younger students were asked to talk among themselves and to try to come up with one description of the situation. This process invited the students to reflect on and discuss the level of responsibility of each person involved in the incident. In some cases, when the written versions continued to be different, students were asked to read each other's version. Then they were given a certain amount of time to come up with a single version.

3. Once the students arrived at a single version of what had happened, they had to propose a way to make amends for their behavior. Initially the students gave themselves traditional punishments, such as "no recess," "stay after school," or "do extra work in a given subject." With time and reflection, the students came to understand that the sanction should be reciprocal; that is, it should make amends for the behavior by taking into consideration the people affected, feelings that were hurt, and damages incurred. It was very important to earn again the trust that had been broken by the student's misconduct. The relationship with the person affected needed to be repaired.

4. The students had to come up with three possible sanctions. After discussion, all parties had to reach consensus on the most appropriate one. Once the students agreed on the sanction, they wrote it down and made a commitment not to repeat the offensive behavior. This contract had to be taken home and signed by the parents. This step kept parents informed and gave them an opportunity to comment on the agreement. If the situation were serious enough for parents to be involved directly, they were asked to come to school and hear the students tell them what had happened.

The change that resulted from these discipline for empowerment steps was evident. As students began taking responsibility for their actions, they also began to develop a sense of personal autonomy. Eventually, when a problem arose, students looked for solutions instead of a scapegoat.

CONCLUSION

We believe that MI is particularly relevant to the context of socioeconomic inequality in a country such as Colombia, where conventional educational structures have imposed methods and curricula that are largely unrelated to the difficult challenges students encounter in their daily lives. Traditional educational structures tend to reinforce a hierarchical system of inequality. They fail to recognize agency in students and teachers. Also overlooked are the needs of communities to have their young educated in ways that will prepare them to address deep societal problems.

MI theory contributed greatly to strengthening interactions among the different players in our school. It helped us identify multiple potentials in our students that contributed to the community at large. In terms of our curriculum, one significant change was the introduction of community-relevant projects. The presence of the students' diverse intelligences became evident as they selected projects. The students chose projects that matched their own strengths and interests. It was also easy to see the personal intelligences at work during these projects. Students demonstrated an honest desire to help one another and to work as a team, even though each student was individually responsible for his or her own project. Instead of an exclusive focus on competition, we found real collaboration and genuine care among students.

The demonstration of positive student behavior as the result of the discipline empowerment program impressed teachers, parents, and community members. For the first time in their lives, many students began to see themselves as agents of change and growth. They saw the consequence of their aggressive behavior and learned alternative prosocial actions. They understood the importance of developing skills to engage in positive social interactions among students, with their teachers and parents, and in their community. As their personal intelligences developed, so did the school community.

Our school provides an active, student-centered curriculum that responds to students' sociocultural context. It is our hope that we have created a positive atmosphere at the school that invites students to learn and enjoy learning. Our ultimate goal is to have a school where the teaching is meaningful to students and what they learn is useful in their daily and future lives outside school. MI theory has helped us move toward achieving this goal.

References

Gardner, H. (1991). *The unschooled mind*. New York: Basic Books.

Kamii, C. (1984). Autonomy: The aim of education envisioned by Piaget. *Phi Delta Kappan*, 65(2), 410–415.

CHAPTER 23

Multiple Intelligences and Constructionism in the Digital Era

Antonio M. Battro

The classic picture of cognitive development provided by Jean Piaget has been recast in terms of two factors: the interest in different profiles of intellectual capacities, as put forth in the MI framework developed by Howard Gardner, and the new forms of expression and communication enabled globally by the new digital media. The One-Laptop-Per-Child Program, directed by Nicholas Negroponte, is providing children in elementary schools around the world with new opportunities to acquire the digital skills required in the new era. Multiple intelligences are in action sharing the wide resources of the network. Many disabled children may have access to education using digital technology. Perhaps a new intelligence, a digital intelligence, is unfolding in the human species.

In this chapter, I examine the way in which the classic picture of cognitive development, as captured in the writings of Jean Piaget, has been recast in terms of two factors: the interest in different profiles of intellectual capacities, as put forth in the multiple intelligence framework developed by Howard Gardner (1983, 1999), and the new forms of expression and communication enabled globally by the new digital media. I share some personal experiences to show how traditional cognitive models and the individual-difference models have unfolded in the past decades. I hope that this testimony will reveal some interesting bridges between the two models and may inspire us to build more, in particular with disabled children.

MULTIPLE INTELLIGENCES: CONSTRUCTIVISM AND CONSTRUCTIONISM

In *The Mind's New Science* (1985), Gardner wrote that Piaget "launched an entirely new field of psychology—concerned with human cognitive development—and provided the research agenda that keeps it occupied until this day. Even disproofs of his specific claims are a tribute to his general influence" (p. 11). At the same time, Gardner also observed that brain-damaged patients "can lose one or the other symbol-using capacity almost completely while other symbolic facilities can remain essentially intact" (Gardner, 1989, p. 95). In Gardner's view, these findings about the dissociation of various cognitive capacities challenged the holistic understanding of the developing mind offered by Piaget. However, along with others (Feldman, 1980), Gardner continues to honor the general Piagetian picture of the construction of knowledge because each intelligence in the MI framework features its own construction of knowledge. In a deep sense, MI is also a constructivist theory.

Multiple intelligences theory emphasizes two dimensions that were minimized in Piagetian developmental theory. First, MI theory claims that various cognitive abilities may, for any number of reasons, develop at different rates and break down under different conditions. Second, rather than focusing on the epistemic subject—the forms of mind common to all human beings by virtue of their species membership—MI theory calls attention to the fact that individuals can and do exhibit quite distinctive cognitive profiles. Put differently, MI is clearly embedded in the current scientific culture of (neuro) modularity while Piaget's focus was on the universals of the cognitive development of children.

As a biologist, Piaget saw all of development as the unfolding of genetic predispositions in the human brain, as modulated by active experimentation in a relatively predictable environment. Unfortunately, during Piaget's lifetime (1896–1980), it was difficult to observe the functioning and growing brain in detail; sophisticated brain imaging technology did not yet exist. It was impossible to imagine what an "educated brain" could be (Battro, Fischer, & Léna, 2008). Even the central notion of neuroplasticity was not fully understood at that time. Today the new field of neuroeducation is thriving, and MI theory is finding fertile soil in this expanding environment.

An important advance on Piaget's work occurred when his ideas of constructivism were conceptualized with reference to learning in an increasingly digital era. In particular, mathematician-turned-educator Seymour Papert expanded the fundamental Piagetian idea of logical constructivism into *constructionism* to cover learning and education. In Papert's words, "From constructivist theories of psychology we take a view of learning as reconstruction rather as transmission of knowledge. Then we extend the idea of manipulative materials to the idea that learning is most effective when part of an activity the learner experiences as constructing a meaningful product" (Papert, 1986). This idea was supported powerfully by Papert's invention and implementation of the computer language Logo in different fields such as mathematics, geometry, music, robotics, language, and visual arts (Papert, 1980; Reggini, 1982, 1985, 1988). Constructionism was embedded in the way children programmed their computers, found new ways for debugging their errors, and reached results that could be integrated in further constructions.

WORKING WITH DISABLED POPULATIONS

Logo became also a powerful tool for working with disabled youngsters, a population in which, as a physician-neuroscientist, I have long had an interest (Battro, 1986, 2000; Battro & Denham, 1989). Working in hospitals and special schools, I have observed many disabled children and adolescents who suffer quite distinctive profiles of abilities and disabilities. Working with computers, many of these young people could find a new significance for their efforts, an intellectual challenge that they might strive to overcome, and a feeling of having accomplished "good work." Many of them are now active in the digital world and integrated at different levels in the society of knowledge.

In several cases I had the privilege of following their path in life for decades, and I am always impressed by the unexpected and often positive growth of their capacities. Recently I met one of my former Logo students, a young man with a mild mental retardation who was quite unable to do any arithmetic calculation but loved computers and had an elaborated language and very good manners. Today he is in charge of the cash flow in a restaurant where he does data entry for the different tables and services. He is still entirely lacking the algorithmic capacity needed in arithmetic, but he became an expert in the heuristics to find the exact item to put into the final account of the client, a kind of multiple-choice program in a practical and demanding setting. This case reinforces the idea that training with computers may lead some disabled individuals to find their way in life and may help to build bridges that overcome the impairment of a cognitive module, like mathematical intelligence in this case.

Of course, any training needs time. It is not always easy to identify what will be the seed of a future and unexpected skill that will be useful later in life. But the core idea of constructionism is that we continuously build cognitive structures, and when they reach a certain stability, they become a platform for a new step. This important achievement opens new perspectives in the study of the relations between development and learning as dynamical systems (van Geert, 1991; van Geert & Steenbeek, 2008). Since Piaget, we know that any particular learning process needs the support of a developmental platform at a specific level of stability (Fischer & Bidell, 1998). We can now explore this issue in more detail with the help of the new digital tools for each of the intelligences described by MI.

My thesis is that both models—neo-Piagetian constructionism and MI—interact at different levels of application. This is very clear in the field of disabilities. In the early 1980s, computers were introduced in education, and one of the first uses of this new tool was to help disabled children (Battro, 1986). I came to understand "the computer as a tool for the brain" (Battro, 2002) at MIT when Seymour Papert and his team created a computer-based learning environment for physically disabled children (Valente, 1983).

As an example of what can be accomplished in a digital environment and how it can be explicated in terms of psychological theory, I describe an admittedly extreme case. Nico, a young Argentinian lad, had his right hemisphere removed by functional hemispherectomy when he was three years old in order to treat his severe epilepsy (Battro, 2000). I worked several years helping Nico to use a computer at school and at home. Many of my interventions were inspired by the MI model: different approaches to reach a target, different ways to deal with a problem, new ways of interacting with the different intelligences with only half a brain.

At one point, I observed that the lack of a right hemisphere was causing a delay in Nico's acquisition of drawing and painting skills, yet he was at the top of the class in logical reasoning. With the help of a computer, I tried to construct a bridge between Nico's spatial and logical-mathematical intelligences. In one activity, Nico used a Logo program to produce a colored border (a logical-mathematical activity) and then manipulated the keyboard mouse to draw the letters in his name (a spatial activity). In this case, MI was used to guide educational practice and inform rehabilitation: Two different intelligences for art and logic were coupled with two different skills, analogue and digital. Each thread of the couple communicates with the other but remains structurally independent. This example clearly illustrates the main point of MI about the modularity of, and possible interactions between, two or more distinct intelligences.

When I met Nico, he was five years old, and neither I nor my colleagues knew what to do to educate an intelligent child with only his left hemisphere. Today Nico is thriving in many aspects of his life; he has finished secondary school, and received a diploma in informatics. His learning path is amazing. His life is a remarkable example of the changes produced by neuroplasticity in the educated brain and a challenge to many traditional views of the developing mind (Immordino-Yang, 2007).

A DIGITAL INTELLIGENCE?

This dramatic example can also serve as a window to observe a "new" digital intelligence as my colleague Percival J. Denham and I have termed it (Battro & Denham, 2007). In fact, the intelligent use of a computer has deep roots in development and even in evolution. It is based in the simple click, what we call the "click option"—the decision to activate (or not) a key, press a button or a lever. When Nico drew through a computer program, a considerable number of clicks were produced using the keyboard and the mouse. This sequence of decisions represents a complex path in the working memory of the individual and constitutes a heuristic procedure, which we think supports the unfolding of a digital intelligence. In particular, the debugging process, that is, the computing experience of correcting the errors of programming, is something essential in the construction of novelty and, more broadly, in the creative process.

The MI perspective also provides some keys for understanding the rapid and massive involvement with computers by children around the world. In my view, MI provides a robust theoretical and experimental framework for our understanding of mental life in a very broad sense—cognitive, emotional, and moral. If the criteria initially laid out by Gardner (1983) can be satisfied, the MI list could be extended to include a "digital intelligence." Essentially we look forward to understand why and how "each generation will become more digital than the preceding one" (Negroponte, 1995, p. 231).

THE SKILLS NEEDED IN A GLOBALIZED WORLD

We live in digital era and in a globalized world where we must find new ways to educate children (Battro, 2004; Gardner, 2004). Continuing in a personal vein, let me mention one highly promising tool for our times. Drawing on many years of research in constructionism and human skills, the nonprofit association One Laptop Per Child (OLPC), founded by Nicholas Negroponte in 2005 (www.laptop.org), is providing low-cost and highly connected laptops, called XO, to millions of children in developing countries. These tools encourage and support the construction and sharing of knowledge and skills in the arts and the sciences.

The OLPC program promises to have considerable impact in the education of disabled children as well. In Uruguay, the first country to launch OLPC for every child and teacher in elementary schools, the computers were first given to children in special schools (www.ceibal.edu.uy) and also in rural areas where some children go to school on horseback. Figure 23.1 shows the joy of these children on horseback with their laptops.

Figure 23.1 Children, Laptops, and Horses in Rural Uruguay
Source: Courtesy of Pablo Flores.

What strikes me is that the new laptop has some key properties related to MI. The XO screen shows several icons: among them a palette for drawing and painting, a drum for music, a copybook for writing, a globe for communicating using the Internet. In a deep sense, this advanced computer design represents several intelligences at work. I see young people working together in art around a palette (spatial intelligence), other groups talking or sharing some information of the Web around a globe (interpersonal intelligence), and one writing alone (linguistic and perhaps intrapersonal intelligence). This environment is always changing; at a certain point, each of the range of intelligences described by MI is represented.

To be sure, the design of the XO was not consciously inspired by MI, but it turned out to be a vivid representation of the basic potentials of the human mind as described by MI. This outcome is not a coincidence. In my opinion, it shows the robust neurocognitive foundations of MI. All children can draw on a variety of intelligences, and each can do so in ways that are consonant with his or her particular profile of capacities. Moreover, this "XO/MI" interface is of great help to the disabled, because many kinds of sensors and motors can also be connected to the XO and may work as prostheses. The disabled may find on the XO all the tools they need to activate some particular intelligence, expand their own modes of representing knowledge, and interact with other people. The OLPC project hopes to realize this educational potential throughout the world.

CONCLUSION

It is clear that we need new cognitive skills to live and work in a digital environment. Today a significant part of the world population is using cellular phones, and in the near future, high-performing portable computers will be available for millions of children. I hope we will approach the United Nations Millennium Goals of providing elementary education to all the children of the world by the year 2015 (Battro, 2007).

In this perspective, the impact of MI and constructionism, individually and jointly, may well grow in orders of magnitude. In recent years, research in experimental neurocognitive psychology has gone beyond laboratories into the schools (Battro et al., 2008). This intervention cannot fail to improve both learning itself and the understanding of how it occurs. However, we still know more about the learning brain than about the teaching brain. Humans teach in a way that other animals do not. In particular, and most important, children teach. They are now teaching their elders how to use a computer. Education, the dialogue between teachers and students, is our great asset as a species.

Each generation must be educated in different cognitive and social environments (Gardner, 2004). Both the general capacities of the human mind that Piaget described and the modularity of the multiple intelligences described by MI theory are part of the unfolding of the new capacities we are constantly developing, in particular those involved in the digital world. We are possibly facing a new kind of evolution because education is changing our individual brains. For instance, our neuronal networks that presumptively evolved to recognize physical objects are "recycled" to read (Dehaene, 2007). A similar process can be predicted in the case of the new skills required in the digital environment today. Perhaps a new intelligence, a digital intelligence, is unfolding in the human species. We certainly need more research on this topic in order to understand our digital era. I am convinced that both MI and constructionism can prove to be powerful catalysts for this endeavor.

References

Battro, A. M. (1986). *Computación y aprendizaje especial. Aplicaciones del lenguaje Logo en el tratamiento de niños discapacitados.* Buenos Aires: El Ateneo

Battro, A. M. (2000). *Half a brain is enough: The story of Nico.* Cambridge: Cambridge University Press.

Battro, A. M. (2002). The computer in the school: A tool for the brain. In Pontifical Academy of Sciences (Ed.), *Challenges for science: Education for the twenty-first century.* Vatican City: Author.

Battro, A. M. (2004). Digital skills, globalization and education. In M. Suarez Orozco & D. Baolian Qin-Hillard (Eds.), *Globalization: Culture and education in the new millennium.* Berkeley: University of California Press.

Battro, A. M. (2007). Reflections and actions concerning a globalized education. In Pontifical Academy of Social Sciences (Ed.), *Charity and justice in the relations between peoples and nations.* Vatican City: Author.

Battro, A. M., & Denham, P. J. (1989). *Discomunicaciones. Computación para niños sordos.* Buenos Aires: El Ateneo.

Battro, A. M., and Denham, P. J. (2007). *Hacia una inteligencia digital.* Buenos Aires: Academia Nacional de Educación.

Battro, A. M., Fischer, K. W., & Léna, P. J. (Eds.). (2008). *The educated brain: Essays in neuro-education.* Cambridge, MA: Cambridge University Press.

Dehaene, S. (2007). *Les neurones de la lecture.* Paris: Odile Jacob.

Feldman, D. H. (1980). *Beyond universals in cognitive development.* Mahwah, NJ: Erlbaum.

Fischer, K. W., & Bidell, T. R. (1998). Dynamic development of psychological structures in action and thought. In R. M. Lerner (Ed.), *Handbook of child psychology.* Hoboken, NJ: Wiley.

Gardner, H. (1983). *Frames of mind: The theory of multiple intelligences.* New York: Basic Books.

Gardner, H. (1985). *The mind's new science: A history of the cognitive revolution.* New York: Basic Books.

Gardner, H. (1989). *To open minds: Chinese clues to the dilemma of contemporary education.* New York: Basic Books.

Gardner, H. (1999). *Intelligence reframed. Multiple intelligences for the twenty-first century.* New York: Basic Books.

Gardner, H. (2004). How education changes: Considerations of history, science and values. In M. Suarez Orozco & D. Baolian Qin-Hillard (Eds.), *Globalization: Culture and education in the new millennium.* Berkeley: University of California Press.

Immordino-Yang, M. H. (2007). A tale of two cases: Lessons for education from the study of two boys living with half their brains. *Mind, Brain and Education, 1*(2), 66–83.

Negroponte, N. (1995). *Being digital.* New York: Knopf.

Papert, S. (1980). *Mindstorms: Children, computers, and powerful ideas.* New York: Basic Books.

Papert, S. (1986, November). *Constructionism: A new opportunity for elementary science education.* Proposal to the National Science Foundation.

Reggini, H. C. (1982). *Alas para la mente. Logo, un lenguaje de computadoras y un estilo de pensar.* Buenos Aires: Galápago.

Reggini, H. C. (1985). *Ideas y formas. Explorando el espacio en Logo.* Buenos Aires: Galápago.

Reggini, H. C. (1988). *Computadoras ¿Creatividad o automatismo?* Buenos Aires: Galápago.

Valente, J. (1983). *Creating a computer based learning environment for physically handicapped children.* Unpublished doctoral dissertation, Massachusetts Institute of Technology.

Van Geert, P. (1991). A dynamic systems model of cognitive and language growth. *Psychological Review, 98,* 3–52.

Van Geert, P., & Steenbeek, H. (2008). Understanding mind, brain and education as a complex dynamic developing system: Measurement, modeling and research. In A. M. Battro, K. W. Fischer, & P. J. Léna (Eds.), *The educated brain: Essays in neuro-education.* Cambridge, MA: Cambridge University Press.

PART FIVE

UNITED STATES

C ontributors in this section expand our understanding of MI application through the creation of schools based on MI principles and by educating specific populations. Representing the home ground of the MI meme, these schools offer opportunities to see MI education in action and to deepen our understanding of multiple intelligences–inspired practices. Work in curriculum and assessment with Latino/a students and Diné (Navajo) children affirms that MI applications can give all student groups meaningful choices in school and multiple ways to succeed. In conclusion, Branton Shearer reflects on his experiences with MI assessment. As noted throughout the book, the use of MI assessments that are intelligence-fair, authentic, and relevant is a challenge for teachers and administrators in countries around the world.

CHAPTER 24

The World's First
Multiple Intelligences School

The Story of the Key Learning Community

Chris Kunkel

*Hope has two beautiful daughters. Their names are anger
and courage; anger at the way things are, and courage
to see that they do not remain the way they are.*
—Augustine of Hippo

We are not preparing children for standardized lives.
—Pat Bolaños, Key founding principal

In 1987, a small urban U.S. public school forever changed the face of education. A few years earlier, in 1983, a report on the failings of education in the United States, *A Nation at Risk,* was published, and government officials soon began enforcing strict guidelines. They hoped these "new basics" would improve achievement and create "a learning society." A group of eight public school teachers in Indianapolis saw this oppressive test preparation curriculum coming and began researching alternatives. After reading Harvard psychologist Howard Gardner's *Frames of Mind,* they found their answer. By developing a theme-based and project-focused methodology within a multiple intelligences curriculum, these teachers began a worldwide movement that revolutionized and changed education. At the Key Learning Community, teachers and students work to identify students' strengths to cultivate learning. Through project work and authentic assessment, students develop real-world competencies and the leadership capacities needed to succeed in today's world.

Current trends in education in the United States are worrisome. In the light of the No Child Left Behind (NCLB) legislation, a growing practice in this country is to use state standardized tests to determine the overall success of each student, each teacher, and each school. Many realize and warn (Gardner, 2006; Popham, 2001; Sacks, 1999) that standardized tests show only a narrow picture of achievement for students. Yet the practice of standardized testing continues to blaze on and indeed intensify. The oppression produced from this narrowly focused practice has been pervasive. Many schools now focus their curriculum to accommodate this arguably invalid measurement of learning—a move that results in a dreary school day for all when drills and rote practice rule the day.

The question, "What is valid assessment in K–12 education?" has been debated for some time now. For decades politicians, school officials, and textbook authors have been producing what they refer to as "teacher-proof" materials to teach and test with. Important here is the 1983 report, *A Nation at Risk* (National Commission on Excellence in Education, 1983), which generated dismal information concerning education and stimulated an effort to standardize education across the educational landscape in the United States.

At the same time that *A Nation at Risk* was published, a group of eight uncommon women who taught in Indianapolis Public School 113 were fed up and decided to do something about it. There simply had to be a better, more authentic way to teach and provide feedback to students. Kathy Sahm, one of the eight teachers, recalls: "Each of us had a story of a child who was successful in the classroom, but when you looked at standardized tests or the progress report, you did not see the success" (Kunkel, 2007). Thus, this 1983 landmark report created a landmark project as the founders of the Key School went on a quest to find a better way to serve the children of their inner-city school district.

THE EARLY JOURNEY

Genius, in truth, means little more than the faculty
of perceiving in an unhabitual way.
—William James

While reading widely, from philosopher John Dewey to theorists Elliot Eisner and James B. Macdonald, these eight educators came across *Frames of Mind* by Howard Gardner (1983). After uncovering this theory of multiple intelligences, they wondered if this might be a logical idea around which to design a school. They decided to ask Howard Gardner himself. After learning that he was speaking in Kutztown, Pennsylvania, late that October, they piled into cars and headed from Indianapolis to eastern Pennsylvania to see what he thought about this idea. Gardner explained that educators were not his intended audience for the theory; but he then admitted that he was intrigued with the notion of designing a school that used the multiple intelligences as the cornerstone for the curriculum. They spoke at length, and thus encouraged and motivated, the Indianapolis 8 headed home to begin the work.

After securing support from the district superintendent, these Key founders launched into grant writing, research, and travel to talk to various educational researchers and visit progressive schools using nontraditional practices. They met researchers at Project Zero at the Harvard Graduate School of Education, Indiana University, and the University of Chicago. They visited places like Pittsburgh Public Schools and the private Carolina Friends School that were reportedly doing interesting work in the field of education.

During the course of their early journey, the Key founders immediately recognized the genius in Howard Gardner's MI theory. They determined the Key School (its original name) was going to be based on the multiple intelligences and each intelligence was going to have equal importance. Applied to the context of education, they could see his theory laid fertile ground in which all students could realize their strengths. In turn, Gardner attributes the Indianapolis 8 with creating the first MI school in the world. Indeed, these eight amazing women came up with that idea; without fully realizing it, they started the MI movement in K–12 education when they opened their doors to 150 K–6 students in 1987.

But the Key founders did not want to trivialize the use of the multiple intelligences; they wanted to provide a program that delved deeply into each intelligence. In order to create rigor in each of the intelligences, appropriate staffing was a must. If the children were to have equal access to each of the eight intelligences, there had to be full-time staffing not only for the generalists, but also for the special areas that include music, spatial arts, and bodily-kinesthetic teachers.

With adequate staffing in place, an appropriate schedule could then be created that would allow the students maximum time in each of the intelligences. "The schedule itself is designed to allow each student to experience all of the multiple intelligences. There is as strong an emphasis on music, physical education, and art class as there is on math and English. Expert, certified teachers are present full time to teach each intelligence. As a result, students are free to deeply explore each intelligence area. Since they are deeply exposed to all the different intelligence areas, they have a good chance to find success in school at an early age, and discover their strengths" (Kunkel, 2003, p. 77). Finally, assessment is wrapped around the multiple intelligences. On each student's progress report, in the place of grades for traditional subject areas, the multiple intelligences are delineated individually.

Key also uses flow theory as a major component of the multiple intelligences curriculum. Flow is an idea identified by Mihaly Csikszentmihalyi (1990) where one becomes so involved in an activity, one loses track of time. Through collaborations with Csikszentmihalyi, the Key School developed the first flow activities center, perhaps the most important feature of the Key elementary program (kindergarten through fifth grade). In flow class, students have the opportunity to explore their intelligences freely, while the flow teacher observes and records choices and strengths. In flow, students learn about the concept of flow as well as the concept of intrinsic motivation. Students and teachers identify where individual interests and strengths lie, and this insight develops intrapersonal knowledge. By developing knowledge of personal strengths and sharpening their intrapersonal intelligence, students set the stage for the further evolution and future use of their own self-knowledge.

The "pod" is yet another part of the K–12 Key program that helps students identify and develop strengths in their multiple intelligences. A Pod class is an elective that students attend four days a week, where they can choose to explore an area of personal strength or any of the intelligences that spark their interest (Kunkel, 2007). Examples of the pods over the years include Planet Fitness, Puppets, Science Wizards, Sing and Sign, and Indy Ambassadors. Pods, then, "are designed to give students an opportunity to engage in work that they enjoy and find challenging. Such efforts can take them into a 'flow' experience. Students face a challenge that is enriching, rigorous, and relevant" (Kunkel, 2007, p. 206). Pod time can be the best time of the day: the students are immersed in an endeavor that they love, and as they work, they have the chance to develop their strengths.

To round out the plan for the Key School, the founders decided that the learning environment at Key was going to be collaborative, not competitive. Multiage classrooms would be used. Parent involvement was crucial so the Key compact was designed to help parents understand and accept their role in the process. Finally, a unique school would need a system in which it could function optimally. The founders studied organizational theorists such as James B. Macdonald, W. Edwards Deming, and Peter Senge. Armed with important ideas, the Key founders were well on their way to taking theory to reality.

THE THEME-BASED APPROACH, THEME PROJECTS, AND ASSESSMENT

Thematic investigation thus becomes a common striving
towards awareness of reality and towards self-awareness, which
makes this investigation a starting point for the educational process.
—Paulo Freire (1970)

From the start, the Key School elected a theme-based curriculum. Each spring, after considerable input by parents, students, and the whole community, the staff selects the themes for the following year. Drawing on a theme to build the curriculum has a number of positive consequences: it helps the students make personal connections to their learning, provides interesting topics that are meaningful and important, and provides a rich foundation for major semester theme projects, such as "This I Believe," "Patterns," "Environments," "Harmony," and "Pathfinders."

As parents began to send their children to Indianapolis-area middle schools after leaving Key Elementary, they expressed their desire for the Key program to be extended to the middle school level. The Key staff saw that expanding the program through high school would make sense as well. Thus, in 1993, the Key Renaissance Middle School opened, and this was followed in 1999 by the Key High School. In 2000, the entire program combined into one building, which became a K–12 site.

As part of the ongoing commitment by Key staff to make research and study a regular part of their tenure, Ernest Boyer's *The Basic School* (1995) became an essential text. In this book, Boyer identified eight commonalities:

> By "core commonalities" we mean those universal experiences that are shared by all people, the essential conditions of human existence that give meaning to our lives. These include: The Life Cycle, The Use of Symbols, Membership in Groups, A Sense of Time and Space, Response to the Aesthetic, Connections to Nature, Producing and Consuming and Living with Purpose. Within these eight themes, every traditional subject or academic discipline can, we believe, find a home [p. 85].

As the Key secondary program was being developed in the early 1990s, it was decided that the middle school would continue to use the themes chosen by the K–8 staff, but high school would use these eight commonalities as themes, with one each semester, as a requirement for graduation. The high school would cycle through the commonalities every four years. Since high school students are admitted only at the ninth-grade level, each high school student would have exposure to each commonality and be able to apply it to each intelligence. As themes, Boyer's commonalities structure a curriculum for Key high school students: students exist in a global community with considerable similarities to one another.

John Dewey (1902) noted, "Education should be child centered; we should begin planning the lesson by looking at where the child is developmentally" (p. 9). Since the Key School project was born in part from frustrations with standardized testing and the concomitant narrowing of the curriculum, another important early concern was the manner of assessment. In light of the test preparation insanity occurring in status quo public schools in the United States since the early 1980s, it was decided that at Key, curriculum would drive assessment.

After two years with a traditional report card, Key faculty decided that there would no longer be report cards with grades from A through F. Instead, teachers agreed on a progress report that gave feedback to the students based on their individual progress. The Key founders wanted assessment to be based on the most authoritative scientific findings, with consideration given to individual cognitive development instead of the more typical bell curve comparisons. This led them to a colleague of Gardner and Csikszentmihalyi, David Henry Feldman. His "universal to unique" theory (Feldman, 1980) helped Key educators to create developmental performance descriptors for each intelligence. These descriptors describe development across a cognitive development continuum in each of the intelligence areas and are used as a rubric in completing the Key progress report.

Instead of subject areas, the progress report lists all of the intelligences. Instead of letter grades, the progress report has a space to indicate the student's motivation (intrinsic, extrinsic, passive, or disruptive) and whether the student is making steady (S) progress, rapid (R) progress, or needs help (N). At the high school level, teachers indicate where the student falls along the continuum of cognitive development in each intelligence. A narrative for each intelligence completes the report.

One of the pieces assessed on the progress report is the semester theme project—each student's major work for the semester. Gardner (2006) has always been supportive of projects at Key:

> At their best, projects can serve a number of purposes well. They engage students over a significant period of time, spurring them to produce drafts, revise their work, and reflect on it. They foster positive cooperativeness in which each student can make a distinctive contribution. They model the kind of useful work that is carried out after the completion of school in the wider community. They allow students to discover their areas of strength and to put the best foot forward; they engender a feeling of deep involvement or flow, substituting intrinsic for extrinsic motivation (Csikszentmihalyi, 1990). Perhaps most important, they offer a proper venue in which to demonstrate the kinds of understandings that the student has (or has not) achieved in the course of the regular school curriculum" [p. 120].

Early on, the Key founders had hoped to avoid standardized testing altogether (though they never did) and to use projects as the main focus for assessment (which Key does). Routine practice at Key has each student complete a major project for each theme during each semester. The theme project must show deep development in one or more areas of intelligence, it needs to show reflection and development through a reflections journal, and it must produce some sort of original work.

These theme projects alone document the development of personal capacities in many areas. For instance, linguistic intelligence is clearly fostered through this work, as students keep journals and then perform verbal presentations of their project. Students also develop their intrapersonal intelligence as they consider the theme and then decide on the topic for their presentation. They research the topic, place it in the context of their own life experience, and then determine how they will present their work to their peers. This presentation becomes an interpersonal experience.

It has also been tradition at Key to have students keep a portfolio of their learning. Students reflect on their work as they make choices to place certain pieces into their portfolio. This self-assessment provides excellent feedback and hones the self-reflective process as the student moves through the program, from kindergarten through to the twelfth grade. At the high school level, Key students are required to gather their work and create a multimedia or digital portfolio that will be presented in exhibition their senior year. This digital portfolio has also been used in the college admission process; students may include a copy of the portfolio with their application and transcript. In many, perhaps most, cases, the student portfolios provide a more authentic look at their work than any other evidence they could submit.

LEADERSHIP DEVELOPMENT AND THE INTRAPERSONAL INTELLIGENCE

Know thyself.
—Socrates

Leadership development remains one of the core goals of the program. In a Ph.D. research project completed at Key, I demonstrated that student project work and the project presentations are an important tool of pedagogy and student assessment.

Project development emerged as a powerful curricular ingredient for leadership development. Students develop confidence and self-awareness by presenting projects; in the process, they develop intrapersonal intelligence, a quality important in people who display leadership (Kunkel, 2003).

One of the unique aspects of the Key program is the deliberate development of self-knowledge, or intrapersonal intelligence. From the first days of kindergarten, teachers begin to help students understand and use their strengths. Generalists work on this process with the students, while special area teachers (music, art, and physical education) look to foster special talents as well. In the flow activities class, the work is most deliberate.

Experiences in the flow activities class lay a foundation that allows students to acquire self-knowledge, and students' intrapersonal intelligence deepens throughout their K–12 experience. After elementary time spent in flow class, students take the next intrapersonal step. In middle school, as they participate in the middle school mentor program, students begin to think about what career they might be interested in. To complement the students' strengths and interests, a mentor who understands the goals of the program is carefully selected. Students spend time each week in the workplace in an area that matches these strengths or interests.

The apprenticeship program is the crowning jewel of the intrapersonal intelligence development program at Key Learning Community. During senior year, students choose an apprenticeship based on their strengths in a field in which they would like to work someday. Sometimes the apprenticeship is a continuation of the mentor experience, but most often the choice is a more mature version of that selection, one based on keener intrapersonal awareness. If students go through the program from kindergarten through the twelfth grade, substantial amounts of time are spent discovering and reflecting on individual strengths and interests. If students use that time wisely, they will have fully developed their intrapersonal intelligence.

Through exploration of the intelligences in flow class, the mentor program, and the apprenticeship program as well as in all of their disciplinary course work, Key students are able to make critical judgments about their educational and career choices. To go one step further, it is our hope that each student will take the strengths he or she discovered and developed to make a positive difference in the community, if not the world. This is part of the work we do to help develop the democratic ideal. Otto Scharmer (2007), a "futurist," agrees with our standpoint when he notes: "We also pour considerable amounts of money into our educational systems but we haven't been able to create schools and institutions of higher education that develop people's innate capacity to sense and shape their future, which I view as the single most important core capability for this century's knowledge economy" (p. 3). But at Key Learning Community, the curriculum is designed to do just that.

REFLECTIONS, EVALUATIONS, AND CONCLUSIONS

Nothing conquers except truth and the victory of truth is love.
—Augustine of Hippo

The Key Learning Community developed from a wonderfully pure and almost completely progressive ideal. In 1987 and in the early years thereafter, whole language, project-based math, and equal time in all of the multiple intelligences were the norm as Key teachers worked to bring students a special experience. While the elementary children still do spend a substantial amount of time in the areas of flow, art, music, and physical education today, we have had to become more concerned with the development of the students' logical-mathematical and linguistic intelligences. Here are the changes we have made recently, and why.

From the beginning, Key has used a lottery-based admissions process. When Key School opened in 1987 with a 32 percent poverty rate, progressive education ruled the day, and our MI curriculum and project-based pedagogy helped our students to flourish in many ways. But even then, high-poverty students' test scores were not flourishing. By and large, these students did not go to preschool, and they did not come to school with well-developed skills in the tested areas of math and English. In comparison to their peers, many of these students (whom we would now call disadvantaged) struggled in the logical-mathematical and linguistic intelligences.

But this lag did not matter so much then. Teaching to the top to challenge all students, peer tutoring, and supporting and scaffolding struggling students in heterogeneously mixed groups were good strategies with respect to the relatively low percentage of youngsters who came from poverty. In addition, with less than a third of students in the low socioeconomic status (SES) category, Key's test scores were just fine overall—above average in comparison to other schools in the district. Thus, in the 1980s and 1990s, low SES students were not the focus or a challenge at Key; they were just part of the community, and they were just fine. We knew that there were more than two intelligences, and we knew that the strengths-based program would do its job. And it did.

Now, twenty-one years later, the number of high-poverty students attending Key has more than doubled. Today, 72 percent of the students at the Key Learning Community come from poverty and are in need of extensive support. This change in demography has brought about a severe challenge for the school. Consider this comparison. In 1987, seven out of twenty-one children in a class needed extra support in basic language and math skills in order to be able to read and compute at basic levels and to perform well on standardized tests. Today this number has jumped to sixteen of twenty-four children—quite a challenge for our teachers. Not surprisingly, this shift in population has caused Key's overall test scores to fall. Pressure from our district to improve scores has become the order of the day.

With a sense of urgency, we have been studying these issues and have had to come to some relatively quick decisions. In the first fifteen years that the Key Learning Community was in existence, our state standardized test scores were good enough to continue our program of progressive and enriching curriculum while never taking a single moment to prepare for the high-stakes tests. In these early days at Key, since we had such a progressive curriculum and pedagogy, standardized test questions and the requisite thought patterns required to answer them were indeed somewhat foreign to most Key students. At the start of the test window each year, they sometimes got "a little freaked out." But in the end they had the wherewithal to sit down, settle down, and do the problem solving needed to answer the questions. In those days, students could usually pull through with good outcomes without preparation. But all this is now changed.

In 2004, we noticed a considerable drop in our elementary standardized test scores. We concurrently noticed lower abilities in all of the intelligences, and in a larger portion of our student population. In an effort to find a better way, "our way," we began by altering our multiage configurations at the elementary level. We now have kindergarten students working in their own group. We have grouped first and second graders in multiage groups, and we have grouped third, fourth, and fifth graders in multiage groups. (Before this, we had grades K to 1, grades 2 to 3, and grades 4 to 5 in multiage groupings.) We hope these new groupings make more sense developmentally, with the new demographic we now serve.

But with the pressures of NCLB and these different demographics, we have also resigned ourselves to a bit of test preparation. We now look at the test scores and the areas that do not score well, and we support the students in these areas. We do give the students opportunity to "scrimmage" with both writing prompts and math facts. We also show students examples of the bubble sheets that they will see during the testing window. We are not happy about this; it takes a big bite out of our project-based class work. But the last thing we want to do is to have the program shut down because we are perceived as stubborn or arrogant. The No Child Left Behind legislation does not care who we are or what we have accomplished.

Yet while these changes have been difficult and pose a threat to our progressive philosophies, our MI curriculum is still intact. Students still spend substantial time in special area classes and daily time in pod class, and teachers still focus on areas of strength. Key also maintains our rigorous K–12 theme-project schedule, and the semester-long theme projects still hold an important place in our program. Lots of energy is given to helping students understand the importance of their project; as before, students are taped (digitally recorded, in the current lingo) and tapes are used as part of their assessment. This focus on meaningful projects and products was an important foundation of the Key program in 1987 and remains so today. Our end-of-semester culminating event is still a priority, and it is invigorating, and sometimes inspiring, to see the wonderful learning that takes place at Key during these events.

Multiage classrooms also are being maintained. Our middle school has grades 6 through 8 in multiage groups and our high school groups ninth, tenth, and eleventh graders together. This is challenging as the district breaks down curriculum to the third-grade test, the fourth-grade test, and so on up to tenth grade. We are permitted to create our own curriculum maps in lieu of the district pacing guides and benchmark tests given by grades every four and a half weeks. We are thankful for this flexibility from the district.

Despite recent struggles, the Key program still sports a theme-based, project-focused MI curriculum, and the popularity of the program has (since 1987) been expanded to include a middle school and high school. In 2006, due to the renown of the program and our long waiting list, Key opened a second elementary campus. So the issue is not whether the Key program is good; it is. The issue is whether the school district is asking for too much and chipping away at the Key program to our detriment. The issue is also Key staff making wise decisions that satisfy current political mandates without destroying the texture of what Key represents. This is all delicate work, as it is critical to our future.

At our twentieth anniversary celebration held in May 2007, Howard Gardner noted that although the Key Learning Community is known worldwide, it is not well known locally. The truth is that even if Key is known in Indianapolis, it is usually not well understood. Many confuse the multiple intelligences with learning styles. Paradoxically Key has been described as a school for the gifted, as well as a school explicitly for students with special needs. It has been characterized as having a bottomless purse from the district—which is far from true. And starry-eyed visitors often assume they have found an educational utopia at Key, which of course is not true either. Key has the same demographics as the rest of the Indianapolis Public Schools in SES, gifted (or not gifted) students, racial differences, and special needs. In short, Key clearly has the same challenges as most other urban public schools throughout the nation.

In this test-score-crazed national environment, a generally progressive urban public school is not always appreciated. Some feel that theme-based and project-focused pedagogy is not the way to educate urban at-risk children; the current catchphrase is that schools should be "standards based." But we at Key feel that this education, one that fosters leadership, self-knowledge, and self-reliance, is just the thing to close the achievement gap and help our students to be successful now and in the longer run. Although our students at the elementary level have struggled recently on standardized tests, by the time they move into our high school, our scores are the highest in our school district. Finally, Key's graduation rate has ranged from 88 to 100 percent since our first graduating class of 2003, a special feat to note considering comparisons to other high schools with similar poverty rates.

The faculty and staff at Key Learning Community have been working hard to examine our practices within the context of our new demographics. Besides looking at our standardized test scores, and unpacking those, we have conducted extensive program evaluations. Through these more authentic program assessments, we are learning that the most important aspect of our work is positive collaboration among staff, parents, community, and students. We are learning that we need to be honest with ourselves and open to evaluation and evolution. And we know we need to find ways to have our parents and students buy into and take leadership in this process. This complex process will ensure a program that will empower students to own their strengths so they can be mindful of choices they make within their own education and ultimately their life paths. We know that this goal cannot be accomplished through a test preparation experience.

The Key Learning Community has been a scholarly endeavor from the start. We see our work as a rigorous exercise in authentically connecting theory to practice. Throughout their educational journey, Key students learn how to execute a successful project, connect their learning to the world they wish to live and work in, and present their finished work to their peers. The primary goal for the students as they move through Key is to identify their strengths and develop them. Through the learning processes in place at Key and with full knowledge of their strengths and how to use them, students learn how to identify problems and effectively solve them. Finally, our grandest hope for our students is that they then use their strengths to build positive changes in both their own lives and in the global community (see Chapter Nine, this volume).

The Key influence on the face of education has been felt far and wide. Key has had visitors from six continents and from forty-two of the fifty states. There has been much media attention, including a piece that appeared on *ABC News,* another on CBS's *Sunday Morning,* two stories that ran on South Korean TV, and still another in the *New York Times Magazine,* to name just a few examples. Key staff have been invited to dozens of other states and countries to share our work. In a continuing effort to foster collaboration with interested educators, we hold an in-depth institute each year and host visitor days bimonthly. Thousands have attended over the years, and many have incorporated Key's ideas into their own schools (see, for example, Chapter Thirteen).

When asked which aspects of the program could be applied universally, we usually recommend the pod elective or creating a flow activities class to help students identify and understand their strengths. We recommend hiring specialists to teach the spatial, musical, and bodily-kinesthetic intelligences instead of expecting each classroom teacher to cover them all. But whenever asked about the transferability of the program at Key, we always caution: you cannot just take the package of Key, wrap it up, and take it back to use it at your school. In order for these ideas to work, you must gather the team who will be implementing the plan and allow them to collaborate to develop the new ideas for the school as a team.

Multiple intelligence schools have changed the way the world looks at education. The late Pat Bolaños, founding principal of Key, once said in a video (quoted in Ward and Associates, 1992), "We really do want to change the direction of education." What has been accomplished at Key Learning

Community is nothing short of extraordinary. It is a tribute to Pat and her colleagues, and their legacy, that Key and all of the other schools represented in this book are doing just that. And by changing the direction of education, we are cultivating students who can indeed change the world.

References

Boyer, E. L. (1995). *The basic school.* New York: Carnegie Foundation for the Advancement of Teaching.

Csikszentmihalyi, M. (1990). *Flow: The psychology of optimal experience.* New York: HarperPerennial.

Dewey, J. (1902). *The child and the curriculum.* Chicago: University of Chicago Press.

Feldman, D. H. (1980). *Beyond universals in cognitive development.* Norwood, NJ: Ablex.

Freire, P. (1970). *Pedagogy of the oppressed.* New York: Continuum.

Gardner, H. (1983). *Frames of mind: The theory of multiple intelligences: The theory in practice.* New York: Basic Books.

Gardner, H. (2006). *Multiple intelligences: New horizons.* New York: Basic Books.

Kunkel, C. D. (2003). A study of community participation and leadership development in an urban public school. *Dissertation Abstracts International, 65*(02), 175. (UMI No. 3122704)

Kunkel, C. D. (2007). The power of Key: Celebrating 20 years of innovation at the Key Learning Community. *Phi Delta Kappan, 89*(3), 204–209.

National Commission on Excellence in Education. (1983). *A nation at risk.* Arlington, VA: ERIC.

Popham, W. J. (2001). Teaching to the test? *Educational Leadership, 58*(6), 16–20.

Sacks, P. (1999). *Standardized minds: The high price of America's testing culture and what we can do to change it.* Cambridge, MA: Perseus Books.

Scharmer, C. O. (2007). *Theory U: Leading from the future as it emerges.* Cambridge, MA: Society for Organizational Learning.

Ward and Associates. (1992). *The wrong stuff* [Video]. Washington, DC.

CHAPTER 25

Multiple Intelligences Around the World

The New City School Story

Thomas R. Hoerr

Multiple intelligences theory was conceived as a way to look at human potential, not as a curriculum or framework for school design. While MI resonates with educators who seek new and varied ways for students to learn, there has been no road map for implementing MI on a schoolwide basis. The experiences at New City School show one way that this can be done. For twenty years, the faculty of the New City School has grappled with how MI can be used to increase student learning. The exploration that began as a faculty reading group has resulted in MI becoming an integral aspect of the school's culture. Today MI frames pedagogy and assessment, informs dialogue among and between educators and parents, and has had a positive impact on faculty collegiality. The school esteems the personal intelligences in particular.

The theory of multiple intelligences (MI) has been implemented at New City School in St. Louis, Missouri, since 1988 and has been a powerful tool in helping faculty look at students in more comprehensive and positive ways. This is not to say that the road to MI has always been easy or smooth; that is not the case. Indeed, the MI journey has not lacked challenges, and even as I write, we continue to grapple with how best to use MI and how to find the right balance among educational goals and approaches. Yet it is clear that our students have gained, our faculty has grown, and New City is a better school since we began to use MI.

The New City School is an independent school enrolling 360 students, age three through grade 6. St. Louis is in the middle of the country in a fairly conservative area. (Missouri's nickname, "the show me state," is proudly indicative of its citizens' skeptical attitudes.) Since the school's founding in 1969, however, its progressive philosophy has embraced joyful learning, a focus on developing character, and an appreciation for human diversity. The mantra "academics, ambience, diversity" is on our stationery because we believe that all of these principles must be embraced in preparing students for the future. Our student body is quite diverse: approximately one-third of our students are children of color; one-third of our students, children of all races, receive need-based financial aid; and our students live in fifty-five zip codes.

For nearly twenty years, we have defined ourselves as an MI school. Beyond using MI as a tool to help children learn, we also see our role as supporting the use of MI by other educators around the world. Our faculty have written two books on how to use MI in teaching and in student assessment (*Celebrating Multiple Intelligences*, 1994, and *Succeeding with Multiple Intelligences,* 1996). I have written a book about how to implement MI on a schoolwide basis, *Becoming a Multiple Intelligences School* (Hoerr, 2001), and scores of articles on MI. We have hosted four MI conferences with Howard Gardner as our keynote speaker, thousands of educators from around the world have visited our school, and we recently opened the world's first MI library. And yet, with both some frustration and some pride, I am very aware that our use of MI remains a work in progress. This frustrates me because we do not have "the answer" (even though I understand there is not one answer), and yet at the same time I feel pride because we continue to reflect on our performance and search for the ways in which MI can help us. Our implementation of MI is very different than it was twenty and ten years ago, and I know that it will continue to evolve over the next decade and beyond.

Our MI journey began when I read *Frames of Mind* (Gardner, 1983) in 1988. I was quickly taken by the implications it offered for educators. Gardner's model made it clear that we need to view students through a broader lens than that which comes from gauging their strength only in the "scholastic intelligences" (Hoerr, 2001) by focusing exclusively on how well they read, write, and calculate. I was aware of some incredibly talented students for whom school seemed to be an ordeal. These children shined in music class or on the athletic field but struggled in literature discussions, for example. Or they might be gifted in painting or in working with others but lackluster in long division. I recalled other students, including some I had taught, who seemed to bide their time in school, waiting eagerly for recess or dismissal because the way they learned did not correspond to the way they were taught. All too often, there was one route to school success, and that route did not correspond to how they learned. Then I remembered the numerous discussions I had with peers of mine, people who had become successful adults and who talked about how they had "survived school."

Indeed, schools do a great job at creating and reinforcing a narrow educational hierarchy. At the top of the pyramid are students who learn through the scholastic intelligences. Further down the hierarchy are students whose talents lie in areas not typically valued in schools. These children may excel in the arts; they might be adept at working with others and knowing themselves; they could be athletes or nature lovers. All too often, however, unless these talents are accompanied by strengths in the scholastic intelligences, schools can be unfriendly places for them, and success can be elusive. This narrowness of opportunity is exacerbated in today's high-stakes testing environment.

In some respects, this hierarchy of intelligences is natural. Many educators learned in traditional ways and did well in school, so it is only natural that they would esteem the traditional scholastic intelligences in their students. Too, schools were designed to produce employees, and the three R's have been assumed to be the keys to economic success. That most schools offer a fairly narrow academic pathway to success is not surprising.

Make no mistake: it *is* important that students do well in traditional academic areas, but an understanding and appreciation of MI makes it clear that the scholastic intelligences do not encompass all of the ways in which children can and should grow. Too often the areas of art, music, and physical education are seen as frills, and students' progress is relegated to the back page of the report card (if these areas survive schools' budget cuts in the first place). Embracing the MI model elevates the role of art, music, and movement in education.

Perhaps most striking to me was the way in which Gardner's conception of the personal intelligences gave a framework for the skills that are so important in every endeavor of life. In particular, his identification of the interpersonal and intrapersonal intelligences seemed to offer rich educational implications. (Indeed, the power of Gardner's personal intelligences was highlighted by the subsequent success of Daniel Goleman's book, *Emotional Intelligence,* in 1995. Goleman used different terminology than Gardner did, but the focus of the emotional intelligences corresponds well to Gardner's interpersonal and intrapersonal intelligences.)

After my initial reading of *Frames of Mind,* my mind was racing with possibilities of ways in which an MI focus might lead to more students learning and to all students learning more. I came away with three beliefs, and they continue to inform our use of MI today:

1. There are many different ways to learn.

2. The arts are important.

3. Who you are is more important than what you know.

BEGINNING WITH MI

I knew that bringing MI to life in my school would require a great deal of hard work. I also knew that it would require buy-in by the faculty; I could not simply mandate that we become an "MI school." (Even if I could have mandated this, I would not have done so because that is not my style.) I made a brief presentation about *Frames of Mind* and MI at a faculty meeting and emphasized the potential that I thought MI offered. I invited teachers to meet with me and read the book. I suggested that we meet a couple of times before the end of the school year and then continue to meet over the summer. "I'll provide everyone with a copy of the book," I said, "and provide food for our meetings. I'll facilitate the first session, and then we'll take turns leading the discussion. Who's interested in joining me?"

Much to my pleasure, over a dozen teachers, approximately a third of our faculty, opted to join the group. I called our group the Talent Committee, and we began to meet after school every other week. The discussions, led by teachers, were rich. We discussed Gardner's definition of intelligence and its implications and tried to use the various intelligences in our learning. We incorporated puzzles in reviewing the chapter on spatial intelligence and used songs to review the chapter on the musical intelligence, for example. Our group was a minority of the faculty, so we took it on ourselves to share what we were learning with the rest of the faculty. At each faculty meeting, I made a point of asking members of the Talent Committee to share what we were learning and discussing. Also, members of the committee made a point of sharing their new knowledge and enthusiasm with their teammates. In 1989 a group of us visited the Key School in Indianapolis to understand how MI could come to life.

How to apply this notion of MI to teaching and learning was challenging. We talked about how recognizing MI would change what happens in classrooms, how student assessment would also have to change, and the impact this would have on communications with our students' parents. We were still enthusiastic but saw embracing MI as a more complex effort than we originally thought.

Teachers began working to find ways to use MI in their classrooms. We quickly found that using MI took place in three ways: teachers using MI in their teaching, students using MI in showing what they had learned, and students working at MI centers created by their teachers. As we began to implement MI, students responded in positive ways, and we became better observers of their interests and how they learned. We recognized that we often can only infer which intelligences a student is using in solving a problem since problems can be solved in multiple ways. It was clear that MI supported our goal of joyful learning, and teachers were enjoying using a new tool to view children and create curriculum. Our use of MI also facilitated faculty collegiality (Barth, 1990) as teachers collaborated and learned with one another.

PARENT EDUCATION

For the first couple of years, our movement to MI was unbridled. We experienced normal frustrations and difficulties but no major obstacles. Our work with MI was limited only by our vision and energies. We had to pace ourselves so that we did not try to do too much too soon. Teachers loved seeing students respond to the different intelligences, and our use of MI continued to gain momentum. Around 1994, however, we began to feel a bit of a pushback from some of our students' parents.

Children learn best when the home and school work together, so I work to keep parents informed and maintain a dialogue with our families. I send a weekly letter to my students' parents and have always been proactive in sharing and in listening. Implementing MI made this even more important since none of our students' parents had attended a school that used MI. I knew that parents needed to be informed, and I made a point of explaining how we were using MI to help students learn. Parents would understand what we were doing and be enthusiastic. Or so I thought.

In fact, I failed to realize that today's parents are different from their predecessors. Many of them are Generation Xers, born between 1965 and 1980. A characteristic of this demographic group is that they are not intimidated by authority and can sometimes be suspicious or cynical. The use of nonscholastic intelligences and an absence of percentiles in depicting student progress can make it hard for these parents to understand and accept MI. The debate about the importance of standardized test results exacerbates that difficulty.

As a result, although I had specifically talked about MI in many of my weekly letters to parents and teachers shared a bit about MI at our open houses for years, most parents did not understand MI. More accurately, they did not understand our implementation of MI and how we were using it to help their children learn. Indeed, what we considered to be positive—students talking about how they were having fun at school—was a cause for alarm in some households. Quite a few parents believed that school should be hard and that students should not enjoy going to class. Although they might not say this, it was clear from their reaction to their students' enthusiasm. Some parents became concerned about our academic rigor and questioned whether their children were being adequately prepared. As students found school to be fun and began to use their "other," nonscholastic, intelligences—musical, artistic, and bodily-kinesthetic—some parents wondered if we were lowering our scholastic standards. It became clear to me that this was a significant problem, and one that I could not solve alone.

I convened a faculty committee to find ways to communicate about our work with MI to our students' parents. When we first met, many of the teachers shared similar experiences, relating times when they had been questioned by some of their students' parents about both the how and why of our MI implementation. This certainly was not an issue for all parents, but the concern was significant enough that we needed to act.

Our committee generated some specific and helpful ideas and suggestions (most of which we continue to use today, more than fifteen years later). Student artwork had always adorned our halls, and we agreed to portray student work in all of the intelligences on the walls and in the halls. In addition, we noted that the presence of student work alone was not sufficient, no matter how attractive or impressive it might be. Beyond simply displaying evidence of student progress, we needed to accompany all of the displays with an explanation of what was being shown and how it fit into our curriculum. "It's not enough for the halls to be attractive," I said, "they must be informative too." Even today, all of our displays are accompanied with signs explaining what is represented and how it leads to student learning.

We also decided to make our welcome back open houses more MI friendly. Rather than just talking about MI and how we were using it, we used MI and let our students' parents engage in some of the same experiences that their children were having. Teachers selected activities and led their students' parents in using MI at the open houses. Parents used their bodily-kinesthetic and spatial intelligences to piece together a puzzle that explained the year's curriculum and goals. Parents worked as teams to talk about issues and raise questions. They worked at MI centers to gain a sense of the kinds of activities their children were doing and to see firsthand how MI helped them learn.

Years later we continue to use some of these parent communications (really, parent education) practices, and others have been eliminated. We no longer use MI at the open houses, despite the fact that parents told us that it helped them understand a bit about how MI was used (and that it was fun). We stopped doing this because teachers were concerned that they did not have enough time at the open houses to adequately present all of the information that parents needed to know (goals for the year, academic and behavioral expectation, channels for communication, and so on). This was reinforced by a comment that one student's parent made to me: "There was so much emphasis on the how at the open house, I never learned what they would be studying that year." Although we still talk about MI and offer an explanation of what it is and why we use it, particularly at the younger grades, it is no longer the focus of the evening.

We continue with some of the other strategies to educate parents, however. We still post explanations to accompany the student work that we have hanging in our halls. I continue to use my weekly parent letter, now an e-letter, which often includes photos of our students using MI (available at www.new cityschool.org), to inform and proselytize for MI. Each grade also sends a weekly e-letter to their students' parents, and teachers use their letters to share their work with MI.

For many—maybe most, perhaps all—parents, what really matters is what they see on their child's report card, yet I have always been struck by the disparity between what principals and teachers say their schools value and what they report to parents. In many cases, school leaders (and school banners and letterheads) talk about developing character and respect, yet these qualities are tucked away on the back of the report card, if they are even listed there. Teachers and principals will say that it is important that students develop an appreciation for others who are different from themselves, for example, yet this capacity is not reflected in what is measured and reported. When there is a disparity between what schools value and what they measure and report, teachers' efforts will be hampered, and this will have a negative impact on student performance and parent support. Lofty goals are well and good and necessary, but teachers' behaviors are naturally framed by the measures of student progress for which they are held accountable (by parents, administrators, students, and themselves). As we moved forward with MI, this meant that we must reflect what we value (students' multiple intelligences) in how we regularly assess student progress and in what we share with their parents.

We determined that our traditional ways of monitoring student progress were no longer adequate; they were necessary but not sufficient. Paper-and-pencil exercises and tests (including standardized tests) have their role but do not provide a full picture of student growth. Our use of MI meant that students were using a range of intelligences to learn, so it seemed only appropriate to also let them show what they learned in these ways too.

Teachers began to search for ways in which nonscholastic intelligences could be used to show what students had learned. Some of our initial strategies are still used today. Our kindergarten students create life-size, functioning human bodies as a way to show their understanding of the systems of the body, just as our third graders build dioramas to show what they have learned about the Native American tribes they have studied. Our first graders create imaginary insects to show that they understand adaptation, and second graders build a monument that should exist to portray an aspect of our country's movement to the West. In studying biographies and citizens who make a difference, fourth graders participate in a living museum in which they dress as the people they have studied and answer questions about their lives. Fifth graders write and perform a musical play about the history of the United

States. Sixth graders create giant murals that capture an "ism," such as racism, sexism, ageism, or "lookism." Each of these projects is accompanied by a written research report so we are able to measure student progress in both nontraditional and traditional ways. Throughout, developing the intrapersonal intelligence became a focus as teachers asked students to reflect on and evaluate their efforts, and talk about how they learned.

Perhaps the most significant change in our assessment practices was that we created a new first page for our report card ("Page One") and devoted it exclusively to the personal intelligences. So many report cards address these crucial areas of human development only with small statements that focus on whether a student "works with best effort" or "is a cooperative learner." In contrast, we believe that the personals are the most important intelligences and that they will make a difference with any task and in every setting. Consequently, an important part of our responsibility is to help students develop their intrapersonal and interpersonal intelligences. Thus we decided to begin the report card, and the subsequent parent-teacher conference, by focusing on students' personal intelligences.

We had lengthy faculty committee meetings to determine what constituted the personal intelligences and what we could reasonably assess and report. Under Intrapersonal Development, "Can self-assess; understands and shares own feelings," our Page One addresses the following areas:

Confidence

- Is comfortable taking a position different from the peer group
- Engages in appropriate risk-taking behaviors
- Is comfortable in both leader and follower roles
- Copes with frustration and failures
- Demonstrates a positive and accurate self-concept

Motivation

- Demonstrates internal motivation
- Is actively involved in the learning process
- Shows curiosity
- Shows tenacity
- Exhibits creativity

Problem Solving

- Shows good judgment
- Asks for help when needed
- Can generate possible hypotheses and solutions

- Shows perseverance in solving problem
- Accepts and learns from feedback

Responsibility

- Accepts responsibility for own actions
- Accepts responsibility for materials and belongings
- Handles transitions and changes well
- Accepts limits in work and play situations
- Uses an appropriate sense of humor

Effort and Work Habits

- Participates in activities and discussions
- Works through assignments and activities carefully and thoroughly
- Keeps notebook, desk, and locker or cubby organized
- Has age-appropriate attention span
- Works independently
- Follows written and oral directions
- Listens attentively
- Uses time effectively

Under Interpersonal Development, "Can successfully interact with others," Page One addresses:

Appreciation for Diversity

- Makes decisions based on appropriate information rather than stereotypes
- Understands the perspectives of others, including those of other races and cultures
- Shows concern and empathy for others
- Respects the individuality of others

Teamwork

- Cooperates with peers and adults
- Works at conflict resolution
- Behaves responsibly in groups
- Demonstrates an ability to compromise
- Expresses feelings and gives feedback constructively and appropriately

When we began using Page One, we were a bit anxious because our parents were used to responding to and discussing students' test scores and percentages of homework completion at their parent-teacher conferences. How would they react, we wondered, to hearing teacher judgments about their children on something as amorphous as "confidence" or "appreciation for diversity"? To our relief, parents welcomed the opportunity to talk about what kind of people their children were becoming. Sometimes, of course, parents see their students differently than we do, perhaps even more so with the personal intelligences. Teachers are prepared to offer examples of why they have marked a child in this or that way. Generally parents understand, even if they are not happy, and they work with us to develop school and home strategies to address areas of need.

Page One has been very successful in helping us focus on what is most important and in reminding everyone what we value. As teachers prepare for parent-teacher conferences, they begin assessing student progress by reflecting on their students' personal intelligences.

Beyond changing what we reported on our report cards, we also decided that student portfolios would make it easier for us to capture growth in all intelligences, and a portfolio committee was formed to decide how best to do this. We began to use portfolios and decided that each year's contents must include a self-portrait or biography and items from all of the intelligences. Each item also needed a tag that would explain the intelligences it required or reflected and the rationale for its inclusion. We initiated a spring portfolio night, an evening in which parents were invited to peruse their child's portfolio.

IT'S DEVELOPMENTAL

In *Corporate Lifecycles* (1988), Ichak Adizes says: "Organizations have lifecycles just as living organisms do; they go through the normal struggles and difficulties accompanying each stage of the Organizational Lifecycle and are faced with the transitional problems of moving to the next phase of development" (p. xiii). It is true that institutions change as they grow and progress—as they meet their goals or do not—and as, of course, they are affected by changes in leadership, demographics, and political milieu. That is true of Apple Computer, Harvard University, and New City School. But Adizes's comments are even more relevant when applied to the implementation of an educational innovation. New City School has gone through several phases in its MI evolution, and more are ahead (these are described in my book, *Becoming a Multiple Intelligences School*).

Our first years of MI implementation were ones of exploration and enthusiasm. Once we gained an appreciation of the potential of MI, it was easy to see how traditional educational practices failed to meet the needs of many students. Teachers began to find ways to incorporate MI into their classrooms. There was a great deal of excitement, accompanied by some hesitancy and some confusion. Changing pedagogical and assessment practices meant engaging in different kinds of work, for sure, and it often meant doing more work too. There were no MI texts, so teachers were brainstorming and sharing tactics that had worked for them, and this was why we published two teacher guides for implementing MI. At the same time, we were identifying and categorizing MI times in the schedule and labeling MI activities and products. In retrospect, it seems clear that it is only due to the power and potential of MI that we persevered.

Ironically, using MI can present difficulties because students invariably respond so well to an MI approach. Even when students have to operate outside their comfort zones or predilections, MI activities are interesting and fun. In addition, many teachers find the student interest and success from using MI to be reinforcing (and sometimes using MI also validates a teacher's intelligence profile). This is well and good, but a difficulty inheres because lessons cannot be driven merely by student or teacher enjoyment and purely for MI experiences. We experienced this lure during our early years with MI. Often I said to the faculty, "It's not enough that students are enjoying the lesson and are excited about coming to school. That's wonderful, but we need to ask how the lesson ties into our curricular goals." (The power of MI is perhaps shown by the fact that I still occasionally need to remind everyone that twenty years later. MI must be used in a thoughtful manner that considers academic goals and curricular expectations.)

As our MI reputation grew, we began to hear from other educators around the country and around the world. We felt (and still feel) a responsibility to help others, and we opened our doors to welcome visitors. Prior to the terrorist attacks of September 11, 2001, we were averaging five hundred to seven hundred educator visitors per year. Today the impact of No Child Left Behind and the vestiges of those attacks have reduced this, and we average more than three hundred educators per year. Hardly a day passes, however, without my receiving an e-mail MI inquiry from somewhere, often from another country.

We have found an approach to MI that works for all of the members of our learning community. Our teachers find MI to be an effective tool, students learn joyfully, and their parents are pleased. Yet our use of MI remains a work in process. Two decades later, we still ask, "What is the right balance between MI and traditional academic skills?" We know that MI is a powerful tool for student development and joyful learning, yet we also know that our students need to perform well in traditional academic areas. These thrusts need not be contradictory, but how time is allocated becomes a crucial factor.

Using MI well requires a significant amount of teacher time in planning and preparation, and it requires ample student time for engagement. The time for MI must come from somewhere, typically from traditional academic exercises. Does spending more time on the personal intelligences mean that students will graduate without being able to spell? Does incorporating the spatial intelligence into social studies lessons mean that students will learn less history? Or does doing this mean that they will have a greater understanding of the topics that have been covered? How do you balance the time that using MI requires against the gains that it offers? We have learned that when MI is used to address curricular goals, it does not have to be viewed as an either-or dilemma. MI can enhance instruction and facilitate student learning.

Our educational balance is always around the corner, and perhaps that is appropriate. After all, there is no one set point that offers educational nirvana; even if such a point existed, it would soon be obsolete as students, staff, and conditions changed. Rather, educational balance is a pendulum, always swinging back and forth. My job is to ensure that we are not satisfied and that we are thoughtful in pursuit of the ever-elusive balance.

LOOKING AHEAD

I continue to characterize our work with MI to be an evolution. We are not there yet, and, in fact, never will be. We have made remarkable strides in some areas, such as with our focus on the personal intelligences. The feedback we receive from the secondary schools to which our students matriculate is that our graduates do well academically, but that is not all: they know themselves well and are strong group members and classroom participants; they know how to learn. Our incorporation of the spatial intelligence into our instruction is quite strong as well. Our use of projects, exhibitions, and presentations in student assessment has become routinized with the use of dioramas, models, and spatial depictions. Student presentations are the norm, and our students achieve well on standardized tests. We recently opened the world's first MI library, and our Centennial Garden is a naturalist magnet to our students. Our use of MI comes together in a wonderful way, and joyful learning is the norm.

In each of these areas, however, we have far more to do. Our use of the musical intelligence is far too often an exception. While our assessment practices are often MI friendly, in some areas, we have not made the progress that I had hoped. With student portfolios, for example, we remain at what I call "the display level": students and parents enjoy perusing the contents of the portfolios, and portfolio night is popular with families, but we do not make good use of them for monitoring student progress. Our Centennial

Garden and MI library are notable physical features that are appreciated by our students and staff and often envied by our educational visitors. However, neither of them has realized its potential. The garden is beautiful and our students enjoy it, but we are still working to use it as a tool to integrate the naturalist intelligence into our curriculum. Similarly, our MI library is visually stunning, but we are still working to find the best way to use it to support MI. We now incorporate MI Centers on a regular basis, and the library abounds with MI opportunities, but we have just begun to realize its potential.

Our school has changed remarkably due to our use of MI, and our students' learning and lives have been altered in powerful ways. They and the school are better because of MI, and our faculty have benefited as well. It has been a wonderful journey, a bit of a wild ride at times, and I am eager for the next steps.

References

Adizes, I. (1988). *Corporate lifecycles.* Upper Saddle River, NJ: Prentice Hall.

Barth, R. (1980). *Run school run.* Cambridge, MA: Harvard University Press.

Faculty of the New City School. (1994). *Celebrating multiple intelligences: Teaching for success.* St. Louis, MO: New City School.

Faculty of the New City School. (1996). *Succeeding with multiple intelligences: Teaching through the personal intelligences.* St. Louis, MO: New City School.

Gardner, H. (1983). *Frames of mind: The theory of multiple intelligences.* New York: Basic Books.

Goleman, D. (1995). *Emotional intelligence.* New York: Bantam Books.

Hoerr, T. (2001). *Becoming a multiple intelligences school.* Alexandria, VA: ASCD Press.

CHAPTER 26

What If They Learn Differently?

Inteligencias Múltiples ¡Despierte el Potencial de Aprendizaje!

René Díaz-Lefebvre

Latinos are the largest minority group in the United States, numbering 47 million (about 15.5 percent of the total U.S. population). Young Latino undergraduates are half as likely as their white peers on campus to finish a bachelor's degree. Many Latino students may be frustrated because they want instruction that is not based on linguistic and logical-mathematical intelligences. Glendale Community College implemented an imaginative approach, Multiple Intelligences/Learning for Understanding (MI/LfU). Including cultural values *(familismo, respecto, simpatia, biculturalism)* proved to be a pivotal and integral component in the effectiveness of the approach that empowers Latino/a students to believe *Sí Soy Inteligente* (I am intelligent).

It just was not working for me and my students. I had to do something. I could no longer rest on the belief that spending most of my career as a community college professor lecturing and giving paper-and-pencil tests was the best way for students to learn. Could it be that I was not teaching or reaching as many students as I thought? I was always prepared for my lectures. I even made it a point to tell jokes, but my students were not "getting it." They were not learning the material, seemed disengaged in class and were doing poorly on tests.

And what about the significant numbers of Latino/a students in class? Was I letting them down? Many were looking to me as a role model, one who came from the same Mexican American background and spoke the same Spanish language. I was someone they could relate to and become excited about learning from. In this chapter, I provide an overview of what happened when a college professor took a risk to try something different and challenging: applying multiple intelligences theory to the psychology curriculum and the learning implications for U.S. Latino/a students in a southwestern urban community college. I start with a few revealing vignettes.

JAVIER'S STORY

I remember it well. Vivid and so real, the experience still haunts me to this day. It was a beautiful spring day, and my introductory psychology class had just ended. I felt good about the review we completed in preparation for the test the following week that would cover the brain and nervous system. "Students who participated in the discussion should do well on the test," I thought to myself, "and the rest, well, I hope they took good notes!"

Javier was in deep thought, busy with what appeared to be a drawing or sketching activity. I could not help but notice his sense of contentment and enjoyment. He seemed to be in his own world—a visual world. As I erased the blackboard and Javier continued his drawing, I wondered how many times people (especially teachers!) stereotype students like Javier because of the way they look, dress, or speak. Javier could have been one of the characters in *Stand and Deliver,* the movie about Jaime Escalante, an inner-city high school math teacher who motivates kids from the wrong side of the tracks to excel in high-level math courses. As I prepared to leave the classroom, I asked Javier if today's discussion on the brain made any sense to him. He shrugged his shoulders as if to say, "Yeah, maybe, but what difference does it make anyway? I don't do well on tests, so who cares?"

As we continued talking about class and school in general, I told him I had noticed that he drew throughout the entire review session. Not wanting to sound too overly concerned for his lack of note taking, I asked if I could see what he had drawn. He opened the sketchbook to reveal incredible drawings of the human brain. I stood in awe of their colorful detail. What was even more remarkable, he had drawn the sketches from memory; his book had been closed throughout the class.

The drawings included the cerebral cortex, the cerebellum, the corpus callosum, the lobes of the brain, and the two hemispheres. I asked Javier to describe what the drawings meant to him. He began to explain in a type of street dialect known as *Caló,* spoken often by young Mexican-descent kids referred to as *Cholos.* "This area is called the cerebellum," Javier explained. "And you know, *ése* [a popular salutary expression to a male friend for hi, hello], it's like when somebody gives you a good *cabronazo en la cabeza* [major blow to the head] and you feel real dizzy. Well, this part of the brain organizes bodily motion, posture, *y tambien* [and also] equilibrium." His example made good sense and demonstrated his understanding of the function of the cerebellum.

In his side-view sketch of the left hemisphere, I noticed a large red arrow pointing to Broca's area, which is located in the lower frontal lobe and is involved in the production of speech. "What's this for?" I asked. *"Pues, tú sabes ése* [well, you know, pal]," Javier replied, "You see, my *nana* [affectionate name for grandmother] suffered a stroke about a year ago on the right side of her body. And as you know, *ése*, the left side of the brain affects the right side of the body, and vice versa! She speaks real slowly as if she is really struggling to get the words out. She makes perfect sense in what she is trying to say. We understand her; it just takes time for her to speak in full sentences. There was damage in that area."

Walking out the door, Javier turned to me and said, "This is what I think you were trying to teach us about the brain *prófe* [professor]."

This exchange occurred fifteen years ago, and it still sends chills up my spine.

Javier "failed" the paper-and-pencil test on the brain, finished the course with a D, took a few more courses, and then dropped out of college. Despite this outcome, I know he understood the brain and its function; he personally understood.

WHAT ABOUT THE BIG KIDS?

I recall listening attentively as fellow teachers talked about how they transformed their classrooms by including MI theory in their curriculum. The conference was on MI and attended exclusively by primary and elementary school teachers and administrators. Their students, the attendees shared, were excited about learning. A ten-year veteran teacher said that since applying the theory, she truly believes her students demonstrate a genuine love of learning.

As I listened to these inspirational teachers describe what they were doing, I could not help but feel a tinge of envy. They seemed to be having so much fun teaching and reaching students. They were elementary school teachers talking about how every child is smart in his or her own way and how MI theory has enhanced their understanding of teaching and how children learn. I thought to myself, "Yeah, okay, this sounds like a great idea for the little kids, but I teach the big kids at the college level. It would never work—or would it?" This question haunted, challenged, and intrigued me to come up with a possible inclusion of MI theory and its benefits in a system of higher learning deeply ingrained in paper-and-pencil testing.

AN EXPERIMENT IN LEARNING

A wide range of efforts has been under way in the United States aimed at providing new and exciting insights into learning. Cognitive scientists are finding that people do not learn in a vacuum; they learn through social interaction. Human development researchers study motivation to discover what makes people exert the effort to learn. Neuroscientists peer deep into how the brain works to redefine learning itself. They have found that brain activity occurs in a number of ways: spontaneously, automatically, and in response to challenge. To learn effectively, this brain activity must be stimulated in at least one of these ways and be combined with useful and suitable feedback systems. Moreover, for learning to continue, the brain must be provided challenging tasks that require significant amounts of reflection or emotional energy. This challenge appears to be an important part of healthy brain functioning (Gardner, 1985).

After completing much reading and research on MI theory, and by attending and participating in a three-week MI Institute at the University of California, Riverside, I was motivated, determined, and ready to take a major risk as a "seasoned" teacher and create something new and different. Could I reach and teach more community college students by utilizing a theory that works so well with children? To explore some of the MI assumptions in the community college setting, an experimental pilot study, Multiple Intelligences/ Learning for Understanding (MI/LfU), was developed and implemented at Glendale Community College (Maricopa Community Colleges) in Arizona between 1994 and 1996. It introduced innovative ways for students to complete assignments and demonstrate learning of essential information. The idea was to incorporate MI theory into a new paradigm where creative forms of learning resulted in real understanding (Díaz-Lefebvre & Finnegan, 1997).

The MI/LfU teaching and learning approach was applied to ten introductory psychology classes with 131 students participating. The class sizes were limited (the average class size was 13 students) to better observe the results of the project efforts. Students were given various learning options to choose from and, most important, demonstrate an understanding and application of core concepts and principles. These learning options were acting/role playing, mime, collage, sculpture, creative dance, original poetry, drawing/ sketching/painting, musical/rhythmic application or performance, computer simulation, book report, interview, creative journal writing, and paper-and-pencil testing.

Students became mini-experts and cofacilitators of learning as they gave "performances of understanding" of the academic content. Assessment for understanding was completed using a creative grading rubric or diagnostic rubric. Reflective student and faculty evaluations provided invaluable insight into the learning and teaching process. Once the pilot study concluded, other teachers enthusiastically joined the initiative. English, art, chemistry, math, child and family studies, communication, psychology, Spanish, anthropology, nursing, music, and biology teachers started to use MI/LfU principles developed in the initial experimental study. Dedicated risk-taking teachers challenged students—and themselves—to get out of their comfort zones while exploring creative ways of learning academic material.

Twenty-five professors have been involved in the initiative. Faculty took part in a six-hour MI/LfU orientation session, and monthly faculty dialogue sessions were held on learning, teaching, and assessment. The sessions were modeled after Parker Palmer's *The Courage to Teach* (1998). Each semester, all participating faculty completed an evaluation, Reflections on Teaching and Learning.

DEMONSTRATION OF STUDENT LEARNING: THE LEARNING OPTION

The learning option incorporates various intelligences proposed by MI theory. Its purpose is to provide students with guidance and an opportunity for learning academic material in a different way. By learning material in a way that makes sense for the student, understanding is achieved. It is difficult to determine whether students actually understand. To understand means that a person can take something learned—concepts, terms, theories, knowledge—and apply it appropriately in new situations.

Within a college setting, the challenge becomes the student's ability to demonstrate an understanding of terms, concepts, and knowledge as they are applied to the real world outside the classroom. Basic premises apply regarding assessment, students, and teaching.

Not all students learn or understand material in the same way. Yet for many, paper-and-pencil testing is the only method used in assessing how they are smart. The purpose of the learning option is to provide choices and creative options that accentuate the different intelligences. Creativity and use of the imagination is highly encouraged, assessed, and rewarded. The written and reflective component of the learning option format is an integral part of the student's learning experience.

The teacher is the content expert and makes the decision on what terms, concepts, and topics students need to know. He or she provides encouragement, support, and confidence in the student's ability to succeed. The teacher provides the guidance, and the student chooses which terms or concepts to incorporate in the learning option. Ultimately the student is challenged to become accountable for his or her own learning and behavior.

The learning option provides the opportunity to reinforce material covered in class, outside reading assignments, and material that may appear on a quiz or test. It becomes a good review exercise for students. Students can explore various ways of learning, get out of their comfort zones, be creative, and have fun. Christina, a nineteen-year-old psychology student, shared, "Because I was given options to choose from, I was not intimidated. . . . I looked at the semester in a positive way. I looked forward to learning psychology the way I wanted to and earning the grade for what I chose to accomplish. MY CHOICE. Everyone becomes motivated when they have a choice."

THE ASSESSMENT MAZE

Effective assessment of student learning outcomes has been a major issue for higher education for a number of years, not only in the United States but abroad as well. Data are collected and made available using traditional measures of student academic performance and progress. With so much information available, it is sometimes tempting to think that many in the higher learning community get caught up in the one-size-fits-all craze that has taken place at other levels of education.

Assessment for understanding helps the teacher and learner set standards. It also creates instructional pathways, motivates performance, provides diagnostic feedback, evaluates progress, and communicates progress to others (Díaz-Lefebvre, 2003).

In reflecting on the resistance I experienced in the early days of the MI/LfU experiment, it seemed that trying something too unfamiliar, without any guarantees, was not compelling enough for some people to take risks and give up the status quo. This belief applies to administrators, students, and faculty alike. Change is tedious, uncomfortable, unsettling, and downright scary for most people. For others, change represents an opportunity to grow, get unstuck, and look at the many possibilities of personal and professional self-renewal.

Too many college students are falling through the cracks because they learn in different ways. Creating multiple approaches to demonstrate how they are smart is at the core of reaching these learners. The reality of what goes on in the classroom is sometimes overlooked or not captured by those far removed from the action. Two stories of different learners illustrate this point.

ROSARIO . . . SÍ SOY INTELIGENTE

Freud's concept of personality structure is always a favorite with introductory psychology students. I recall how one of my students, Rosario, creatively captured the essence of her understanding of Sigmund Freud's id, ego, and superego by writing a poem. She explained:

> My poem, "Quarrel," creatively interprets the voices of the Superego, the Id, and the Ego. The first stanza is the Superego complaining about the Id. The next stanza is the Id antagonizing the Superego. Finally, the last stanza is the Ego urging his feuding brothers to realize their mistakes. The Superego loathes the Id's threat to his world. The Superego must constantly pick up after the Id's mess. "Trash the glass, then make it mold" is a line that can be interpreted in different ways. One would say the Superego must make the glass mold again after the Id ruins it. The Id lashes back to say the Superego has no courage and will never take the risk. The audience will note the Id will continue to entice the Superego: "Do you know the extreme of numb?" The Ego steps in as referee. He attempts to show them the big picture. The line, "Last this long—less than years," is saying "you've gotten this far but you won't last much longer." I chose to print the poem with a visual aspect as well. The audience will see the Superego's words clear to the left but sliding to the right. Id's words are displayed in an opposite format and looking a bit haphazard. Ego's words are down the middle in a very compromising tone. This presentation builds upon the characteristics of the three positions.

By providing Rosario the different entry point of poetry for her understanding and application of a challenging Freudian concept, she proved her understanding at a deeper level of reflection than most students. She continued:

> I will never forget these Freudian concepts after working on my poem. To be able to interpret the three characteristics correctly, I had to understand the ideas. However, the reinforcement and creative freedom of the learning option allows it to be more significant than words in a thick book. My poem has also sparked more concept realization and ideas for a different creative learning option. I can honestly say I have a much stronger hold on the concepts of the Id, Ego, and Superego. This was one of the most enjoyable assignments I have had the opportunity to do throughout my entire educational career.

Rosario's classmates and I listened attentively and were in awe as she recited her incredible poem. A few students came up to me and indicated they had a better understanding of Freud after listening to Rosario's poem and the discussion that followed. Carlos offers how his motivation has changed once he had options in demonstrating how he is smart:

> Siento que he tenido más motivación para aprender psicología debido a las diferentes opciones de conocimiento. La razón para esto es porque me fue

"concedida" la oportunidad de aprender a "mi" manera. Al serme concedida esa oportunidad, aprendí mucho más que si yo fuera que tomar examines escritos cada semana [Díaz-Lefebvre, 2006b]. [I feel I have had more motivation to learn about psychology because of the different learning options. The reason for this is because I was "given" the chance to learn "my" way. By being given this chance, I learned a lot more than if I were to have taken paper and pencil tests every week.]

In this evaluation, Carlos indicated the importance of being encouraged to express oneself in Spanish: "I am allowed to express my true feelings and thoughts about the material I am learning."

CREATIVE GRADING RUBRIC, OR HOW DO YOU GRADE THIS STUFF!

A rubric is a set of guidelines for comparing students' work. It provides descriptors for varying levels of performance and answers these questions: By what criteria are performances judged? What does the range in quality of the performance look like? How are the different levels of quality described and distinguished from one another? Rubrics have been used at the elementary level of education for quite some time, whereas the use of rubrics at the college level is relatively recent.

The grading rubric developed in the pilot study assesses student completion of the learning option and evaluates progress for the following criteria: (1) creativity/imagination, (2) demonstration/performance, (3) organization/format, (4) reflection/metacognition, and (5) evidence of understanding. Teachers complete a grading rubric for every student who selects a learning option (Díaz-Lefebvre, 1999).

In addition, after every learning option, each student is required to complete and turn in responses to three reflective questions. In general, the questions challenge the student to:

- Identify or define, explain, and show examples of how specific terms and concepts were creatively incorporated into the learning option
- Justify, explain, and use examples of how and why the particular learning option selected (for example, mime, poetry) assisted or reinforced the understanding of academic material mentioned in the textbook or discussed in class
- Provide a paragraph (or longer) of reflection and evaluation of the learning option experience (for example, by creating a sculpture, the opportunity of learning nursing concepts in a different way)

REVISITING JAVIER AND OTHERS LIKE HIM

I began the chapter with Javier, an incredibly bright, intelligent man. I owe a lot to this young Latino. What I learned from him about how people learn has changed my idea of how MI theory can be applied to different groups of learners: Spanish-speaking Latino/as. I must admit that in the past, I have resisted the notion of there being separate populations or groups of people (Asians, Native Americans, Latinos, and so on) who could benefit from MI instruction. After all, an intelligence is a biological and psychological human potential possessed by all of us. Correct?

MI does not apply only to Latino/as. But my interaction with Javier led me to wonder what might happen if I presented the MI/LfU approach to learners who speak a different language and whose cultural values and mores represent a significant part of the community my college and district serve. About two-thirds of the total Latino population in the United States is of Mexican descent (born in either the United States or Mexico). According to the Pew Hispanic Center, a nonpartisan fact tank that provides information on the issues, attitudes, and trends shaping America and the rest of the world, about a quarter of Hispanic adults are undocumented individuals, most of them arriving as part of a heavy wave of immigration that began gathering force in the 1970s (Pew Hispanic Center, 2007). High school dropout rates and low levels of college attendance pose critical challenges for this burgeoning segment of American society. There are major differences among Latino subgroups in terms of their cultural characteristics, immigration experiences, history, socioeconomic levels, and other important factors. It is no longer appropriate to negate these differences or to assume that all Latinos share similar psychological issues (Fry, 2005).

Over the twelve years of the MI/LfU initiative, I have provided material in Spanish for a small segment of Latino/a students taking my psychology classes. I am seeing some encouraging and promising results by including cultural values like *familismo* (strong family orientation, involvement, and loyalty), *personalismo* (preference for personalized attention and courtesy in interpersonal relations), *respeto* (emphasis on respect and attention to issues of social position in interpersonal relationships, for example, respect toward elders), *simpatia* (a deferential posture toward family members and others in efforts to maintain harmony in family and in interpersonal relationships), *enculturation* (an orientation toward a return to ethnic core culture), and *biculturalism* (the capacity to function effectively and to switch adaptively between two cultures) (Velásquez, Arellano, & McNeill, 2004).

By including examples of prominent Latino/a leaders representing various intelligences, Latino/a students are able to see and relate to exemplary individuals who share similar cultural backgrounds. For example, I have featured novelist Gabriel García Márquez for linguistic intelligence, neurologist Santiago Ramón y Cajal for logical-mathematical intelligence, painter Frida Kahlo for spatial intelligence, star athlete Ana Guevara for bodily-kinesthetic intelligence, guitarist Carlos Santana and opera singer Plácido Domingo for musical intelligence, Mexico president Vicente Fox and union organizer César Chávez for interpersonal intelligence, and environmental activist Chico Mendes for naturalist intelligence.

Although the number of Spanish-speaking Latino participants in MI/LfU has been small, I see incredible *potencial* in reaching this segment of the college population. When material is presented in the language that one feels most comfortable in, it provides an excellent entry point for the student to enter the fascinating world of MI possibilities. I believe MI/LfU can make significant and positive changes in the academic and personal lives of Latino/a learners. I am excited about pursuing application, evaluation, and research into this new horizon.

OUTCOMES, REPLICATION, AND LESSONS LEARNED

In 2004–2005, the MI/LfU initiative celebrated its tenth anniversary at Glendale Community College as a viable, alternative academic approach to learning, teaching, and creative assessment. Although many data have been collected and analyzed over this period, primarily through student and faculty evaluations, it was time to conduct a large-scale survey on former and current students. In June 2004, a ten-question survey gathered data from students who participated between fall 2001 and spring 2004. A total of 1,239 questionnaires were distributed: 1,034 mailed and 205 handed out in classes. We had a 34 percent return rate.

The results show increased student motivation, longer retention of academic material, and high satisfaction of learning with MI/LfU compared to traditional methods. Average scores on all questions relating to their learning experience were 4.0 or higher on a 5-point scale. Most significant were the findings from students taking courses in the hard sciences (math, biology, and chemistry). Eighty-four percent of students completing biology classes indicated that their ability to retain information was better by completing a learning option. Students completing chemistry classes indicated a 93 percent retention rate, and math students stated an 86 percent retention rate. In response to another survey question, *In your opinion, what is more of a meaningful and effective method of assessing student learning, paper/pencil testing or MI/LfU Learning Options?* 84 percent of students in all disciplines thought MI/LfU was better than traditional methods for assessing student learning. Within each discipline, the percentages of those favoring MI/LfU were: math (94 percent), child/family studies (94 percent), anthropology (89 percent), Spanish (88 percent), psychology

(87 percent), English (84 percent), nursing (80 percent), music (79 percent), chemistry (77 percent), and biology (71 percent).

Throughout the initiative, students using a variety of learning options demonstrated more positive risk-taking behavior in applying the different ways of learning academic material. In particular, students were more interested in exploring different learning options when the instructor modeled, encouraged, and rewarded their getting out of comfort zones. The instructor taught using multiple and creative methods and took chances himself or herself. In evaluation documents, students shared that their motivation and out-of-class effort increased because they saw more clearly the value of their learning experiences, they enjoyed the opportunity to be creative, and they began to develop their own love of learning. Student evaluation and reflective papers on the learning options showed more depth and analysis than with previous assignments. Although there were a few who resisted the notion of attempting something new, students in general welcomed the opportunity to try something different. For many of them, it made common sense to offer a curriculum based on how well each individual is motivated and learns.

In addition, I learned a lot about teachers and teaching during the initiative. Most colleagues supported my efforts to attempt something new. Others thought I was just another "wacky" psychologist doing something weird. I convinced a few instructors in my own department and faculty in other disciplines to experiment with the learning options and see what happens. My biggest satisfaction as a teacher came as I watched Latino/a students become empowered and confident and develop a *Sí Se Puede* (Yes I Can!) attitude about themselves and learning.

CONCLUSION

Change and research take time and come hard-won in academia. Teachers and administrators interested in replicating this approach should be reminded that when challenging long-practiced methods and deeply ingrained paradigms, they will face resistance and argument. Resistance can come from colleagues, administrators, and students to maintain the status quo without ever looking at the possibility of asking "What if?" Nevertheless, the possibilities are endless and exciting (Díaz-Lefebvre, 2006a).

References

Díaz-Lefebvre, R. (1999). *Coloring outside the lines: Applying multiple intelligences and creativity in learning.* Hoboken, NJ: Wiley.

Díaz-Lefebvre, R. (2003, August). In the trenches: Assessment as if understanding mattered. Learning Abstracts. *League for Innovation in the Community College*, 6(8). Retrieved July 11, 2008, from http://league.org./istreamsite/info_form.cfm.

Díaz-Lefebvre, R. (2006a). *Inteligencias múltiples en el proceso de enseñaza ¡Despierte el potencial de aprendizaje!* Phoenix: Editorial Orbis Press.

Díaz-Lefebvre, R. (2006b). *The multiple intelligences/learning for understanding approach: Some pieces to the puzzle of learning.* Retrieved January 10, 2009, from http://www.mi-lfu.com/Video percent20Files.html.

Díaz-Lefebvre, R., & Finnegan, P. (1997). Coloring outside the lines: Applying the theory of multiple intelligences to the community college setting. *Community College Journal, 68*(2), 28–31.

Fry, R. (2005, November). *Recent changes in the entry of Hispanic and white youth into college: Chronicling Latinos' diverse experiences in a changing America.* Washington, DC: Pew Hispanic Center.

Gardner, H. (1985). *The mind's new science: A history of the cognitive revolution.* New York: Basic Books.

Palmer, P. (1998). *The courage to teach.* San Francisco: Jossey-Bass.

Pew Hispanic Center. (2007, December). *2007 National Survey of Latinos: As illegal immigration issues heat up, Hispanics feel a chill.* Washington, DC: Pew Hispanic Center.

Velásquez, R. J., Arellano, L. M., & McNeill, B. W. (Eds.). (2004). *The handbook of Chicana/o psychology and mental health.* Mahwah, NJ: Erlbaum.

CHAPTER 27

Problem Solving and the DISCOVER Project

Lessons from the Diné (Navajo) People

C. June Maker
Ketty Sarouphim

Solving a wide range of problems is a key aspect of demonstrating multiple intelligences. Observation of children and adults engaged in problem solving is the most valuable way to discover their varied strengths and expression of abilities. In the Diné (Navajo) culture, the use of an assessment based on this philosophy has resulted in a greater understanding of how abilities are expressed in children growing up in a rural environment and in a culture that places high value on visual arts. We describe our experiences during these assessments, give examples of children's performances, and provide a recent analysis of the relative strengths of Diné children from a cross-cultural perspective.

When June Maker walked down the hall at Chinle Boarding School in the Diné Nation and saw the sign "Testing, Do Not Disturb" on the door of the class-room in which our team was assessing children, she was puzzled. "Testing? Oh, no, we don't tell the children we are *testing* them! We tell them we are watching them as they work on problem-solving tasks. I thought I explained this to the teachers and children. How come the sign says 'testing'?" Inside the classroom, June, Ketty, and other researchers from the University of Arizona presented a series of tasks to the children, including solving tangram puzzles, telling stories, and writing stories. At the end of the work, several children came up to June and asked, "Did you test us today?" Careful not to use the word *testing,* she described what she and her colleagues had done.

"No, no," the children said, "it's okay if you did. If you *did* test us today, will you please come back and test us again tomorrow?"

This was not an isolated instance in our work with Diné children. They thoroughly enjoyed solving the problems we presented and always asked when we were coming back. Evidently the problem-solving tasks, designed as part of our assessment for identifying diverse giftedness, are inviting, engaging, and challenging. When children are motivated to participate in activities, they are more likely to do their best, and we are more likely to identify their true capabilities and potential.

The scenario also showed the compatibility between our assessment approach and Diné people's beliefs about the meaning of *testing.* In their culture, testing does not mean asking someone questions you already know how to answer yourself. The practice of mainstream American parents who ask their children to name colors and count with numbers, for example, is strange in this cultural context. To Diné children, testing means to give a person something to do and then to watch how the person does it. That is, testing means observation of problem-solving abilities in real-life situations.

In this chapter, we focus on the importance of problem solving as the defining construct of intelligence. We show how Howard Gardner's definition of intelligence influenced our approach to examining problem-solving abilities in a project named DISCOVER. We further illustrate the value of observation in developing an understanding of the abilities of children, especially children in remote areas of the land of the Diné people in northern Arizona. We believe these experiences can be helpful for others interested in cultural and geographical influences on the use of multiple intelligences.

DINÉ NATION: THE GEOGRAPHICAL AND CULTURAL CONTEXT

The Diné people live in the area designated as the Navajo Nation, approximately twenty-seven thousand square miles in northwest New Mexico, northeast Arizona, and southeast Utah. Based on the Treaty of 1868 and subsequent administrative rulings, court orders, and congressional acts, the Diné people live in a separate nation and have the right to govern themselves even though they reside within the territorial boundaries of the United States. In the year 2000, approximately 180,000 Diné lived in the geographical area bounded by the Four Sacred Mountains. An additional 118,000 lived in towns and communities bordering the Diné Nation and in other states and countries. The median age of Diné people is 22.5 years.

The landscape at lower altitudes has mostly desert shrubs, while at higher altitudes, pinion pine and other trees are found. Near rivers and streams, cottonwood and other larger trees can survive in this mostly dry climate. The mountains and salmon-colored sand with ribbons of white, gray, and dark red provide a sharp contrast to the green of the trees and shrubs. The land is breathtaking in its beauty and majesty. In recent years, towns have become larger, and more people are living near them. Because of the importance of sheep herding and farming, most people still live in small communities or in remote areas where there is less competition for scarce water.

Often families have several homes close together, and one can see the generations in the structures—grandmothers and grandfathers live in a traditional hogan, mothers and fathers live in a house or mobile home, and children are beginning to build modern hogans, some with two stories and new types of construction. Children in this culture are respected and given great freedom to grow up. The responsibility of family members (grandparents, parents, and siblings) is to identify children's natural gifts and find ways to nurture these seeds so they will grow and blossom. In turn, each individual is expected to use her or his gifts for the good of all.

Diné people have four types of schools: public schools that are governed by the State of Arizona, boarding and day schools funded and operated by the federal Bureau of Indian Education (BIE), BIE grant schools funded by the BIE but locally operated, and "freedom schools" governed by locally elected boards (Begay & Maker, 2007). The boarding schools were the first forms of education provided by the U.S. government, and many still exist, although they are much less common now than in the past. In our projects, we worked with the first three types of schools. Some schools were in traditional rural communities with relatively intact families, language, and culture. Others were in communities on the border of the Nation, with much more influence from the majority culture and language.

THE DISCOVER PROJECTS: DEFINITION OF GIFTEDNESS AND ASSESSMENT DEVELOPMENT

Funded by both federal grants and funds from the Diné Nation, DISCOVER stands for Discovering Intellectual Strengths and Capabilities while Observing Varied Ethnic Responses. As the name signifies, the primary purpose of the project is to identify diverse giftedness among ethnic groups, particularly groups that often are excluded from traditional programs for gifted students. The primary means used in the project is the observation of children's ethnic responses to problem-solving tasks.

Defining Giftedness

MI theory was the inspiration and framework for creating our definition of giftedness. Gardner (1983) defines intelligence as "a set of skills of problem solving enabling the individual to resolve genuine problems or difficulties that he or she encounters . . . , to create an effective product, and . . . the potential for finding or creating problems—thereby laying the groundwork for the acquisition of new knowledge" (pp. 60–61). Guided by MI theory, we defined giftedness as *the ability to solve the most complex problems in the most efficient, effective, or economical ways.* According to this definition, gifted or highly competent individuals also *"are capable of solving simple problems in the most efficient, effective, or economical ways"* (Maker, 1993, p. 70). Later, we added *elegant* to the definition because when we worked with Diné children, often we found ourselves saying "that's simple, but *elegant!*"

Developing an Assessment Tool

Armed with a clear definition of giftedness, DISCOVER researchers launched a series of efforts to develop forms of assessment that would help us identify varied ethnic expressions of intellectual strengths and capabilities. In the first study, with bilingual Spanish speakers and monolingual English speakers, Maker and Schiever studied individuals who were nominated as highly competent in using specific intelligences, asked them to solve a series of problems ranging from structured to open-ended, observed them as they solved increasingly open-ended problems, interviewed them about their problem-solving processes, and finally analyzed videotapes of their performances (Maker, 1993; Maker & Schiever, 2005). The continuum of problem types, a modification of the early work of creativity researcher Mihalyi Csikszentmihalyi (Getzels & Csikszentmihalyi, 1967, 1976), was effective in eliciting varied problem-solving competencies. Using this tool, we found that participants, both those considered highly competent and those considered competent, exhibited the core capacities outlined by Gardner in his description of multiple intelligences (Gardner, 1983), but in varying degrees or at different levels. This study served as a validation of our belief that multiple intelligences are observable during problem solving.

In the next series of studies, using the same general strategy of presenting problems and observing the behaviors of problem solvers, our team worked with children and adults from a variety of cultures. At the end of each series of activities we presented to children, each observer was asked to designate the child or children who were "effective, efficient, elegant, or economical" problem solvers, and to describe what those children did or said that led to this conclusion. If someone used a term such as *highly motivated,* he or she was asked to describe observable behaviors. For example, terms such as "follows through to completion," "continuously working," and "doesn't want to quit when time is called" are observable behaviors that lead one to believe someone is "highly motivated." We recorded only the observable behaviors. After we had observed over five thousand children from various cultures and no new behaviors were listed, we categorized and classified them according to intelligences and whether they were characteristics of the problem-solving process or the products. Studies of the reliability and validity of this assessment have continued, and the assessment is accepted in several states and various countries as a valid way to measure abilities and to place children in programs for the gifted. This assessment has a number of unique features:

- The assessment includes a set of engaging, developmentally appropriate activities from kindergarten to twelfth grade. Activities are specified for four levels: kindergarten to second grade, third to fifth grades, sixth to eighth grades, and ninth to twelfth grades.

- The activities are designed to be intelligence fair. Rather than requiring a verbal response to all questions, observers present tasks and use materials appropriate to the particular intelligence being measured.

- During the assessment process, children use two kinds of knowledge: their first-order knowledge, deriving from experiences, and their second-order knowledge, resulting from learning in academic contexts (Gardner, 1992).

- Assessment tasks progress naturally from closed questions with right answers and correct methods to tasks in which the problem itself needs to be defined and solutions are completely determined by the problem solver.

- The assessment takes place in small groups in regular classrooms, environments most authentic to children's learning and therefore most likely to reveal children's real intellectual capabilities. Students working in these small groups are encouraged to interact, and their interpersonal strengths are noted.

- The assessment includes standardized procedures and directions as well as a behavior checklist. Observers record behaviors of each child to designate the child's level of "effective, efficient, elegant, or economical" problem solving. For example, the designation of "highly motivated" would be suggested by observable behaviors such as "follows through to completion," "works continuously," and "doesn't want to quit when time is called."

At this point, the DISCOVER problem-solving assessment at the elementary level includes the following sets of activities:

- Tasks to measure spatial artistic abilities by involving children in constructing a variety of objects, animals, and scenes using brightly colored cardboard pieces and black plastic connectors

- Tasks to measure spatial analytical abilities by inviting children to make geometric shapes and solve puzzles of increasing difficulty using tangrams
- Tasks with a focus on oral linguistic abilities—providing opportunities for children to talk about the toys they are given and to tell a story about any or all of them
- A worksheet with math problems that range from those with one correct answer to those with an unlimited number of appropriate answers
- An open-ended writing task in which children write about any topic and in any format they choose

Our identification of a set of problem-solving behaviors closely matched the core capacities Gardner (1983) identified for linguistic, spatial, logical-mathematical, interpersonal, and intrapersonal intelligences. They also resemble traits found in the creativity literature (for example, fluency, flexibility, elaboration, and originality) and research on eminent individuals (for example, task commitment) (Amabile, 1996; Charles & Runco, 2000; Renzulli, 1978; Simonton, 2000; Torrance, 1972, 1981; Weisberg, 2006; Zuckerman, 1977). (See Maker, 1994, 1996, 2005; Rogers, 1998, for more information about these behaviors and how they are part of the assessment. See Maker, 2005; Sarouphim, 2000, 2001, 2002, 2004, for information about the validity of this assessment.)

RELATIONSHIPS AMONG INTELLIGENCES

The results of our research on relationships among the intelligences using the DISCOVER assessment supports MI theory. We have found that in general, correlations between diverse activities are low, ranging from .00 between spatial artistic and math activities at grade 2 to .29 between spatial analytical and written linguistic activities in grades 9 to 12 (Sarouphim, 2000, 2002, 2004). Correlations between scores on activities that assessed the same intelligences were low to moderate, ranging from .02 between spatial artistic and spatial analytical at grade 5 to .52 between spatial analytical and math at grade 4. Interestingly, the correlations between oral linguistic and written linguistic were low to moderate, increasing from .29 at kindergarten to .43 at grade 4, then decreasing to .25 at grades 6 to 8 and .28 at grades 9 to 12. These results and the case studies of Diné children we observed from grades 2 through 10 indicate that interactions and relationships among the intelligences may be highly individualistic and may develop over time or change as a result of schooling. Most children, for instance, exhibit profiles similar to Crystal, in which they have one or two dominant intelligences. When we use the

DISCOVER assessment, 26 percent demonstrated the highest level of abilities in one activity while only 14 percent demonstrated this level in two activities. Children like Alex were rare; only .3 percent of children in our samples demonstrated the highest level of performance in all five activities. (Crystal and Alex are profiled in the next section.)

CASE STUDIES: THE IMPORTANCE OF OBSERVATION

To make the statistical data more accessible, we provide two examples to illustrate varied intellectual profiles among Diné children. We chose children we have observed every year for nine years and with whom we worked closely in special classes and programs. In the first case, Crystal reveals her strong tendency to work through one dominant intelligence. In the second case, Alex combines different intelligences and appears to be equally proficient in all of them.

Crystal

Crystal is exemplary in the use of her strong interpersonal intelligence to approach the world around her. One day when June was assessing a group of students, Crystal asked: "Where did you sleep last night?" "Do you like ice cream?" "Do you like chocolate?" "Where do you live?" "How old are you?" "Are you married?" "Do you have children?" Toward the end of this series of questions, the other children told her she should not be asking those questions, and she replied with a grin, "She answered, didn't she?"

On another day, Crystal asked for June's address so she could write to her. June gave her address to Crystal, not expecting to hear from her, as June had given her address to many children before. A week after returning home, June received a wonderful letter from Crystal, telling how much she missed her and how she would love for June to live in Rock Point. Later that week, June was telling her colleague Ketty about Crystal's wonderful letter, and Ketty pulled out her own Crystal letter! Crystal had been busy writing to all of her observers. Years later, when June attended graduation ceremonies for the group of students we had followed, she saw Crystal, who said, "I saved all your letters to me." Crystal saved the letters because personal relationships are the essence of her life.

Crystal's strong interest in personal relationships was evident in the DISCOVER assessment process. In the spatial artistic activities, children are asked to construct a variety of objects. Crystal made people and only people—people with different personalities, people from different cultures and age groups, and people in different kinds of relationships with each other. In one assessment, she convinced all the students in her group to make "people exercising" and the group had great fun with that. Often she was so focused on encouraging and helping others during the tangram puzzle activity that she did not finish working her own puzzles. Her storytelling was about people. Her insights about their personalities and motivations were far beyond those one would expect for a child her age. Crystal even made up word problems about people for her math exercises. People—their relationships, needs, stories, and emotional states—colored Crystal's mode of learning and understanding the world.

Alex

In contrast to Crystal, Alex's case represents students who seemed to work through all intelligences—at least all those we were assessing—with equal facility. As a young child, he made complex products during the spatial artistic assessment, often consisting of thirty to forty pieces in contrast to the three- and four-piece constructions typical for this age. He worked the tangram puzzles with ease, completing the challenge page (given to those who complete the puzzle book before time is called) before most reached the fifth (out of six) puzzle page. When he was in high school, we had created two more challenge pages to ensure we assessed the highest ability levels of these bright students. For Alex, we had to develop a third challenge page on the spot because he had completed all of the puzzles with ten minutes remaining.

In the area of language and literacy, Alex excelled as well. Over the years, he created a variety of written products: poetry, short stories, autobiographies, descriptive accounts, and fantasy. His vocabulary was extensive and his plots complex and clear. His imagery was rich, and his humor was contagious.

His logical-mathematical abilities are revealed through his creation of a computer program that called the name of the librarian. One night, the librarian working in the media center suddenly heard a voice calling softly, "Kyla," "Kyla," "Kyla." For several days, she looked all over the library to find the child who was calling her name. After a long search, she finally realized that the sound was coming from one of the computers rather than from a real child. She thought it sounded like Alex. When asked, he admitted he had done it, and explained how.

The main point of these stories is to emphasize the importance of observation—observation with an open mind and respect for who and what one is observing. Educators like us must continually dust off the lenses of our perceptions so that we can see clearly what the other is telling us, not what we want to see based on our beliefs and values. What we learned from these children could not have been learned if we had approached them with a strong belief in what intelligence is or how the various intelligences *should* be expressed.

EXPRESSION AND LEVEL OF INTELLECTUAL COMPETENCE: EFFECT OF CULTURAL AND GEOGRAPHICAL CONTEXT

After we expanded the use of the DISCOVER assessment to other cultures in the United States and other countries, we compared the performance of students in each activity with the Diné students we knew so well. Specifically, we analyzed the results of the DISCOVER assessment for 941 students from grades K to 5 from six ethnic groups (Sarouphim & Maker, 2008): white Americans (14.7 percent), African Americans (13.9 percent), Hispanics (9.9 percent), Native Americans (12.9 percent), South Pacific/Pacific Islanders (12.8 percent), and Arabs from Lebanon and Bahrain (35.9 percent). Using a 5 × 6 MANOVA (activity × ethnicity), we found a significant interaction effect for ethnicity by activity ($F[5,793]$, $= 6.98$, $p = .03$), with a moderate effect size of 0.24. The result particularly relevant to this chapter is that plots of the interaction revealed that Native Americans scored significantly higher than the other groups on the spatial artistic activity. No main effect for activity ($F[5,793] = 1.21$, $p = .215$) or ethnicity ($F[25,3965] = 4.98$, $p = .03$) was found.

How is this finding connected to the cultural and geographical context? Many who are familiar with American Indian groups in general will recognize the high value placed on artistic expression in most of these cultures. Rug weaving, jewelry making, basket weaving, and other crafts have long been a source of income and artistic expression in American Indian cultures. Perhaps less known is the use of symbolic sand painting in Diné healing and blessing ceremonies. In connection with these paintings, the spiritual leader weaves a complex ceremony connecting songs, prayers, and herbs with sounds, scents, and images from the natural world to produce a "protective, peaceful, and optimistic state of mind" through which the individual and her or his family can "overcome physical, emotional, and psychological ill health" (Begay & Maker, 2007, p. 143). This constant focus on wholeness and connection, we believe, is the essence of spatial intelligence—the ability to see or create a connected picture or symbols in which relationships are shown among seemingly disparate elements.

In addition to the cultural context, another factor to consider is how the environment influences the development of intelligences. In this vast geographical area with very few paved roads, finding a name or number on any road except main highways is impossible. For individuals growing up in the city, where everyone finds their way around by reading street signs, this environment can be confusing indeed. But for those growing up here, reliance on images and a deep knowledge of the cardinal directions makes the task simple. We became accustomed to being told to go to the rock that looks like a hand and turn north, or go up two hills and at the bottom of the second hill turn south. A memorable experience for my graduate assistants was when they were lost and asked an old gentleman for help. He volunteered to draw them a map. On the map, he drew the bumps in the road, the holes to avoid, and the main rock formations they would encounter as they followed his directions. They found their way and in the process, learned an important lesson about differences in cultures and environments.

The geographical context also influences the development of intelligences in Diné children. Recall that in the spatial artistic portion of the DISCOVER assessment, the tasks range from structured to open-ended. During the more structured part of the activity, we showed pictures and asked students to use brightly colored cardboard pieces to make what was in the pictures. For the open-ended activity, students could "make anything they wanted to make." The Diné children never said, "I don't know what to make." We found that most were reluctant to stop creating and go on to another activity. However, in other ethnic groups we observed, some children either made the same things they had made in the structured activities or simply did not make anything.

One of June's most memorable experiences was watching a tenth-grade girl work the tangram puzzles during the spatial analytical assessment. First, she placed all the large pieces where they would fit on the puzzles and then she placed all the parallelograms. After the parallelograms, she used the squares, then the medium triangles, and finally the small triangles. While working on the entire six pages of puzzles, she never removed a piece or rearranged a puzzle. All were placed correctly on her first attempt, and she worked the puzzles more quickly than anyone else in her group. After the activity was over, June asked her to reflect on how she completed the puzzles. This was the basic strategy she used: find places for the most difficult pieces first and leave the most versatile pieces to finish the puzzles. Instead of working each puzzle separately, this girl worked all of the puzzles on each page at the same time.

This tendency to work holistically also influences the Diné children's performance in activities to assess other intelligences. One example can be seen from the results of the DISCOVER linguistic assessment. In the oral part of the assessment, each child is given a bag with different kinds of toys from the same categories (people, animals, vehicles, objects). Children are asked to tell a story about the toys in the bag. In the written linguistic assessment, children are asked to write about anything they want to write about and in any form they wish. Both are holistic assessments rather than batteries of questions about isolated vocabulary words.

Many Diné children who performed poorly on reading and language arts portions of achievement tests received high ratings on the DISCOVER linguistic assessments. One dramatic example comes from a third-grade girl, Melissa. Her verbal score on the Developing Cognitive Abilities Test was the ninth percentile and her scores on the Iowa Test of Basic Skills were eleventh percentile in vocabulary and first percentile in language. When told she could write any-thing she wanted to write in the DISCOVER assessment process, she wrote the following poem:

My autumn eyes behold
Spooky costumes skipping in Halloween night
White ghost dancing by my house
Orange pumpkin nestled on my window
Black witches gliding across the full moon
Red golden leaves falling softly from the tree.

Clearly culture and environment have pervasive effects on the develop-ment and expression of intelligences. The DISCOVER assessment tapped these varied intellectual expressions through observing children engaging in problem-solving tasks. Identification of culturally sensitive intellectual strengths and capabilities helps to pave the way for more culturally responsive education.

CONCLUSION

A central theme in this chapter is observation. Two kinds of observations are reviewed: children observe to learn and adults observe to learn. One of the reasons Diné children and children from many other indigenous cultures are overlooked in classrooms is that in their culture, they are taught from an early age to learn by observing. They are taught to watch closely and not to interrupt with questions. This kind of behavior is not understood or valued in mainstream society in which gifted children are described as verbally preco-cious: they answer questions quickly, elaborate on ideas with richness and detail, and, most important, they ask a lot of questions. Native children and children from other cultures with a high degree of spatial intelligence are keen observers, and much of their learning comes through this intelligence. Their abilities and preferences must be respected more in our verbally ori-ented academic programs.

Parallel to the need for better understanding of Diné children's use of observation in learning is the need to increase our own awareness of the importance of observation and hone our ability to observe. For educators and psychologists, quietly watching the children in a classroom instead of con-stantly organizing and orchestrating their activities can help us see the pat-tern of children's behavior. Watching a couple interact can give us valuable clues about how to help these children build social skills. Reading a child's story, without a red pen in hand and a critical eye for mistakes, can lead to important insights and interesting surprises. The essence of an assessment is observation—observation with respect, openness, and a desire to learn.

References

Amabile, T. M. (1996). *Creativity in context: Update to the social psychology of creativity.* Boulder, CO: Westview Press.

Begay, H., & Maker, C. J. (2007). When geniuses fail . . . Na-Dené (Navajo) conception of giftedness in the eyes of the holy deities. In S. N. Phillipson & M. McCann (Eds.), *Conceptions of giftedness: Socio-cultural perspectives* (pp. 127–168). Mahwah, NJ: Erlbaum.

Charles, R. E., & Runco, M. A. (2000). Developmental trends in the evaluative and divergent thinking of children. *Creativity Research Journal, 13,* 417–437.

Gardner, H. (1983). *Frames of mind: The theory of multiple intelligences.* New York: Basic Books.

Gardner, H. (1992). Assessment in context: The alternative to standardized testing. In B. Gifford & M. O'Connor (Eds.), *Changing assessments: Alternative views of aptitude, achievement, and instruction* (pp. 77–120). Norwell, MA: KluWer.

Getzels, J., & Csikszentmihalyi, M. (1967). Scientific creativity. *Science Journal, 3*(9), 80–84.

Getzels, J., & Csikszentmihalyi, M. (1976). *The creative vision: A longitudinal study of problem finding in art.* Hoboken, NJ: Wiley.

Maker, C. J. (1993). Creativity, intelligence, and problem-solving: A definition and design for cross-cultural research and measurement related to giftedness. *Gifted Education International, 9,* 68–77.

Maker, C. J. (1994). Authentic assessment of problem solving and giftedness in secondary school students. *Journal of Secondary Gifted Education, 6*(1), 19–26.

Maker, C. J. (1996). Identification of gifted minority students: A national problem, needed changes and a promising solution. *Gifted Child Quarterly, 40*(1), 41–50.

Maker, C. J. (2005). *The DISCOVER Project: Improving assessment and curriculum for diverse gifted learners.* Storrs, CT: National Research Center on the Gifted and Talented.

Maker, C. J., & Schiever, S. W. (2005). *Teaching models in education of the gifted* (3rd ed.). Austin, TX: Pro-Ed.

Renzulli, J. S. (1978). What makes giftedness? Re-examining a definition. *Phi Delta Kappan, 60,* 180–184, 261.

Rogers, J. A. (1998). Refocusing the lens: Using observation to assess and identify gifted learners. *Gifted Education International, 12*(3), 129–144.

Sarouphim, K. M. (2000). Internal structure of DISCOVER: A performance-based assessment. *Journal for the Education of the Gifted, 3,* 314–327.

Sarouphim, K. M. (2001). DISCOVER: Concurrent validity, gender differences, and identification of minority students. *Gifted Child Quarterly, 45,* 130–138.

Sarouphim, K. M. (2002). DISCOVER in high school: Identifying gifted Hispanic and Native American students. *Journal of Secondary Gifted Education, 14,* 30–38.

Sarouphim, K. M. (2004). DISCOVER in middle school: Identifying gifted minority students. *Journal of Secondary Gifted Education*, *10*, 61–69.

Sarouphim, K. M., & Maker, C. J. (2008). *Ethnic and Gender Differences in the Use of DISCOVER.* Manuscript in preparation.

Simonton, D. K. (2000). Creativity: Cognitive, personal, developmental and social aspects. *American Psychologist*, *55*(1), 151–158.

Torrance, E. P. (1972). Predictive validity of the Torrance Tests of Creative Thinking. *Journal of Creative Behavior*, *6*(4), 236–252, 272.

Torrance, E. P. (1981). Empirical validation of criterion-referenced indicators of creative ability through a longitudinal study. *Creative Child and Adult Quarterly*, *6*, 136–140.

Weisberg, R. W. (2006). *Creativity: Understanding innovation in problem solving, science, invention and the arts.* Hoboken, NJ: Wiley.

Zuckerman, H. (1977). *Scientific elite: Noble laureates in the United States.* New York: Free Press.

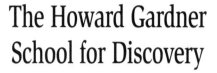

CHAPTER 28

The Howard Gardner
School for Discovery

Vincent Rizzo

The Howard Gardner School for Discovery (HGSD) has adopted multiple intelligence theory as a founding principle. As a laboratory school, HGSD chooses to focus on practice. MI's impact on how and what we teach is integral to our program. In this chapter, I explain what the theory looks like in practice and how students in a school are advantaged by its use. Specifically, I address our attempt to incorporate MI seamlessly into our work. The school's staff adopted an apprenticeship model that helps us clarify our own theoretical bases for curriculum writing, project-based learning, authentic assessment, and use of more traditional measurements of student achievement. Finally, I demonstrate the practicality of MI-inspired practice for all schools, as well as its potential for whole school reform.

The Howard Gardner School for Discovery was founded in 2005, converting from a former laboratory school for the University of Scranton's education department into the only independent, nonsectarian, private school in Scranton, Pennsylvania. The Gardner School is one of only two laboratory schools on the International Association of Laboratory and University Affiliated Schools roster that is not university affiliated. Laboratory schools are training schools for new teachers. What makes the school stand out even more as a laboratory school is our organization around multiple intelligences (MI) theory. MI's influence is more systemic than obvious. There are few overt signs of MI in the school's common areas. Only a small book shelf in the hall outside the director's office has a compilation of MI texts and other Gardner titles.

We have chosen MI for two reasons. First, it affirms what educators observe and believe about children: all children can and do learn. Gardner (1991) alludes to how even very young children can grasp complex phenomena when it is presented in an accessible way: "Within the cognitive realm there are forms of understanding that have a distinctly abstract flavor and that the child seems pretuned to appreciate. Understandings of causal relations, of the nature and constituents of objects, and of the world of numbers can all be elicited in the first years of life" (p. 52). MI affects not just what we do and how we do things, but makes us ask why and whether those practices are in the best interests of students.

Second, organizing classroom practice around MI theory offers a much more hopeful view of students' abilities to demonstrate their mastery of subject matter. Gardner (1991) posed a challenge: "Much of what we have discovered about the principles of human learning and development conflicts sharply with the customary practices of schools" (p. 143). Schools tend to provide unchallenging materials and ineffective tests to gauge understanding. By identifying discrete intelligences children possess, MI assessment extends beyond what or how much is learned to include the myriad ways children can demonstrate their understandings according to their individual intelligence profiles.

At the Gardner School, we base our educational decisions on the concepts of authenticity and relevance. Authenticity addresses how each child is an individual with a particular profile of intelligences and interests. To be authentic, assessments should tap into the actual intelligence without being channeled through other capabilities. That is, a bodily-kinesthetic intelligence assessment is less authentic if done through a linguistic paper-and-pencil test. Children should be allowed to demonstrate their understanding of material in a way that fits with their profiles.

Relevance addresses how each child resonates with different opportunities in his or her environment. Some contextual elements are perceived as more important than others. It speaks to a child's questioning why the lesson or subject matters to them. If we cannot satisfactorily answer this question, the effort may be lost. In *A Different Kind of Classroom: Teaching with Dimensions of Learning* (1992), Robert Marzano notes that a key characteristic to making schoolwork meaningful to students is the extent to which students are able to direct and construct the tasks at hand. The application of skill or knowledge addresses this concern: subject matter is relevant to the extent that a child senses he or she can use it.

The more authentically schools can tap into students' individuality and can reproduce the type of relevant product or problem solving required in a real-world application, the better prepared the student will be when he or she is asked to respond within his or her chosen vocational or life field. Marzano (1992) makes a similar claim: "These tasks require students to use their knowledge to accomplish specific goals or to apply their knowledge when answering specific questions. Their emphasis is not learning for learning's sake, but learning as a by-product of trying to accomplish something, of trying to answer questions that are common human concerns. This is always the most powerful kind of learning" (p. 124).

Schools are not isolated, but rather are part of larger communities and societies (Gardner, 1991). Schools are a microcosm of their society in how they assess schoolwork. In schools, teachers and parents assign value to a student's work. These assessments are a precursor to the professional, vocational, and other fields that exist in society. After students graduate, and thereby become practitioners, their work will be judged by experts and other practitioners in their chosen field. Authenticity and relevance in school breed a confidence in learners that their solutions can be trusted to work in real world applications.

In this chapter, I describe how the Gardner School realizes these notions of authenticity and relevance through individuality, apprenticeships, projects, and assessments that trust the learners to engage with their world in meaningful, productive ways.

INDIVIDUALITY

Molly Perry, an eighth grader at the Gardner School, writes: "The single biggest difference between The Gardner School and other schools I attended is the movement. There is constant change. . . . When you finish your work, there is always something else to do. Communication is important as well. Teachers know your strengths and weaknesses, likes and dislikes. They know you. In moving to the Gardner School from my other school, it was like the sensation of getting out of a pool. At first, it is shocking, because of the change in temperature. Then, when you get used to it, you remember how easy it is to walk and breathe.

While many private schools have an elite or upper-middle-class population, the Gardner School is decidedly middle class. In this way, the school is much nearer in demographic makeup to public schools, such as the Key Learning Community in Indianapolis, than most private independent schools. As a teacher-training laboratory school, it is important that our student demographic closely mirror the community we serve. Scranton was settled by immigrants from eastern and southern Europe, and later by families of Hispanic or Latino/a origin. Schools historically were important for immigrant children to prosper socially and professionally in the future, and they continue to be an important community resource for attracting new families and businesses.

The Gardner School is more diverse than most other schools in our area, with approximately 15 percent minority and foreign-born students. The school provides tuition assistance to approximately one-third of our students. But the Gardner School goes further than class and ethnic diversity. We also embrace a diversity of abilities. The school admits students with autism, attention defi-cit hyperactivity disorder, and limited English language proficiency. We find that our MI-inspired classrooms, along with small class size and adult aides, work well for all students.

Many schools identify themselves as "child centered" and extol the virtues of working with children as individuals and developing unique skills they may possess. Yet few adapt their curriculum and assessment model to reflect each child's uniqueness and perspective of the world. Instead, children are given a general curriculum to follow and must adapt their skills accordingly. Assessment is often a default to logical-mathematical and linguistic intelli-gences when schools generalize about "intelligence." In contrast, the Gardner School takes individuality to heart.

Molly's statement at the start of this section suggests that students mov-ing into an MI environment are in for a pleasant surprise. Our classrooms at first glance appear very different from traditional classrooms. The individual contributions of students are visible everywhere. Projects line the halls and walls. There are soaring roller-coasters made of K'nex Building Kits blocks (see http://www.knex.com/Thrill_Rides, http://www.knex.com/Thrill_Rides/) sitting beside geometric shapes held together by hardened marshmallows. On the walls hang paintings and clothing designs by third and fourth graders to sell in a Walmart-like school mall. Visitors do not find a room dominated by desks until they reach the senior room, for grades 7 and 8, in the basement. Chairs, tables, and wide expanses of floor make up most classroom teaching areas. Rugs are spattered with the paints and other learning media children use to build, draw, and assemble their demonstrations of what they learned that day.

In the Gardner School, students realize that their role is quite different than it is in other schools. Children are arranged in a multiage setting starting with preschool and kindergarten. There is considerable movement and conversa-tion throughout the day. Some children study in small groups, while others may be working alone or listening to their teacher discussing the day's lesson. Children freely walk the halls and converse as they complete a day's work in the school. The exchanges between children and adults sound more conver-sational than didactic, and sometimes they show how children and adults are learning. An observer might conclude that students seem quite involved in their education—and that is our goal.

APPRENTICESHIPS

Every Tuesday, Harold walks into the school carrying an old, beaten carry-on bag. Nearing his ninety-first birthday, he is an expert in economics, and he trades daily in the stock market. Today he will be teaching third and fourth grade students about the volatility of the stock market. Harold serves as a "master," and students have been apprenticed to him and other volunteers since the Gardner School opened.

The school has adopted apprenticeships, based on Gardner's description in *The Unschooled Mind* (1991), as a framework for the learning process. Apprenticeships make the interpersonal and intrapersonal intelligences central by emphasizing how we learn from each other. Gardner (1983) stipulates the importance of apprenticeships because they bring novices together with experienced practitioners. The novices not only receive didactic information but can watch practitioners in action, test their own growing skills scaffolded by the practitioner, and gain a sense for authentic and relevant real-life work situations. Children apprentice to "masters" from the community. Teachers, parents, university students, coaches and moderators, college students, and experts from Scranton come to the school to guide children.

Harold, featured in this section's opening vignette, mentors third and fourth graders who run a student store. Students have the responsibility for purchasing, designing, pricing, and marketing pencils, pens, and small toys to our school community. Other students manage a birthday party business aimed at doting parents who bring snacks and treats on birthdays. The six-person "Birthday Blast" Company surprises birthday boys and girls with these snacks, songs, and confetti within a three-minute period. After cleaning up the confetti, the revelers return to class.

A newer endeavor is our Upper Class framing and art display company. Students from all grades submit items from their portfolios that they feel merit display in our school halls and offices. Under the tutelage of a local framing shop owner, fifth and sixth graders critique the works submitted, select a display format, then matte, frame, and hang each selected work. All works hang for at least a month. Parents are invited to view our gallery on specific evenings throughout the year.

Although no longer associated with a university, the Gardner School still serves as a training ground for teachers from three local colleges. This situation offers an even more pointed example of apprenticeships in learning. Preservice teachers are both apprenticed in their field experience studies and at times serve as teacher assistants and mentors to the children in the class. Furthermore, the children can function as both novice and master, mentoring one another based on their individual profiles of skills and abilities. For both students and preservice teachers, we maintain a common rubric, which evaluates novice through master performances as material is mastered and demonstrated to others in the school. Although grading is still done in most classes, its focus is more as formative assessment. It is important to us that these status indicators are descriptive in the format of a rubric and not ordered in the format of grades.

PROJECTS

The HGS Insider *staff works feverishly to meet their publishing deadline. In the center of the classroom, editors are busily reviewing their beat writers' story submissions. Huddled around a computer, the layout staff and advertising group discuss space configurations for ad placements procured by salespersons. Writers are busily writing and researching as they review their editors' notes. In the midst of this activity, teachers walk from group to group encouraging students and helping with questions about formatting, timeliness of the topic, or a Web citation.*

Projects provide vehicles for several intelligences to develop concurrently. For example, although language arts obviously draw heavily on linguistic intelligence, they also can nurture intrapersonal, interpersonal, and other intelligences when placed within a project. We aim to make the writing experience as authentic and relevant as possible. A class writing project anchors the curriculum at each level. Writing is organized around the concept of audience, and students focus on the particular audience assigned to their class. Students consider themselves storytellers and authors.

In the early childhood and primary years, audience is defined as parents, teachers, and community mentors. Preschoolers through second graders prepare and share stories about themselves through pictures, written words, and verbal storytelling. Such stories can help build self-awareness. Teachers gather these stories into little books. Students who are not yet ready to compose a story are assigned a mentor: a community volunteer, parent, or older student who assists them in putting their thoughts into written words. Some students draw illustrations for their mentors and then have mentors record their stories in print.

Students read their stories to the audience. Usually they also read them to a very interested principal. I recall Rachel and Mara walking into my office. Both are preschool/kindergarten students. "Can we come in and read our books?" Rachel asks. I invite them in, and they hoist themselves onto the oversized chairs that are meant for adults. Both five year olds look proud, if a bit nervous. Each reads her story, which is bound by staples and amply illustrated in crayon drawings. Rachel wrote about a butterfly—probably a topic in science class that week. Mara told a story about a princess and a castle. As they left, they assured me they would be back as soon as they finished another "book."

In association with the student store apprenticeship, the third and fourth graders' audience is consumers. Students prepare advertisements and write descriptive copy for online catalogues and design brochures for the student store. Such writing requires taking the prospective customers' perspective into consideration, which can build interpersonal intelligence. It also advances logical thinking by presenting information in an organized, persuasive manner.

Our senior class produces a quarterly newspaper for an adult audience. Students apply for positions using résumés based on their work. Student editors and teachers hold interviews before selecting applicants for open positions. Local newspaper and photojournalist professionals mentor these seventh- and eighth-grade students. During their two project periods each week, the newspaper staffers conceive, write, lay out, and publish each online edition for other students, parents, and interested community members to read. Creating a newspaper calls on not only linguistic intelligence but spatial and interpersonal intelligences as well.

ASSESSMENT

As faculty gather before the opening of a new school year, we find ourselves on our own learning curve as teachers. We thought we knew about portfolio assessment. Warned by our mentor, Carol, to avoid the tendency of thinking "I do that (already)," we begin. We will be using a process portfolio in classes this year, and we will be expected to maintain our own portfolio along with the children. We look at one another and smile, considering Michelangelo's observation, "I am still learning."

Gardner (1983) criticizes psychometric tests' limited usefulness for evaluating the many ways a student could demonstrate understanding and mastery. Harvard Project Zero's Project Spectrum created evaluative tools for measuring the intellectual profiles of young children—a task Gardner deemed worthwhile but nevertheless arduous and time-consuming. Our own interpretation of MI theory suggests that MI legitimizes certain assessment methods such as projects, portfolio, and integration because they allow a more balanced, more accurate picture of what a child knows and has learned through understanding performances. The practical aspect of doing bridges knowledge and application. A school curriculum's usefulness is that it be used for some purpose.

The authenticity of an apprenticeship model and collaboration among students in real-world projects supports an MI vision of assessment. As Gardner (1999) acknowledges in *Intelligence Reframed* "What matters is the use of intelligences, individually and in concert, to carry out tasks valued by a society. Accordingly, we should be assessing people's success in carrying out valued tasks that presumably involve certain intelligences. . . . We should observe people in real life situations where they have to be sensitive to the aspirations and motives of others" (p. 208).

An MI approach provides experiences, such as running a store, newsroom, or business, that not only provide engaging hands-on learning but also determine understanding of algebra, science, or language arts. These experiences allow students and their teachers an opportunity to determine aptitude for carrying out tasks that have value in the real world. How well students write for a teacher is not as powerful an indicator of success as whether the writing sample is clearly conveyed to an appropriate audience.

Student understanding is gauged in as many formats as possible. We use a range of evaluation tools: state and nationally standardized tests, teacher-created and -graded tests and projects, and process portfolios. A process portfolio is a collection of drafts that show works in progress. We maintain longitudinal data on our test results from both Terra Nova tests and Pennsylvania's state assessments. Our students generally exceed the grade-level norms and show steady growth as they proceed from grade to grade in each of the core areas of the curriculum. Unlike schools that feel challenged by state tests and comparative annual yearly progress statistics, the Gardner School uses the information to improve practice and learning. Assessments are treated as opportunities for building strengths, improving curriculum, identifying deficits, and planning.

In addition to observable data from apprenticeships and projects as well as test scores, we assess our students' success through their experience as they make the transition to other schools following graduation. Each of the past two years, our graduates have been contacted and asked to report on their high school experience. Of the twenty graduates, more than half of them attend private schools that require rigorous entrance examinations. Except for one student, all have been accepted and continue to progress normally in their new schools, which tend to have more structured surroundings than the Gardner School. Reports from graduates who chose to attend public school are similarly positive. In two incidences, students who attended the Gardner School and were classified as having educational disabilities (dyslexia and behavioral disabilities) have excelled and attained honor role status at their new schools.

TRUST THE LEARNER

I once attended a week-long summer training program that focused on service-learning. The training's reflection model included a midweek Q&A through which attendees questioned what planners had considered basic and obvious points in the program. As the session drew to a close, one of the planners seemed despondent and wondered if the daily sessions were being appreciated and understood. Another member of the planning team counseled, "Trust the learner."

⌒

At times, my experience in education suggests that educators have lost confidence in our young charges to learn what is being taught. Especially in a high-stakes testing environment, doubting our students' abilities calls into question our own proficiencies as teachers. What doubters seem to be saying, in effect, is, *How can one prove that MI-inspired schools work?*

A critical consideration in our methodology is our commitment to patience. MI argues for a more open perspective on learning and time. I am reminded of William, a fourth-grade student who came to us as a student with severe learning and behavioral disabilities. His performance on standardized tests suggested that he was more than two years behind his peers in the critical subject areas of math and reading. William spent four years in our program. Each year his knowledge base and performance on varied assessments improved to the point that at graduation, he was on par with his classmates and showed little signs of his previous "disabilities."

Now in high school, William is a solid student who has achieved honor roll status several times. It may be easy to suggest that the most important factor in his development as a student is related to our school and its program. But a more honest perspective, and one just as complimentary of the school, is that William needed more time to demonstrate his knowledge and abilities. Time is something young students surely have in abundance, but it is something rarely afforded them in schools.

At the Gardner School, we are affirmed that our practice is successful not because we are adept at teaching more or that our students are naturally brighter, but because we offer students more options for understanding and more opportunities to assess their learning. Our understanding of an MI approach implies that real understanding of a concept occurs over time. It involves an initial engagement, a period of trial and error during which the concept is viewed from multiple perspectives, and a period for reflection. For all children, especially those like William, those times are approximate and uncompromising. MI gives us reason beyond intuition or our own self-doubt to be patient with our learners. By recognizing the diversity of intelligences that are available for students to tap into their understanding of the world, and by creating an environment that encourages students to develop and express those intelligences, we can be more confident and hopeful of our own work.

References

Gardner, H. (1983). *Frames of mind: The theory of multiple intelligences.* New York: Basic Books.

Gardner, H. (1991). *The unschooled mind.* New York: Basic Books.

Gardner, H. (1999). *Intelligence reframed.* New York: Basic Books.

Marzano, R. J. (1992). *A different kind of classroom: Teaching with dimensions of learning.* Alexandria, VA: ASCD.

CHAPTER 29

The Challenges of Assessing the Multiple Intelligences Around the World

C. Branton Shearer

Since MI theory was introduced, educators around the world have desired an assessment that they could use to better understand students' MI profiles and inform classroom instruction. The complex nature of each intelligence makes the creation of a valid, reliable, and practical assessment a great challenge. This chapter describes the various ways that people have approached this task and the barriers that differing cultural contexts have presented along the way.

To better understand the difficulties of MI assessment in various cultures, surveys were e-mailed to educators and researchers in twenty-two countries. Three general types of barriers were identified: cultural bias against some of the intelligences, philosophical views of education that may be less congruent with MI, and cultural variation with regard to focusing on individuals' strengths. Despite such challenges, MI assessment can be a useful tool for understanding students' strengths and validating the theory itself.

A discussion of the challenges inherent in assessing multiple intelligences must first address the question, "Why assess MI at all?" Since that theory has always operated on the margins of education, revered by a few, disregarded by the majority, what purpose is served by assessing MI in the way that general intelligence is traditionally assessed?

In brief, MI assessment can serve three useful functions: it can provide ammunition for educators who are trying to validate and promote the theory. It can help teachers understand students' strengths and needs and thus support instruction. Finally, it can enhance each student's self-understanding and educational planning.

THE CHALLENGES

Acceptance and implementation of multiple intelligences have been impeded in part by the dominance of psychometric traditions in intelligence research. For over a hundred years, Western science has conceptualized intelligence as little more than logical and verbal thinking that could be conveniently captured by an IQ test score. The moderate correlations among IQ, academic grades, and occupational status (Block & Dworkin, 1976; Herrnstein & Murray, 1994; Sternberg, 1985[1]) were deemed sufficient to validate IQ and assign an individual's intellectual and economic potential.

In contrast, the validity of multiple intelligences theory rests not on statistics, but instead on a qualitative review of many, very diverse sources of data (neurological, anthropological, psychometric, developmental psychology, and others). As a result, many cognitive scientists view MI as less than scientific. Given such marginalization in the scientific literature, policymakers and administrators can dismiss MI as unproven and exclude it from educational practice.

A related obstacle to MI's acceptance is that there is no practical MI test that teachers can use to understand each student's unique MI strengths and limitations. Teachers who embrace the idea of multiple intelligences typically rely on their intuition, informal observations, and unvalidated instruments. This leaves them vulnerable when it comes time to defend their use of MI to parents and administrators. In turn, this limits the growth of MI practices.

ASSESSMENT DRIVES IMPLEMENTATION

Assessments bring the power of an idea directly into organizational decision making, structures, and functions. For example, scores on IQ-type tests influence how intellectual potential is defined, and thus they influence curriculum placements, achievement, and career paths. Throughout most of the twentieth century, a huge industrial-scholarly complex supported the development of IQ testing and its implementation, which typically followed top-down mandates by government officials and school administrators.

In contrast, since its introduction in 1983, MI has been largely a grassroots movement that individual teachers and small-scale, alternative MI schools have struggled to grow. Educators find MI reverberates with their classroom experiences: children display a multitude of skills, abilities, and intellectual styles that an IQ score cannot fully explain.

For more than twenty years, my work has focused on the creation of valid and practical MI assessments that could enable educators to move MI into practice for the benefit of students.

I have been privileged to travel throughout the United States and across many other countries, sharing educators' delight and pain as they struggled to realize the power of MI in the midst of cultures, traditions, and testing regimes that discourage its growth. I have seen MI bloom at the margins of the educational establishment, thus enabling the design of more effective schools and benefiting small numbers of fortunate students. I have been impressed with these inspired initiatives, but I have been frustrated by the difficulty of transferring these efforts into the larger world of underfunded mass public education.

MI's marginalization is partially a result of the assessment tools that have accompanied it. Most MI assessments are nonstandardized, performance based, and individually administered. They focus on describing the quality of a student's classroom work or a student's MI profile, or sometimes both. This potentially useful information stands in stark contrast to the mandate for more high-stakes, quantitative, standardized tests (as with the American No Child Left Behind legislation). The tension between these two positions leads to an unfortunate misunderstanding of MI as a revolutionary approach that is incompatible with the development of academic skills.

VARIETIES OF MI ASSESSMENTS

Since MI was introduced, a number of assessments that are compatible with its emphasis on real-world ecological validity have been developed. These include performance tasks (Chen, Krechevsky, & Viens, 1998); portfolios (Meisels, 1993; Stefanakis, 2002); presentations, exhibits, and projects (Díaz-Lefebvre, 1999; Hoerr, 2000); observation scales (Bolaños, 1996); checklists (Armstrong, 1994; Kagan & Kagan, 1998; Silver, Strong, & Perini, 2000), and surveys and interviews (Montgomery County Public Schools, 1990; Shearer, 2007).

Portfolios and Performance-Based Assessments

Portfolios are widely used in MI schools because they provide a rich source of information about students' skills and learning. A portfolio is a collection of performance samples gathered together for evaluation by an outside "expert." Because they are time-consuming and labor intensive, they are often used more as final exhibitions rather than formative assessments. Rating scales or rubrics are often used by a trained person, such as a teacher, coach, or supervisor, to describe or measure performance within a specific context (for example, during a sporting event, on the job, during a dance performance or debate, or to evaluate creative writing). The development and use of rubrics to measure performance, projects, and portfolios require significant expertise, time, and energy.

A good example of a performance appraisal system was developed over a period of several years by the faculty of the Key Learning Community (http://www.616.ips.k12.in.us/). This system provides a detailed set of developmental performance descriptors to evaluate the progress of primary age students in each of the eight intelligences. This framework provides teachers with a common set of variables to describe a child's ability level as evidenced by his or her performance on typical classroom tasks. The Key Learning Community also employs extensive videotaping of student presentations and performances that serve as a cumulative video portfolio.

The Project Spectrum assessment was first described by Gardner (1993) and later extended by Chen et al. (1998) as a means to "measure the profile of intelligences and working styles of young children." Young children are observed over a period of time interacting with a carefully designed set of problem-solving materials that embody each of the multiple intelligences. A trained evaluator completes a set of rating scales describing various aspects of the quality of the child's performance (interest, skill, outcome, and so forth). A composite report is produced at the end of a long period of time that varies according the classroom situation. Some of the fifteen to twenty activities can be integrated into the standard curriculum but others are unique to Spectrum.

Another well-known performance assessment for the identification of gifted and talented children is DISCOVER (Maker, 1992). This package of materials and activities requires that an assessment team visit the school to observe students performing many different activities. It takes between eight and nine hours to complete for each child and results in an in-depth evaluation of the student's abilities.

The MI portfolio approach described by Stefanakis (2002) provides a structure for collecting a child's work efforts in a systematic way. Using a "process-folio," the teacher can provide feedback at each step of the way, and the child reflects on each piece in the collection. In this way, the portfolio can be more of a formative assessment rather than merely evaluative. Products in the portfolio may be assessed against an external standard (say, the math skill expected of third graders) or compared to the child's own previous performance.

Observation Checklists

MI checklists are provided in many books and are freely available on numerous Web sites. Gardner (1993, 1995) has argued against the use of these checklists, however. They serve to promote a superficial and distorted understanding of MI and to foster a quick-fix approach to instruction, curriculum, assessment, and school renewal. They also tend to conflate MI with a range of learning styles and personality constructs. Despite such problems, MI checklists have been fairly widely used because they are cheap, easy to use, and quick.

Structured Interviews, Questionnaires, and Self-Reports

Structured interviews, questionnaires, and self-reports have a long history in personnel selection and clinical assessment (Anastasi, 1979; Owens, 1976). They rely on a respondent's perceptions and memory and thus are not always reliable. To ensure a valid assessment, they need to be used in conjunction with other sources of information, such as test results and school history. An advantage is that they are relatively easy to conduct and time efficient. A lot of information can be gathered in single interview or by way of a questionnaire.

In 1987, I began conducting clinical interviews with relatives of traumatic brain injury survivors who were undergoing cognitive rehabilitation. As a counselor, I needed to understand the survivor's MI strengths and limitations prior to injury so that strengths-based cognitive remediation strategies could be employed. This MI structured interview evolved into a self- (or parent-) report questionnaire, the Multiple Intelligences Developmental Assessment Scales (MIDAS; Shearer, 2007), that produces a qualitative and quantitative profile of the person's "intellectual disposition."

Teachers have used the MIDAS to better understand their students' intellectual strengths (and weaknesses) and thereby guide students to use their strengths to promote learning. Counselors use the MIDAS Profile to help students enhance their self-understanding, self-esteem, and career planning. Educational researchers in numerous countries have validated cultural adaptations and translations of the questionnaire for use in their primary and secondary schools, as well as in higher education.

An advantage of the MIDAS is that a lot of MI-related information can be gathered in a short time and applied to educational issues. Yet several cautions must be exercised in conjunction with the MIDAS. As a self-, or parent, report, the information it yields must undergo a verification process. In addition, the profile can be misinterpreted as being equivalent to standardized test scores rather than as qualitative information. The MIDAS, like all other MI assessments, might be misused simplistically to label students or might be incorrectly viewed as a substitute for the sustained attention needed to integrate the assessment information into classroom teaching and guidance.

CHALLENGES TO ACCEPTANCE AND IMPLEMENTATION OF MI ASSESSMENTS

Alongside the dominance of IQ, high-quality MI assessment is challenged by the need to consider varied cultural contexts and differences in educational traditions. I have learned of these interrelated variables through direct personal experience, by reading reports from many countries, and through data I collected in a survey e-mailed to seventy-five educators and researchers in twenty-two countries. Fifty responses were received. Half of these were from educator-researchers who used an MI assessment as part of their master's thesis or doctoral dissertation. The other respondents were educators, psychologists, or counselors who have used an MI assessment for many years. Some respondents have worked with an assessment for adults and teenagers, while others worked with children. Because the sample was not random, the results are not generalizable. Nevertheless, they give some insights into barriers, as well as affordances, to the use of MI assessments in different cultures. I integrate excerpts from survey responses to capture diverse viewpoints.

Cultural Bias Against Several of the Intelligences

In a number of countries, there has been a marked bias against several of the multiple intelligences. For example, working with one's hands has been equated with manual labor rather than intelligent, bodily-kinesthetic endeavor. Artistic pursuits associated with the spatial and musical intelligences are labeled "mere aptitudes." If a culture has little association with animals, then the assessment of an individual's naturalist abilities will be quite difficult. Winnie Pong of the Nice Studio in Hong Kong described the latter problem: "According to the living environment in Hong Kong, the residents in most estates are prohibited from having pets; therefore, the naturalist intelligence will easily be underestimated."

The naturalist and kinesthetic intelligences were deemed problematic in Iran and Arabic countries, where individuals (especially women) are discouraged from engaging in activities that depend on these strengths. Alireza Manzour of Azad University in Iran also noted, "[Assessment] questions regarding musical intelligence are a problem for Middle Eastern countries where music is not only omitted from the National Curriculum, but in some societies discarded as an educational medium." Implementing and identifying multiple intelligences thus depends on a culture's appreciation for varied activities that are likely to engage those intelligences.

Intra- and interpersonal skills are sometimes considered "personality characteristics" and not on par with "higher cognitive functions." C. C. Wan of the Asian Association for Lifelong Learning reports that academic test scores in Hong Kong are of paramount importance. Thus, parents may undervalue the interpersonal and intrapersonal intelligences of their children because of their high expectations for academic accomplishment

Philosophical Views of Education Incongruent with MI

Acceptance of MI is often a problem in countries where the entire education system follows a tradition of standardized paper-and-pencil skills tests. Such systems by design allow little room for performance-based assessments. It is a common refrain that conducting MI assessments is a distraction from the more important business of intensively preparing students to attain high scores on college and university entrance examinations. This issue was described by Mania Ziridis: "MI theory is perceived by some people as being too innovative, especially when considering the Greek educational system that focuses a lot on mathematics and Greek language; there is a very tight curriculum that must be followed. Exams to enter a Greek university are based on pure memorization of facts."

A related problem is cited by Joseph Tan of Hwa Chong Institution in Singapore:

> In the past, there were several challenges to the acceptance of multiple intelligences assessment in Singapore. The principal factor was that Singapore, as a society constantly adapting to an era of great change, had come to value productive "efficiency" over "innovation." Historically, the arts were often pursued as pastimes for one to rest and recreate, and we applied much higher rigour (and priority) to academics. . . . In the end, I think that the mind-set of the various stakeholders has to be transfigured. With time and a clear direction, we are confident that this challenge can be overcome.

In contrast, some nations have their own unique historical characteristics and cultural ideals that may not be congruent with an education dominated by standardized academic tests. There, schools are more than just factory-like institutions that produce children who can read, write, and multiply. They are also the means by which rich cultural knowledge (implicit as well as explicit) is passed on from one generation to the next. Mary Ann Toledo-Pitre of Caribbean University notes, "A Spanish heritage nation like Puerto Rico can be described as artistic, musical and kinesthetically oriented. . . . Addressing the multiple intelligences is just what 'the doctor ordered.'" This observation accords with the views of many arts educators in the United States who are attracted to MI because of its appreciation for creative thinking.

Variations in Cultures with Regard to Focusing on Individuals' Strengths

Another barrier to MI and its assessment is that respecting each child's unique intellectual abilities is not an inherent value across cultures. Often academic test results inform curriculum planning and placement without regard to the child's other potential strengths. Alrezia Manzour described the problem this way: "The MI Profile has some cultural issues due to the fact that in some Middle Eastern and Asian cultures . . . moving within to discover inner abilities is thought of as a trivial waste of time."

In contrast, two Catholic school educators highlight how they value individual strengths. Sister Martha Moss in the United States eloquently noted, "A greater understanding of multiple intelligences strengthens the self-acceptance of young people and gives them a key to how they might best learn." Similarly, Brother Robert Fanovich of Presentation College in Grenada stated, "I used an MI assessment in church youth groups to help them realize their gifts. I suppose the Biblical equivalent of MI is 'talents.'"

While there are cultural variations with regard to focusing on individual strengths, the value of recognizing each learner's unique profile of abilities was reiterated by a number of survey respondents in disparate parts of the world. Most teachers tend to teach how they themselves were taught and this is usually well aligned with their own MI profiles, accentuating their strengths in the linguistic, interpersonal, and intrapersonal intelligences. MI assessment helps teachers to understand that their classrooms are populated by students with a wide variety of learning strengths and needs. In Ireland, researcher and teacher Declan Kelly noted, "For teachers, there is a need to change instructional strategies in a dynamic way. The slogan, 'The student is not like me' is very useful as MI brings home the idea that how the teacher learns may not be the way the student learns."

Romanian teacher-researcher Sorin-Avram Virtop noted the value of helping parents see students' strengths: "One of the main benefits [of the MI assessment] for parents was that we succeeded in making them understand and be more open to know their children better."

Knowledge of individual students' strengths was seen as important to the students themselves. Zahra Zarata of the University of Applied Science and Technology in Tehran, Iran, reports, "There were many cases among respondents who told me that before responding to the MI assessment, they themselves were not fully aware of their abilities or using those abilities in learning." In Hong Kong, C. C. Wan has used MI assessment to overcome "the notion that once you are identified as a 'failure' under the traditional academic assessment, then you are forever doomed. Instead, my students learn that there are other areas where they are strong. . . . This is the beginning of the learner's journey to gain self-confidence."

As these examples illustrate, MI assessment can be a powerful means to increase this self-understanding. The examples also indicate that a need to identify at least some individuals' strengths may be a useful route to the theory's implementation in varied cultures.

CONCLUSION

In contrast to a "testing society," I think that the assessment approach and the individual-centered school constitute a more noble educational vision. . . . I define assessment as the obtaining of information about the skills and potentials of

> *individuals, with the dual goals of providing useful feedback to the individuals and useful data to the surrounding community.*
> —Howard Gardner (1993)

Despite technical challenges and cultural complexities, researchers and experienced educators from around the world have described their positive experiences with MI assessment and its benefits to students, teachers, and parents. Students benefit from learning more about themselves and about the practical manifestations and uses for their multiple intelligences. Teachers and parents benefit from having a better understanding of students' MI strengths and limitations and the corresponding instructional implications. Conducting high-quality MI assessments may not be quick and easy, but it can certainly be worthwhile to enhance learning and instruction. It can take time and effort for educators to learn how to make good use of this information within their particular cultural setting, so a long-term commitment is essential to achieving success.

MI assessment can also serve as a means of investigating the scientific validity of MI theory itself. Ninety-two percent of international respondents (thirty-three of thirty-six) report that the American MIDAS assessment could be successfully adapted or translated for their cultures. Sixty-nine percent (twenty-two of thirty-two) of international researchers report that there was either good or strong evidence that the MI profile produces a valid measurement. Eight of these researchers conducted large-scale empirical studies of students (340 to 7,500 participants for each researcher). Somewhat surprisingly, 72 percent of respondents report that people are able to accurately self-report their MI abilities most of the time. International validity data often parallel the research results obtained from similar U.S. samples, providing support for the cross-cultural validity of MI theory.

After twenty-five years, MI is still a young idea, and researchers in the field must continue to work hard to establish it as a respected scientific theory in the educational reform debate. An authoritative instrument can play an important role in demonstrating the efficacy of MI instruction to school officials and educational decision makers.

As psychologists have long debated the legitimacy of various intelligence theories (most recently, IQ versus MI versus triarchic versus emotional intelligence), classroom teachers and educational reform initiatives have been caught in the crossfire. Their efforts to bring MI to life in their classrooms and schools have often been stymied because sustainable change in schooling requires more than good theory.

If teaching is equal parts art and science, it is nevertheless embedded in a world dominated by quantitative science. For this reason, a quantifiable assessment of MI must be available to support educators' efforts to implement the theory. Teachers need tools that will guide their use of the multiple intelligences to maximize students' potential. Such tools will also help teachers, parents, schools, and community leaders to work together to the ultimate benefit of each student, and thus to the benefit of society as a whole.

Note

1. Portfolios and other performance measures are often supplemented with standardized paper and pencil tests of knowledge and basic skills. Even the most thoroughly MI-inspired school will use a hybrid of performance assessment and written tests. Testing is employed for varied reasons, including meeting state standards, satisfying parental expectations, and because of its familiarity to teachers and other stake-holders (e.g., for admission to other schools). An obvious advantage of standardized tests is that they require minimal expertise and investment in staff time to administer and score.

References

Anastasi, A. (1979). *Fields of applied psychology* (2nd ed.). New York: McGraw-Hill.

Armstrong, T. (1994). *Multiple intelligences in the classroom.* Alexandria, VA: ASCD.

Bolaños, P. (1996). Multiple intelligences as a mental model: The Key Renaissance Middle School. *NASSP Bulletin, 80,* 24–29.

Block, N. J., & Dworkin, G. (1976). *The IQ controversy.* New York: Pantheon.

Chen, J., Krechevsky, M., & Viens, J. (1998). *Building on children's strengths: The experience of Project Spectrum.* New York: Teachers College Press.

Díaz-Lefebvre, R. (1999). *Coloring outside the lines: Applying multiple intelligences and creativity in learning.* Hoboken, NJ: Wiley.

Gardner, H. (1993). *Multiple intelligences: The theory in practice.* New York: Basic Books.

Gardner, H. (1995). Reflections on multiple intelligences: Myths and messages. *Phi Delta Kappan, 77,* 200–209.

Herrnstein, R., & Murray, C. (1994). *The bell curve.* New York: Free Press.

Hoerr, T. (2000). *Becoming a multiple intelligences school.* Alexandria, VA: Association for Supervision and Curriculum Development.

Kagan, S., & Kagan, M. (1998). *Multiple intelligences: The complete MI book.* San Clemente, CA: Kagan Cooperative Learning.

Maker, C. J. (1992). Intelligence and creativity in multiple intelligences: Identification and development. *Educating Able Learners: Discovering and Nurturing Talent, 17*(4), 12–19.

Meisels, S. J. (1993). Remaking classroom assessment with the Work Sampling System. *Young Children, 28*(5), 34–40.

Montgomery County Public Schools. (1990). *Observational checklist for multiple intelligences.* Silver Spring, MD: Author.

Owens, W. (1976). Background data. In M. Dunnette (Ed.), *Handbook of industrial and organizational psychology* (pp. 609–644). Skokie, IL: Rand McNally.

Shearer, C. B. (2007). *The MIDAS: A professional manual* (rev. ed.). Kent, OH: MI Research and Consulting.

Silver, H. F., Strong, R. W., & Perini, M. (2000). *So each may learn: Integrating learning styles and multiple intelligences.* Alexandra, VA: ASCD.

Stefanakis, E. H. (2002). *Multiple intelligences and portfolios.* Portsmouth, NH: Heinemann.

Sternberg, R. J. (1985). *Beyond IQ: The triarchic theory of human intelligence.* Cambridge: Cambridge University Press.

PART SIX

SYNTHESIS, REFLECTION, AND PROJECTION

I n this final section, three experts on MI theory and practice reflect on patterns found across chapters and in the book as whole. They address questions that underlie the work of individual contributors: Why is it important to develop and educate multiple intelligences? How will applications of MI theory affect educational policy? What helps to explain the differences in cultures' responsiveness to MI-based education? Deep reflections on these questions stimulate readers around the world to move toward new initiatives and appropriate, generative applications of MI theory.

CHAPTER 30

Why Multiple Intelligences?

Seana Moran

Intelligences are often thought about as an individual property. However, they are less a property or end in themselves and more a tool to achieve cultural goals. This chapter examines what individuals do to affect their cultural environments: how interactions of intelligences end in contributions that benefit culture. Each of us offers a profile of intelligences that interact with each other within one person's mind, intelligence profiles of other individuals with whom the person works and plays, and cultural, cross-cultural, and technological resources employed for various purposes. These interactions create further opportunities for us to make contributions to the common good and to expand our own and others' horizons for accomplishing positive community aims. As more than just logical-mathematical and linguistic intelligences are valued and developed in various cultures, the array of potentials, capabilities, and performances grows exponentially.

The chapters in this book provide a vibrant picture of the strategies used to date to implement multiple intelligences (MI) theory in countries around the world. I applaud the vision, passion, and perseverance of the policymakers, researchers, and practitioners who have built strong foundations for the theory's success. In this chapter, I take a step back to examine why the development of multiple intelligences is important to cultures.

I do not address why intelligences are important to particular cultures, as this within-culture focus has been the purview of many of the other chapters in this book. Battro, Pogré and Rogé, Vialle, Knoop, and Fleetham focus on inclusion, allowing and inviting more people from more diverse backgrounds to become productive contributors to their cultures. Chen emphasizes harmony—how we each contribute to the well-being of others and our culture. Barrera and León-Agustí, K. Cheung, Kim and Cha, and Craft discuss

365

self-awareness and personal meaning, coming to better understand who we are, direct our own efforts agentically, and evaluate our progress. Barrera and León-Agustí, Howland et al., Kim and Cha, Shen, and Craft suggest creativity in terms of both self-expression and effecting change on our environment. And Sahl-Madsen and Kyed, and Canon-Abaquin, discuss making the world a better place by addressing our societies' most pressing problems.

Instead of within-culture purposes, I consider how the interaction of many intelligences within and across individuals and cultures contributes to the development of culture in general. How do intelligences compose the ways of being and knowing that we call culture among a group of people? Thus, I attempt to broaden the book's discussion to a bird's-eye view of culture and its relationship to intelligences.

Intelligences are resources that span the interaction of person and culture. Because individuals share a culture, they are not completely independent. Culture is not "out there," but rather is carried within the minds and behaviors of individuals. A culture is alive to the extent that people internalize and use the language, values, and customs. Through socialization, education, parenting, feedback, and other mechanisms, each of us reinforces our culture to others. We interact through "communities of practice" (Lave & Wenger, 1991). Thus, culture is not separate from individuals: we compose each other's cultural environment.

Intelligences are often thought about as an individual property: a person "has" linguistic or musical intelligence. However, they are less a property or end in themselves and more a tool to achieve cultural goals. Gardner (1983) insisted that intelligences must be employed to fashion products or ideas within cultural contexts. Individuals' intelligences are resources to be developed to make a contribution that benefits not only the individual but the wider community. As K. Cheung said, intelligences must be "put to good use."

What makes intelligences so powerful, and people's diverse profiles of intelligences within cultures so powerful, is the pattern of interactions among them. Most performances of a task do not isolate one intelligence but rather combine intelligences to achieve a purpose. Similarly, most performances are not completely done by one person. He or she assimilates tools from artifacts or from other individuals. Through his or her contributions, this person alters the cultural landscape and makes available further artifacts and resources for others to assimilate (Moran & John-Steiner, 2003). These interactions drive both cultural stability and cultural evolution.

INTERACTIONS AMONG INTELLIGENCES WITHIN INDIVIDUALS

Each of us offers a profile of intelligences to be employed for various purposes. But a profile is not a bar chart of separate intelligences. The intelligences affect each other's development and expression. Interactions may help explain why, even within a particular intelligence, there is much diversity in expression. A gifted orator and a talented writer both have strong linguistic intelligences, although each may be valued differently in different cultures. In the orator, linguistic intelligence may mix with musical, bodily-kinesthetic, and interpersonal intelligences to give him or her a mesmerizing stage presence. The writer may mix linguistic intelligence with existential and logical-mathematical intelligences to design a well-structured, broad-minded narrative. This interactive nature of intelligences suggests that intelligences can be expressed in a variety of ways depending on cultural context, and tests that isolate intelligences may not do justice to individuals' true potential within a culture.

Intelligences interact with each other in three broad ways: bottlenecking, compensation, and catalysis (Moran & Gardner, 2006a). Intelligences can bottleneck each other: one can interfere with the expression or development of another. A "universal" test may bottleneck expressions of an intelligence because the test requires strength in one particular intelligence or because the intelligence studied may be expressed in different ways, depending on how it interacts with other intelligences a student may have and the values of the student's culture. Bottlenecking may occur when nonlinguistic intelligences are assessed using language-based paper-and-pencil tests. Similarly, a teacher with strong linguistic intelligence who forces students to respond only in writing may be creating a bottleneck. One student may express his strong linguistic intelligence well only orally, whereas another expresses it well only in writing. And neither may score well on tests that isolate linguistic intelligence abstractly.

Intelligences can compensate for each other: a strength can offset the effects of a weakness. The mind is plastic; it can adapt to different situations, constraints, and goals in various ways. Shen's example of a student with poor linguistic plus strong bodily-kinesthetic intelligences in drama highlights compensation. A person with weak linguistic intelligence may still function well in society due to strong interpersonal intelligence (I have a dyslexic but very charismatic friend, for example) or vice versa (consider the autistic author Temple Grandin, who holds a doctorate). A person relatively weak in logical-mathematical intelligence may still make significant contributions in science because of a strong naturalistic intelligence (Charles Darwin, for example). Thus, there are multiple pathways to the same end point of "success" or "quality performance" that need to be accounted for in educational interventions and assessments. We must take care not to write off a student who is weak in a particular intelligence. In interaction with other intelligences, it may not be a weakness at all, and it may actually turn into a benefit if employed toward certain purposes. For example, creative people tend to show how intellectual weaknesses can be benefits by helping them see aspects of the world in nonstandard ways. H. Cheung's comment about how "bad students can become famous" may allude to such situations.

Finally, intelligences can catalyze each other: one can stimulate further growth in another. Musical or spatial intelligence can make a writer's poems more rhythmic or imagistic. Spatial intelligence can make naturalistic intelligence more "3D," helping the person categorize natural phenomena in a maplike, rather than a table-like, way. Vialle's story about how Peter's personal and spatial intelligences catalyzed each other within drama is a good example of catalysis, as is Battro's suggestion that Nico bridges spatial and logical-mathematical intelligences. If we aim to maximize students' potentials and turn those potentials into performances, accounting for catalysis can help us achieve that aim with less external support to the child. Integrative projects and real-world problem solving—described by several authors, including Maker and Sarouphim, Hoerr, Kunkel, Barrera and León-Agustí, and Canon-Abaquin—may be a particularly fruitful way to make visible catalytic interactions.

INTERACTIONS AMONG INTELLIGENCES ACROSS INDIVIDUALS

In addition to recognizing intelligence interactions within a person, it may be helpful to look at intelligence interactions across individuals. After all, in the work world, most people's work is done in relation to the work of others. Effective teams are built based on complementarity of resources and skills among diverse workers, not on a collection of identical individuals. To use an analogy, a jigsaw puzzle is interesting because different images and shapes fit together to form an overall image, not because all pieces have the identical image and shape. From this interactionist perspective, an educational system with universal standards makes little sense (and many extraordinary achievers do not reminisce fondly about their school days; see Gardner, 1993; Moran, 2006). It becomes more difficult for individuals to figure out how they fit in the bigger picture of their cultures if they are demanded to become like everyone else.

All three types of interactions can also be seen in teams. When one student demands that all members of the team must persuade others of their ideas' merits, his strong interpersonal intelligence may bottleneck the contributions of others who may be less socially skilled. When students with different strengths work together on a project and respect each other's differences, compensation can lead to an outcome better than if anyone had completed the assignment alone. One student's mathematical wizardry can stimulate a more spatial-oriented painter to include geometry or fractals in her work, thus catalyzing the painter's learning and performance. Or a strong naturalist student paired with a strong existential student and a strong interpersonal student probably could create an amazing environmental awareness-raising public service campaign. As Knoop said, we can achieve much more together than by ourselves.

A child with a nascent bodily-kinesthetic intelligence may not blossom until she works with another child with a strong rhythmic, musical intelligence. Kaya and Selçuk describe how one student, Mehmet, could influence other children, despite his poor linguistic and logical-mathematical intelligences. Díaz-Lefebvre's heart-wrenching story about Javier and his drawings of the brain suggest a missed opportunity for him to enlighten his classmates because of rigid standards of "high" and "low" performance. We may be limiting the resources we have in the classroom—the various intelligences of class members—when we restrict interactions to be one way from "better" to "worse" students on a unidimensional criterion.

INTERACTIONS AMONG INTELLIGENCES ACROSS CULTURES

Cross-cultural interactions of intelligences also provide a rich arena for expression and development of intelligences. The introduction of MI as a scientific theory and a foundation for educational practice is a cross-cultural phenomenon. Yet its application, as shown in this book, is primarily intracultural—how the intelligences are interpreted and valued within one particular culture. Children are educated within a culture. Most children interact with people of another culture only late in their formal educational careers—in high school or college exchange programs. A few who live in cosmopolitan cities or travel may be exposed to cultural differences sooner. However, as transportation, immigration, and electronic media grow, people from diverse cultural backgrounds can interact more often and in more varied ways.

In cross-cultural interactions, not only their intelligences, but also the meaning and value of those intelligences, may differ. Such interactions add a new level of possibility for learning and understanding because values and meanings cannot be taken for granted. I have visited several American schools where principals have told me how they have to now "deal with" refugees from another country. I understand that language barriers and prejudices might make social interactions a challenge at first. However, from an MI-interactionist perspective, this cross-cultural situation is not a problem but an educational opportunity that has yet to be fully realized if educators view it in terms of compensation and catalysis rather than create bottlenecks based on preconceptions.

These interactions become all the more intriguing as technology affects them. Battro describes how computers can be used as an extension of one's intelligences, compensating for weaknesses or enhancing strengths. Sahl-Madsen and Kyed describe how personal digital assistants help visitors to Danfoss Universe make the most self-reflective use of their time within Explorama activities. In work on youth civic engagement, I commented on how the Internet has become the civitas, the town square, and the political arena for young adults, changing the opportunities and strategies for those seeking to lead (Moran, 2007). Technology extends personal resources and bridges the person-culture boundary.

CONTRIBUTION TO CULTURE

The intelligences themselves are not goals. Intelligences are resources invested in a task or product and valued by a culture. If the task or product is not valued, it is not a contribution. Contributions are the goal. Cultivation of intelligences makes sense in the context of how they are used to affect the community. Contributions can range from proficiency to expertise in the maintenance of existing cultural practices, to creativity, or cultural transformation (Moran & Gardner, 2006b), to wisdom, or particularly astute actions that consider multiple perspectives within a situation or culture to have a positive effect on the common good (Moran & Connell, 2008).

Many schools fall short of supporting contribution. Contribution is a step beyond engagement, performance, demonstration, and display of work, which are more often lauded as goals or benefits of an educational practice. Engagement makes learning more enjoyable, and students take more responsibility for their learning. Hoerr's chapter even alluded to how such engagement might be misinterpreted by parents as lacking rigor since students were having too much fun! Performance and demonstration make learning and competencies visible; they show what students can do. Several chapters describe mentorships, apprenticeships, portfolios, and learning performances through which students can demonstrate competencies. And public display shows pride in student work. The American schools, in particular, make a point of using their hallways to exhibit student progress. But engagement, performance, demonstration, and display do not have an impact on the wider school community, neighborhood, or beyond. These programs still keep students segregated from the potential they have to play a real role in their cultures. As Rizzo proclaimed, what is needed is relevance.

MI implementations seem to focus on the adults in educational settings—which would be considered the "environment" for the child. Many use an expert-novice zone of proximal development model where the older, more experienced person does most of the contributing, and the younger, less experienced person does most of the assimilating (Vygotsky, 1987). Several chapters in this book suggest that for particular cultural practices to be maintained or changed, contributions are required at every level of power within the educational establishment: policymakers, researchers, and teachers. What is described less often is how students contribute. Albeit less experienced, students *are* cultural members. They may be limited in what they can do: some of those limitations are due to unfinished development or immature abilities, but some also are due to cultural constraints. For example, there are legal or other institutional constraints on young people's participation in driving, voting, working, and other common contributions (Moran, 2007).

Keinänen alludes to what can happen to students when contribution is not considered. She described how some students in Norway drop out and rebel because they have nothing to lose. They are disconnected; what they do or do not do, from their perspective, does not matter. Díaz-Lefebvre's story of how Javier's potential contribution was not valued led to his dropping out of college. On a more positive note, Kim and Cha's story of Ji-Min's naturalist intelligence and love of insects shows what contribution can do for a child. When students see that the use of their intelligences has real impact, they blossom. As Barrera and León-Agustí so eloquently put it, young people can "pronounce themselves as people."

Many young people can and want to contribute, if given the opportunity. Several chapters in this book describe wonderful ways young people are fully contributing members of their communities. In Colombia, students from poverty backgrounds contribute to a less violent, more just society by reflecting on and solving their own conflicts. In Argentina, students created an anthology of written work that was distributed to others. In Denmark, young people helped design exhibits in a science park. In England, scouts earn badges through taking action, not just doing activities. In the Philippines, students become each other's heroes and heroes for others outside school, and day care centers reduce environmental impact through recycling programs. Students are not learning "about" a topic; they are learning to truly engage an issue, be part of a solution, and see the effects of their actions.

Particularly strong examples of contribution in this book are the book-making, frame business, birthday bashes, and newspaper endeavors at the New City School and the Rainforest Café Project that planted trees and the White Elephant Sales to raise money for books for poorer children in the Philippines. Each of these programs requires the interaction of individuals and their intelligences toward a culturally valued outcome. Students see that they are important, understand how their actions matter, and receive feedback to help them improve their contributions in the future.

Another strong example comes from my visits to various schools. One state has a vocational education center that not only trains young people in various skills, such as drafting, media production, or child development. It also contains a kitchen where student chefs cook lunch for the faculty, an auto mechanic bay where students fix faculty and community members' cars, and a day care facility where faculty bring their toddlers. Construction students go into the community to build sheds and other buildings; when they drive around town, they can point to examples of their contributions. Health care students work in hospitals half a day. Drafting and preengineering students design solutions for community organizations, including the police department. As Maker and Sarouphim suggest in their depiction of the Diné culture, perhaps the best "testing" is real-life problem solving.

CONCLUSION

It may be simpler to have one general intelligence and one set of rules, standards, or pathways for all. If we set a policy, such as the U.S. No Child Left Behind or Norway's "not excel too much" ethos, to bring everyone up to a "norm," and we assume that norm equals "maximizing potential," then we have done our job. But people are not identical. Each of us has a set of resources and potentials different from others. The potential of one student is not simply higher or lower, but perhaps on different dimensions, than another student. Each of us can contribute to our cultures in diverse ways. And the roles a culture affords are quite varied. Becoming an expert carpenter or mother or pianist or friend requires far different skills and resources than a poet or statistician does. And most cultures need all of these roles.

The commitment of individuals' multiple intelligences to contribute to the greater good creates a more complex situation for educators. The educational trajectories of students, the training of teachers, and the outcomes of learning become more interactionist, nonlinear, and harder to predict. But a multiple intelligences approach also offers a more vibrant future of opportunities for everyone. We can achieve more by collaborating with people dissimilar but complementary to us than by surrounding ourselves with like-minded copycats: a saxophone and piano playing in harmony is more provocative than two violins in unison.

Perhaps we are poised for the intellectual equivalent of the Cambrian explosion, a prehistoric period characterized by an immense diversification of biological species. As more than just logical-mathematical and linguistic intelligences are valued and developed in various cultures and as individuals and cultures increasingly interact, the array of potentials, capabilities, and performances grows multiplicatively. Rather than just labels and measures of separate intelligences, the relationships between intelligences, between individuals, and between cultures become the focal point of intellectual and cultural development.

One of the greatest hopes of MI theory is that it can help catalyze all of us from various cultures to consider, reflect, and ideally contribute to ongoing cultural achievement writ large. That is, MI theory makes visible the wider range of possibilities open not only within our own cultures but to culture in general. Our profiles of intelligence matter because of what ends we put them toward in sustaining or changing aspects of the cultures of which we are a part. Culture is a process, and multiple intelligences create a broader horizon to aim for.

References

Gardner, H. (1983). *Frames of mind.* New York: Basic Books.

Gardner, H. (1993). *Creating minds.* New York: Basic Books.

Lave, J., & Wenger, E. (1991). *Situated learning.* Cambridge: Cambridge University Press.

Moran, S. (2006). *Commitment and creativity*. Unpublished doctoral thesis, Harvard University.

Moran, S. (2007). *Commitment in democracy*. Paper presented to the Symposium on Social Understanding, Trust and Commitment at the Association of Moral Education Conference, New York.

Moran, S., & Connell, M. (2008). *All the wiser: Wisdom from a systems perspective.* Presentation at the University of Chicago Arete Initiative, Chicago.

Moran, S., & Gardner, H. (2006a). Multiple intelligences in the workplace. In H. Gardner, *Multiple intelligences: New horizons* (pp. 213–232). New York: Basic Books.

Moran, S., & Gardner, H. (2006b). Extraordinary cognitive achievements: A developmental and systems analysis. In W. Damon (Series Ed.) & D. Kuhn & R. S. Siegler (Vol. Eds.), *Handbook of child psychology, Vol. 2: Cognition, perception, and language* (6th ed., pp. 905–949). Hoboken, NJ: Wiley.

Moran, S., & John-Steiner, V. (2003). *Creativity in the making: Vygotsky's contribution to the dialectic of creativity and development*. In R. K. Sawyer, V. John-Steiner, S. Moran, R. J. Sternberg, D. H. Feldman, J. Nakamura, & M. Csikszentmihalyi (Eds.), *Creativity and development* (pp. 61–90). New York: Oxford University Press.

Vygotsky, L. S. (1987). *Mind in society.* Cambridge, MA: MIT Press.

CHAPTER 31

What's Policy Got to Do with It?

A Policy Perspective on the Theory of Multiple Intelligences

Mindy L. Kornhaber

The theory of multiple intelligences, advanced as a new conception of human intelligence, soon became a framework for pedagogy and school reform. This chapter explores the intersection between the theory of multiple intelligences and social policy. I first consider the policy environment for the theory's development in the United States and then examine the trajectory of the theory's implementation, given policies within the United States and in other countries. I claim that from a policy perspective, the theory of multiple intelligences serves as an agent of cognitive equity. When soundly implemented, MI enables diverse people to use their minds well. In turn, the theory is a democratizing tool: it enables the development and expression of ideas by those who might otherwise remain unheard.

In this chapter, I focus on the intersection of the theory of multiple intelligences (Gardner, 1983) and policy, that is, the means of promoting or limiting actions in pursuit of a social goal (Pal, 1997). I consider the theory's development and its use in schools in response to existing social problems and policies and also the theory's adoption as a policy tool itself. The central theme is that from a policy perspective, use of the theory is meant to develop the minds of a much wider array of students than traditional psychometric conceptions. To the extent that various implementations of MI succeed in doing this, the theory is an agent of cognitive equity (Kornhaber, 1998): it enables a greater diversity of individuals to use their minds well. In turn, the theory is a democratizing tool: it facilitates the development and expression of ideas by those who might otherwise remain largely unheard in their communities or in the wider society.

As Gardner has often noted (see, for example, Chapter One, this volume), although MI was intended to influence thinking within the sphere of academic psychology, it was far more readily adopted in the world of educational practice. There, MI soon became a means to address policy problems. Only four years after Gardner published the theory, the Key School established itself largely on MI in response to *A Nation at Risk* (National Commission on Excellence in Education, 1983) and its ensuing regimen of standardization and testing (see Chapter Twenty-Four, this volume).

Although this change of venue surprised the theorist, it is worth noting that MI, and all other conceptions of human intelligence, are creatures of social contexts. Central to such contexts are issues of leadership, the interactions of people and groups within a social order, socialization of children into that order, and the bases on which such things rest. Thus, while MI is revolutionary both methodologically and politically, it also follows a tradition dating back to Plato, who claimed that the quality of metal that comprises each individual's capacities should determine his place in society (Plato, 1960). Furthermore, to place a man of iron in a position requiring a man of gold would surely have dire consequences for the state. In essence, the way in which one's "metal" is ascertained is fundamentally an issue of social policy.

DEVELOPMENT OF THE THEORY IN THE UNITED STATES

As Thomas Armstrong noted in Chapter Two, MI is an American export. It makes a great deal of sense that the theory was produced in the United States. American society is notable for its focus on individual, as opposed to collective, identity (Bellah, Madsen, Sullivan, Swidler, & Tipton, 1985). (For a contrasting case, see Chapter Three, by Jie-Qi Chen, on intelligence as a family versus individual characteristic in China.) Culturally, it is a place that has long lauded rugged individualists such as Teddy Roosevelt. Americans' cherished individuality is legitimized in, among other places, their constitutional right to free expression. Certainly not all people were equally free to exercise this and other rights. However, the long-term, albeit uneven, trajectory of American domestic policy has been to expand rights to those in formerly excluded sectors of the society (Patterson, 1995) and to further individuals' "right to life, liberty and the pursuit of happiness."

Against this distal historical backdrop, other powerful, proximal events were taking place in American society. From about the time Howard Gardner entered Harvard College in 1961, a series of political movements took aim at the limited educational and employment opportunities that commonly confronted African Americans and other minority groups, women, and individuals with disabilities (Farber, 1994). It is fair to say that few intellectually engaged Americans were unaffected by these efforts to gain civil rights and to correct laws that had consigned many fellow citizens to inferior roles.

Clearly Gardner's research in neuropsychology, cognitive development of normal and gifted children in various domains, and the arts and human cognition was central to the theory's development (see Chapter One, this volume). In the course of this research, he often saw contradictions with the traditional notion of general intelligence. These led to his awareness, as he noted in Chapter One, that "something is rotten in the state of intelligence." It is evident that the development of the theory drew deeply on Gardner's expertise in psychology and his interdisciplinary review of a wide range of research. Yet alongside this scientific investigation, I would argue that he and his theory, just as it is with all other theorists and theories, are also products of both distal and proximal social influences (see Gould, 1981).

INITIAL ADOPTION AND TRAJECTORY IN THE UNITED STATES

Gardner notes in Chapter One that his theory was not warmly embraced and widely accepted in all quarters. It was, in fact, quite harshly criticized by some fellow academic psychologists. A number of them saw MI as diluting or obscuring "Intelligence" (with a capital I), a construct central to psychology. The theory did not even rest on the approved methods of the field (Miller, 1983; Scarr, 1985). Such criticisms continue here and abroad (White, 2005; Willingham, 2004), and their ferocity is not surprising. From a policy perspective, Gardner's questioning of human "metal," and the traditional methods used to assay it, is tantamount to an attack on the gatekeepers of the state.

In other quarters of learning, the debate among academic psychologists hardly mattered. Most teachers do not see themselves as strict methodologists or gatekeepers. Instead, they focus on the ground-level challenges of engaging and developing students. For them, the theory and the evidence underlying it were clearly compelling. It accorded with their experience that students differ along a number of dimensions, they learn in different ways, and many have their own particular genius (Kornhaber & Krechevsky, 1995).

The American education system was fertile ground for the initial application of the theory to educational settings. Precisely because of its statistical infrastructure and its touted potential to bring rational decision making into organizational settings (Terman, 1919; see Callahan, 1962), the psychometric view of intelligence and its armamentarium of assessments have not always rested comfortably within American society. From the initial administration of mass testing in the military and schools, vociferous critics have regarded the tests and their results as dubious ways of limiting individuals' rights and opportunities (see Lemann, 1999; Lippmann, 1922a, 1922b). In contrast, the theory of multiple intelligences suggests no inherent hierarchy of abilities or, therefore, of rights and opportunities. Furthermore, in Gardner's theory (1983), "intelligence" is not reflected by a score obtained from an hour or two of short-answer questions, but by how one solves problems or fashions products that are culturally valued. As Armstrong suggested in Chapter Two, the theory is well suited to Americans' pragmatic, optimistic worldview.

For nearly fifteen years after the Key School's initial adoption of MI, U.S. educators working with every conceivable population—students in urban, rural, and suburban schools across the nation; gifted learners; low-literacy adults; youth in juvenile detention centers; college students; preschoolers— sought out the theory. They used it to develop students' minds and disciplinary knowledge and to connect students to school and the wider society. Chris Kunkel speaks of this process in Chapter Twenty-Four: "It is our hope that each student will take the strengths he or she discovered and developed to make a positive difference in the community, if not the world."

However, as Kunkel indicates, existing pressures to raise students' test scores, exacerbated by the Bush administration's signature domestic law, the No Child Left Behind Act of 2001 (NCLB), have narrowed many educators' goals. This constriction is greatest in schools serving high-poverty and minority students (see Booher-Jennings, 2005; McNeil & Valenzuela, 2001; Neal & Schanzenbach, 2007). The effect of these policies, in the United States as in every other setting they have been used, is to pull schools, teachers, and students into a much more uniform line of operation. Yet the emphasis placed on the test scores, or any overly weighted social indicator, corrupts the processes by which they are generated (Campbell, 1976). Thus, in the eight years of the Bush presidency, while billions of dollars (see General Accounting Office, 2003) were spent in pursuit of NCLB's single-minded approach, much of it going to corporate entities that produce tests and test preparation materials, almost no meaningful gains in achievement materialized on independent assessments of national achievement (Fuller, Gesicki, Kang, & Wright, 2006; Lee, 2006; National Center for Education Statistics, 2007).

As a result of NCLB and related policies, work with the theory has contracted in U.S. public schools. This is evident from Kunkel's chapter. Another indicator is that of the forty-one schools that participated in lengthy interviews for the Project on Schools Using MI Theory (SUMIT) in 1998–1999 (Kornhaber, Fierros, & Veenema, 2004), only fourteen replied to Gardner's follow-up inquiry in 2006 (Gardner, personal communication, 2006). For now, most thoughtful applications of MI in the United States are restricted to preschools, private school settings, or the college level, which remain outside the purview of the high-stakes accountability testing that affects U.S. public schools.

We see examples of such work in this book in Chapter Twenty-Five by Tom Hoerr, Chapter Twenty-Eight by Vincent Rizzo, and Chapter Twenty-Six by René Díaz-Lefebvre. The theory also continues to flourish in the United States outside school settings, such as in museums and arts organizations.

POLICIES SUPPORTING THE ADOPTION OF MI BEYOND THE UNITED STATES

As the case of the United States illustrates, policies that embrace narrow, uniform standards and hierarchical rankings are not consistent with the widespread adoption of MI. In contrast, policies that seek to diminish hierarchy, broaden standards, and embrace diversity are hospitable to the theory and to genuine cognitive equity. In many parts of the world, such policy trends are in place. That said, there is considerable variation among such policies, including their systemic scope and their immediate aims. This section considers uses of the theory now operating at a national level, then at more local levels. The particular policy aims are considered within each level.

Implementation of MI at the Level of National Policy

Even as national-level policy in the United States since 2001 has reduced the use of MI, in other countries, with other national policies and programmatic stances to them, the theory began to take hold and even to flourish. In Norway, as Mia Keinänen writes in Chapter Twelve, the existing culture favored egalitarianism and democratic organization, and it was thus "fertile ground for MI." In line with this culture, Norway's Ministry of Education during the 1990s produced a core curriculum that was not informed by MI but very hospitable to it. The curriculum's seven dimensions included "social," "creative," "environmentally aware," and liberally educated and an education law that required the school to adjust to the individual child. Once it became clear that MI was not just a means to serve gifted children, a group whose needs are not readily addressed within Norway's egalitarian culture, educators gravitated toward the theory. Their immediate impetus was that the theory presented a clear route to meet Norway's policy demand to become more inclusive and address the individual needs of each student.

Several contributors to this book have noted that the adoption of MI in schools, teacher education programs, or other settings accompanied their nation's transition from autocratic governments to more participatory ones. At the national level, Paula Pogré and Marcela Rogé illustrate this point in Chapter Twenty-One: after the Argentinean junta ended, the new 1993 Federal Education Law set out "the principles of education for all." In turn, they write, "A group of educational researchers and practitioners working in private schools and later in public schools saw the potential of the theory to help transform the educational system, making it more democratic and inclusive," and to meet the aims of the new policy. Not long after, the Ministry of Education itself realized that MI aligned with its aim of "education for all" policy. It has since begun to promote its use.

In Ireland, there was a similar trajectory: a national policy aimed at promoting educational inclusion spurred the adoption of MI, and afterward the theory was adopted into national policy. As Áine Hyland and Marian McCarthy detail in Chapter Seventeen, the Education Act of 1998 and the University Act of 1997 were implemented largely in response to a great wave of immigrants who had been attracted to Ireland's new-found wealth and opportunity. These new laws called on every level of the education system to meet the needs of learners, "regardless of their abilities or disabilities, or their cultural, social, linguistic, ethnic, or religious background." As Hyland and McCarthy show, MI provided a framework by which educators could put this policy into practice. Following Hyland and her colleagues' efforts to implement MI and the teaching for understanding framework (Blythe, 1997; Stone-Wiske, 1997), and to educate policymakers about the positive results they obtained, several national policy documents have incorporated the theory.

In Scotland, Brian Boyd describes in Chapter Eighteen the gradual diminution of social class and high-stakes testing influences on precollegiate educational opportunity in his country. The increasing inclusiveness of the system has encouraged efforts to enhance learning among a broad range of the population. To meet this challenge, Scotland's local education authorities have undertaken steps to incorporate the theory. In 2004, with Boyd's participation, the Ministerial Review Group generated a national curriculum framework that called for a broad set of academic, emotional, and social competences. The group embraced MI as a means for achieving these ends.

Turkey and Korea would seem unlikely places for MI to have been included in national policy. Each has long had a narrow, exam-driven curriculum. In both, test scores largely determined students' educational fates and future opportunities in the economic sector. Yet in Chapter Twenty, Osman Nafiz Kaya and Ziya Selçuk reveal that MI made inroads in Turkey over the course of twenty years. Initially MI was implemented in a laboratory school affiliated with Selçuk's university and in other private schools, which have fewer curricular constraints. In the schools that first employed MI, educators began carrying out more interdisciplinary work, reoriented assessment from measurement to evaluation, and became more inclusive in their views of intelligence. Given these changes, teacher education programs incorporated the theory into their educational psychology courses. In 2003, Selçuk was appointed to Turkey's Board of Education and has helped encourage MI in a major revision of the national curriculum. The national adoption has been accompanied by broad professional development efforts for teacher educators and textbook publishers, so that the theory could be soundly implemented in ways that foster disciplinary understanding. MI has moved from the margins of school practice to a prominent resource for addressing policy problems, which range from the expansion of technology to imperatives demanded by the European Union.

In Korea, as in Turkey and Ireland, the theory's incorporation into practice and then into national policy began with researchers and teachers working toward its implementation in a few private schools. In these schools, as Myung-Hee Kim and Hyung-Hee Cha report in Chapter Eight, there were improvements in achievement and attitudes toward learning. Policymakers began to see MI as a way of addressing a variety of educational problems, including underachievement by students who lost interest in learning in a highly competitive test-driven system. In 2005, the Korean Ministry of Education put forth its Seventh National Curriculum, which "pursues diversity and individuality. It tries to provide customized education for individuals, changing education from teacher-centric to student-centric. It calls attention to respecting individual differences and adapting curriculum to differences among students." The curriculum includes MI as a theoretical and implementation framework.

Although China has not embraced MI in official policy documents, the theory is extremely well known and widely used throughout the country, even in some remote, poor areas, described by Zhilong Shen in Chapter Five. Several chapters in this book highlight China's cultural traditions, including Confucian educational philosophy and the varied expression of human abilities and talents that have been widely valued there. Jie-Qi Chen in Chapter Three and Happy Cheung in Chapter Four also note the importance to China's economy of an education that fosters individual development, problem solving, and creativity in addition to high test scores. For these and other reasons, China has produced a number of policy documents that make MI a reasonable tool for their implementation. For example, K. C. Cheung of the University of Macao draws attention in Chapter Six to China's 2001 mathematics curriculum, which states that "each student will have his/her own distinctive kind of development." In line with this tradition and the direction of China's central government, Macao's chief executive gave a major policy address that promoted MI "as an important means to foster all-around development for the new generation." Both Happy Cheung's and Zhilong Shen's chapters make mention of China's Quality Education Policy, introduced in 1999. The policy calls for educators and parents to attend not just to academics but to promote all-around cultivation, including the arts, sports, and moral education. As Happy Cheung writes, "In the effort to find theoretical support [for the China Quality Education Policy], the theory of multiple intelligences has served virtually as a magic elixir."

In the world of policy, it is not uncommon to find national policies colliding with each other. The China Quality Education Policy coexists with a continuing tradition of high-stakes college-entrance exams. Drawing on Jie-Qi Chen's chapter, the answer to the question of how MI coexists with such tests may inhere partly in the traditional Chinese balance of individual and collective needs. Contemporary Chinese education reform underscores the need to develop each person so that he or she can contribute to the society as a whole. The answer may also partly be explained by the fact that the great majority of Chinese students will not be attending higher education, and thus the exams may have somewhat less force on the system as a whole than America's NCLB policy, which is designed to evaluate each public school and school district.

Such a national policy contradiction also appears to hold in England. Both Anna Craft in Chapter Fifteen and Mike Fleetham in Chapter Sixteen take note of England's Every Child Matters policy, initiated in 2000. The policy, as Fleetham describes it, is aimed at helping every child to "enjoy and achieve, make a positive contribution, and achieve economic well-being." The policy also underscores "personalized learning" and calls for schools to address students' diverse needs. Although MI offers a framework that would complement these goals, it is not specifically mentioned in the policy. Furthermore, Fleetham questions the genuineness of the policy. It coexists alongside England's system of high-stakes testing in math, English, and science. Research on that system finds that England's teachers feel compelled to teach to the test, as do many American teachers (Booher-Jennings, 2005; Pedulla, Abrams, Madaus, Russell, Ramos, & Miao, 2003; Neal & Schanzenbach, 2007; McNeil & Valenzuela, 2001). Although China may have found a way to have its tests and MI too, efforts in England and the United States to educate inclusively and address each child's needs, coupled with high-stakes testing of a narrow range of disciplines, reflect a fundamental policy contradiction.

Implementations at the Programmatic and Local Levels

Many chapters in this book reflect local, programmatic, or schoolwide efforts to implement MI. Such efforts, like their larger counterparts, seek to improve individuals' opportunity to learn, diminish hierarchy, embrace diversity in thinking, and enhance cognitive equity. Although the immediate targets of these efforts are more local, I would argue that they often have broad national, or international influence (as is true of the Key School and the New City School in the United States).

For example, in Romania, the work of Florence Mihaela Singer and Ligia Sarivan's teacher education program arose in response to the education policies of that country's communist era. At that time, schooling consisted of silent rows of students who "memorized the single view of the single textbook" and then reproduced it on tests. Once communism ended, genuine desires to implement meaningful educational change were frustrated by a new policy problem: teachers educated in the old system had difficulty acquiring, and therefore using, other pedagogical approaches or deep understanding of their disciplines. Singer and Sarivan's programmatic effort, which they describe in Chapter Twenty-Two, is aimed at enabling prospective teachers to develop rich understandings in their disciplinary content areas and build competence in curriculum design. MI has been used to help preservice teachers develop multiple representations of disciplinary knowledge and translate declarative disciplinary knowledge into procedural knowledge. Rather than having minds aligned to the state's directives, these future teachers are helped to develop and possess their own minds. This has a multiplicative effect. As Singer and Sarivan write, "the unique voice of the teacher provides space for the multiple voices of the students."

Mary Joy Canon-Abaquin's MI International School, a private school in the Philippines, combines the theory of multiple intelligences with the ideas of the GoodWork Project (Gardner, Csikszentmihalyi, & Damon, 2001). This is done to nurture intellectual capacity, character, and commitment in young people, so that they can address the multiple policy problems of the wider society. In this school, students' multiple intelligences are engaged in social entrepreneurship to address genuine social problems, such as the diminishing rain forest and child poverty. Canon-Abaquin, like several other contributors to this book, combines MI with other frameworks developed at Project Zero. Her school draws as well on the GoodWork Project which emphasizes "the use of knowledge and intelligences to make a difference" through good, socially responsible work (Gardner et al., 2001). The children from this school have already had a multiplier effect, and although only time will tell, it is reasonable to expect they will continue to do so.

MULTIPLE INTELLIGENCES AND POLICIES AROUND THE WORLD

In the conclusion to Chapter Twenty-Two, which powerfully describes their work in developing a school for impoverished children in Bogotá, Colombia, María Ximena Barrera and Patricia León-Agustí write: "Traditional educational structures tend to reinforce a hierarchical system of inequality. They fail to recognize agency in students and teachers. Also overlooked are the needs of communities to have their young educated in ways that will prepare them to address deep societal problems." These authors, and the other contributors to this book, underscore that MI offers a powerful approach to educating diverse students in ways that enable them to use their minds well. When used thoughtfully, the theory promotes cognitive equity and is a force for democratization.

As such, from a policy perspective, the use of the theory will come in and out of fashion. In various places and at various times, leaders will seek to develop or diminish deep, genuine thinking among their citizens. To the extent that hierarchy most depresses the voices of those lowest on the ladder, one must wonder about the growing influence of high-stakes exam policies in many parts of the world.

The opportunity to use MI often conflicts with policies that require uniformity in teaching and learning, whether they are NCLB's high-stakes tests or the tightly controlled curriculum of communist-era Romania. Nevertheless, there is now substantial empirical evidence to show that the route to developing powerful forms of understanding is not through an increasing reliance on uniformity-inducing policies (Bransford, Brown, & Cocking, 1999; Pellegrino, Chudowsky, & Glaser, 2001). Instead, the development of deep understanding relies on a host of thoughtful approaches, some illustrated in this book, that enable teachers and students to engage, reflect regularly on their learning, and see learning as a purposeful activity. In an era of complex policy problems, each nation, and the world as a whole, will benefit by rising to this challenge.

References

Bellah, R. N., Madsen, R., Sullivan, W., Swidler, A., & Tipton, S. M. (1985). *Habits of the heart: Individualism and commitment in American life.* Berkeley: University of California Press.

Blythe, T. (1997). *Teaching for understanding.* San Francisco: Jossey-Bass.

Booher-Jennings, J. (2005). Below the bubble: "Educational triage" and the Texas accountability system. *American Educational Research Journal, 42*(2), 231–268.

Bransford, J. D., Brown, A. L., & Cocking, R. R. (Eds.). (1999). *Brain, mind, experience, and school.* Washington, DC: National Research Council/National Academy Press.

Callahan, R. (1962). *Education and the cult of efficiency.* Chicago: University of Chicago Press.

Campbell, D. T. (1976). *Assessing the impact of planned social change.* http://www.wmich.edu/evalctr/pubs/ops/ops08.html.

Farber, D. (1994). (Ed.). *The 60s: From memory to history.* Chapel Hill: University of North Carolina Press.

Fuller, B., Gesicki, K., Kang, E., & Wright, J. (2006). *Is the No Child Left Behind Act working? The reliability of how states track achievement.* http://eric.ed.gov/ERICDocs/data/ericdocs2sql/content_storage_01/0000019b/80/1b/d6/59.pdf.

Gardner, H. (1983). *Frames of mind: The theory of multiple intelligences.* New York: Basic Books.

Gardner, H., Csikszentmihalyi, M., & Damon, W. (2001). *Good work: When excellence and ethics meet.* New York: Basic Books.

General Accounting Office. (2003). *Characteristics of tests will influence expenses: Information sharing may help states realize efficiencies.* http://www.gao.gov/new.items/d03389.pdf.

Gould, S. J. (1981). *The mismeasure of man.* New York. Norton.

Kornhaber, M. L. (1998). *A return to cautious optimism: In the black-white test score gap.* http://www.prospect.org/cs/articles?article=the_blackwhite_test_score_gap.

Kornhaber, M., Fierros, E. G., & Veenema, S. A. (2004). *Multiple intelligences: Best ideas from research and practice.* Needham Heights, MA: Allyn & Bacon/Pearson.

Kornhaber, M. L., & Krechevsky, M. (1995). *Expanding definitions of teaching and learning: Notes from the MI underground.* In P. Cookson & B. Schneider (Eds.), *Transforming schools* (pp. 181–208). New York: Garland.

Lee, J. (2006). *Tracking achievement gaps and assessing the impact of NCLB on the gaps: An in-depth look into national and state reading and math outcome trends.* http://www.civilrightsproject.ucla.edu.

Lemann, N. (1999). *The big test: The secret history of the American meritocracy.* New York: Farrar, Strauss, & Giroux.

Lippmann, W. (1922a). The mystery of the "A" men. *New Republic, 32,* 246–248.

Lippmann, W. (1922b). The abuse of the tests. *New Republic, 32,* 297–298.

McNeil, L. & Valenzuela, A. (2001). The harmful impact of the TAAS system of testing in Texas: Beneath the accountability rhetoric. In G. Orfield & M. L. Kornhaber (Eds.), *Raising standards or raising barriers?* (pp. 127–150). New York: Century Foundation Press.

Miller, G. A. (1983). Varieties of intelligence. [Review of *Frames of mind* by H. Gardner]. *New York Times Book Review,* December 25, p. 5.

National Center for Educational Statistics. (2007). *Mapping 2005 state proficiency standards onto the NAEP scales.* http://nces.ed.gov/nationsreportcard/pdf/studies/2007482.pdf.

National Commission on Excellence in Education. (1983). *A nation at risk.* http://www.ed.gov/pubs/NatAtRisk/.

Neal, D., & Schanzenbach, D.W. (2007). *Left behind by design: Proficiency counts and test-based accountability.* National Bureau of Economic Research, working paper no. 13293. http://www.nber.org/papers/w13293.

Pal, L. A. (1997). *Beyond policy analysis: Public issue management in turbulent times.* Scarborough, ON: Nelson.

Patterson, O. (1995). *For whom the bell curves.* In S. Fraser (Ed.), *The bell curve wars.* New York: Basic Books.

Pedulla, J., Abrams, L., Madaus, G., Russell, M., Ramos, M., & Miao, J. (2003). *Perceived effects of state-mandated testing programs on teaching and learning: Findings from a national survey of teachers.* http://www.bc.edu/research/nbetpp/reports.html.

Pellegrino, J. W., Chudowsky, N., & Glaser, R. (Eds.). (2001). *Knowing what students know.* Washington, DC: National Research Council/National Academy Press.

Plato. (1960). *The republic, Book 3* (B. A. Jowett, Trans.). Classics.MIT.edu/Plato/republic.

Scarr, S. (1985). An author's frame of mind. *New Ideas in Psychology, 3*(1), 95–100.

Stone-Wiske, M. (1997). *Teaching for understanding: Linking research with practice.* San Francisco: Jossey-Bass.

Terman, L. M. (1919). *The intelligence of school children.* Cambridge, MA: Riverside.

White, J. (2005). *Howard Gardner: The myth of multiple intelligences.* London: Institute of Education, University of London.

Willingham, D. T. (2004). Reframing the mind. *Education Next, 4*(3), 18–24.

CHAPTER 32

Cultural Zone of Proximal Development

A Construct to Further Our Understanding of MI Around the World

Jie-Qi Chen

As this book documents, MI theory has been introduced and implemented successfully in numerous countries around the world. The diversity that characterizes these countries is striking. No single characteristic is common to all contributors' work. Seeking a means of analyzing and reflecting on their work, this chapter proposes the construct of cultural zone of proximal development (CZPD). An extension of Vygotsky's individual zone of proximal development, the CZPD focuses on the relationship between a culture and the MI meme. The chapter explores the power and utility of the CZPD construct for better understanding the interactive and dynamic relationship between multiple cultural forces and MI implementations. Three specific issues are addressed: the multiple forces that shape the CZPD, the developmental course that shifts it, and applications that enrich it. Insights and lessons learned from applying the CZPD construct to the MI implementation processes described in this book are discussed.

In Chapter One, Gardner brought our attention to the phenomenon of the MI meme. A meme is a unit of information, such as a theory or a set of practices. Generated at a particular place and time, a meme can be transmitted from one person to another, one place to another, and across generations. This book presents stories of MI meme travel around the world during the past two decades. While Gardner developed MI theory in 1983 based on a set of criteria and a series of claims, the focus and application of the MI meme take new forms as different people encounter it in diverse cultural and educational contexts. As the MI meme travels, new applications emerge.

Although Gardner did not intend to develop a theory of the human mind with implications for educational practice, educators have enthusiastically embraced the MI meme. With the meme, they find justification and affirmation of what they believe to be true about students and the best approaches to education. They use MI theory for a variety of purposes: as a conceptual framework for educational reform, a blueprint for curriculum and assessment innovation, an alternative perspective on educating gifted and special needs children, and a guide for developing museum education and media programs, to name a few.

The scope and impact of the MI meme vary with characteristics of the culture it encounters. The term *culture* in this chapter refers to the behaviors and beliefs characteristic of a particular group of people or setting: citizens in a society, residents in a community, and teachers in a school, for example. Every school has a culture, and different schools have different cultures. The same is true of institutions, communities, and societies. Each has its own distinctive culture. The stories in this book are embedded in distinctive cultures of a society as well as cultures of schools and communities within the society.

Aware that each culture is distinct, I was curious about whether cultures that adapt the MI meme also have commonalities. If so, could these shared features help to explain why and how some cultures have advanced further than others in implementing MI? Reviewing the chapters, I found shared characteristics among some cultures, such as the effects of national educational policy in China, England, Scotland, and South Korea. More revealing than the search for attributes across cultures, however, is observation of the different developmental stages in which a school, community, institute, or society engages in MI-related activities. From this point of view, a culture's readiness for MI theory shapes the extent of MI infusion and implementation. Unlike shared characteristics across cultures, readiness describes the development of a single culture. It emphasizes that a culture's level of functioning influences its openness to MI theory. Neither the correctness of the theory nor the sophistication of the culture determines outcomes of MI meme application. Instead, outcomes are based on interactions between characteristics of the MI meme and priorities of the culture.

To help us conceptualize the interactive relationship between the MI meme and the cultural context, I extend Vygotsky's (1978) notion of an individual's zone of proximal development and propose a cultural zone of proximal development (CZPD). An individual's zone of proximal development represents the relationship between the learning and the development of a child. It refers to the distance between a child's actual developmental level on a learning task and the potential developmental level the child can reach with the guidance of adults or in collaboration with more competent peers (Vygotsky, 1978).

Referring to this relationship as a zone, Vygotsky thought of development not as a linear scale but as a terrain with many pathways to a destination. Describing the zone as proximal means behaviors that are ready to emerge will develop with appropriate support (Bodrova & Leong, 2007).

Analogous to the concept of an individual's ZPD, the CZPD contributes to understanding the relationship between cultural development and the MI meme. A cultural ZPD refers to the distance between a culture's level of functioning and the level that may be reached with additional support, such as innovative leadership, exposure to new models, and access to relevant expertise. In relation to the MI meme, CZPD indicates the level of a culture's readiness to accept new ideas about teaching and learning and engage in alternative educational practices. The greatest receptivity and most effective germination of ideas and practices occur within the CZPD.

Cultural readiness for a new idea or practice is not a fixed state. It develops through interactive processes with multiple forces such as political climate, historical influences, and educational priorities. The CZPD develops through exposure to outside stimuli as well as through opportunities and pressures that emerge within the culture. The question of readiness is not an either-or proposition. It is an indicator of cultural capacity. Readiness is a matter of degree.

In this chapter, I explore issues related to the cultural ZPD, a construct proposed to help organize our thinking about MI theory's travels around the world. For this purpose, I regard contributors' chapters as data that can be understood through analysis based on the CZPD construct. Specifically, I explore the multiple forces that shape the CZPD, the developmental course that shifts it, and applications that enrich it. My aim is to use the construct of CZPD to explore the underlying structure of MI implementations across the wide range of cultures represented in this book. If CZPD contributes to a greater understanding of MI implementations in diverse cultures, the construct may be usefully applied by others engaged in or considering the MI implementation process.

FORCES AFFECTING A CULTURE'S READINESS TO SUPPORT MI IMPLEMENTATION

As the MI meme travels, it comes into contact with varied CZPDs. A CZPD is affected by multiple forces, including ideologies and values, political activity, state of the economy, historical factors, organization of the educational system, and performance status of schools. Forces act on different levels, ranging from national to community levels. To understand why the MI meme does or does not take hold, multiple factors must be considered. Identifying either the MI meme or a culture as the primary cause of the meme's acceptance or rejection assumes the meme and the culture can be separated and understood in isolation. Thinking in these terms obscures the relationship between the culture and the meme. That relationship is shaped by characteristics of both.

Numerous contributors to this book describe the interactive relationship between particular educational policies and the infusion of MI ideas (see Kornhaber's chapter for detail). The Every Child Matters strategy in England, the Curriculum for Excellence report in Scotland, the Seventh National Curriculum in South Korea, and the character education movement in China demonstrate that national educational policies can become an impetus for educators to introduce and activate the MI meme. We also find motivation for activating the MI meme in internal demands for more competitive economic development as described in the work of Kim and Cha in South Korea, Craft in England, and Chen in China.

National education policies have widespread effects. Activity at the community level is also vital. Translating MI theory into new practices requires input and support from individuals I call "MI meme bearers." Many contributors to this book play this role. They are sources of local contagion about MI and its applications, generators of excitement about the power of MI in educational practices, and active disseminators, delivering workshops and making MI ideas accessible to the public. The enthusiasm, dedication, and visionary leadership of these "meme bearers" create attraction at the local level that draws the MI meme into the culture's ZPD.

MI meme bearers cannot function alone. Successful MI implementation requires the coordination of many additional forces: teacher buy-in, family involvement, business and community partnerships, support from local government officials, and collaboration between school personnel and university researchers. Pogré and Rogé's work on L@titud, the Latin American Initiative Toward Understanding and Development, provides one example of these forces working in tandem. Collaborating with universities and corporations across the country, the L@titud network in Argentina has created widespread MI teacher networks and implemented MI practices in numerous private and public schools. Gatmaitan-Bernardo also clearly demonstrated the value of coordinating forces to form coalitions among schools, families, local communities, and government agencies. These strong alliances have made important contributions to successful day care center reform in the Philippines. Coordinating multiple forces generates momentum, diversifies the range of expertise, and often increases the pool of resources.

Though powerful when interactions are in sync, multiple forces do not always move in the same direction. When forces are opposed, their interactions create fractures and cause dissension. If MI conflicts with the culture's priorities, response from the culture is likely to be weak and the impact small. Kunkel struggled to promote diverse ways of learning under No Child Left

Behind legislation in the United States. Shearer describes the sizable obstacles he has encountered in efforts to introduce alternative assessment to schools and teachers in the United States. Keinänen expresses concern that greater emphasis on quantification in education in Norway may dilute MI-inspired practices and other forms of progressive education. The poor performance of Norwegian students on the Programme for International Student Assessment (PISA) study prompted this shift in educational priorities. Conflicting values and goals make it difficult for the MI meme to move into the CZPD. Opposing forces tend to create tension in the zone and make it less flexible.

By locating MI implementation efforts in relation to the multiple forces that shape cultural contexts, educators can identify the origins of obstacles to implementation and find opportunities to extend successful applications of MI theory. For example, educators in China and South Korea determined that the MI meme fell within the CZPD of their countries when they recognized opportunities for educational reform created by political shifts toward a more open society. They also observed societal needs for an educational approach that prepares citizens to contribute to rapid development in a global economy. These shifts in political position and workforce demands helped close the distance between cultural priorities and MI-related practices. As the distance closed, readiness grew, and more and more educators have opened their schools to MI theory and practice. Because they found opportunities to integrate the MI meme with the national educational reform movement, educators in South Korea and China have made significant changes in relatively short periods of time.

The chapter authors wholeheartedly agree that MI theory is appealing and favorable for dissemination. Yet the MI meme travels successfully only when it meets the needs or matches the interests of a culture. When MI relates directly to cultural needs and priorities, the culture is relatively open to the MI meme. Reception tends to be strong, and implementation is effective. Exemplifying the success of MI implementation when the MI meme fits cultural priorities, Hyland and McCarthy say that because it arrived during a decade of curriculum reform in Ireland, MI was a theory in the right place at the right time. It is important to note that the relationship between the culture and the MI meme is not a one-time consideration. Following the initial implementation of MI-related practices, the MI meme remains influential only if it remains consistent with cultural priorities.

Understanding a culture's zone of proximal development and the specific factors that inform educators' thinking about where the fit with MI will be close and what aspects of the theory will require the most extensive adaptations is important. Understanding a culture's ZPD will also help educators anticipate reactions from different members of the school culture, including administrators, teachers, and parents. If the MI meme falls outside the CZPD, educators can increase the probability of successful implementations by deter-mining how to integrate MI with existing school practices. They can help shift the CZPD by providing opportunities for the public to see MI in action and inviting the involvement of community leaders and parents.

RELATIONSHIP BETWEEN CZPD AND THE MI MEME

The culture is an active contributor to encounters with the MI meme, not a passive receiver. What the culture contributes reflects the multiple forces that shape its CZPD. In relation to the MI meme, the culture brings, for example, prevailing models of the teaching-learning process, current educational prac-tices, and a system for training educators. Within the CZPD, the culture inte-grates the MI meme in ways that are consistent with its values, goals, and priorities. The relationship between the culture and the meme is dynamic rather than static, interactive rather than unidirectional.

Although the term *zone* connotes a fixed space, the CZPD changes con-stantly. The zone changes through exposure to external cultural forces as well as in response to emerging opportunities and new pressures from within. Battro's work in Argentina was initiated in response to external cultural forces and the new opportunities they created. Specifically, the initiative was a response to the emerging digital revolution. Prior to the momentum of the revolution, it is unlikely that Battro would have focused on MI-related prac-tices in the digital age.

The Key Learning Community presents another example of CZPD's change in relation to MI meme implementation. Twenty years ago, eight women in Indianapolis read Gardner's *Frames of Mind.* Committed to offering their stu-dents a better school experience, they drove ten hours to attend Gardner's MI theory talk in Kutztown, Pennsylvania. Returning to school with new ideas and fresh enthusiasm, they were ready to pursue their ideas about MI theory in the classroom. Today the Elementary Key School has grown into the K–12 Key Learning Community. Under Kunkel's leadership, the school has reached a new readiness level—nurturing a wide range of intellectual potentials in the diverse student population it serves and engaging these students in discipline-based learning for school success. In every school, the relative readiness for MI practice reflects the varied needs and goals of specific cultural contexts, as well as the motivation and preparedness of the educators involved.

The CZPD represents a leading edge of cultural development. Within the zone, interactions with internal forces and the MI meme tend to stimulate development and push the upper limit of the zone to new levels of function-ing. The zone's development does not follow predictable linear progressions. Rather, the zone is a terrain with possibilities for movement in different directions

(Engestrom, 2008). The characteristics of unpredictability and emergence help to explain the reports in this book that the process of MI implementation can be a bumpy road. Ups and downs are found in patterns of normal development.

An uneven pattern of development within the cultural zone may emerge when a culture is ready to advance in one area of educational change but not in others. As depicted in H. Cheung's chapter, China is encouraging multiple ways of learning and teaching through MI. However, the country is not ready for alternative ways of evaluating student learning. Because a large population of high school students is competing for limited enrollment in higher education, the college entrance exam is deemed an indispensable tool for identifying the most appropriate forms of career development for diverse students. It would be neither practical nor reliable to base these decisions on MI's individual intellectual profiles. The decision to apply MI to teaching, but not to evaluation, is not perceived as inconsistent. It is seen as combining the best tools and techniques to meet student needs.

In addition to effects of interactions between larger cultural issues and the MI meme, MI implementations are also affected by activities of specific schools and institutions. Recognized for their success in applying MI theory, the Key Learning Community and New City School welcome several hundred visitors from across the world each year. Observation and informal conversation stimulate thinking about the possibilities of MI theory. Visitors gain access to practices in action that they can take back to their school. For example, adapting the idea of flow activities centers from the Key Learning Community, Rosenlund Municipal School in Denmark implemented the practice of flow workshops with materials and activities organized to exercise students' different intelligences.

As described in numerous chapters, the Harvard Project Zero Summer Institute provided critical scaffolding for the development of cultural ZPDs by offering new ideas about MI practices such as teaching for understanding. Gardner's travel to different countries is another example of outside influences affecting CZPDs. He transmitted the essence of the MI meme to educators, expanding its reach and benefits to students.

As important as the outside forces are, the advancement of a culture's ZPD is pushed as well by the people within it. The internal dissatisfaction with what is and the need for something new, whether within a country or a school, is the ultimate driving force for change. Six contributors describe MI applications within an individual school setting: Colegio Del Barrio School in Colombia, Rosenlund Municipal School in Denmark, Multiple Intelligence International School in Philippines, and New City School, the Key Learning Community, and Gardner School in the United States. Despite dramatic differences in the population each school serves and how MI theory was implemented, all six schools share a key characteristic: educators in the schools were dissatisfied with existing practices and were determined to make improvements. It is this motivation and determination that drives schools to work with MI theory and adapt it to help students learn and succeed.

EXTENDING THE CZPD OF MI PRACTICE THROUGH APPLICATIONS

The cultural zone that the MI meme enters is a land of learning and development for everyone who is part of it. While committed educators work diligently to grasp the essence of MI theory and adapt it to meet national and local needs, they broaden its applications and contribute to its development. The MI meme is elaborated and enriched through applications. The extensions have taken many forms. For example, adapting MI-related practices for use at different grade levels, integrating MI with other instructional practices, training teachers, and involving parents have required different approaches to the use of MI. Less common but equally important are adaptations involving local government officials and learning outside the walls of the classroom. Contributors to this book offer examples of these forms of elaboration.

Consider adaptations of MI practice in terms of grade levels. Teachers at every grade level adapt MI practice to align it more closely with the developmental characteristics of students. At the same time, teachers at different grade levels work to meet different educational goals. Examining applications in preschool through high school, we see how grade level influences the way MI is implemented. We also understand better the range of extensions and elaborations required to adapt MI for all grades.

At the preschool level, the curriculum is more flexible, and the use of high-stakes standardized testing is relatively infrequent. Through daily routines and play activities, teachers emphasize development of the whole child. At this level, MI ideas usually are applied to strengthen the design of learning centers and further the development of multiple symbol systems. Stories from Canon-Abaquin and Gatmaitan-Bernardo in Philippines give evidence of the power of learning centers inspired by MI principles. By exposing young children to a range of learning experiences rather than limited academic areas such as reading and math, children gain a greater understanding of themselves and their surroundings. They also develop more tools for thinking, communication, and expression.

In elementary school, a project-based approach is often employed to provide students with multiple entry points to concept learning. In the Gardner School for Discovery described by Vincent Rizzo, a class writing project anchors the curriculum at each grade level. Writing is organized around the concept of audience. Students focus on the particular audience assigned to their class, such as parents, teachers, community mentors, and the public at large. Although the writing projects draw heavily on linguistic intelligence, they also can nurture intrapersonal, interpersonal, and other intelligences. Project-based learning not only invites students to study a particular topic by using different media; it also encourages them to express their understanding of the topic through diverse representational methods such as writing, three-dimensional models, and dramatizations. This approach, according to Rizzo, makes it possible for students to find ways of learning that are attuned to their predispositions and therefore increase their motivation and engagement in the learning process.

Toward the end of middle school and in high school, the challenge for MI educators is interfacing with well-established, compartmentalized curriculum teaching. Emphasizing students' in-depth understanding of content knowledge is the priority. To ensure mastery of content knowledge, curriculum has been organized traditionally around goals for a group of students at a particular grade level. MI applications shift attention away from these group goals toward the individual student. The many benefits of these shifts have been described by numerous authors in this book. Retaining an emphasis on content, the teaching for understanding framework has been integrated successfully with students in upper grades. Teaching disciplinary knowledge with attention to big ideas, key concepts, and critical skills of subject matter is reported by Pogré and Rogé of Argentina, Kunkel of the United States, and Hyland and McCarthy of Ireland.

To implement MI practice in classrooms, teacher training is critical. Many contributors report on preservice and in-service MI programs for teachers. The MI meme in teacher professional development emphasizes the interplay of curriculum, instruction, and assessment. Because all intelligences are equally valuable, teachers need to develop curricula that encompass a broad range of subject areas, including and then going beyond skill development in reading, writing, and arithmetic. With children varying in their ways of perceiving and processing information, teachers are most effective when they emphasize multiple pathways in teaching and learning. Following the purpose of developing intelligences, which is to fashion products and solve problems, assessments true to the MI spirit are performance-based, instruction-related, and developmentally appropriate ways of knowing and understanding students. Enriching teacher development through pursuit of these and related objectives is a natural extension of MI theory applications.

While teachers extend and elaborate MI applications to help students meet developmental and educational goals, the MI meme is also applied to increase the involvement of parents. Parent involvement has long been documented as a key to student success in schools. Recognizing its critical role in education, MI educators have devoted great attention to parent education. Clearly illustrated in Hoerr's chapter, parent understanding of MI helps them support teachers and classroom activities. It also helps them to reinforce classroom learning through experiences at home. Although MI theory is focused on the individual, understanding a student in the context of the family can benefit students, teachers, and parents. Becoming more familiar with the family context, teachers gain a more complete understanding of the range of a child's interests and competencies. Such understanding works as a bridge between the home and school environments and enhances the child's learning opportunities at school and at home.

The involvement of government representatives is not typically necessary for the implementation of an MI-related program. However, elaboration that invites the participation of government officials can increase the credibility and sustainability of a program. In China, Turkey, and Tagbilaran City, Bohol, Philippines, the voices of top educational leaders and government officers attracted attention, gained support, and had considerable impact on educators' thinking and action. These leaders were also effective in spreading the word about MI-related education because they belong to well-established networks that are linked on regional and national levels.

Described by Armstrong, Happy Cheung, Sahl-Madsen and Kyed, and Boyd, the culture of MI practice is not limited to schools, but extends to museums and media such as television programs and radio shows. The Explorama, a science park, brings MI to life by inviting visitors to experience the use of various intelligences to solve problems in everyday life. Through engaging in fun, exploratory activities, visitors develop a basic understanding of how different intelligences work. The outside school that Armstrong encountered at Kollmyr School in Skien is a learning environment for the naturalist that goes far beyond the occasional field trip. The work of these contributors reminds us that environments designed to educate MI are not limited to the boundaries of traditional classrooms. Our assumptions about the location of education need to be expanded.

As these elaborations illustrate, MI theory has a life of its own. It continues to develop and meet educational needs in new ways. MI educators offer a wellspring of ideas. They contextualize the MI meme to better serve the needs of a particular school, institution, or community. MI theory enhances educational practice. In turn, educational practices enrich the MI meme across different cultural zones.

CONCLUSION

As attested to in this book, MI theory has been introduced and implemented successfully in numerous countries around the world. This is the first collection to review, synthesize, and reflect on this unique cross-cultural and educational phenomenon. Through synthesis and reflection, we gain a fresh and fuller understanding of MI theory. As well, we develop more specific knowledge about why MI theory has been welcomed in so many countries, how its use can be appropriate in such diverse cultures, and what has supported and fueled travel of the MI meme. Synthesis and reflection can take us a step further to consider what happens after the meme's successful travel. At some point, it may become desirable for the MI meme to do more than visit. How does the transition from visitor to resident meme take place? Do the same factors that support MI meme travel also contribute to its residency?

Becoming a resident means that MI will permeate the educational process and enter a new developmental phase. This change requires a qualitative shift in what educators do. For example, additional planning and new strategies are required when taking the MI approach from one classroom or one school to schools systemwide. The prospect of moving from traveler to resident raises several questions. First, can the MI meme become a local resident without being distorted through assimilation to existing views and practices? Second, are the skills used by the initial innovators of MI-related programs the same ones needed to shepherd MI programs toward local permanence? Finally are some more philosophical and speculative questions. Is it desirable for MI to become a resident rather than remain a visitor? Is MI-related education the best approach for all students? These concluding questions for reflection sample from the many uncharted territories in the cultural ZPDs of MI concepts and practices.

In this chapter I have proposed and applied the construct of cultural zone of proximal development. Suggested initially by contributors' references to the relationship between their initiative and the cultural context, I explored that relationship by extending Vygotsky's conception of ZPD for the individual. The value of the construct is using it to explore features of MI implementations that at first appear to be characterized only by differences. Perceiving commonalities helps us to understand more about each contributor's work and more about the travels of the MI meme. Along with all of the contributors and members of the editorial team, I hope readers will go beyond the readings in this book to explore the many questions related to MI practice and use the knowledge gained to lead MI to new places around the world.

References

Bodrova, E., & Leong, D. J. (2007). *Tools of the mind: The Vygotskian approach to early childhood education* (2nd ed.). Upper Saddle River, NJ: Pearson.

Engestrom, Y. (2008, September). *The future of activity theory: A rough draft.* Paper presented at the Third Congress of International Society for Cultural Activities and Research, San Diego, CA.

Vygotsky, L. (1978). *Mind in society.* Cambridge, MA: Harvard University Press.

Appendix
Chapter Topics and Issues

C hapters in the book are organized in terms of geographic region. The basis for this grouping of chapters is to be sensitive to cultural context and to be readily understood. For readers interested in particular topics, the table provides an overview of the content in each chapter. Note that all chapters address more than one topic. Most focus on several educational issues with students of a specific age group in a particular setting. Use the table for a quick reference to chapter topics and issues.

Cross Categories

Region and Country — Educational Issues / Setting / Educational Level

Region and Country	Assessment	Cultural Analysis	Curriculum and Instruction	Educational system	Focusing on Arts	Parent Involvement	Policy Influence	Special Population	Teacher Training	Technology Use	Independent School	Network of Schools	Public School	Venues Beyond	School	Elementary	Middle School	High School	Higher Education
Overview																			
U.S. (Gardner)		✓	✓	✓	✓	✓							✓	✓					
U.S. (Armstrong)		✓	✓			✓	✓												
Asia and Pacific Areas																			
China (Chen)		✓	✓	✓	✓														
China (H. Cheung)		✓	✓						✓					✓					
China (Shen)		✓	✓	✓															
China (K. Cheung)		✓	✓	✓	✓				✓		✓								
Japan (Howland, Fujimoto, Ishiwata, and Kamijo)	✓		✓	✓						✓							✓	✓	✓
Korea (Kim and Cha)		✓	✓	✓					✓		✓					✓	✓	✓	
Philippines (Canon-Abaquin)	✓	✓	✓	✓		✓	✓	✓				✓	✓		✓	✓	✓	✓	
Philippines (Gatmaitan-Bernardo)	✓					✓	✓	✓	✓						✓		✓		
Australia (Vialle)		✓	✓																
Europe																			
Norway (Keinänen)		✓	✓													✓	✓	✓	
Denmark (Knoop)		✓						✓		✓						✓	✓	✓	
Denmark (Sahl-Madsen and Kyed)	✓		✓						✓										
England (Craft)		✓	✓	✓		✓	✓	✓	✓				✓			✓	✓	✓	
England (Fleetham)	✓	✓	✓				✓						✓						✓
Ireland (Hyland and McCarthy)	✓	✓	✓				✓	✓					✓	✓	✓	✓	✓	✓	
Scotland (Boyd)					✓		✓	✓					✓	✓	✓	✓	✓	✓	
Romania (Singer and Sarivan)	✓	✓	✓	✓					✓				✓			✓	✓		
Turkey (Kaya and Selçuk)		✓		✓			✓		✓		✓					✓	✓	✓	✓

South America										
Argentina (Pogré and Rogé)					✓					
Colombia (Barrera and	✓	✓		✓			✓			
León-Agustí)	✓	✓		✓	✓		✓			
Argentina (Battro)				✓	✓		✓			
			✓							
	✓			✓		✓	✓			
	✓									
	✓	✓		✓	✓		✓			
		✓		✓						
	✓	✓		✓	✓					
		✓		✓		✓				
				✓				✓	✓	✓
				✓		✓				
United States										
Kunkel	✓	✓		✓			✓		✓	✓
Hoerr	✓	✓		✓	✓	✓	✓	✓		✓
Díaz-Lefebvre	✓	✓		✓	✓	✓	✓	✓	✓	✓
Maker and Sarouphim	✓	✓			✓	✓	✓	✓		
Rizzo										
Shearer										
Synthesis, Reflection, and Projection										
Moran										
Kornhaber										
Chen										

NAME INDEX

SUBJECT INDEX

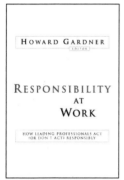

RESPONSIBILITY AT WORK

How Leading Professionals Act (or Don't Act) Responsibly

Howard Gardner, Editor

ISBN 978-0-7879-9475-4
Hardcover | 368 pp.

"In this remarkable collection of essays, Gardner and his colleagues have given us an astonishing array of penetrating insights into the responsibilities, meaning, and ethics of work. Everyone, anyone, in any organization, can learn and profit from the wisdom in these pages."
—Warren Bennis, Distinguished Professor of Business and University Professor, University of Southern California and author, *On Becoming a Leader*

"Gardner and his colleagues boldly confront the ever-present tensions between professional action and professional responsibility with superbly crafted individual case studies as well as broad theoretical arguments. Taken together, the writers deepen our understanding of the challenges of leadership—from classical ethical dilemmas to the seemingly mundane question of how to allocate one's time."
—Lee S. Shulman, President, The Carnegie Foundation for the Advancement of Teaching

Filled with original essays by Howard Gardner, William Damon, Mihaly Csikszentmihalyi, and Jeanne Nakamura and based on a large-scale research project, the GoodWork® Project, *Responsibility at Work* reflects the information gleaned from in-depth interviews with more than 1,200 people from nine different professions—journalism, genetics, theatre, higher education, philanthropy, law, medicine, business, and pre-collegiate education. The book reveals how motivation, culture, and professional norms can intersect to produce work that is personally, socially, and economically beneficial. At the heart of the study is the revelation that the key to good work is responsibility—taking ownership for one's work and its wider impact.

The authors examine how responsibility for work is shaped by both personal and professional components and explore the factors that cause a sense of responsibility, the obstacles that lead to compromised work, and the educational interventions that can lead to a greater sense of responsibility. Most important, this volume provides strategies for cultivating greater responsibility in both seasoned workers as well as the young people who will one day enter the workplace.